T0371591

The Material Atlantic

In this wide-ranging account, Robert DuPlessis examines globally sourced textiles that by dramatically altering consumer behavior helped create new economies and societies in the early modern world. This deeply researched history of cloth and clothing offers new insights into trade patterns, consumer demand, and sartorial cultures that emerged across the Atlantic world between the mid-seventeenth and late eighteenth centuries. As a result of European settlement and the construction of commercial networks stretching across much of the planet, men and women across a wide spectrum of ethnicities, social standings, and occupations fashioned their garments from materials old and new, familiar and strange, and novel meanings came to be attached to different fabrics and modes of dress. *The Material Atlantic* illuminates crucial developments that characterized early modernity, from colonialism and slavery to economic innovation and new forms of social identity.

Robert S. DuPlessis is Isaac H. Clothier Professor of History and International Relations Emeritus at the Department of History, Swarthmore College.

The Material Atlantic

Clothing, Commerce, and Colonization in the Atlantic World, 1650–1800

Robert S. DuPlessis
Swarthmore College

CAMBRIDGE
UNIVERSITY PRESS

CAMBRIDGE
UNIVERSITY PRESS

University Printing House, Cambridge CB2 8BS, United Kingdom

Cambridge University Press is part of the University of Cambridge.

It furthers the University's mission by disseminating knowledge in the pursuit of education, learning and research at the highest international levels of excellence.

www.cambridge.org
Information on this title: www.cambridge.org/9781107105911

© Robert S. DuPlessis 2016

First published 2016

Printed in the United States of America by Sheridan Books, Inc.

A catalogue record for this publication is available from the British Library

Library of Congress Cataloguing in Publication data
DuPlessis, Robert S.
The material Atlantic : clothing the New World, 1650–1800 / Robert S. DuPlessis.
  pages   cm
Includes bibliographical references and index.
ISBN 978-1-107-10591-1
1. Clothing and dress – America – History – 18th century.   2. Fashion – America – History – 18th century.   3. Textile industry – America – History – 18th century.
4. Textile fabrics – America – History – 18th century.   5. Material culture – America – History – 18th century.   I. Title.
GT601.D86   2016
391.0097′09033–dc23

2015014698

ISBN 978-1-107-10591-1 Hardback

Contents

Plates

Figures

Maps

Tables

Acknowledgements

Over the many years that this book has been underway, I have been the grateful recipient of assistance from many institutions and individuals. Swarthmore College generously helped underwrite several leaves; in addition, I received fellowship support from the John Simon Guggenheim Foundation, the National Endowment for the Humanities, the Camargo Foundation, and the William C. and Ida Friday Fellowship from the National Center for the Humanities. The staffs of libraries and archives too numerous to mention have gone out of their way to locate materials, but I want to recognize the outstanding interlibrary loan staff of McCabe Library at Swarthmore College, in particular Sandra Vermuychuk, who has tirelessly obtained books, articles, and images from places near, far, and impossible. My former colleague Diego Armus helped me find two excellent research assistants. Rodolfo González Lebrero in Buenos Aires provided superb transcriptions of documents in Buenos Aires archives as well as leads to (and on occasion copies of) secondary works and useful textile vocabulary; Christiane Maria Cruz de Souza did similar yeoman work in Salvador da Bahia. I was equally fortunate to have the assistance of Courtney Dunn and Denise Finley, my outstanding Swarthmore research assistants; I am again obliged to Swarthmore College for granting me summer research grants to hire them. Sophie White has graciously shared documents and references. Tim Burke has been prompt to suggest relevant readings. Trevor Burnard generously provided copies of the transcript of Thomas Thistlewood's diary as well as stimulating conversation and keen questions. Marshall Joseph Becker has offered ideas and information on Native Americans and read several chapters with great acuity. Pierre Gervais and Pierre-Yves Saulnier have stimulated my thinking on a variety of matters pertinent to several chapters of this book. Dean Anderson's gift of a copy of his computerized records of Montreal trade cargoes saved me an enormous amount of labor. Time and again, Heather Dumigan has given me technical assistance and trouble-shooting. I also owe thanks to the patience, care, and good sense of two anonymous referees for Cambridge University Press who forced me entirely to rethink and rework my manuscript, and to my patient, persistent, and perspicacious editor Michael Watson.

I would like to thank my hosts for and commentators on drafts of portions of this book presented in lectures, seminars, and conferences in Antwerp, Baltimore, Brussels, Buenos Aires, Charleston, Cholet (France), Columbus (Ohio), Dakar, Ghent, Greensboro (North Carolina), Helsinki, La Rochelle, Lisburn (Northern Ireland), Midland (Ontario), Montreal, Paris, Philadelphia, Poitiers, Princeton, Providence, Research Triangle (North Carolina), Rouen, St. Augustine, South Bend, Stellenbosch, Sydney (Australia and Nova Scotia), Washington, DC, and Wolverhampton. Early (often very early) versions of some materials included in *The Material Atlantic* have been published in *Monde(s); Afro-Ásia; The Spinning World: A Global History of Cotton Textiles 1200–1850*, ed. Giorgio Riello and Prasannan Parthasarathi; *The Atlantic Economy during the Seventeenth and Eighteenth Centuries: Organization, Operation, Practice, and Personnel*, ed. Peter A. Coclanis; *The European Linen Industry in Historical Perspective*, ed. Brenda Collins and Philip Ollerenshaw; *French Colonial History; Actes du Colloque International: Le mouchoir dans tous ses états*, ed. Jean-Joseph Chevalier and Elisabeth Loir-Mongazon; *Revue du Nord*.

My deepest gratitude is to my wife Rachel who in the midst of multiple writing and publishing commitments of her own not only kept up my spirits but several times found time to apply her fine literary sensibility, astute editorial skills, and judiciously wielded red pencil (actually, this being 2015, bright yellow text highlight) to the entire manuscript. Grazie tante.

Abbreviations

ADG	Archives départementales de la Gironde, Bordeaux
Aff. Am.	*Affiches Américaines* (Saint-Domingue)
AGN	Archivo General de la Nación, Buenos Aires
AndD	Anderson data: computer printouts of original data on forty-seven cargoes sent to eight Great Lakes posts by Montreal merchants between 1715 and 1758 assembled by Dean Anderson and used in his "Documentary and archaeological perspectives on European trade goods in the western Great Lakes region," Ph.D. dissertation (Michigan State University, 1992). One cargo was dispatched in 1715, forty-five between 1721 and 1748, and one in 1758; they were destined for Detroit, Green Bay, Michilimackinac, Michipicoten, Nipigon, Ouiatenon, Rainy Lake, and Sioux Post. In the text I often use specified subsets of these data.
ANOM	Archives Nationales d'Outre-Mer (formerly Centre des Archives d'Outre-Mer), Aix-en-Provence
APEB-JI	Arquivo Público do Estado da Bahia, Salvador da Bahia, Judiciário, Inventories
BANQ-M	Bibliothèque et Archives Nationales de Québec, Centre d'Archives de Montréal

CCA	Chester County Archives and Records Services, West Chester, Pennsylvania
CCWB	Charleston County Will Book, SCDAH
CO	Colonial Office papers, TNA
doss.	dossier
EcHR	*Economic History Review*
FSC	French Superior Council records, LHC
GHS	George Historical Society, Savannah
GN	Greffes de notaires, Fonds Cour supérieure, District judiciaire de Montréal, BANQ-M
GS	Genealogical Society, Salt Lake City, Utah
HAHR	*Hispanic American Historical Review*
HSP	Historical Society of Pennsylvania, Philadelphia
IB	Inventory Book, JA
JA	Jamaica Archives, Spanish Town
Jam. Gaz.	*Jamaica Gazette* (Kingston)
JR	Reuben Gold Thwaites, *The Jesuit relations and allied documents: travels and explorations of the Jesuit missionaries in New France, 1610–1791*, 73 vols. (Cleveland: Burrows Bros., 1896–1901)
Kask. Mss	Kaskaskia Manuscripts, Randolph County Courthouse, Chester, Illinois
LAC	Library and Archives of Canada (formerly National Archives of Canada), Ottawa
LHC	Louisiana Historical Center, New Orleans
MCC	Middelburgse Commercie Compagnie, Middelburg, Zeeland
mf.	microfilm
Monson 31/1–31	Thomas Thistlewood's manuscript diaries; the originals are in the Lancashire County Archives
MOOC	Masters of the Orphan Chamber (Cape Colony), Cape Archives, Cape Town (MOOC 8 = Inventories; MOOC 10 = Vendu Rolls)
Ms.	manuscript
NJSLA	New Jersey State Library and Archives, Trenton
NONA	New Orleans Notarial Archives, Louisiana
Not.	Notary
Pa. Gaz.	*Pennsylvania Gazette* (Philadelphia)
RAC	Royal African Company (United Kingdom)

RSP	Records of the Secretary of the Province, SCDAH
RWP	Registrar of Wills, Philadelphia City Archives, Pennsylvania
RWSC	Record of Wills, Surrogate's Court
SCDAH	South Carolina Department of Archives and History, Columbia
S. C. Gaz.	*South Carolina Gazette* (Charles Town)
SDOM	Saint-Domingue collection, ANOM
SL	Sucesiones legajos, AGN
STB	Stellenbosch Inventories, Cape Archives, Cape Town, Republic of South Africa, transcribed in Annemarie Krzesinski-De Widt, *Die boedelinventarisse van erflaters in die distrik Stellenbosch, 1679–1806*, 5 vols. (Stellenbosch Museum, 2002)
TNA	The National Archives, Kew (England)
VOC	Verenigde Oost-Indische Compagnie (Dutch East India Company)
W	Will
WI	Wills and Inventories
WMQ	*William and Mary Quarterly*
ZA	Zeeuws Archief, Middelburg, Zeeland

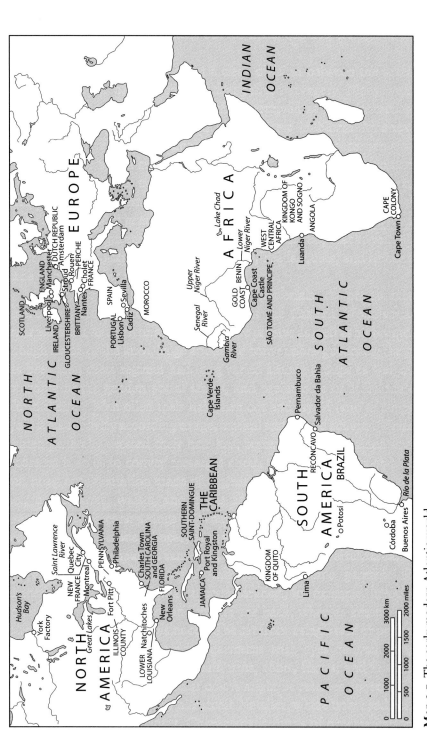

Map 0.1 The early modern Atlantic world

INTRODUCTION: FASHIONING THE ATLANTIC WORLD

On October 6, 1761, the newly widowed Luiza Maria da Conceição witnessed the drafting of an inventory of the estate left by her late husband Manoel João Viana.[1] Born in a northern Portuguese village, Viana had emigrated to Salvador da Bahia. São Salvador da Bahia de Todos os Santos, to give its full and proper name, was capital of colonial Brazil between 1549 and 1763, a refreshment and refitting stop (*escala*) for ships traveling to and from India, port for the sugar plantations of a substantial hinterland, and distribution center for licit and contraband Asian goods throughout the South Atlantic, notably cloth for the massive Angolan slave trade.[2] In that bustling city, Viana married, fathered at least two children, and set up as a *comerciante*, apparently specializing in fabrics.[3]

Following accepted practice, the inventory itemized and valued the decedent's movable and immovable possessions, both private and professional. Apparel and textiles made up a substantial part of Viana's assets. His own garments included a suit comprising breeches, jacket, and waistcoat of black *droguete* (a mixed fabric of wool and silk or wool and flax linen), along with a pair of silk stockings, all in good condition; eleven "rather worn" shirts, some of Indian cotton cloth, others of *bertanha* (a fine linen); four pairs of white linen breeches; and an item whose identity time has effaced from the fading archival page.

Viana's shop stocked an impressive array of textiles. Dozens of pieces of handkerchief material each contained a dozen or more individual kerchiefs that could be used as shawls or scarves, as headwraps, or as nose wipes. Many handkerchiefs were silk, others Indian cotton, some French linen, yet others of unspecified material, but nearly all were colorful: blue, red, light yellow. Of the many lengths of cloth catalogued, nearly a hundred were noted as "pieces" (a few of them 40 meters in length), while dozens more were measured in *côvados* (0.68 m) and *varas* (1.1 m); together, they totaled at least 5,000 meters of fabric woven from diverse natural fibers. Cottons included expensive chintz, cheap French *ruam*, coarse and smooth Indian muslin, and yet other kinds at all price points. Linens, too, ran the gamut from choice dazzling white cambric and Hamburg *bertanha* through medium-priced French *crês* and Indian types to rock-bottom rough *linhagem* and fibery tow (*estopa*). Viana had some expensive silk chintz on offer, but his customers could also select medium-priced silks such as shiny taffeta or colorful blue, green, red, or white shagreen for lining. Similarly, while shoppers for woolens might fancy very high-end blue or green broadcloth or slightly less expensive but still pricey black baize, they could also find much more reasonable varieties: cheaper baize (in various colors), smooth but durable serge, or plain-weave camlet.

Interspersed with handkerchiefs and fabrics were ready-made garments: fifteen frilled cotton shirts and five that were striped, eleven pairs of red linen breeches lined with cotton, four cotton *penteadors* (*peinadors* or dressing gowns), ten muslin cravats, a cotton and lace nightcap, and a blue silk with silver sprigs front piece for a waistcoat. Two bed coverings also put in an appearance: an extravagant flame-colored satin coverlet embroidered, fringed, and otherwise ornamented with silk and lined with pearl-colored taffeta, and a modestly priced white linen counterpane (bedspread).[4] The report wound up with a tally of several dozen French and other semifine hats; a few dozen pairs of men's and women's stockings (some French), white and colored, made from silk, linen, and cotton; and length upon length of tape, fringe, lace, silk twist, cord, and braid, amounting to several thousand meters in all.

The inventory was drawn up only to assure the appropriate succession of one individual's property. Yet beyond their workaday purpose, the dry and formulaic entries that enumerate Viana's estate provide tantalizing clues about trade patterns, fabric consumption practices, and sartorial cultures that came into existence once Europeans constructed commercial networks stretching across much of the planet, settled throughout the Atlantic, engaged in massive cultural and population transfers and disruptions, and established new economies and societies. Those commercial patterns, appropriative usages, and dress mores are the subjects of this book. Focusing on cloth and apparel in delimited locations between the mid-seventeenth and late eighteenth centuries, *The Material Atlantic* investigates the ways in which women and men of diverse ethnicities, statuses, and occupations fashioned their apparel from materials old and new, familiar and strange, in a variety of geoclimatic, political, and sociocultural environments that presented both innovative possibilities and severe constraints. This book describes the fabrics and attire that became available to consumers, traces the modes and occasions of their acquisition, interprets the meanings of their deployment, and explains the effects of these developments on global textile industries. By analyzing the dress that disparate Atlantic residents fashioned, *The Material Atlantic* explores crucial developments that characterized early modernity: the material effects of colonialism, proliferation of new and widely sourced goods, massive enslavement, deep and prolonged intercultural transfers, changes in consumer behavior and attitudes, new expressions of social identification, and innovations in manufacturing before the onset of factory industrialization.

But how can studying cloth and clothing in the Atlantic basin shed light on these subjects? Why examine locations scattered across four continents facing onto a vast body of water? Why privilege the seventeenth and eighteenth centuries? What kinds of sources are available to help answer these questions? What bodies of scholarship can help apprehend the phenomena under consideration, and what theories explain them?

Textiles and dress

Among the first human manufactures, textiles were both independently developed in many parts of the world and diffused among cultures beginning in early prehistory.[5] In most societies, production was focused on local needs. But some textile raw materials, semi-processed cloth, and finished fabrics long circulated within sizeable trading regions such as West Africa, the Indian Ocean, the Mediterranean, or Mesoamerica. In addition, knowledge of raw materials and techniques slowly disseminated over great distances, as did small quantities of luxury cloth, such as the Chinese silks and Indian cottons occasionally found in medieval Europe.[6]

European colonial and commercial expansion of the early modern era (roughly the late fifteenth through the late eighteenth centuries) eroded the relative isolation of existing commercial regions, and fabrics and garments became the pre-eminent interculturally exchanged consumer manufactures. Cloth and clothing constituted more than two-thirds of English exports to West Africa in the eighteenth century, cotton goods alone the same proportion of French imports from India.[7] So central were textiles to the deerskin trade between Muscogulges (Creeks) and European settlers, Kathryn Holland Braund proposes, that it "could have been termed the cloth trade . . . for fabrics of various weights, colors, and designs were the staples."[8] Beyond commercial exchanges, all manner of gifting – official and private, clerical and lay – assured that woven fabrics were increasingly present and prominent in societies around the globe.

Textiles and items made from them were major consumption items for individuals in all segments of the population. Enhanced levels of domestic comfort raised demand for bed and table linen, window and door curtains, floor and table rugs, while traders and agriculturists depended on sails, sacks, and strainers all made of fabric.[9] For most people, however, clothing was their most considerable and most regular consumer expenditure apart from food and drink. In late seventeenth- and eighteenth-century England, for instance, apparel represented by far families' biggest outlay for manufactures, accounting for up to 15 percent of their annual budgets; across the Atlantic, clothing for enslaved persons was estimated at 11 percent of a model Georgia rice plantation's yearly costs in the mid-eighteenth century.[10]

The economic significance of apparel is evident. Its meanings are less so. Clothing is materially and metaphorically multivalent. Besides fulfilling utilitarian needs for warmth and protection, it affords considerable if diverse aesthetic satisfactions. By virtue of the sundry properties – texture, quality, color, pattern, density, to name a few – of the many substances out of which it can be fashioned, apparel is remarkably protean, available for multiple expressive and symbolic projects.[11] It can denote an individual's personal style or participation in a group's fashion, declare autonomy or exhibit conformity or subordination, reveal aspiration for economic and cultural capital or attainment of wealth and status. What one wears may announce deliberate syncretism or simply reflect the selection at hand, manifest an eager social assimilation or a scornful rejection of norms, disclose one's identity or disguise it. In fact, both *clothing* ("the items of apparel" that one puts on) and the more comprehensive *dress* (everything worn on and over the body to cover, add to, or alter it) are likely to convey several messages at once, not all of them intended and some probably mixed.[12]

Though rules formal and informal have long sought to prescribe dress and its meanings, most sartorial items, whether singly or as part of an ensemble, have no fixed signification: what they denote is defined by interaction among wearer, situation, and norms of attire. If, moreover, dress may reflect conscious choice and fashioning, it may equally be a matter of unmindful, virtually automatic routine.[13] And even when an individual does exercise choice, its outcome is shaped by a congeries of mainly implicit values, dispositions, and practices (the know-how proper to the person's social situation, or what Pierre Bourdieu calls her or his "habitus").[14] So with few exceptions, dress incorporates personal expression and social standard, individual statement and collective convention.

Not only, finally, are the meanings of dress ambiguous but our knowledge of dress in the past is mediated by problematic sources, as we shall see below. Still, the effort is well worth undertaking. What individuals and groups wore imparts much about the social and cultural imperatives and meanings that governed quotidian experience in general, and about the impact of early modern Atlantic commerce and colonialism in particular. Fortunately, textiles and attire left abundant documentary traces, because early modern people regarded dress as a critical guide to understanding both their own societies and those newly encountered. Even though dress is essentially a visual, even fugitive, means of communication, it provoked a great deal of written commentary and a myriad of pictorial representations.

Places and period

Merchant networks that traversed the globe brought a plenitude of fabrics and garments like those listed in Viana's inventory to localities throughout the great Atlantic basin. Nearly a dozen of these sites figure most prominently in *The Material Atlantic*. Two were in regions of independent indigenous states: Cape Coast Castle on the West African Gold Coast (now littoral Ghana), which from 1672 was the English Royal African Company's operations center for the entire region, and Angola and neighboring kingdoms in west Central Africa, where merchants from several European states trafficked, Catholic orders established missions, and the Portuguese undertook colonization, with mixed results.[15] The others were European settlements and the commercial hinterlands they developed: Spanish Buenos Aires and the areas under its jurisdiction in the Río de la Plata region of today's Argentina; Dutch Cape Town and inland agricultural regions in present-day South Africa; Salvador da Bahia and the Recôncavo, a sugar and tobacco plantation zone that arcs around the Baía de Todos os Santos west of Salvador in Portuguese Brazil; the southern district of French Caribbean Saint-Domingue (today's Haïti), which had multiple small towns and ports rather than a single center; British colonial Port Royal, its successor Kingston, and the island of Jamaica that they dominated commercially as well as socially; the continental North American French colonies of New Orleans and rural lower Louisiana, and Montreal with the nearby settlement zone that grew along the Saint Lawrence River and its tributaries in New France; and the British mainland North American settlements of Charles Town (present-day Charleston, South Carolina), whose trading zone reached into what is today the neighboring state of Georgia, and Philadelphia and its commercial hinterland that eventually stretched west into present-day central Pennsylvania and east into New Jersey.

While hardly an exhaustive registry of places engaged in Atlantic commerce and colonialism, these ports and colonies encompass all the populated continents facing on that basin, as well as its major non-polar geographic and climatic zones, economic structures, socio-cultural ecologies, and European colonial empires. They were, moreover, economically and geographically dynamic. Not only did trade and colonial settlement continually expand – or at least attempt to – but the economic and cultural reach of Atlantic ports and settlements always extended into contact zones beyond current commercial and colonial borders. Most important, the locations studied in this book exemplify the diversity of dress cultures affected by the materials, manners, and modes introduced by early modern Atlantic commerce and colonization.

In the mid-seventeenth century, clothing in many Atlantic societies was tailored from woven-fiber textiles, but in others it was fashioned from furs, skins, and beaten tree bark. Even when woven fabrics were the dominant dress materials, moreover, societies had different preferred fiber types and favorite cloth sources, which might be local, regional, or far distant. Apparel styles ranged from what Europeans considered nakedness or shockingly minimal coverage of the body to degrees of envelopment that at their most pronounced left little save extremities visible. Similarly varied were the forms of alternate or additional types of corporeal adornment and their place within overall clothing ensembles. Together, this diversity and dynamism enable *The Material Atlantic* to analyze the impact of colonialism and globalizing commerce not only on sartorial goods and styles but on cultural practices of both long-established and nascent societies.

Early modern Atlantic colonialism and commerce reached their apogee in the period from the mid-seventeenth to the later eighteenth centuries. European exploration of the basin dates back to the fifteenth century, colonization and exploitation of natural resources to the sixteenth. But only from the 1640s did "a shared Atlantic world," which Pierre Gervais has defined as a "thick web of relationships, linking a number of people on each side of the Atlantic Ocean," come into existence.[16] Beginning in those years, proliferating settlement and rapid expansion of the plantation economy greatly increased commerce and migration while both supplying and demanding a much broader array of trade goods.[17] That Atlantic world reached its height across the first three-quarters of the eighteenth century. Whereas some 1,144,000 Africans and Europeans left for the Americas in 1640–1700, about 3,666,000 departed between 1700 and 1760.[18] Between the early eighteenth century and the early 1770s the Atlantic trade of England about sextupled and France's rose at least eightfold; in both cases, growth in Atlantic commerce was at least double the gains registered in other commercial zones.[19]

The Atlantic cloth and clothing trades were particularly dynamic. Overall, England's textile exports and re-exports (of which more than three-quarters of the cottons and some of the silks were Asian) grew less than twofold between 1699–1701 and 1772–74 – but they rose more than sixfold to the Americas and West Africa. Across that period, textiles always comprised more than half of total English exports and re-exports, and about three-fifths of manufacturing exports and re-exports. In every major fiber category, Atlantic markets were more buoyant than any other. Exports and re-exports of cottons and calicoes more than quadrupled, of woolens and linens more than sextupled, of silks jumped nearly sevenfold. By 1772–74, Atlantic locations took more than 90 percent of British linen exports and re-exports, as well as nearly half of all silks and more than a quarter of all woolens, cottons, and calicoes.[20] Across the late seventeenth and eighteenth centuries, in short, merchant networks delivered all manner of woven-fiber textiles from Europe and beyond to the diverse populations of the rapidly developing Atlantic world. How, why, and what sorts of dress were made from these goods are the subject of this book.

Sources and complications

Studies of dress during the early modern era can draw on a wide variety of sources. The multitude of fabrics, apparel, places, and populations in the early modern Atlantic invites – indeed, mandates – consideration of and comparison among sources as diverse as possible, with the proviso that many are more pertinent for some groups than for others. Before modern marketing surveys (which have their own shortcomings), direct evidence about consumer preferences – the motives behind appropriation acts – is at best scanty, necessitating reliance on inference from traces and clues left in an assortment of documents, written and pictorial. Yet all pose problems for analysis and interpretation, thanks to the different purposes for which they were created, the discrete conventions on which they draw, and the manifold dispositions that inform them. Moreover, none includes every group in all locations across the entire period, and even the most widely available have many local idiosyncrasies.

Probate or post-mortem inventories like Viana's are the most numerous and typically the most detailed documentary sources. Usually drawn up shortly after death by notaries paid a small proportion of the total value of the estate, by court-appointed executors when the decedent left a will, or by administrators when the decedent died intestate, numerous similarities in form and content obtained among them. No matter where prepared, they customarily contained information about the decedent and heirs; lists of movable property, including cash and financial instruments; declarations of credits, debts, and items that were missing or on loan; sworn signatures of those responsible for drafting the document, appraisers (if any), and witnesses; and (less often) values for some or all of the goods enumerated. Some also listed real property, though unimproved land – and sometimes all real estate – might not be appraised.

Though inventories are compendious and widely found, only a minority of deaths generated one. The goods of children, indentured servants, the enslaved, and indigenous people were almost never inventoried, nor were many estates of adult free settlers, particularly married women. Inventories were most likely to be prepared when a dispute over a decedent's property had emerged or was anticipated: when heirs disagreed about division of goods; when creditors required satisfaction; when a community of goods dissolved upon the decease of one of the partners; when minor children needed non-parental guardians; or when there were children from more than one marriage. Keeping in mind as well the many documents lost over time, it is clear that surviving inventories do not constitute random samples of the populations in the places from which they originate.

Nor are the inventories that were created trouble-free. The local authorities or notaries who composed them used current terminology that sometimes proves impenetrable to twenty-first-century scholars. Textiles are especially fraught. Fiber composition often changed over time: thus the fabric called a "rouen" or "ruam" after its initial French place of production was made of linen in the seventeenth century but usually, though not always, of cotton from some point in the eighteenth. Equally, cloth could be made of diverse materials in the same period (an eighteenth-century "check" could be a linen, a cotton, or a combination of both, and was often simply but unhelpfully denominated "check" in an inventory), or be referred to by an attribute such as its pattern (e.g., "damask") with the fiber – which in this case could be linen, silk, wool – left unspecified. Apparel terminology could also be ambiguous: in New France, an *habit* could be a coat or a suit, while in the Cape Colony *rok* might signify a skirt or a coat.

In addition, listings could be incomplete or lack historically significant information because heirs accepted items en bloc, compilers were ignorant or negligent, decedents granted items in wills. Appraisers, often neighbors of the decedent, might be ill-informed, and though merchants or artisans were often called in for specific expertise, they might be unable to provide price or other needed data. Worse for the purposes of this book, many inventories either omit clothing altogether or lump it into one catchall category such as "purse and apparell." A growing problem everywhere as the eighteenth century progressed, this defect was most pronounced in Britain and the Netherlands and their respective colonies. Finally, even the most accurate and thorough inventory cannot provide an account of the process of consumption: it is a snapshot not a film, a record of accumulation rather than a narrative of acts of appropriation.

For all that, inventories are invaluable.[21] They incorporate a broad selection of social groups, occupations, and locations from both genders among free adult European and European-descent populations around the entire Atlantic, and in some places include free people of color as well. Moreover, the most common reasons for which inventories were compiled cut across lines of age and wealth: the need to provide for minor children, for instance, resulted in many inventories of decedents who were neither affluent nor old. Comparisons of estimates and actual sale prices show that valuation errors were minor, very rarely more than a few percent, while detailed merchant inventories permit interpolation of fabric price data where needed. And if it is impossible to track individuals' sartorial behavior over time, sufficient inventories have survived from determinate periods in both the later seventeeenth and later eighteenth centuries to permit identification of significant group trends and patterns in many places.

One inventory makes a cameo appearance when Native American dress is investigated in Chapter 3. The most substantial Atlantic populations appear very rarely in inventories, however, and then almost always fortuitously and inferentially. It is likely that the coarse *linhagem* and *estopa* linen in Viana's holdings, for instance, were destined to dress enslaved men and women – that was, after all, a leading use for such fabrics in Brazil – but such information is not found in the document itself. To learn it, we must turn to other sources, including merchant papers, official and personal letters and reports, and newspapers, in which Africans both free and enslaved, as well as indigenous inhabitants of the Americas, feature more consistently, overtly, and intentionally. Unlike inventories, however, which were created by, for, and within European and free settler societies, all of these other documents, no matter how anodyne, were created by outsiders to the communities on which they reported.

On the whole, commercial records are most straightforward, not least because they consist mainly of information about trade to or aggregate supply in particular locations. For this reason, they figure centrally in analyses of textile commerce in Chapter 2. Along with inventories, they allow a kind of paper-based (occasionally parchment-based) archeology that supplements material remains or even substitutes for those that have been lost.[22] Still, like inventories, merchant archives reveal little about the uses to which the items on offer were put. They disclose the availability of cloth and clothing, as well as the conditions and situations of exchange. But commercial records do not tell why people acquired textiles and apparel or what customers did with their new possessions.

Some of these deficiencies in information about consumer demand can be remedied with the aid of contemporary narrative works. Missionaries, officials, and visitors usually took an interest in the dress worn by those whom they evangelized, administered, or observed because apparel was widely considered a reliable marker of civility and thus of suitability for allegiance, conversion, or respect. To be sure, these sources must be used with care. Very seldom are African or Amerindian voices heard (no matter whether free or enslaved), and then usually in translation and virtually always in transcription, with all the inevitable difficulties entailed by such processes no matter how forceful or well informed the speaker, no matter how attentive or sympathetic the scribe. Further, many works are palimpsests of primary, secondary, apocryphal, and even invented materials, and they may concentrate on the exotic, picturesque, and bizarre. Authors who never saw the lands or peoples they ostensibly described retailed mis-understandings, exaggerations, and outright fabrications, as did writers who sought to enhance the reputation of themselves or their group or to denigrate others.

Few commentators were disinterested. The *Jesuit Relations*, annual reports on the Society's missionary activities throughout the world, have rightly been regarded as invaluable proto-ethnographic reports. But on occasion they tried to advance one of their principal objectives – increasing lay support and funding for evangelization – by detailing the difficulties the Fathers faced and the strangeness of the customs they encountered. Descriptions of plantation societies often overtly or covertly defended chattel bondage, or bitterly assailed it, by one-sided characterizations of the material life of the enslaved. Other

accounts – whether for colonial proprietors, for mother country govern-
ments, or just for wider anonymous reading publics – could be yet more
overtly moralistic, propagandistic, or sensational.

Invaluable information on clothing and its uses can nevertheless
be extracted from such documents. They can be collated within and
across time and space, though because authors routinely – but usually
without acknowledgement – copied from one another, agreement may
only reveal a common source; fortunately, scholars have begun to
produce critical commentaries on or editions of some of the most widely
cited of these sources.[23] Moreover, many writers were conscientious,
making use of information gathered first-hand, talking to or compiling
information from others with direct experience, using sources that are
now lost. Then, too, partisan and prejudiced works can be read against
the grain by exploiting contradictions or by extrapolating from information subsidiary to their authors' intent. And because such reports are
particularly interesting for what they reveal about the outlook of their
writers, they figure prominently in Chapter 1 (dress at the beginning of
our period) as well as in Chapters 3 and 4, which focus on dress
practices among groups that Europeans regarded and treated as savage
or subordinate.

Newspaper advertisements are a rich source for sartorial
knowledge, notably listings seeking the return of fugitive slaves, servants, and apprentices, who for ease of recognition were frequently
described in terms of their clothing as well as (and in many cases more
than) by their physiognomy. Of course, runaway listings are not
necessarily inventories of all the clothing owned by the individuals
described: they may simply note what was worn at the time of escape
or the apparel that masters or mistresses considered distinctive and
thus easily recognizable. Yet when and where they are sufficiently
abundant they give an excellent sense of the array of garments held
by those in permanent or temporary bondage, and they permit developments to be followed over time. The rub is that whereas newspapers
were becoming common in western Europe as the seventeenth century
progressed, they only appeared in British colonies in the early eighteenth century and in French colonies in the 1760s; what is more, in the
Caribbean only a small minority of the runaway advertisements mentions dress.

Myriad paintings, engravings, woodcuts, and other images
portray the early modern Atlantic and its inhabitants. Frequently

more vivid and captivating than written documents, the realistic style of many of these depictions can give the impression of transparent reproduction of their subject matter free from representational distortions. Yet if exempt from the linguistic issues bedeviling written sources, these pictures raise problems of their own. Not only were many images of Africa and the Americas and their inhabitants not based on direct observation. Artists also frequently deviated from or entirely ignored the passages that they were purportedly illustrating, and publishers were wont to recycle depictions among different texts, typically without acknowledgement.

Even apparently straightforward renderings "from life" or "on the spot" were shaped by a host of artistic conventions derived from European models. Take, for instance, the verisimilitude of the paintings of the Italo-English Agostino Brunias (c. 1730–96), whose oeuvre provides the best extant portfolio of the quotidian activities of eighteenth-century indigenous, enslaved, and colonizing inhabitants of the West Indies. Despite its Caribbean subject matter and setting, Brunias's work was firmly rooted in such metropolitan genres as the so-called urban "cries" and fashion illustrations that delineated types rather than individuals, as well as in the romantic idealization of both figures and landscapes.[24] Patron participation also modified art works. For their portraits, Timothy Breen has argued, colonial sitters typically selected the garments and fabrics in which they were to be depicted, and they had aspirational rather than representational objectives in mind. This imagistic self-fashioning intended to show them not as they physically and materially existed but as they wanted to be visually perceived, with dress denoting the status and wealth they sought to project.[25]

But if visual images cannot be taken as objective representations of the subjects depicted, artists were not mere tools of conventions or clients. Neither were the images they created simple flights of fancy unworthy of serious study. Art works often violated or complicated established norms, and in ways productive for historical analysis. In addition, many times artists, like writers, had access to sources that have since disappeared, and, like texts, visual depictions can be compared and contextualized. Many images, too, were created by observers with minimal or no formal artistic training but with excellent knowledge of the localities in which they found themselves, and their depictions frequently turn out to have been remarkably accurate.[26]

Equally important, even stylized and distorted representations helped both to produce and to reveal contemporary understandings and practices. The circulation of images of clothing shaped and was shaped by sartorial cultures, while also making evident attitudes about the dress worn by specific groups, if not individuals. As John Styles has noted, stereotyped portrayals are compelling because they evoke characteristic attire: Artists might caricature particular items of apparel, but their images got their force by being rooted in "the typicality of the clothes they depicted."[27] It would be hazardous to take any image – even or especially a portrait – as the literal likeness of a particular person, much less of her or his wardrobe. But together with the wealth of information that can be retrieved from written documents, the copious clues about fabrics, garments, dress habits, and cultural values encoded within visual materials enable textured insight into early modern clothing cultures.

Approaches and debates

The Material Atlantic enlists, modifies, and extends recent scholarship on early modern globalization, the Atlantic world, and consumption. Though each has a distinct intellectual genealogy, focuses on disparate issues, and relies on different sources, they can provide insights that help interpret trends, patterns, and consequences of textile and apparel practices in the seventeenth and eighteenth centuries.

Early modern historians have long studied European overseas expansion and foreign commerce and the sundry effects that they occasioned. Increasingly, these developments are subsumed under the capacious rubric of "globalization" to spotlight not only the "intensification of commercial, economic, social and cultural connections between different areas of the world" but also the integration of innovative or newly available goods into the daily lives of substantial groups of people even before the advent of factory industrialization.[28] Intended to displace hierarchic, diffusionist, and Eurocentric explanations, the global turn has not been unanimously embraced. Among early modernists, its proponents have with some justice been faulted for slighting European primacy in constructing, coordinating, and sustaining global connections; ignoring unequal power relations among participants; and anachronistically exaggerating the extent and significance of intercontinental commercial and related exchanges.[29] Yet if early modern globalization often differed from what is sometimes claimed for it, its emphasis on interaction, polycentric agency, and hybridity is productive for understanding some modes and meanings of innovative dress practices.

Though a form of textile-based globalization arguably linked together much of the medieval Indian Ocean, it was Europeans who established networks that greatly heightened worldwide movements of people, products, images, and styles in the early modern era.[30] Moreover, Europeans retained a principal role in the operation of these networks, even when neither producers, sellers, nor purchasers were European, as with East Indian companies' intra-Asian trade or the cotton cloth woven and dyed under Portuguese supervision in the Cape Verde Islands for consumers on the West African mainland. Many globally traded commodities came as well from producers in Europe or European colonies: manufactures from the former, so-called "colonial groceries" (sugar, coffee, tobacco) and raw materials like indigo and cotton from the latter. Within and between networks, power was asymmetrically distributed and exercised: Europeans and free settlers typically commanded more resources, notably capital (usually in the form of credit flows), the physical assets required for long-distance oceanic transport, and relevant technologies.

Yet if Europeans and colonists of European descent dominantly structured early modern globalization, its personnel, contents, and customers were remarkably heterogeneous. Much of the commercial activity associated with global trade was not in European hands, and much of whom and what was traded – slaves, most cotton and many silk fabrics, spices, and tea – came from societies that Europeans did not control. Goods, fashions, and usages did not circulate unilaterally or unidirectionally, for societies with customs and concerns not dictated by Europeans accounted for a great deal of supply and demand. *The Material Atlantic* demonstrates that early modern worldwide trade fostered the wide availability of some similar items – certain textiles in particular were global goods par excellence – but they were consumed within specific imperial, regional, and local contexts. Convergence and divergence were equally intrinsic to early modern globalization.

Early modern globalization should not be confused with today's. Not only did it entail very different forms of production, commercial organization and conduct, and transport and communications. It took place without formal liberalization of markets or creation of transnational political and economic organizations; in fact, imperial, mercantilist, and other barriers shaped and limited its extent. It also proceeded slowly and unevenly, sharply contrasting in both scale and scope with more recent manifestations, and it encompassed a more circumscribed array of places and phenomena.[31] But then as now, this book argues, globalization provoked diverse strategies among both sellers and buyers. Some involved provision and acquisition of goods that replaced indigenous products and cultures; others entailed customization that targeted or domesticated imported commodities to diverse environments, a process now often termed (g)localization.[32] At times, European goods and standards proved authoritative; in other situations, consequential products and influences emerged from different locations; in yet others, producers and consumers far distant from one another mutually refashioned the goods that global trade circulated.[33] Any given outcome depended on a host of circumstances; as the chapters of this book document, only empirical investigation of concrete dress practices can establish which held true in a given situation.

All these processes can be observed again and again throughout the Atlantic basin. As with the topics now encompassed by the study of globalization, historical attention to the societies located around the Atlantic is hardly a novelty. But "Atlantic world" or "Atlantic system" histories propose that the basin constituted not simply an aggregate of places but an increasingly integrated community; a new world created by encounters, fusions, and transformations of old worlds; an entity particularly characterized and joined by intercontinental and transnational flows of people, objects, and concepts. Sundry approaches have been essayed. All, however, insist on the primordial significance of interactive rather than unilateral relationships that transcended geographic, cultural, and imperial borders.[34]

As critics have not been shy to point out, Atlantic histories have often fallen short of their programmatic claims, or even the promise of their titles. All too often remaining within national and colonial frameworks (the Spanish Atlantic, the French, the Dutch), with preponderant attention devoted to the British North Atlantic, many are little more than the traditional topics of European expansion or imperial studies renamed – and even then are likely to ignore the European metropoles. At the same time, the "Atlantic" epithet has been misapplied to processes that were broader or narrower. Early modern European political and commercial expansion was worldwide, not solely located in the Atlantic, while early modern merchants built networks – commercial relationships – that were not primarily demarcated by physical or political borders.[35]

The early modern Atlantic was, moreover, neither self-enclosed nor boundaryless; nested within a globalizing world, it was continually, intimately, and necessarily articulated with other zones. A substantial number of the commodities that circulated within the Atlantic came from outside that basin; indeed, the existence of most colonies therein depended on massive imports of Indian cotton fabrics that were traded in West and west Central Africa for the enslaved men and women who toiled on plantations in the Americas. As a result, trends within the Atlantic were inevitably influenced by wider global patterns. At the same time, political units significantly oriented trade and thus material cultures. Hence no matter how global their aspirations or how personal their networks, merchants found it "easiest and most cost-effective" to do business "within imperial boundaries and alliances."[36] The contours of the Atlantic were, finally, fluid over time and space. Some areas extending far inland eventually became strongly integrated with coastal ports and posts, whereas others much closer to littorals remained largely untouched by Atlantic influences.

But if the Atlantic was both part of a wider history and contained numerous diverse ecologies each with its own development, it was also a zone of especially dense networks of interconnections and interactions. While no merchant (or anyone else) thought in specifically "Atlantic" terms, Atlantic routes and operations were the core of their networks, and their headquarters were situated in the Atlantic basin.[37] No European colonial empire was restricted to the Atlantic arena, yet all (with the exception of the Dutch) had their demographic centers and their most important settlements there. Because of the thick intermingling of colonies and commercial networks, and the humming reciprocal connections forged among disparate economic, social, and cultural systems, the Atlantic focus of this book advances understanding of processes that unfolded globally, throughout the basin, and in more delimited locations.

A meaningful activity by which individuals and groups acquire and make objects their own (that is, "appropriate" them), consumption is a central cultural practice and process of symbolic communication in all societies.[38] Many scholars have proposed, however, that a "consumer revolution" involving qualitative as well as quantitative changes occurred in the early modern era.[39] Though numerous aspects of the thesis remain in debate, it is now widely accepted that at least across the seventeenth and eighteenth centuries, growing numbers of people in Europe and its colonies evinced the ability and the propensity to purchase consumer goods in an expanding array of commercial venues. Shoppers selected from an ever-wider variety of items, many of them previously unknown foodstuffs and manufactures from Atlantic and global producers, in a profusion of materials, qualities, and finishes from suppliers using innovative techniques of promotion and presentation.

An Atlantic perspective, however, raises questions about the geographic and social reach of the changes, and the modernizing teleology that underlies it. How many buyers exhibited novel attitudes, values, and habits, a behavioral complex frequently termed "consumerism"? Did enhanced social mobility and shifting gender roles increasingly encourage all consumers to act according to individualistic motives, ignore or reject time-honored strictures about purportedly morally dubious and economically harmful "luxury" expenditure, and display a marked taste for the new (an aggregate of dispositions usually designated "fashion")? Analyses of the package of changes summed up by the term "consumer revolution," this book proposes, must take account of selective adoptions and adaptations that occurred around the Atlantic.

The evidence deployed to demonstrate that fundamental changes in practices and meanings of consumption occurred during the early modern era has been mainly drawn from northwestern Europe and colonial British North America and has featured populations enjoying personal autonomy. Examining a broader range of societies, *The Material Atlantic* revises existing interpretations to account more accurately for appropriations of dress undertaken not only by metropolitans and free settlers but also by the substantial populations around the basin that were held in bondage and by indigenous people living beyond the boundaries of European settlements and stations yet engaged in exchange with them.

In any society, admittedly, the significance of consumption acts is never unambiguous. For one thing, all goods are polysemic; their meaning depends on how, when, and where they are employed and which consumers use them. For another, consumers' motives are always formed and expressed in complicated ways, in a jostle of conscious reasons and unconscious forces. In short, consumption acts involve more than simply acquisition: they also entail appropriation, that is, taking possession of an item's panoply of utilitarian, symbolic, and aesthetic properties. Appropriation, however, is rarely autonomous.

Rather, it is shaped not only by climate and geographic environment but by multiple overt and unseen sociocultural factors including wealth, profession, status, gender, and ethnicity; supply and demand conditions; imperatives toward imitation and toward originality; the operation of forcible or discreet power relations.

The Material Atlantic decodes practices of dress acquisition and appropriation. It documents sartorial choices that intended to affirm norms, and others that set out to disrupt them, practices that signaled inclusion and those that marked exclusion. The book traces the results of sumptuary laws designed to mandate certain garments or fabrics, and to forbid others. Most of all, in the Atlantic world, where identities were particularly fluid thanks to the continual intercultural movements and mixtures of peoples, goods, styles, and ideas, this book shows how dress practices emerged out of and promoted identifications – both chosen collective self-representations and imposed categorizations – increasingly defined by some combination of gender, ethnicity, status, occupation, and class.[40]

Beyond the inherent intricacy of all appropriation, moreover, Atlantic trade involved repeated encounters between disparate material goods, cultural conventions, and sociopolitical projects. As a result, the sartorial practices analyzed in The Material Atlantic involved a good deal of the material and behaviorial intermingling that scholars have denominated hybridization, syncretism, or bricolage.[41] To capture the complexity of both the processes at work and the material results, this book delimits what it calls "dress regimes." Such regimes consist of objects (garments and related items of dress), practices by which they were appropriated and deployed, and verbal and pictorial discourses that sought to direct, explain, and justify (or delegitimize) both objects and practices. Dress regimes could be widely eclectic or narrowly selective, highly innovative or strikingly traditional, broadly diffused or of more circumscribed ascendancy. But like the identifications they expressed, all were dynamic, incorporating contributions from old and new materials, imperatives, and styles.

Claims and chapters

On the basis of these objects, places, period, sources, and approaches, The Material Atlantic investigates the ways in which novel as well as well-known cloth and clothing were disseminated and taken up around the Atlantic basin during the seventeenth and eighteenth centuries and explains how and why they supplanted, modified, or sustained existing dress regimes. Each chapter opens – as this one has – with a visual or written document that highlights dress both in a specific place and time and within a larger Atlantic context. Most generally, *The Material Atlantic* argues that by supplying an increasing variety of similar fabrics to diverse locations and populations, early modern globalization enabled both standardization and diversification of dress styles. Concomitant trends toward material cultural homogenization and heterogeneity were inherent in early modern globalization. Though typically considered a recent phenomenon, concurrent convergence and divergence of material cultures was a defining characteristic of the pre-industrial Atlantic.

As people living throughout the Atlantic basin incorporated imported woven-fiber fabrics into their sartorial imaginary and prac- tice, they all, this book demonstrates, created fashions from specific amalgams of habitus, needs, desires, conventions, rules, and available supplies.[42] Sometimes these fashions entailed little more than existing items rearranged into new styles,[43] but frequently they were inventive combinations of novel apparel, fabrics, and styles. Many fashions were intended to express group identifications or at least aspirations, yet others were designed to manifest difference, mark subordination, or civilize savages. Atlantic fashions included striking innovation as well as affirmation of convention, boundary crossing and border drawing, affiliation and proscription: Involving conformity and dis- tinction, imitation and differentiation, they prescribed, governed, and expressed behavior and attitudes of a wide array of groups rather than providing a uniform template.[44] Free settlers were particularly anxious, and able, to follow metropolitan fashion signals. Enslaved and indigenous people were more creative. Using imported cloth and clothing as well as other materials and practices of adornment they developed syncretic dress regimes rather than, as contemporaries usually insisted, misinterpreted versions of European styles. In fact, these hybrids displayed a level of sartorial creolization – the creation of a new cultural form appropriate to a new environment – that eluded most free settlers.[45] But as a whole, *The Material Atlantic* posits, the dress regimes of Atlantic indigenous peoples, enslaved men and women, and free settlers left an ironic legacy for textile manufacturers. While promoting innovation in some sectors, it sustained long-established products and forms of production in others. Neither globalization in general nor its Atlantic iteration embodied an intrinsic modernizing impetus.

These propositions are elaborated in chapters that describe and interpret the causes, components, and meanings of transformation and persistence in the dress regimes in Atlantic colonies, trading posts, and metropoles. Chapter 1 outlines the variety of appareling practices, contemporary understandings of proper garb, and social, economic, and cultural forces that would both foster and retard sartorial change on the eve of the vast increase in commerce and colonialism that characterized the later seventeenth and eighteenth centuries. Imported woven-fiber textiles were the most important element enabling changes in dress, so Chapter 2 investigates the multiple means, agents, and occasions that distributed these fabrics around the Atlantic basin, the factors that complicated textile supply, and the merchant stocks that resulted.

The next two chapters examine clothing practices among groups subjected to broad and prolonged attempts at redressing not only under European and settler initiative but also on their own. Amerindians were engaged in voluntary and involuntary appareling almost from first contact. Chapter 3 examines the fashions that emerged across the Americas from the goods and processes involved in the material cultural encounter between missionaries, officials, merchants, and Indians. Enslaved and indentured men and women likewise experienced compulsory attiring, yet they too dressed themselves both by necessity and by choice. Chapter 4 explores the content, extent, and ambiguities of sartorial agency in the diverse experiences of life and labor that slaves confronted throughout the Atlantic.

Free settler dress in the tropical Americas and in more temperate colonies including southern Africa are the subjects of Chapters 5 and 6 respectively. Considering the influence of climate, occupation, wealth, gender, and race on appareling habits, they evaluate changes in the dress regimes that free settlers imported from Europe, the disparate ways in which "luxury" and place of residence influenced colonial attire, and the extent to which metropolitan fashions were emulated. After reviewing the scope and import of changes registered in dress regimes of diverse indigenous, colonial, and European societies that constituted the Atlantic world, Chapter 7 concludes by identifying some paradoxical results for textile manufacture: these developments retarded as well as stimulated industrial innovation.

* * *

Most societies located on the Atlantic had long experience with textiles, all with dress. But their sartorial regimes differed greatly, from almost total bodily covering to what Europeans considered nakedness but denizens deemed satisfactory dress. This variety of practices, perceptions, and attitudes formed the backdrop of the nascent material Atlantic.

1 DRESS REGIMES AT THE DAWN OF THE SHARED ATLANTIC

> Women [of the court] wear three kinds of wrappers [*traverse*] from the waist down, one down to the heel, the second shorter, the third shorter yet, each one fringed, tied diagonally, and slit in front: from breast to waist they are dressed in a doublet, and all these garments are made of palm cloth, and over their shoulders a cape of the same material. They walk around with faces uncovered and with a little cap similar to men's. Middling women dress in the same way, but of cheaper cloth, and slaves and low-class women are apparelled only from the waist down, otherwise going naked.[1]

So announced Filippo Pigafetta in a passage on "the clothing of that people, before they became Christians, and after" in his 1591 *Account of the Kingdom of Kongo and Surrounding Lands, Based on the Writings and Words of the Portuguese Duarte Lopez*. A Portuguese merchant who spent 1578–83 in west Central Africa, Lopez then served as envoy of King Alvare I of Kongo to papal Rome, where he met and frequently conversed with the Italian Pigafetta, himself a one-time papal emissary; out of these meetings was born the *Account*.[2] Lopez was one of many European merchants, missionaries, and travelers who reported on the lifeways of the diverse peoples with whom they came in contact across the nascent Atlantic world. Some of their works were sketchy, superficial, filled with errors and fabrications. Others, however, were discerning, richly detailed, proto-ethnographic expositions, frequently accompanied by engravings that illustrated or supplemented the text. Despite inaccuracies, omissions, and blind spots, writings of the latter type make it possible to delineate Atlantic dress regimes just as movement and exchange began to intensify throughout the basin from the early seventeenth century.

Dress encounters: cues and codes

The authors of these works had good reason to comment upon dress. Readers expected information about commercial possibilities in newly explored regions, particularly for goods like apparel textiles that had long been valuable and valued trade commodities. Their own experience, moreover, had taught Europeans that social and cultural cues and codes were woven into clothing, adornments, and their deployment. Hence knowledge about dress practices would yield insight into such crucial matters as class and gender structures, receptivity to unfamiliar religious, diplomatic, and material influences, and level of development of peoples previously unknown to them.

Dress was taken to be a particularly accurate – not to mention immediately apparent – marker of "civilization" or "civility" – or its absence.[3] Like its opposites, "savagery" and "barbarism,"[4] the concept of civilization embraced a congeries of ideas, assumptions, and values about sociocultural institutions and practices that normatively employed dominant conventions and prescriptions of Christian Europe as templates for understanding other peoples (typically as a prelude to converting, conquering, trading with, or trafficking them). With respect to dress, Europeans presumed that near-total coverage of the entire body with an abundance of predominantly shaped garments made of woven-fiber textiles, along with certain adornments of but not in the skin, both comported with and promoted the moral, religious, and social imperatives that fulfilled the appropriate demands of civilization in its most complete, desirable, and correct iteration.

When applying these criteria, Europeans did not necessarily condemn the dress of their contemporaries elsewhere in the Atlantic; on the contrary, they often praised innovative materials, superb craftsmanship, striking colors, and imaginative fashions as they sought to interpret the economic, social, and moral messages they received from other Atlantic peoples and to gauge the commercial, religious, and political potential of engagement with the societies that sustained such material cultures. At the same time, however, commentators regularly expressed dismay over two usages that they found not just uncivil but disconcertingly widespread: nakedness (as well as the attire and fashions that embodied it) and oft-associated forms of corporeal modification, notably tattooing.

Early modern Europeans were certainly familiar with both public undress and artistic nudity.[5] But just as knowledge both true and false about Atlantic societies and their diverse mores was growing, public displays of nakedness, always limited and temporary, were disappearing within Europe itself, as the socially shaped but increasingly internalized self-restraint that Norbert Elias has termed "the civilizing process" took hold.[6] Public nakedness therefore became associated with newly discovered Others. As such, it was subject to religious as well as civil opprobrium, for condemnation of undress was deeply rooted in Judeo-Christian tradition, beginning with the biblical creation story. After Adam and Eve ate the forbidden fruit, according to Genesis 3, their realization of their now ignominious nakedness caused them to fashion fig leaves into loincloths. These were subsequently replaced by animal-skin garments personally tailored by God Himself just before He expelled the first couple from Eden into the world of further sinful disobedience, punishment, and historical change. Hence wrongdoing, retribution, submission, awareness of the body, shame, and modesty – along with both nakedness and clothing – had all originated from the same transgressive act. In this view, to be naked after the Fall was to be at once defiant, reprobate, and indecent, as well as simply uncovered.

What early modern Europeans understood by nakedness included a variety of practices.[7] Sometimes the term signified a complete lack of clothing; in this age of Atlantic encounter, in fact, this meaning became synonymous with lack of European-style civility, as witnessed by the French catch-phrase "Savages go entirely naked."[8] In many accounts, however, "naked" denoted partial (un)dress – typically, garbed in some way below but not above the waist. According to that usage, one could be naked even when "that which modesty wants one to hide" was concealed.[9] Writers who began by flatly affirming the complete exposure of their subjects' bodies regularly went on to qualify their initial claim. "The men go about stark naked," announced the Dutch merchant Pieter de Marees about residents of Cape Verde, West Africa, "except that they cover their private parts with a little piece of Linen."[10] Conceptually, dress and undress seem polar opposites. But in early modern usage they were points on a spectrum of human bodies revealed and concealed, for uncover and vestiture were understood to be as intimately and inherently linked in the present as they prototypically had been in Genesis. No matter what usage of nakedness was under consideration, however, what always distinguished and defined the practice for Europeans was the shocking fact that those who engaged in it "have not the least Shame to be seen naked," but "rather seem to glory in it."[11]

Despite the publication of works such as those describing and illustrating the elaborate corporeal decorations of ancient Britons, most early modern western Europeans were unfamiliar with markings inscribed directly on the skin, whether in prehistoric, classical, and medieval iterations of the practice, or in its presumed survival in Christian communities in some parts of the Ottoman empire. Admittedly, a minority acquired epidermal badges of their own. Pilgrims to the Holy Land and even to western European holy sites such as Loreto in the Italian Marches often had themselves tattooed with crosses, stigmata, or other Christian symbols; sailors sported tattoos (particularly after voyages to the South Pacific); and in some parts of Europe indelible marks identified prisoners.[12] Still, corporeal manifestations were mainly known second-hand and were associated with exotic peoples in newly discovered lands. A handful of Amerindians with body ornamentation visited Europe. But much more influential were printed works, notably the engravings in the first two volumes of Theodore de Bry, *Travels in the East and West Indies*, for these widely distributed compendia were often translated and reprinted.[13]

The predominant European view, then, was that epidermal marking signaled the outsider, never mind if that outsider was found within European society of the day or in its historical genealogy. Besides the biblical prohibition (Leviticus 19:28) of tattooing, understood as a Gentile abomination, the growing practice among European settlers of branding slaves emphasized that to be imprinted on the body was to be immediately recognizable as alien in both status and culture. Some accounts and images presented tattooed bodies benignly, even favorably. But in most, such corporeal alteration was viewed as a deformity that evoked "moral and aesthetic disgust."[14] To seventeenth-century writers, many contemporary Africans and Amerindians – like ancient Britons – were barbarians as much by virtue of their artfully patterned skin as because of their nakedness.

Facts (frequently fallacious) and commentary (frequently prurient) about nakedness and body modification thread through representations of newly encountered peoples, testifying to the simultaneous fascination and repulsion they exercised upon early modern Europeans. As we shall see in later chapters, anxiety about these earmarks of savagery informed efforts to transform the dress regimes that evinced them. For all their disquietude, however, the same depictions provide abundant information about garment and adornment materials, items, and styles, as well as suggesting some of the principles that governed their presentation. If unwittingly, the accounts and images also reveal just how anomalous, in the Atlantic context, western European dress regimes were in structure and in practice.

Yet as a result of European commercial, political, and diplomatic initiatives, it was European modes of dressing that were to be most widely distributed around the Atlantic world. Among traders, missionaries, and settlers, as well as beyond their intentions and the borders of their settlements, missions, and outposts, Atlantic European dress items and habits became available for scrutiny and acceptance – or rejection – in whole or in part. By virtue of these encounters in new environments, European dress regimes themselves were also exposed to conditions and materials of vestmental alteration, and the commodity, epistolary, and personal networks that fostered their pan-Atlantic presence likewise transmitted news of innovations back to the metropoles – even if many of the innovations were largely ignored.

In order properly to evaluate the means and the consequences of these processes, it is necessary first to understand the contours of dress regimes around the Atlantic as confrontations among them got underway. Each of these regimes involved specific materials, formed into characteristic dress items, and arranged in particular shapes according to distinctive rules. At the same time, each shared general attributes. Over the Atlantic basin as a whole, attire and adornment were composed out of two basic materials – woven textiles and animal skins and furs; while dress regimes might mix items made of or trimmed with both materials, for the most part they were kept separate. There were also two basic garment types: shaped or tailored and wrapped or draped. Norms of appropriate corporeal coverage were likewise twofold: full torso or below the waist. Decoration or ornamentation also bifurcated, being either essential parts of a basic outfit or extra adornment, and, finally, as we have seen, nakedness was considered either publicly acceptable or not, and direct corporeal manipulation was also deemed normal (at least for some in a society) or aberrant. Each dress regime had evolved in response to a singular configuration of climatic conditions, raw materials supplies and manufacturing or crafting possibilities, socioeconomic structure, and informal as well as organized values, rules, and institutions. At the same time, each was to some extent receptive to novel material and cultural influences.

Woven textile dress regimes in the Atlantic

"Civility" and coverage: western Europe

The western European states that dominated commerce and colonization in the Atlantic did not form a single entity. Besides being political and economic rivals, Spain, Portugal, France, England, and the Dutch Republic were politically, socially, and religiously dissimilar. Internally, too, they were shot through with religious, social, and cultural differences. Dress reflected and contributed to this diversity. Woolen garb was long associated with England, for example, silks with Spain. In contrast to the distinctive and in some cases elaborate costumes of Catholic clergy, Protestant ministers favored simple dress that differed little from that of laymen. Whereas well-to-do individuals boasted high-heeled shoes, the laboring majority wore simpler, rougher footwear with low heels. Dress also evolved disparately according to place and group, with elites, influenced by Italian styles and Spanish courtly culture, increasingly attuned to fashion in the modern sense with its emphasis on change and novelty. At the same time, common features helped to define a characteristic western Europe dress regime. These shared attributes were particularly pronounced in terms of the materials, structure, and content of dress, as well as the distinctions encoded in and the evolution of specific dress regimes.[15]

As it had since antiquity, early seventeenth-century Atlantic Europe continued to depend for sartorial materials mainly on wool and linen (both flax and hemp) that was produced, woven, finished, and traded throughout the region. European linens and woolens came in a dizzying array of qualities, finishes, and prices, so some type of both fabrics constituted the great majority of the wardrobe of virtually every individual, rich or poor, merchant or peasant, man or woman. Wool

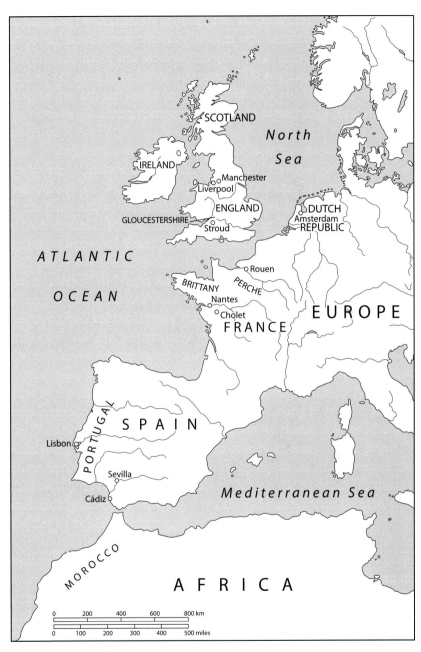

Map 1.1 Atlantic Europe

was beginning, however, to acquire a gendered identity as a symbol of masculinity and therefore particularly suitable for male garb, while still remaining the preferred fabric for female outerwear. Cottons and silks had become available in the later Middle Ages, often imported from India or (more often) the eastern Mediterranean, and centers of production had also emerged in Europe itself, though usually relying on imported raw materials. A number of factors limited the use of silks and cottons, however. No matter where manufactured, silks were expensive and often reserved by law and economics to elites. Because Europeans had yet to master cottons technology, their cottons had to add another fiber, usually linen but on occasion wool or silk, and they were demonstrably inferior in quality and finish to Asian imports.

Atlantic European garments might also be fashioned from furs and leather. By the early modern era, however, such materials were largely restricted to specific items (for instance, leather shoes or fur hats), occupations (such as artisans' leather aprons), or ceremonial occasions (e.g., ermines for coronation cloaks). As garments were singly made (mass production of garments appeared in the later seventeenth century and then initially for military garb), most clothing was made and adorned at home, usually by women. More elaborate clothing, notably that of the affluent, did, however, require the efforts of specialized artisans, who also frequently tailored outer garments, notably coats.

No matter what the materials that composed it, or who fabricated it, pre-contact Atlantic European dress enclosed nearly the entire body of both men and women, leaving only face and hands exposed to sight – and even these might be covered by gloves and, as among Iberian women, *mantillas*, shawls or veils drawn over the face. Lack of covering was taken to denote moral depravity, as well as extreme poverty and danger of sickness from cold, so if possible all but minimal public nakedness was rigorously eschewed. At the same time, clothes most visible to observers were shaped to reveal the body's contours, whether by tailoring or (more recently) by knitting, as knitted stockings increasingly supplanted those made by sewing pieces of cloth together. The male shirts and female smocks or chemises that were starting to appear were interchangeable in style and material, and men's and women's draped outerwear was similar in appearance. But most garments were clearly gendered – at times in sexualized ways, as with the codpieces worn by some men or some women's décolleté. Women had fitted bodices, men doublets. In the main, breeches were reserved to men, skirts or gowns to women aside from a few male professions such as the Catholic clergy and some practitioners of the law.

Wealth and occupation likewise influenced the contours of clothing. The leisured minority dressed in more form-fitting garments than the laboring majority, for whom ease of movement was important and tailoring more summary. Similarly, the affluent boasted more and different garment embellishments than others: though decreasingly, laced ruffs at wrists or neck, for instance, or complicated embroidery rather than ribbons. Both rich and poor might wear adornments, though the wealthy boasted greater amounts and more precious materials. With very few exceptions, ornamentation was worn over the body rather than being directly inscribed on or embedded in it; apart from hair dressing and cosmetics, corporeal manipulation and alteration were taboo.

Whenever possible, men and women wore colorful garments, with red and blue the most favored colors. Once more, however, class and wealth intruded. The apparel of the less affluent was duller – for example, unbleached rather than dazzling white linen – and often purple (sometimes red) was reserved for monarchs and/or nobles. Under the influence of both the Spanish court and Protestant moralism, moreover, black and other muted tones were gaining favor among the middling as well as elites, a development facilitated by technical innovations and the importation of new dyestuffs. Materials and total costume always lent distinctive local, regional, and national touches, and in the early modern period specific garments appeared and vanished. Still, a great deal of dress consistency obtained over all of Atlantic Europe, and in each gender's distinctive sartorial silhouette.

Women dressed in a long skirt below the waist and above it in a short jacket with sleeves or in a bodice perhaps stiffened with bone, reed, or wood. Elite women often added a one-piece robe or gown that reached the floor over the bodice and skirt, whereas working women's skirts came to only mid-thigh to facilitate movement. From the middle third of the seventeenth century, a partial reorganization occurred, particularly in elite dress, as the bodice-jacket-skirt combination started to give way to the gown, and the skirt became a kind of petticoat or underskirt revealed by fastening back the gown. Women also wore stockings and footwear (increasingly shoes, usually made of cloth uppers with leather soles and heels), a cap or hat, and an apron – long and plain for working women, short and decorated for others. Women also might wear an outer garment, typically a cloak or mantle.

Men's costume was also evolving, if within existing shapes and materials. Previously it had included a doublet, breeches, hose or stockings, and usually a draped outer garment, typically a cloak. Waist or hip-length, padded or lying flat, the doublet was fitted with sleeves and various forms of decoration; breeches were tied to it. Breeches themselves were more or less baggy, thigh or knee length, but like doublets always shaped; hose was attached to breeches by garters above or below the knee. From the mid-seventeenth century, the doublet gave way to the vest or waistcoat, which was long, fitted, and usually sleeveless. The vest also extended over the top of the breeches, which were not attached to it, but became more fitted to the waist and usually simpler, particularly among the laboring majority. Worn over both vest and breeches, the coat was typically knee-length and fitted, though lengths and contours of coat bodies, sleeves, and skirts varied; coats also might be hooded or not. As decreed by both Louis XIV of France and Charles II of England, the court version of this predecessor of the three-piece suit included cravats and wigs, though the adoption of these accessories was incomplete among other classes for reasons of practicality as well as resources. Like women, men also wore stockings and shoes (though men's were usually cobbled entirely from leather), and usually some sort of headgear.

Across Atlantic Europe, new attire was supplementing the basic outfit. Undergarments, formerly worn mainly by elites, were becoming more common among the general populace, particularly in the form of a shirt for men and a chemise or smock for women, which for both genders had a similar T-shape with long sleeves and extended well below the waist. An emerging concern with cleanliness, achieved by laundering undergarments that had absorbed bodily secretions rather than washing the body, understood as dangerously porous, designated unsoiled undergarments as a sign of "civility." As shirts gained favor, ruffs at the neck yielded place to folded or upright collars. Shoes supplanted other forms of footwear. Among elites, the appearance of fashion publications and the cultural and political influence emanating from courts and cities hastened these changes, as did controversies engendered by the greater public attention devoted to sartorial innovation.

Finally, similar distinctions among dress regimes obtained across Atlantic Europe. In nearly all states, some form of sumptuary law intended to restrict the wearing of specific materials, adornments, and colors. These regulations sought to manifest and codify in material objects the class, professional, and gender correlates of a hierarchic social structure, reflecting a widespread belief in the power of dress to identify, define, and classify individuals and groups as well as elites' desire to safeguard their cultural distinctiveness. Repeatedly violated and repeatedly renewed, sumptuary laws were never successful in their own terms. Most were repealed or went unenforced in the seventeenth century, as new fabrics and fashions that early modern globalization made available to increasingly broad segments of the populace rendered the sumptuary project impossible. The disparity between the more fitted and tailored affluent dress and the looser garments of the working majority was likewise found across the region. At the same time, however, the reliance of many people on second-hand clothes, obtained through inheritance, purchase, or theft, helped diffuse materials and styles across social barriers, as well as imparting an ongoing dynamism to dress regimes in Atlantic Europe and more widely, as colonists carried metropolitan garments, styles, and conventions throughout the Atlantic basin.

"Wonderful craft": West and west Central Africa

Like Atlantic Europeans, Africans in the Gold Coast and west Central Africa had long worn textile-based apparel made of imported as well as local fabrics. They lived, too, in regions that were politically divided, socially hierarchic, commercially vibrant, and receptive to external cultural influences. Some rules and practices of their dress regimes, and differences expressed within them, likewise evoked those of Europeans. In overall structure, however, as well as in component parts, styles, treatment of the body, conventions, and some apparel materials, Atlantic African dress was very unlike that of the Europeans who reported on it.

Many European observers – including some of the best informed – claimed that pre-contact Atlantic Africans, lacking woven

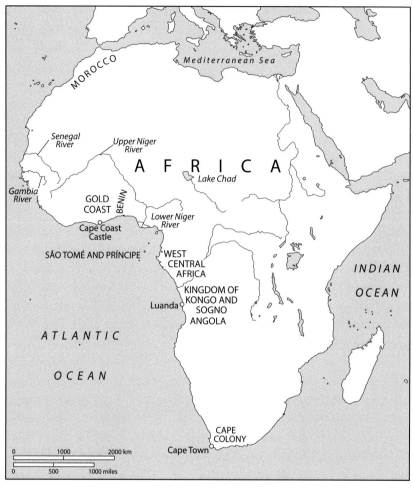

Map 1.2 Atlantic Africa

fabric textiles, had gone partially or wholly unclothed before the arrival of European cargoes. The illustrated 1602 *Description and Historical Account of the Gold Kingdom of Guinea,* for instance, written by the Dutch merchant Pieter de Marees on his return from the Gold Coast, remains an invaluable source thanks to its author's generally judicious information-gathering and ethnographic detail.[16] Yet though Marees had spent time at several posts on the Gold Coast at least in 1601 and perhaps earlier, and avowedly had consulted reliable local informants, he opined that before the advent of Portuguese traders the people of the region "made do with what they produced locally, which was nothing very notable, especially with regard to anything to clothe themselves with; for in the olden days they used to go around naked."[17]

Marees was mistaken about both cloth supplies and pre-contact nakedness. On the early modern Gold Coast, bark cloth ("the barke is of that nature, that it will spin small after the maner of linnen," according to the mid-sixteenth-century English trader William Towerson) and perhaps cotton textiles were locally woven on narrow looms and then sewn together to make pieces of suitable size for garments.[18] In addition, from as early as the eighth century CE, trans-Saharan trade had brought to the Gold Coast woolens and silks from North Africa (particularly Morocco and Egypt) and – albeit in small quantities – Europe. Starting about 1000 CE, dyed and plain cottons had also been imported from major West African manufacturing centers along the upper Niger, Gambia, and Senegal Rivers and, further to the east, around Lake Chad and the territory of the early Hausa kingdom. No later than the fifteenth century, cottons were also available from the lower Niger region, known from at least the ninth century also for raffia and bast cloth.[19]

Some Europeans wrote accounts similar to, and equally as incorrect as, Marees's on the Gold Coast about the textile and dress histories of west Central Africa.[20] There, in fact, artisans in numerous locations had long practiced what other commentators admired as the "wonderful craft" of palm (raffia) cloth weaving, producing both "very beautiful" colorful silk-like stuffs resembling fine velvets, damasks, satins, and brocades, and lighter, coarser varieties made from shorter threads; common as well as superior types were traded throughout the area.[21] In places where raffia cloth was neither woven nor sold, cloth was fabricated from the inner bark of the *enzanda* or *insanda* tree, an evergreen said to have resembled the laurel. In some regions, finally, select males wore special garments of animal skin.[22]

From the late fifteenth century, Europeans added their cargoes to these long-available textiles. On the Gold Coast, the Portuguese merchants who enjoyed a de facto monopoly between the 1470s and about 1540 offered fabrics of global provenance: European linens, woolens, and satins; cottons from distant India and closer Benin, São Tomé, and Príncipe; Moorish fustians. But most of all they imported North African woolens, for which demand was already well established: these accounted for four-fifths of their textile sales. If some of these fabrics came from sources new to West Africans, most were familiar, and the French, English, and Dutch who supplanted the Portuguese continued to supply similar well-known goods, though European woolens largely replaced those formerly obtained from North African centers.[23] The wool, linen, silk, cotton, and mixed fabrics that Europeans traded introduced a greater degree of novelty into Angolan dress, which had previously embodied a narrower range of fibers. But woven fiber attire was no innovation.

As in Europe of the time, so in Atlantic Africa sumptuary regulations sought at times to order the social hierarchy by materially reproducing it. On the Gold Coast, the wearing of woolens, silks, and imported sewn garments such as hooded cloaks, caps, and leggings was often restricted to ceremonial occasions presided over by political elites, while cottons served for the quotidian apparel of all groups and for every type of commoner clothing. In west Central Africa, rules seem to have been even more elaborate, at least in the kingdom of Kongo. The best varieties of palm-leaf cloth were reserved for kings and their entourage, as were footwear, headgear, and special forms of adornment. Other males wore only less good palm-cloth wraps, and not only were the rest of their bodies left uncovered but they went unshod and without any head covering.[24]

Atlantic African dress regimes – like those in Europe – thus both shared basic characteristics and subtly but legibly differentiated by gender, status, occupation, and likely wealth. For all that, they did not resemble European dress. Both men and women wore mainly untailored draped apparel, lengths of cloth that were wrapped around part or all of the trunk, though males and females were clearly demarcated by the quantity and shaping of the individual garments, and even more by the accessories and adornments that both genders boasted. Everyone had as well distinctive headgear or hairstyles; all displayed some form of body decoration, whether incised into or painted on the skin or worn over it. At the same time, social group correlated with amount of fabric worn, presence or absence of an upper-torso garment, manner of draping apparel, specific variety of head and/or hair treatment, type of jewelry or corporeal modification, and whether and in what situation footwear might be worn.

On the Gold Coast, men's basic garment was a loincloth or breechclout fashioned from a length of 2 fathom (1.75 yard) cloth that passed through the legs and wrapped around the waist.[25] Minimal or absent among slaves (Figure 1.1 A), it was also summary among peasants (B), fishers (C), palm-tree tappers, and other laborers. Among those of greater status, amount of fabric in and elaborateness of the arrangement of the loincloth signaled rank, distinguishing, for example, "nobleman" (Figure 1.2 A), from interpreter/intermediary (C), from inland merchant (B). All women wore below-waist wrappers, again socially differentiated by length and intricacy of structure, from short belted pieces that covered only the genitals and buttocks of the wives of peasants (Figure 1.3 B) and other laborers through the knee-length skirt of women of middling status (D), to the much longer skirt of highly placed women (C).[26] Marees claimed that mixed-race commonlaw wives (A) of resident Portuguese were maintained "in grand style" and kept "in splendid clothes, and they always dress more ostentatiously and stand out more than any other Indigenous women."[27] Elite individuals of either gender might wear draped mantles, but some went partly uncovered above the waist, commoners wholly so. Even slaves boasted singular hair arrangements, as did all ordinary males and females. But the size and degree of complexity of the hats or caps made from bark, cane, reed, or animal skin atop elite men corresponded to their social position. Jewelry such as bracelets, earrings, necklaces, and ankle and leg rings, though displayed on every body, was likewise distributed by wealth and rank (rich men, Marees wrote, sported ornaments of gold, Venetian beads, and coral) as well as gender: A young unmarried woman like C, he declared, would wear 30–40 iron bracelets, while the mulatta wives of Portuguese boasted "many beads." Though in Marees's images direct body markings (both tattooed and painted) were a feature of non-elite women, his text reports that all females had them on their faces, arms, and upper trunks. Finally, Marees emphasized, proper attire on the Gold Coast included a clean and glistening body, achieved both by washing with water and by rubbing with "Palm oil or animal fat."[28]

Similar in garments and in the presence of socially shaped variation to the Gold Coast, west Central African dress was distinct in materials, adornments, and specific practices formal and informal, and the boundary between elite wear and that of commoners was drawn more sharply.[29] Despite their difference in status, male courtiers and commoners alike wrapped palm-fiber fabric around their waists, but elite men alone added decorative small animal skins worn apron-style, crocheted and tasseled knee-length capes worn over the right shoulder,

1.1 Dress of male commoners in early seventeenth-century Gold Coast.

Drawn by an unknown author, Figures 1.1, 1.2, and 1.3 illustrate descriptions of dress in Pieter de Marees's long-authoritative account of the Gold Coast, *Beschryvinghe ende Historische Verhael van het Gout Koninckrijck van Gunea anders de Gout-Custe de Mina genaemt liggende in het Deel van Africa* (The Hague: Cornelis Claesz, 1602). For evaluations of both text and images, see Iselin 1994; Marees 1987. The original Dutch text was reprinted in Marees 1912.

1.2 Dress of elite men in early seventeenth-century Gold Coast.

1.3 Women's dress in early seventeenth-century Gold Coast.
Dress was an important topic in Marees's book, and is depicted in numerous additional scenes of war, labor, ritual, and other activities.

palm-fiber sandals, and small four-sided red and yellow ceremonial caps that were showy but provided little protection against rain or sun. While poor and "common" men wore the same type of below-waist loincloth as "the king and his courtiers," it was made of cheaper raffia cloth, and except for it they went entirely naked. Women observed a similar hierarchy. As cited in the opening passage, the attire of elite women included three pieces of fine-quality raffia cloth worn below the waist, doublet, cape, and cap. Women of the middling orders wore the same outfit, if of less good fabric, while females at the bottom of the social hierarchy were, like male commoners, garbed only below the waist. Pigafetta is silent on the subject of body adornment among the mass of the population, but later accounts indicate that carefully treated and lustrous skin was an integral part of dress, and that "very varied" corporeal ornamentation, involving feathers, bones, animal skins, tree bark, and elaborate multicolored body painting, was widely practiced.[30]

The arrival of Christianity, which led the king to model his court on the Portuguese, did provoke some changes in dress in Kongo, as "great men" and their ladies sought to mimic Portuguese fashions.

But apart from the addition of women's veils, men's swords and, arguably, short boots (*stivaletti*), the novelties were modifications or elaborations of existing elite dress. Imported scarlet woolen and silk and (among women) bejewelled black velvet cloaks and capes replaced those made of the best palm cloth (which Pigafetta had previously compared to fine expensive silks), velvet and leather slippers and buskins supplanted male palm-fiber sandals, new styles of caps and hats took the place of old. The innovations did, however, consolidate or perhaps widen the gap between the elite and the rest of society, for they were socially limited. Even among the "*grandi*," "everyone" adopted new items "according to his means." They were wholly out of reach for "the common people," who therefore "retain their former practices," which would have included raffia cloth.[31]

In the Gold Coast and west Central Africa about 1600, then, a proper outfit was both less and more elaborate than in Atlantic Europe. Less in that many individuals typically wore only a single short garment around the waist, albeit of diverse sizes and complexity; less, too, in the general absence of footwear. More in that headgear and hair arrangements were more elaborate and more differentiated socially, and more because of the greater use of body adornments, including direct corporeal markings, which comprised essential components of proper wear. Europeans expected garments to cover the entire torso on virtually all occasions. In most situations, however, the great majority of inhabitants of Atlantic Africa were clothed only below the waist though adorned elsewhere. So whereas Europeans achieved proper dress largely through appareling – featuring as well attire that enclosed the entire body – inhabitants of the Gold Coast and west Central Africa satisfied the same imperative by a mixture of attire and somatic ornamentation that left significant portions of the skin unappareled.

Non-woven dress regimes in the Atlantic

Though not examined in *The Material Atlantic*, other Atlantic societies had woven textile dress regimes. In substantial parts of the basin, however, pre-contact populations had little or no acquaintance with woven fabrics as clothing materials and none at all with those that were the mainstays of contemporary Atlantic Europe. They constructed their dress from other substances, mostly animal skins and furs but at times including plant matter such as grasses, bark, and woody fibers that could be variously twined (or, in a small minority of cases, woven). In contrast to the societies with woven textiles examined above, these decentralized societies lacked formal sumptuary rules. Nevertheless, their dress obeyed distinct conventions that emphasized wrapping parts of the body and adorning or incising others. Europeans were wont to label these peoples as naked. In most cases, this referred to greater exposure of the epidermis than the European norm. But in a few societies, adults as well as children voluntarily and unabashedly wore no garments at all in daily public life; save in exceptional circumstances, they consistently went unclothed.[32] For all that, they were dressed, often quite elaborately, even if their dress regimes have to be uncovered from reports that presented them as stark naked.

"As naked as they come out of their mother's womb": coastal Brazil and Río de la Plata

Among the best known of the peoples in which "the men, women, and children not only do not hide any parts of their bodies," but "habitually live and go about their affairs as naked as they come out of their mother's womb" were the Tupinambá of coastal Brazil (Figure 1.4); the less well-known Guaraní who inhabited the Río de la Plata area likewise went uncovered.[33] First-person reports both sympathetic and hostile described Tupinambá dress customs in detail, and Michel de Montaigne ruminated upon them in his essay "Of the custom of getting dressed."[34] According to Jean de Léry, a French Huguenot missionary who wrote a particularly influential account, Tupinambá men and women used the same materials and the same techniques, but clear gender distinctions obtained, with male dress generally more ornate.[35] Thus both genders plucked all hair from their bodies, including eyebrows and eyelashes, yet whereas men went on to shave hair off the front of the scalp, women did not. Likewise, each gender inserted adornments into the skin: but men stuck bone, later replaced by gemstones, in their lower lips and sometimes their cheeks, along with white bone earrings, while women inset heavy shell earrings that hung to the shoulders or even lower. Women also painted their entire faces with blue, red, and yellow spirals, whereas men would "mottle" their torsos with red paint and dye their legs deep black; in addition, the "greatest warriors" were tattooed with black powder on their chest, arms, and thighs. Decorative pieces worn over the body obeyed a similar logic.

1.4 Tupinambá man, woman, and child (1580).

Men might don necklaces strung with pieces of shell, but their distinguishing ornament was a crescent-shaped neckpiece made from brilliantly white polished bone. Though women had the same strings of shell as men, they wore them as belts or twisted around their arms, and they also fashioned white bone into armbands up to a foot and a half long. And men alone, it seems, bedecked themselves with bright yellow toucan feathers glued near their ears, multicolored feather headbands, and on occasion bird feathers dyed red glued all over their torsos, arms, and legs.

Though not constructed by specialized artisans, garments and tailoring were not entirely unknown to the Tupinambá and Guaraní. On the contrary, Tupinambá "dexterously" sewed together bird feathers of many colors into robes, caps, bracelets, "and other adornments" that appeared to be made of long-pile velvet. But they only put on such robes for festive occasions, notably ceremonies before eating war prisoners who had been "ceremonially killed"; among the Guaraní, animal skin or feathered robes were essentially reserved for shamans in ceremonial settings. Again, though Léry wanted to believe that the penis sheaths that some old Tupinambá men wore indicated "that there remains in them some spark of natural shame," he concluded that they were "rather to hide some infirmity" than "on account of modesty." For the Tupinambá and Guaraní, that is, the wearing of apparel was reserved for ritual or other extraordinary situations rather than being a quotidian experience; ordinarily, they dressed fully, even elaborately, without garments.

"Trinkets and trifles": indigenous Cape of Good Hope

More often than going unapparrelled, Atlantic peoples wore attire wholly or mainly made of non-woven materials. Among them were the

---

Caption for 1.4   (cont.)

A Huguenot pastor who was briefly in a French colony in Brazil in the mid-1550s, Jean de Léry was both sympathetic to and critical of the Tupinambá in his *Histoire d'vn voyage faict en la terre du Bresil* (Geneva: Antoine Chuppin, 1580), in which this image appeared. Though his account of their beliefs is often (and usually evidently) biased, his descriptions and depictions of their material culture are even-handed, even when he found it strange or shocking. Additional information and bibliographic guidance can be found in the editor's introduction to Léry 1578/1990.

groups of transhumant pastoralists and hunters comprising the Khoikhoi (Khoekhoe, long called "Hottentots" by Europeans), who lived in the area Europeans named the Cape of Good Hope and its hinterland (today in the Republic of South Africa).[36] Even before the Dutch East Indies Company (Verenigde Oost-Indische Compagnie or VOC) arrived in 1652 to establish a provisioning stop for crews of outbound and homeward ships, passing European merchants had described Khoikhoi dress, and European engravers illustrated it, with varying degrees of inaccuracy. But in the first decades of the nascent Cape Colony appeared several accounts based on extended personal observation, discussions with settlers and other visitors, and/or sources now lost.[37] Recently discovered snapshot-like drawings and commentary likely made in the 1690s by an unknown but skilled and empathetic if apparently non-professional visitor confirm, in some instances correct, and most importantly manifest in greater detail, both pictorial and verbal, the information available in written descriptions. Together, these sources show the Khoikhoi dress regime just before the combined impact of epidemic disease, military operations, and colonial land acquisition and settlement fatally disrupted it.[38]

Based on animal skins and furs, Khoikhoi apparel comprised a basic garment worn on all occasions by every member of society as well as a variety of other items whose possession or deployment varied by gender and wealth, weather and season, occupation and activity. The central item, seen on all the individuals in Figure 1.5, was the "*kaross*," sometimes described as a blanket or coat but better understood as a cloak that was typically worn across and down the back and secured around the throat, though if necessary it could be worn over one shoulder or even wrapped entirely around the body; its mutability meant that it could also serve as a ground cover at night or even as a canteen-like sack to hold liquids. At least knee-length, the *kaross* was made from up to three animal skins sewn together with gut. The *kaross* of the more prosperous Khoikhoi were fashioned from tiger, leopard, and dassie (hyrax) skins, often fringed with leather strips, those of the poorer from the undecorated skins of sheep, goat, oxen, small antelopes such as springbok, steenbok, and duiker, or rabbit and other small mammals.

Women might add a second *kaross* around the waist, but more often they donned several short "aprons" over both genitals and buttocks. Men wore fur penis sheaths (*kull-kaross*); more affluent males

1.5 Khoikhoi dress (1690s). Anonymous.

Depicting a family of herders and their animals, this image gives an excellent sense of not merely what Khoikhoi wore but how they wore it during everyday activities. Most other drawings in the series that includes this scene also depict Khoikhoi dress in a variety of settings, but a few show Cape Colony farmers. Smith and Pheiffer 1993 is the best guide to the works of the unknown artist.

favored otter and badger, others fox. Most of the time, women wore floppy peaked and tasseled leather caps with earflaps that tied under the chin with thongs. Men would put on caps in rainy weather and in winter (and, in some accounts, at night). But usually they went bareheaded with greased hair decorated with beads, copper plates, shells, bone, wood, and other small objects and often shaped into a topknot or shaved into diverse shapes; when women went hatless they too bedecked their hair. Men usually wore flat sandals, which settlers called "field shoes," made of hard elephant, rhinoceros, or ox skin and secured with two straps across the foot. While women had the same footwear, they were said to wear it only to traverse the harshest terrain, otherwise going unshod.[39] Men went barelegged; women boasted leggings made of rings of dried rawhide, the number of rings indicating the wealth of the wearer. Only men, it seems, owned the useful item displayed in the male's right hand in Figure 1.5, an ostrich feather or animal tail attached to a stick used to wipe the nose, dry sweat, and drive away flies.

Not only on their heads was the ornamentation of men and women, rich and poor, similar in material yet subtly distinguished by quality, quantity, and modes of display. Both genders had small, decorated skin bags to carry tobacco, flintstones, and other "trinkets and trifles" (to Europeans), men usually hanging theirs on their chest, women over the back.[40] All sought to paint their faces with red ochre and spread animal fat over their bodies. But those who owned more livestock could afford to smear on more fat to achieve a more lustrous appearance; in addition, they could coat the outside of their garments, while the poorer stood out for their dry apparel. Arm and wrist bracelets as well as necklaces were widely worn. But affluent individuals sported more items, of more costly materials (elephant tusk ivory elbow bracelets, for example, or multiple copper-bead neck chains). Thus, if diversely in terms of garments, ornamentation, materials, and practices from other Atlantic peoples, the Khoikhoi dressed from head to toe; little of the body was left uncovered, even when unattired.

"No difference between the garments": Atlantic North America

The inhabitants of the Eastern Woodlands of North America, the large region east of the Mississippi and south of the Arctic, lived in climates ranging from sub-Arctic to sub-tropical, spoke myriad dialects and languages, engaged in diverse economic activities, obeyed social arrangements ranging from largely egalitarian to rigidly stratified, and often found themselves at war. Nevertheless, at the time of their first encounters with merchants, missionaries, and officials based in settlements such as New Orleans, Charles Town, Philadelphia, and Montreal, they had largely similar dress regimes.[41] The basic outfit for post-pubescent adults comprised a wrapped or draped garment below the waist: a breechclout for men, worn over a sash or belt, and a knee-length skirt for women. This was supplemented as needed by protective leggings (by some accounts originally a male garment attached to a breechclout belt), "matchcoats" (robes draped over one or both shoulders and sometimes referred to as blankets, mantles, or shawls), and moccasins particularly for hunting or traveling, in snowy regions supplemented by snowshoes. Like the Khoikhoi, Eastern Woodlands men and women carried leather or twine pouches or bags holding various personal items, including food when on the road. Headgear was rarely worn apart from ceremonial occasions. Natchez men sometimes put on short-sleeved mid-thigh-length tunic-like shirts made of deerskin, but this was unusual and in warm weather both genders wore nothing above the waist.

Most garments were constructed from animal pelts. Deerskin, abundant almost everywhere, could be made into any and all apparel, for once dressed it was easily cut and sewn with thread made from animal tendons and needles of bone. Depending on local climate conditions and animal availability, matchcoats were also fashioned out of buffalo, bear, moose, elk, beaver, and other skins, and in the southeast of what is today the United States some spectacular robes were laboriously constructed from bird feathers. Animal fiber (notably bison and opossum hair) was favored for accessories such as breechclout and skirt sashes, garters for leggings, and pouches. Though much less prevalent, apparel might be made from interlaced vegetable and animal fibers (both separately and mixed), notably in the southeast. While they did not have "true" looms familiar to Europeans, Native women were skilled at braiding, twining, and plaiting. They fabricated skirts, shawls, breechclouts, and sashes from grasses; from the bark of mulberry, basswood, white cedar, willow, and elm trees; from hemp, thistle, and nettle bast; and, along the most southerly Atlantic and Gulf coasts, particularly in Florida, from braided palmetto leaves, draped palm fronds, and tufts of Spanish moss.[42] In addition, in the lower Mississippi cotton shawls were worn; most likely they were imported from Pueblo Indians further west. Still, the great majority of woven fibers were used not for garments but for mats, baskets, storage bags, nets, and cordage.

For Europeans the lack of a clear division between the sexes had long been one of the attributes that defined savagery. Many were confirmed in that opinion by what they perceived as a disconcerting similarity of indigenous male and female dress in North America. According to one Jesuit missionary, "there is no difference between the garments of a man and those of a woman, except that the woman is always covered with her robe, while the men discard theirs or wear them carelessly, in warm weather."[43] This impression was strengthened by the fact that both genders decorated skin and fiber garments with a wide variety of figurative and abstract designs in red, black, yellow, russet, as well as adorning them with shells, beads, quills, and ribbons made from tree fiber and other natural objects.

Yet for all that garments and materials of pre-contact Amerindian dress were much alike across the Eastern Woodlands, ornamentation and sartorial practices were diverse as well as elaborate. Though much of the knowledge about the conventions governing them has been lost, dress regimes had long varied among groups as well as according to the gender, social status, and preferences of individuals within them.[44] Men oiled their hair then cut and styled (and at times dyed) it distinctively according to age, marital status, and activity. While women generally dressed their hair less, sometimes they braided and decorated it so as to convey messages about their status. Women and men hung ornamentation made of a great variety of materials around their necks, arms, waists, and heads as well as from (occasionally inserted in) their ears: strings of white or purple wampum, feathers, bone, shell, pearl, stone, copper, each gender following its own rules.

For all its apparent sameness, too, attire was diversely created and deployed. Different peoples fashioned the same garment in distinctive ways. In the Powhatan confederation, for example, breech-clouts were draped, fringed, and tied in the back, whereas among the Sauk they were fitted. Moccasins could be cut from a single skin or pieced together from several. Decorating garments with dyes derived from ochreous earth, charcoal, shells, bark, nuts, roots, leaves, and flowers was widely popular, but particular colors might be reserved for specific groups, as among the strongly hierarchic Natchez, where only headmen could wear black breechclouts. Characteristic forms of ornamentation likewise distinguished the clothing of particular groups. Southeastern Ojibwe men had embroidered and painted buckskin shirts; both female and male Abenaki elaborately decorated virtually all their garments with "bands of parallel lines, realistic and geometric motifs, and lacelike patterns."[45]

Corporeal decoration was fundamental to dress in some cultures, but even within them it was likely to be disparately practiced. Tattooing, whether partial or over the entire body, was generally reserved for men, as Louis Nicolas illustrated based on his missionary experience in the Great Lakes (Plate 1). Nevertheless, southeastern Ojibwe women boasted characteristic facial designs. In many instances, body painting signaled special occasions such as war, ritual gatherings, dances, and games, which were particularly male. Gender could also differentiate how a given garment would be worn: Whereas men commonly draped their matchcoats over both shoulders, at least in the southeast women looped and tied them so as to allow both arms free movement. Gender could also specify the materials out of which attire was made, such as the short cloaks crafted from flamingo or other colorful bird feathers worn by Lower Creek women or apparel made from Spanish moss, also gendered female.

The dress regimes of Eastern Amerindians rested firmly upon plentiful local materials and deep cultural knowledge, as well as being well adapted to particular social and natural environments. But they were not static. Exchange among peoples and cultural zones provided new materials and styles. On the eve of contact, for instance, some women, notably in the Great Lakes area, were replacing the skirt with a straight dress with attachable sleeves, while some men were beginning to add a tunic-like shirt to their basic wardrobe, both garment changes remarkably paralleling innovations occurring in Atlantic Europe in the same years. At the same time, Amerindians eagerly engaged in trade with Europeans from the time of first contact, and the well-articulated trade networks that had long crisscrossed the Eastern Woodlands meant that new goods could be quickly moved long distances: As surprised Europeans often reported, in their initial meetings their Native interlocutors already boasted cloth garments and other imported items. This commercial and cultural engagement was only to increase as trade, evangelization, and settlement increased Europeans' economic, material, diplomatic, and demographic presence. Like all Atlantic peoples, the inhabitants of the Eastern Woodlands were beginning to experience the onslaught of forces that challenged their existing way of life.

Atlantic dress regimes and the forces of change

On the eve of the shared Atlantic, each of these diverse dress regimes had preferred materials, attire, adornments, styles, conventions, and practices, and each subsisted within a specific geoclimatic, socioeconomic, and cultural environment. At the same time, all were becoming subject to commercial, colonizing, and cultural enterprises promoted and at times imposed by Europeans. These were powerful forces indeed, not only because they mutually sustained one another throughout most of the Atlantic but also because they expanded impressively in scale and scope across the seventeenth and eighteenth centuries. For all that, the outcomes of encounters between existing dress regimes and the goods and usages introduced by Europe's Atlantic projects varied considerably, as we shall see. Some characteristics of both dress regimes and their host societies visible in the early seventeenth century hint at possible reasons for the differences.

Long acceptance of new textiles and garments, as well as a growing fascination with fashion, indicates that Atlantic Europeans, to begin with, were receptive to sartorial innovation. At the time, moreover, barriers to the availability and acceptance of novelty were being lowered: Witness both the chartering of companies for direct trade with Africa, the Americas, and the East Indies and the indifference to and disdain for sumptuary rules. Nevertheless, Europeans' convictions about civilization and savagery, and their concomitant notions about proper somatic presentation and corporeal alteration, suggest that they might have resisted many of the materials, styles, and practices of other Atlantic peoples.

As woven textiles and apparel were already widely deployed to signal status in Atlantic Africa, groups involved in Atlantic encounters – political elites, commercial intermediaries, converts, for example – might likewise welcome novel varieties of cloth and attire to express their new situation. Moreover, pre-contact textile supplies, imported and local, appear to have been insufficient to satisfy demand among both coastal and inland populations, thus further hinting at markets for imported goods.[46] Still, Pigafetta did mention that cost limited Angolans' adoption of sartorial novelties, while some seventeenth-century commentators claimed that cultural values, at least in west Central Africa, emphasized passivity over industriousness, "bare necessity" over the accumulation of material possessions, and reproval of Europeans for their devotion to luxury.[47]

During the brief, unsuccessful mid-sixteenth-century Huguenot settlement venture of which Léry was a part, the Tupinambá did accept some new dress items, notably colored glass beads, mirrors, and combs for women's adornment. But they showed no interest whatsoever in garments. Léry expressed particular surprise that women, who ornamented their bodies less than men and thus presumably were less attired even within their own schemata, never wanted to wear the robes and shifts that the French gifted to them. In fact, they were "obstinate in refusing to dress themselves in any way at all," so much so that "it has never been in our power to make them wear clothes." Female slaves whom the French bought "would choose to bear the heat and burning of the sun, even the continual skinning of their arms and shoulders carrying earth and stones, rather than to endure having any clothes on"; only "great strokes of the whip" could compel them "to dress themselves" – and at nightfall they would "strip off the shifts" and "promenade naked all around" the settlement. And though Tupinambá men had put on some of the colorful fabric shirts, hats, and sailors' breeches that they had traded for, they soon took them off.[48] Still, with the advent of substantial and sustained European colonization and commerce from the late sixteenth century in Brazil and Río de la Plata, new goods, economic relations, and cultural projects confronted both the Tupinambá and the Guaraní.

How imported dress items would affect Khoikhoi dress remained an open question in the Cape Colony's early years. The Khoikhoi had long engaged in commodity trade among their constituent groups and were linked to long-distance routes that supplied ornamental materials like copper and, once the Portuguese introduced them into Angola and Mozambique in the sixteenth century, glass beads. Moreover, Khoikhoi soon began to barter livestock with the Dutch for "favourite and most desired articles," namely "tobacco, brandy, beadwork and copper," not to mention bunches of coral, and they often found work on settlers' farms.[49] But if these activities gave the Khoikhoi access to new goods, other factors worked to limit their impact. It is notable, but not surprising, that neither apparel nor textiles appeared on the list of their preferred articles in trade. From their herds and the surrounding environment, the Khoikhoi had the materials for their garments and adornments readily at hand.[50] No matter what the Khoikhoi wanted or needed, moreover, as the colony expanded, many moved or were pushed into the interior, away from easy commercial intercourse with settlers.

The indigenous inhabitants of the Eastern Woodlands likewise enjoyed abundant access to dress materials, with long-established Native trade relations supplying others. Many of their items of apparel, uniquely suited to North American climatic conditions, had no European equivalent. From earliest contact, nevertheless, Amerindians evinced an attraction for textiles, garments, and adornments that Europeans bartered or gifted them. Utilitarian considerations (ease of drying or cleaning, warmth, flexibility of material, for instance) may have recommended those novelties, as many Europeans asserted. But they were also suitable for expressing existing Native symbolic concerns and aesthetic values. At the same time, religious conversion as well as economic engagement with settlers and merchants, particularly through the production and exchange of pelts and skins, provided means, opportunities, and motives for acquisition of imported dress objects that could travel well-trafficked trade routes far into the interior.

The seventeenth-century Atlantic world, in sum, encompassed a plenitude both of conditions that promoted the transformation of dress and of circumstances that worked against that result. The contest between them played out across the various geoclimatic zones, economic ecologies, imperial boundaries, and social groups. The resulting dress regimes were rooted in the commercial networks, sites of acquisition, and commodities that are examined in the next chapter.

2 ACQUIRING IMPORTED TEXTILES AND DRESS

Fifteen hundred ells of *limbourg*, half blue, half red ...
Eight hundred trade shirts for men, as long in front as in the back ...
One hundred ells of well-chosen scarlet woolen cloth; that which has
   been sent previously being only a double linen serge ...
Eight hundred ells of [woolen] *sempiterne*, blue, red, and plum ...
Fifteen hundred two-and-a-half point blankets ...
Four hundred lengths of scarlet woolen ribbon ...
Two thousand ells of St Jean linen
Two hundred shirts for male slaves
Two hundred shifts for female slaves ...
Three thousand ells of fine thread linen
Eight thousand ells of common thread linen ...
Two hundred ells of striped cotton cloth ...

On 31 December 1758, the leaders of the Louisiana colony submitted their
yearly "Statement of Requests" for supplies to the French king. Some 127
notations in all (of a total of about 400), the listings of cloth, clothing,
adornments, and associated items included 25 designated for "Annual
Presents that are Given to the Indians"; another 8 for "Extraordinary
presents"; 16 to exchange with Choctaws; 15 for commerce with
Alabama, Attacapa, Kickapoo, Mascoutern, and Shawnee Indians
together; and 14 "For the Projected Trade with the Cherokee Indians." A
further 43 items would be for officials, their enslaved laborers, and the
military, while a final 6 would furnish hospitals and pay the nuns who
staffed them.[1]

   This order from a remote corner of the Atlantic world opens a
window onto the abundance of textile goods available to early modern

consumers throughout that space. The entries suggest – if barely – the great variety of types, colors, qualities, and finishes of woven-fiber fabrics, garments, and notions distributed throughout the Atlantic world; the diverse consumers of those goods; the configurations of their particular cloth and clothing demand; and the commercial and non-commercial ways by which that demand would be satisfied: gifting, market exchange, compulsory attiring, recompense for services rendered. Fleshing out clues provided by the Louisiana document, this chapter investigates the venues, occasions, participants, and procedures involved in supplying cloth and clothing to sites around the seventeenth- and eighteenth-century Atlantic; the composition of the merchant textile stocks thereby assembled; and the ways by which consumers acquired them. It demonstrates that as institutions and practices governing both long-distance trade within and local outlets around the Atlantic world became more efficient and more alike across the seventeenth and eighteenth centuries, the textiles to which consumers had access concomitantly developed greater homogeneity and distinctive imperial, regional, and local characteristics. New, revised, or retained, post-contact Atlantic dress regimes were rooted in material possibilities at once similar and disparate.

Supply

Merchants specializing in long-distance trade controlled the supply of non-local fabrics around the Atlantic. Admittedly, some textiles were in other hands for part of their journey to consumers. Hoping to supplement their wages or provide a little extra capital for colonial ventures, some sailors, ships' officers, and passengers included marketable textiles and finished garments in the small assortments of goods (*pacottes* or *pacotilles* in French) that traditional privilege allowed them to carry free of freight charges.[2] What can be termed "quasi-merchants" also participated. Most often they were European civilian officials and military officers, whose positions enabled them to conduct some trade, typically alongside the gifting to state clients and allies associated with their official duties.[3]

Yet even in these instances, the knowledge, connections, and resources of long-distance merchants were indispensable, given an economic environment defined by non-uniform goods, mutable and stratified markets constantly vulnerable to unforeseen events, considerable intervals – months, even years – between orders, sales, and settlements, and problematic yet indispensable credit relations. Merchants and their representatives drew up and received orders, located manufacturers who could supply fabrics appropriate to diverse destinations, assembled capital and negotiated credit terms, arranged for packing and shipping, contracted for insurance, paid duties and fees, collected rebates and drawbacks (refunds), and found retail-level outlets. It was merchants, in short, who set in motion and managed the long chains of relationships that connected producers around the globe with consumers around the Atlantic.

Not all these merchants were Europeans. Arab and African traders maintained or even expanded the large-scale trans-Saharan caravan routes that for centuries had brought fabrics and items of apparel from the Mediterranean to West Africa, while professional merchants from several ethnic groups (notably the Dioula, the Hausa, and the Diakhanke) moved cloth and other goods over great distances in the West African interior.[4] But Europeans and their descendents monopolized intercontinental trade, both within the Atlantic and along the vital Asian feeder routes.

"European," of course, meant individuals hailing from states that competed as fiercely in commerce as in most other areas. But across the later Middle Ages and Renaissance, their commercial cultures had adopted what in the West was an Italian institutional innovation (related systems were found outside Europe): the replacement of itinerant traders who accompanied their goods even to quite distant markets by sedentary merchants who did business by correspondence with networks of far-flung representatives.[5] These agents were – or were intended to be – trustworthy, endowed with good judgment, and therefore able to generate the reliable information, profitable orders, and access to credit that were the lifeblood of long-distance commerce.

In the early years of global trade and colonization, merchant networks (like settlement schemes) had commonly been embedded in chartered companies enjoying monopolies awarded by national states. But most of the companies operating in the Atlantic foundered in the course of the seventeenth century, their privileges routinely violated by interlopers even before their dissolution. The only chartered companies that persisted viably across the period were the East India companies of Britain, the Netherlands, and France. If rarely very profitable,[6] they did supply goods – notably cotton textiles – vital for trade throughout the Atlantic.

Private networks, in contrast, proved well suited for responding to the specific challenges of Atlantic commerce: dispatching or locating intermediaries in places previously unknown; doing business with new groups

of consumers, whose needs and preferences were at first poorly understood; mastering geographies, climates, and distances that complicated
both communications about market and price conditions and the delivery
of goods at the appropriate time.[7] Together with contemporaneous technical, infrastructural, and institutional advances that decreased shipping
costs,[8] early modern networks enhanced the efficiency of long-distance
trade, helping to diminish risk, reduce costs, and thereby cut prices. For
one thing, members' multiple roles and partnerships – often individuals
were principal and factor, or partner and agent, in sundry trading ventures
at the same time – endowed their networks with webs of connections to
diverse suppliers, shippers, markets, and thus gave them the knowledge
and flexibility to master inevitably shifting market conditions.[9] Operating
across cultural and ethnic boundaries, merchant networks proved particularly adept at establishing and managing the relations of trust that underlay
the credit flows requisite for commerce of every type.[10]

Of singular importance was network affiliates' expertise about
the quality and suitability of specific goods for particular markets and
the credit arrangements necessary to effect a profitable junction between
them. Such expertise was, of course, at the root of all viable commercial
relations. But it was especially salient in the context of both the early
modern Atlantic and early modern textiles. Thanks to the increase of
trade with Africa and Asia and to a proliferation of new varieties of
cloth by European producers (many of them in response to African and
Asian textiles), the range of fabrics expanded dramatically, as did the
ethnic and sociocultural spectrum of consumers and the economic and
climatic environments in which they lived. The growth of the networks
themselves, along with the increasing amount and sophistication of the
information that they transmitted, also stimulated enlargement of the
product lines that they handled.[11] Similarly, the extension of trade networks necessarily created demand for credit, while distinct local conditions ranging from farming rhythms to traditions of trust directed
debt management and settlement. No one individual could possibly
possess the detailed knowledge of textiles, customers, and credit
required for accurate market decisions all around the Atlantic.
However, the collective knowledge of a network could, so merchants
built and assiduously maintained networks with the aim of better understanding and thus more profitably exploiting the markets that they were
simultaneously developing.[12] Beyond advancing network members'
private goals, the amalgam of specialization and breadth that they

represented helped markets function more effectively, thereby widening access to imported goods socially and geographically.

Insofar as merchant networks sought both desirable and profitable goods wherever they could find them, they promoted Atlantic-wide homogeneity of textile stocks. At the same time, however, they operated within constraints that cut against this trend. In particular, the laws and edicts analytically bundled together since Adam Smith as the "mercantile system" or "mercantilism" encouraged merchant networks to source their products and focus their operations within imperial boundaries. Mercantilist enactments attempted to make empires into protected commercial zones by sharply curbing, if not outright banning, the import of foreign goods and the participation of foreign merchants and shipping in imperial trade.[13] They also sought to promote industries in the national metropoles by measures including prohibitive tariffs, export payments, and governmental grants or investments.

Such laws experienced mixed success. According to Ralph Davis, the Navigation Acts "fulfilled the purpose of confining all important trade with the [British] colonies to Britain."[14] The outcome for the Iberian empires was rather different. Within the large colonial commercial domain that Spanish authorities sought to wall off, substantial and lucrative merchant networks did develop smartly. Before the mid-eighteenth century, however, they were controlled, albeit illegally, by English, French, Dutch, and other foreign merchants, resident initially in Seville and from the early eighteenth century in Cádiz. Only those merchants could efficiently provide – or in the case of textiles, could provide at all – the manufactures that colonists demanded, because they alone had the capital, credit, and connections that were out of reach of all but a handful of Iberian merchants, whose usual role was to serve as a front for these unlawful foreign ventures.[15] Not until the 1740s did Spanish merchants begin to build their own networks and win ascendancy over a great part of their own imperial trade, and even then they remained dependent on cloth made abroad. Similarly, from the late sixteenth century British-dominated merchant networks centered in Lisbon and Porto commanded a sizeable part of Portuguese commerce with the Americas, and some individual Britons were even allowed to join the Portuguese Brazil Company, chartered in 1649. Winning broad legitimate access to trade with Brazil in 1703 simply allowed them to tighten their grip and assure the continued export of British textiles to Brazil.[16] Moreover, Atlantic Africa lay largely outside mercantilist systems; the Cape Colony of the free-trade Dutch wholly so. In Angola and the Gold Coast, European companies did build forts and relationships with rulers, officials, and local merchants. Nevertheless, the ease of interloping, along with Africans' skill at playing off Europeans against one another, defeated any pretensions to national monopolies.

Perhaps the major – if unintentional – impediment to mercantilist pretensions was the smuggling in which virtually every European nation and colony engaged. In many parts of the Atlantic, smuggling was banal: according to Zacarias Moutoukias, contraband was "an essential phenomenon in the commercial life of Buenos Aires"; in that imperially peripheral yet bustling port, it was "neither occasional or circumstantial, nor secret and clandestine" and enjoyed the studied blindness or even active connivance of numerous officials.[17] The same situation often obtained in Dutch Curaçao, British Jamaica, ports on French Saint-Domingue, and New Orleans, among other places.[18]

Despite statutory, administrative, and military efforts, many textiles (especially cloth in high demand) circulated as contraband. Some cloth was smuggled within Europe itself: most famously calicoes from India or from other parts of the Continent. This activity became substantial after laws designed to protect existing woolens and silk industries by prohibiting the weaving, importing, and wearing of cotton fabrics took effect in France, Britain, Spain, and Prussia in the late seventeenth and early eighteenth centuries.[19] Large amounts of contraband textiles also circulated in the wider Atlantic world. Usually unnecessary in the more open and competitive commercial environment of Atlantic Africa, cloth smuggling did occur in places where Portuguese officials sought to restrict trade, as with the cottons woven in the Cape Verde Islands illicitly carried to coastal West Africa or with Asian cloth equally illegally shipped from Salvador da Bahia to Luanda in Angola.[20] Contraband was more prevalent in the Americas – according to one scholar, it "often overshadow[ed] legal trade between 1600 and 1800" – fostered by the close proximity of many colonies operating under disparate trade rules and supply conditions.[21]

Though accelerating when war, hurricane, or some other event human or natural disrupted regular supplies, contraband was structural to early modern commerce thanks to the distortions introduced by mercantilist and related laws in concert with the shortcomings of metropolitan industries. Authorities intercepted some bootlegged goods, but because the techniques of successful smuggling rang just minor changes on regular merchant practices, they were easy to master. Textiles, for example, could be intermingled with or wrapped in legal goods, and false invoices were readily composed.[22] Paradoxically, by seeking to cut off imports, mercantilist restrictions often encouraged producers injured by them to reduce prices, thereby increasing the allure of smuggling the goods affected. Noting that since English bans had been imposed a few years earlier, linens bought in France had become "much cheaper then formerly," in 1679 the London merchant William Freeman admitted that this "doth incorage us the more in goeing upon itt," that is, bootlegging them to the West Indies.[23]

Contraband of expensive cloth and clothing could be particularly lucrative, for such activity evaded weighty tariffs. A cargo seized at Philadelphia in 1726, for example, included pricey fine kenting and Holland linens, silks, and silk hose.[24] But even inexpensive items might be bootlegged. The advantageous price situation that William Freeman found made it worthwhile for him to smuggle low-priced linen "dowles" (dowlas, a heavy, coarse linen for shirts) and "canvis" (an equally rough, unbleached linen).[25] Evading tariffs and trans-shipment costs imposed by mercantilist regulation could make the difference between gain or loss on goods that faced strong competition among many quite similar varieties or could enhance otherwise thin profit margins. The confiscated 1726 Philadelphia cargo, for example, included numerous cheap linens.[26] Even Irish linens, which enjoyed a bounty when shipped via English ports, were smuggled into North America, suggesting just how lucrative bootlegging was perceived to be by the calculus of gain and loss.[27] By virtue of its ubiquity, interest in every type of cloth, and acute sensitivity to potentially profitable but unfulfilled consumer needs and desires, contraband helped expand both the variety and the uniformity of the fabrics found around the Atlantic.

Stocks

Interplay between local structures of demand and trade licit and illicit constituted Atlantic textile stocks.[28] To be sure, not all cloth was supplied by European-dominated merchant networks – or by any merchant network at all. In much of Atlantic Africa, unknown quantities circulated largely outside the ken of Europeans, not to mention usually beyond their control. From all evidence, these channels of supply were more important on the Gold Coast, which participated in regional as well as long-established trans-Saharan and West African textile trade, than in west Central Africa, peripheral to many African trade routes and also home to some local clothmaking. In a few European colonies, too, settlers either wove a small portion of the fabrics they needed or had it made by itinerant or nearby resident weavers. At the same time, not all the fabrics found in warehouses, shops, and peddlers' sacks were destined for apparel. Some ended up in household furnishings as well as in agricultural, commercial, and artisanal uses.

Yet if comprising both less and more than the totality of woven-fiber clothing fabrics, the stocks of textiles assembled by merchants and shopkeepers do reveal the profile of the imported cloth that became available throughout the Atlantic, enabling change in existing dress regimes.[29] Thanks to merchant inventories and cargo manifests, the contours of these supplies can be calculated. These sources nearly always list textile values; much less often, however, do they specify dimensions. Moreover, many size descriptors found in the documents ("piece," "remnant," "length") are unquantifiable. Though pieces were at times characterized as "entire," many textiles were not produced or sold in standard lengths: an uncut piece of Indian calico, for example, might be 12 ells long, 15, or 18.[30]

Any attempt to measure and compare commercial textile stocks must therefore rely on values. Of course, even within the same fiber category – within, indeed, the same fabric – quality, width, color, finish, and thus price could vary, often considerably.[31] The precise mix of textiles within a category also differed across place and time. Detailed analysis of the sources used in Tables 2.1, 2.2, and 2.3 indicates, however, that the hierarchy of relative textile prices remained remarkably stable, as textile prices on the whole declined.[32] On average, linens were cheapest per yard or ell, followed in ascending order by woolens, cottons, and silks. Hence the physical stocks of the textiles anatomized in the tables below included more linens than suggested by the figures, fewer of those made from more costly fabrics. Yet textiles had many non-apparel uses, linens more than the rest. As a result, the fiber composition of dress regimes was not a simple multiple of relative value but was subject to many influences. As outlined in the third section of this chapter, finally, woven-fiber clothing supplies also included second-hand garments disseminated through formal and informal but non-commercial channels. All these caveats notwithstanding, the great

Table 2.1 *Types of textiles commercially available in the late seventeenth-century Atlantic*
Percentages of total stocks by value (in parentheses, number of merchant probate inventories or cargoes)

Type of fabric	Cape Town 1693–1707 (4)	Angola 1676–93 (37)†	Cape Coast Castle 1685–94 (23)†	Buenos Aires 1670–97 (10)	Kingston 1683–99 (49)	Charles Town 1684–94 (4)	Philadelphia 1686–99 (16)	Montreal 1677–97 (12)
Cottons	49	83	16	1	4	10	9	5
Linens	21	6	35	11	44	30	38	20
Misc.	6	1	0	1	4	2	5	0
Mixed	0	0	0	0	4	0	1	3
Silks	7	1	1	43	24	8	6	6
Woolens	17	9	48	44	20	51	41	66
Total	100	100	100	100	100	101	100	100

† Cargoes
Sources: See Appendix 1

majority of apparel fabrics, whether consumers acquired them new or in the form of inherited or gifted attire, came originally from the types of merchant stocks discussed here. So whether distributed as a length of cloth or made into a garment, the textiles available in commercial sites were the materials for but hardly the sole determinants of potential dress change.

The figures reported in Table 2.1 indicate a considerable degree of difference in the composition of textile stocks around the late seventeenth-century Atlantic.[33] Local needs and tastes shaped the evident diversity. But so, to a degree, did network inertia and mercantilist restrictions: these directed English fustians to Charles Town and Philadelphia, for instance, and French *serge de Nîmes* to Montreal. At the same time, some patterns can be seen. Linens and woolens were widely and for the most part abundantly stocked, even in the tropics, cottons and silks much less so. Analysis beyond the vagaries of nomenclature also uncovers similarity among individual fabrics: fustians and *serge de Nîmes*, in fact, were comparable coarse cotton-linen blends. Divergence with some convergence defined imported textile supplies on hand in the initial stage of the shared Atlantic.

Stocks of cottons and silks were both regionally circumscribed and disparate. At the end of the seventeenth century, the significant Atlantic destinations for cottons were African, but these were far from identical, either in characteristics or in source.[34] Royal African Company cargoes for Angola and Cape Coast Castle contained many identical cottons, but the quantities involved reveal that the two locations had distinct preferences. In Angola, just three of eighteen types accounted for nearly three-quarters of cottons in the cargoes. By itself, the fustian-like blue and white striped *annabasse*, a varying blend of cotton and linen or wool manufactured in Manchester (England), Rouen (France), and Holland specifically for Africa, perhaps in imitation of an African cloth (the Benin *ambasis*) comprised half the cottons by value (and, because it was relatively cheap, considerably more in physical quantity); more expensive blue and black *bafts* and blue and white striped *neconnees* – both made in western India – each totaled an eighth.[35]

At Cape Coast Castle, about a quarter of the cottons included in RAC cargoes comprised *tapseils* from western India (often white with blue stripes), but otherwise supplies were dispersed across the remainder of the dozen imported cottons, some from Europe, others Asian.[36] Thanks to its original purpose as a refreshment and repair stop for

VOC ships, as well as the origins of many of its early residents, enslaved and free, Cape Town was heavily oriented to Asia, from which it took both cultural cues and goods, notably cotton textiles.[37] So in contrast to Angola and Cape Coast Castle, whose cottons were as likely to have been made in Europe as in Asia, tastes in the Cape Colony ran to Indian cottons: colorful calicoes for the affluent, plain white or solid blue or red *sallampores* for the poor and the enslaved. In the Americas, the exiguous amounts of cotton cloth available included Indian calicoes and muslins, though very few of the best sellers in Angola and the Gold Coast, as well as European-made mixed cotton-linens; in these years, much was destined for curtains, bed coverings, and other domestic uses rather than attire.[38]

Interest in silks was also regionally focused, albeit in the Caribbean and in Iberian America rather than Africa; like cottons, too, silks were widely sourced from outside as well as inside imperial borders. Customers in Buenos Aires seem to have been partial to three varieties: expensive multicolored Italian brocades with woven designs that resembled embroidery; fine, shiny, less expensive Spanish taffetas, often black; and soft, long-napped Asian plush. Jamaican merchants, though relying on the same sources as well as France, did not focus on any individual type of silk, perhaps because a good part of their holdings was intended for very lucrative smuggling into a variety of mainland Spanish American ports.[39]

In light of their centrality to European textile manufacturing and dress regimes, it is hardly surprising that linens and woolens generally enjoyed much the largest presence in textile stocks assembled by European and colonial merchants, nor that the great majority of the abundant choice of up to three dozen distinct varieties in nearly every location were imports from the European metropoles. Stocks in the Americas offered linens and woolens from across the price spectrum, yet the most widely favored were very similar if not identical in weave and finish though offered under different names. First among fine woolens, for example, ranked what was variously denominated broadcloth, *drap*, or *paño*; some version of serge (or its equivalents, perpetuana or *sempiterna*) was most frequently selected when hard-wearing cloth was required.

Once again, however, diversity in specific preferences accompanied some overall similarity. In plantation colonies such as Jamaica and South Carolina, about two-thirds of merchants' linen stocks comprised cheap, coarse, usually hempen varieties such as ozenbrig and harford, the rest focusing on holland and other dearer flax types (some of Jamaica's destined, like equally expensive silks, for contraband to Spanish colonies). The Philadelphia and Montreal areas had less polarized profiles, with shops in both stocking considerable quantities and numerous types of middling-value linens. Charles Town, Philadelphia, and Montreal also housed notable amounts of middling-quality woolen stroud (*limbourg* or *escarlatine* in New France) and coarser duffel or thick flannel-like *molleton* (melton) used in the peltry trade with Native Americans. For their part, Buenos Aires merchants relied heavily on Andean workshops (*obrajes*) for all but the highest-priced woolens, while fine bright white French *bretaña* and batiste featured prominently in linen stocks.

With respect to cottons, as we have seen, Cape Town had a different textile profile than other European colonies in the Atlantic. Its linen and woolen stocks, in contrast, bore greater resemblance, though with a somewhat greater admixture of rough, less expensive sorts, such as hempen canvas and light, thin, napless stuffs and *estemijn* (estamine), not to mention a modicum of expensive *laaken*, the Dutch variant of the broadcloth that won elite favor throughout the Atlantic. Cape Coast Castle had a strong orientation to moderately priced woolens and linens. There, durable twilled woolen perpetuanas or perpets were especially in vogue, apparently for the rainy and windy seasons and for dispatch to interior upland areas, as well as second-hand linen sheets worn as full body wraps and, according to some contemporaries, torn and used by women during their menstrual periods.[40] Even Angola participated in woolens and linens consumption, if at a modest level, as the RAC stocked some fine, usually scarlet, broadcloth and dazzling white silesia linen (also known as platilla or *platille*).

Late seventeenth-century Atlantic textile stocks were characterized by some consistency, then, but even more by diversity. Predominance of woolens and linens across many climatic, imperial, legal, and ethnic frontiers, together with wide presence of quite similar individual fabrics within these fiber categories, coexisted with pronounced regional bounds to the appeal of cottons and silks, as well as with disparate local configurations of even the most popular woolens and linens. Data from three more locations, for which sufficient usable information first becomes available in the 1730s, are displayed in Table 2.2. They disclose the wider existence of some patterns of woven textile availability seen earlier and the emergence of some new trends grounded in similar socioeconomic circumstances.

In all three of these colonies, where plantation slavery was rapidly developing, cloth stocks exhibited a marked degree of price

Table 2.2 *Types of textiles commercially available in the Atlantic in the 1730s*
Percentages of total stocks by value (in parentheses, number of merchant probate inventories)

Type of fabric	Salvador da Bahia (3)	Southern District, Saint-Domingue (4)	New Orleans (10)
Cottons	19	29	15
Linens	40	40	36
Misc.	1	1	1
Mixed	1	2	1
Silks	15	10	1
Woolens	24	18	46
Total	100	100	100

Sources: See Appendix 1

and quality polarization, much like that already manifest in the slave societies of Jamaica and South Carolina. The phenomenon was especially striking among linens, where at least two-thirds of the merchant holdings consisted of a plethora of similar coarse, cheap, often hempen varieties – many unbleached, others striped or checked, most often in blue and white – as well as an admixture of equally rough cotton-linens like *ruão* in Salvador da Bahia, and the analagous *rouen* and striped or check *siamoise* in Louisiana and Saint-Domingue. Also corresponding to what had already become apparent in the late seventeenth century, the 1730s figures exhibit the greater availability of silks in Iberian America and the Caribbean; further paralleling the earlier contrast between the Río de la Plata and Jamaica, pricey varieties were a larger presence in Brazil than in Saint-Domingue.

Table 2.2 likewise signals two trends that not only altered previous patterns but would ever more strongly mark eighteenth-century textile cultures throughout the Atlantic: the growing importance of cottons and declining significance of woolens.[41] As merchant stocks of cottons expanded in size and variety, the fabric shed its regional identity.[42] As before, however, cotton stocks were not uniform on the two sides of the Atlantic. Whether pure Indian cottons or European imitations, the *bafts*, Guinea stuffs (plain, blue and white checked or striped, or solid blue), and printed *pintado* version of calico (among many more types) that were popular in Gold Coast and Angola rarely found their way to the Americas; conversely, generally plain varieties such as *bazin* (sturdy, ribbed but fine dimity), finely woven muslin, and coarse heavy *cotonade* were favored only in the Americas. Calico did bridge the ocean to a degree, yet it was much more popular in European colonial settlements than among indigenous Africans. Despite the lesser presence of woolens in the three plantation colonies included in Table 2.2, broadcloth retained its primacy; at the same time, merchants in all three stocked considerable quantities of cheap, coarse woolens. Finally, like their counterparts in Montreal, New Orleans merchants had large holdings of both expensive *limbourg* and more moderately valued *molleton*, reflecting the deep involvement of both places in the fur trade.

By the end of the second third of the eighteenth century, the interplay of European commercial rules and conventions, diversely evolving colonial socioeconomic structures, and changing consumer preferences had significantly affected the relative composition of merchant textile stocks around the Atlantic even while in absolute terms the quantities of imported textiles had sextupled and the number of fabric varieties available at least doubled. Table 2.3 shows the situation obtaining in all eleven areas previously examined in Tables 2.1 and 2.2; in the nine European colonies, the figures include stocks found in the commercial zones that had developed around the original port settlements. As elaborated in Appendix 1, imported textile supplies in Angola likely included more woolens and fewer cottons, and perhaps more linens, than presented in Table 2.3, and Cape Coast Castle fewer woolens and more mixed-fiber cloth. Still, the adjustments for any category in any of these locations would be no more than 5 percent and thus would not substantively alter the contours of the imported textile stocks portrayed here.

Among the diverse fiber types, greater uniformity than earlier obtained both across the Atlantic and within specific regions, though these processes of convergence coexisted with still-marked individuality of local textile cultures. The contrasting fortunes of cottons and woolens already becoming visible earlier in the eighteenth century persisted in 1760–74. Cottons comprised at least a seventh of merchant offerings in all eleven areas, and in most considerably more – including New France with its often frigid temperatures – but African stocks remained proportionately much larger than anywhere else in the Atlantic.[43] Woolens, once dominant in many locations, had lost that position almost everywhere, yet they retained a much greater presence in Atlantic continental North America than elsewhere. Other types of fabrics experienced more regionally disparate fortunes. Linens had firmed up their position within

Table 2.3 *Types of textiles commercially available in the Atlantic in 1760–74*
Percentages of total stocks by value (in parentheses, number of merchant probate inventories or cargoes)

Type of fabric	CapeCol. (14)	Angola (20) †	Cape Coast Castle (32) †	Río de la Plata (19)	Salv. da Bahia and Recôncavo (6)	Jamaica (64)	South Dist. S-Dom (25)	Lower Louisiana (7)	South Car. (26)	Philadelphia Area (86)	Montreal Area (27)
Cottons	45	95	60	18	17	12	44	30	19	15	23
Linens	13	1	16	51	28	66	45	60	43	25	34
Misc.	1	0	0	0	0	0	0	0	1	3	1
Mixed	8	0	3	0	3	11	0	1	9	5	0
Silks	6	1	7	12	34	4	5	2	3	7	8
Woolens	27	3	14	19	18	7	5	7	26	45	34
Total	100	100	100	100	100	100	99	100	101	100	100

† Cargoes.
Sources: See Appendix 1

plantation slavery colonies while yielding to cottons in Africa. Silks remained consequential only in Iberian America as reforms in Spanish trading regulations sharply reduced the attractiveness of textile smuggling from the West Indies and thus the stocks of silks in Jamaica and Saint-Domingue. In the trans-imperial Caribbean (Jamaica, southern Saint-Domingue, lower Louisiana), cottons, linens, and/or cotton-linen mixtures overwhelmingly predominated, the three lighter fabrics together comprising about 90 percent of all textiles in merchant stocks, yet the proportion of each category varied markedly from place to place.

Greater similarity also characterized stocks of individual fabrics everywhere in the Atlantic as well as within its discrete zones, but without erasing the distinctiveness of local textile cultures. For instance, calicoes, including the more expensive types sometimes distinguished as "chintz," became the most popular cotton in a majority of places and one of the top three nearly everywhere else: To a significant extent, the eighteenth-century rise of cottons was actually the rise of calico – often at the expense of an earlier favorite, muslin. Again, the British plantation colonies depended increasingly on cheap cotton checks, the French on equally inexpensive *siamoise*, the Iberian colonies on *ruan* or *ruão*. Yet Angola was largely impervious to the appeal of any of these; even though late eighteenth-century stocks there contained only a tiny number of any of the once-dominant *annabasses* and *bafts*, their place was taken by European copies of long-established favorites of Indian origin, such as *neconnees, tapseils*, and blue or blue and white striped Guinea cloth.[44]

Several overlapping trends defined linens. Cheap, coarse, often hempen types now became the largest component of stocks around most of the Atlantic; in the British colonies, many of these less expensive linens were single-fiber checks. In plantation colonies, costly types of linens could still be found, but stocks of medium-priced varieties waned, suggesting polarization of demand; in the Buenos Aires, Philadelphia, and Montreal areas, however, stocks of more equal qualities and prices continued to be available. A declining part of cargoes to Atlantic Africa, linens nevertheless became a favored material for handkerchiefs and neckcloths; in Cape Coast Castle second-hand sheets were largely supplanted by new sheeting (whether this was due to supply or demand is unclear), and colorful printed linens supplemented chintz, the post's preferred cotton. Finally, thanks to several forms of mercantilist assistance, Irish linens swept the market throughout the

British colonies, with offerings at every price point in varieties suitable for each locality.

Among mixed-fiber textiles, cotton and silk combinations such as strong, plain weave *alpine* (alapeen) and poplin with its corded surface won favor in the Cape Colony and the Philadelphia area respectively, while cheaper linen-cotton checks (along with the single-fiber cotton and linen types) became a very popular low- to medium-priced cloth in British Caribbean and North American colonies. In the general decline of silks, medium-priced taffetas (or, in Salvador da Bahia, the very similar *canelões*) held out best. Though also a decreasing presence across most of the Atlantic, woolens stocks remained important outside Angola and the Caribbean. Moreover, broadcloth under its diverse nomenclature stayed the most widely held woolen. Perpetuanas, *sempiternas*, and similar durable but cheaper woolens largely disappeared, yet demand for cloth of that quality did not. At Cape Town it was fulfilled by various types of napped *baaij* (baize), including very coarse "slave baize"; at Cape Coast Castle by long ells, and in South Carolina by plains (also known as kendal cottons and "Negro cloth") that – together with other very similar kinds of fabric – comprised half by value (and much more by length) of woolens stocks in that colony. Finally, both British and French America now featured glossy, brightly dyed, often striped or patterned worsteds like calimanco and its equivalent *calamande* intended to imitate – and compete with – calicoes.

Increases of every nature in the availability of textiles – sheer quantities, newly invented varieties, more widely distributed well-established fabrics – thus permitted the development of distinctive, if constantly changing, local stocks of imported cloth. Equally striking was the growing convergence of woven-fiber cloth supplies beyond individual locales. Early modern globalization concomitantly promoted greater similarity of textile supplies within regions and in the Atlantic basin as a whole. Cape Colony evidence shows tellingly how these processes played out. There, the proportion of woolens in merchant stocks actually rose between the end of the seventeenth century and 1760–74, while that of cottons declined. These sharp contrasts in trend compared to developments elsewhere in the Atlantic brought the Cape Colony's textile supply profile closer to that obtaining on both sides of the ocean, even while continuing to endow the Cape Colony with a particular balance of fabrics that was neither simply colonial nor wholly African.

Access

No matter how assembled, where located, or what their composition, throughout the Atlantic world textile stocks became available to consumers by both market and non-market methods. Depending on local conditions and local needs, market-based trade in cloth was carried out by a variety of agents, ranging from wholesalers to retailers, planters to peddlers, slaves to auctioneers. On occasion, long-distance merchants themselves, or their sedentary and itinerant representatives, sold goods directly to individuals. In Atlantic Africa, this seems to have occurred where fixed trading places such as forts did not exist; the practice decreased in importance when and where trade became more regular, though it never completely died out.[45] In late eighteenth-century Kongo, for instance, African sellers negotiated directly with ship captains "at the water's edge," pricing slaves in multiples of *marchandises*, which were 10–14 ell lengths of cottons or calicoes.[46] In the Americas, import merchants were among the few sources of consumer goods during early periods of settlement, and some wholesalers always continued to sell retail as well.[47] Planters could also be important suppliers of consumer goods in colonies with few sizeable settlements. Generally their role diminished as other forms of retailing spread in the eighteenth century, though in poorly served backlands some continued to sell cloth to their slaves.[48]

In the few Atlantic places where chartered companies survived, their monopolistic pretensions led them to try to control consumer purchases. Thus between 1722 and 1731 New Orleans residents could only lawfully shop at the warehouse of the Compagnie des Indes, while throughout the century and a half (1652–1795) that the VOC ruled the settlement at the Cape of Good Hope, it sought to obstruct the development of retail shops.[49] Though they raised prices and vexed consumers, these restrictions were repeatedly evaded, notably by women who traded from their own homes.[50] At the other extreme were the informal, casual, or adventitious exchanges in which all sorts of individuals engaged: criminals disposing of stolen goods, runaway slaves or servants who took with them a few pieces of fabric or a spare garment to finance their new lives, settlers seeking to round out their farming incomes by selling to their Amerindian neighbors, artisans doing a bit of trading on the side.[51]

Apparel and occasionally textiles were also bestowed as remuneration for work. Native American translators, canoemen, porters, and other laborers typically received in-kind wages, including a substantial textile component; Amerindians also earned rewards of cloth for returning runaway slaves or turning over enemy soldiers.[52] Just as such payments helped diffuse standard types of cloth and garments among Native Americans, so metropolitan styles were disseminated among free and enslaved colonials when affluent settlers, hoping to participate in European fashion or just to circumvent colonial tailors ("bunglers," in the words of one Georgia planter), ordered bespoke clothing directly from the metropole, or (if rarely) furnished slaves with garments imported from Europe.[53]

For all that, some kind of professional retailer handled most cloth and clothing transfers. Between the seventeenth and eighteenth centuries, historians have argued, all types of formal retailing proliferated in town and country in western Europe and colonial North America, with the shop at the forefront. Shops expanded in number, spread from cities into small towns and rural villages, specialized in select lines of goods, and took on a new physical configuration; together, these developments helped create integrated consumer markets in which similar kinds of goods were widely available, though cities always offered wider choices than country districts. As shopkeeping became a distinct occupation, a new breed of proprietors presented their goods and themselves in innovative ways, using print advertising and offering fashion advice and easier credit to induce customers to buy an expanding array of fashionable goods. The shopper emerged as a recognized social role and shopping as a discrete and valued cultural practice, as a new ideal transformed simple buying based on a utilitarian calculus into a pleasurable activity stimulated by advertising, featuring choice, fashion, and aesthetic values, and promising access to new cultural styles and social subjectivities.[54] Figure 2.1, showing the interior of a late seventeenth-century millinery shop in Paris, epitomizes the new establishments – or at least the image that their proponents wished to diffuse. The engraving displays at once the elegant retail space, the fashionable consumers who were to frequent it, and the desirable fabrics and garments they were to acquire. To guide the consumer, the chic clothing is numbered and the modish fabrics lettered, with accompanying text detailing colors, finishes, and occasionally the elegant person with whom the commodity was associated.[55]

Some version of these developments appeared in the wider early modern Atlantic world, at times precociously. The vigorous early

2.1 *Intérieur d'une boutique contenant des étoffes et des vêtements pour hommes / Interior of a shop containing fabrics and men's garments.*

This engraving was originally published in *L'extraordinaire du mercure galant* (January quarter, 1678), 342, before being sold separately. Founded in 1672, the *Mercure galant* aimed at upper-class society with news and guidance about court life and etiquette, current intellectual and artistic matters, and fashion. For the cultural impact of the journal, see DeJean 2005.

growth of Spanish America meant that even Buenos Aires in the late sixteenth century, though recently founded, and with a population of no more than 2,000, already boasted *tiendas*, shops that handled imports (notably garments, textiles, iron implements, and wine), as well as *pulperías* focused on local foodstuffs. It is not known, however, whether the yet more numerous retailers in seventeenth- and eighteenth-century Buenos Aires undertook further expansion, specialization, and transformation of shop premises and shopkeeper practices.[56] As economic and demographic growth accelerated from the late seventeenth century on, shops proliferated elsewhere in the Atlantic, first in ports and larger towns, then even in small inland settlements.[57]

As central to colonial as to metropolitan retailing, credit helped translate wishes (or just needs) into purchases.[58] To be sure, shopkeepers were squeezed between demands by wholesalers, who considered six months the limit of a proper term of payment, and consumers' expectations of a more casual settlement schedule, which they often obtained simply by not settling debts for extended periods of time. Nevertheless, most of the time shopkeepers – like wholesalers – presumably incorporated a credit charge into their normal prices, hinting at the practice by offering discounts to purchasers with cash, even if the very ubiquity of credit normally rendered it invisible and the operation of its mechanisms unarticulated.

As in European metropoles, so too in some mid-eighteenth-century colonial towns incipient shopping districts began to form: along rues Notre-Dame and Saint-Paul in Montreal; on Front and Second Streets both north and south of Market Street in Philadelphia; on the three parallel streets closest to the waterfront in Kingston (Port Royal, Harbour, Water); in a rectangle formed by Tradd, Broad, Church, and Bay Streets in Charles Town.[59] In the same years, shopkeepers in British colonies started to apply flattering descriptors such as "large" and "commodious" to their establishments in advertisements, thereby imaginatively characterizing them as suitable for exhibiting goods – fabrics most of all. The fabrics themselves were characterized as desirably "neat," "choice," "fashionable," "fresh," or "newly imported."[60] Many shopkeepers promised a consumer cornucopia by listing dozens of distinct textiles, exploiting a language of novelty, modishness, and quantity, and heightening the sense of magnificence by comments about colors, designs, finishes, and sizes. The kinds of competitive comparison and interchange bred by these developments fostered at least broader knowledge of textiles considered desirable elsewhere in the Atlantic and very likely played a role in encouraging their acquisition.

These innovations seem to have taken hold first and most extensively in the British Atlantic.[61] Elsewhere the picture is mixed. Even in the eighteenth-century Parisian luxury and semi-luxury trades, the most recent study concludes, "commercial dynamism" coexisted with "very traditional" practices, regulations, and establishments.[62] Change advanced rather less in other places. Shops in Cape Town were typically nothing more than rooms in private homes, operated by part-time shopkeepers, typically wives of respectable citizens and VOC officials, who sold heterogeneous lots of goods obtained at irregular intervals from passing ships, local auctions, or on occasion directly from the Netherlands. Because they did not get their stocks from the inadequately provisioned, overpriced VOC stores, these shopkeepers had to operate in secrecy or at least without attracting official attention by signs, advertisements, or accoutrements.[63] In Salvador da Bahia, too, many retail establishments were nothing more than barely furnished rooms, while New Orleans shops were not embellished in any respect, did not adopt new ways of organizing their interiors or presenting goods, and did not even make a clear division between personal and retail spaces.[64] Nor do innovations seem to have affected the unspecialized general stores found widely in North American frontier forts or the petty retail establishments selling cheap cloth and other goods in *presidios*, the rudimentary military garrison settlements found all along the Spanish empire's many frontiers in Central and South America.[65]

Outside British possessions, moreover, colonial newspapers, which offered the potential for advertising to a broad audience, remained rare before the 1760s. Once they began to appear, however, advertisements in them quickly adopted the same kind of colorful language as their counterparts in the British empire.[66] Again, it is difficult to find traces in the colonies of the clothes brokers specializing in second-hand apparel whose activities in Europe are thought to have diffused metropolitan elite materials, attire, and fashions to broader social groups. Still, something similar may have occurred in the Americas, where tailors and seamstresses, often claiming to be well versed in the latest European styles, marketed used garments after repairing and updating them.[67]

Many retailers, in any event, did not operate shops. Often they had stalls in public markets, or simply set out their wares in open space in or near a marketplace. Among the oldest organized commercial sites around the world, markets were nearly ubiquitous throughout the Atlantic.[68] Found even in small localities, they dominated retailing in Atlantic Africa apart from that conducted by Muslim women inside their compounds.[69] Marees described and illustrated the market at Cabo Corso (subsequently Cape Coast Castle), which he characterized as "the freest market in all the towns" of the Gold Coast and thus a "good place to trade." Figure 2.2 shows an orderly, well-policed (P) area under the guardianship of a "Fetish" ("their God": N), where both Africans and Dutch (O) buy fresh and prepared food (C–F, H, M), water (I), wood (G), sugarcane (K), and where, at the center, "measurers" (L) cut imported "Dutch linen" into the lengths desired by local consumers.[70]

Markets also grew up quickly in most colonies, informally at first, then regularized by statute.[71] Despite discriminatory laws designed to hobble retailing by slaves, Sunday markets, scheduled to minimize disruptions to field labor, became particularly vibrant and central economic, social, and cultural institutions in American plantation colonies, where they were mainly staffed by enslaved women and men and free persons of color.[72] As images like Agostino Brunias's painting (Plate 2) suggest, and innumerable regulations and a great deal of written commentary confirm, lengths of fabric, kerchiefs, and new and used garments were chief among the manufactures exchanged at such Sunday markets. Similarly, in eighteenth-century Portuguese Angola, enslaved and free market women (*quitandeiras*) in rudimentary street stalls dealt not only in local palm oil and dried fish but pricier imported chinaware and Indian cottons. Together with their merchandise, their willingness to work long hours led to an outcry from licensed shopkeepers whose business was allegedly harmed by this competition.[73]

Markets were dramatic – and, by many contemporaries, dramatized – sites for retailing, yet itinerant huckstering was probably as important for distributing goods. Some slaves combined peddling on their own account with selling in Sunday markets.[74] Others were trained and dispatched by their masters or hired by merchants. So much cloth did such ambulatory hawkers allegedly sell in Salvador da Bahia that in 1724 shopkeepers petitioned the authorities to stop them, only to be refused on the grounds that women, who in the large and spread-out city often could not easily get to shops, depended on them.[75] In the kingdom of Issyny on the Gold Coast, according to the French Dominican Godefroy Loyer, it was the king who organized peddling.

2.2 *Market at Cabo Corso*, from Pieter de Marees, *Beschryvinghe ende Historische Verhael van het Gout Koninckrijck van Gunea anders de Gout-Custe de Mina genaemt liggende in het Deel van Africa* (The Hague: Cornelis Claesz, 1602).

Marees carefully described this market, already long a center for exchanges with Europeans as well as between Africans, before the RAC established their Cape Coast Castle trading post nearby.

Arrogating to himself, his brother, and his chief official the right to buy imported textiles and tobacco, he then sent his slaves to sell the goods "in the mountains and far distant lands," cash only, with no risk to him and no expenses but a handsome profit.[76] White marketers (*feirantes*) in Angola got around limits to their activities by hiring enslaved factors (*pumbeiros*), granting them goods on credit to exchange for slaves in the interior.[77]

Peddling was not, however, an occupation reserved for the enslaved; in French colonies in particular, free people of color were often chapmen.[78] Occasionally in the Caribbean, but more commonly in the mainland colonies of every nation, hawkers were of European or mixed descent. Shops, markets, and other fixed sales points were scarce in much of Brazil, but chapmen (*mascates*) with mule trains and canoe fleets distributed textiles, apparel, and goods throughout the country.[79] In North America, peddling became a crucial mode of selling to Amerindians once the depletion of fur stocks near settlements curbed informal trade between colonists and native trappers, as well as to settlers, particularly in thinly populated rural and frontier districts distant from other sources of goods, where bad weather and worse roads further complicated shopping.[80] As one petition in support of a peddler's application for a license expressed it, "ye Severall Inhabitants of the province [Pennsylvania], Living in remote places & far Distance from any Stores Enjoy A great Advantage by [peddlers] . . . furnishing them with goods & Necessaries at Reasonable prices."[81] Some packmen were independent operators, others employees of merchants in port cities or trading posts. But all their packs – as those of their European counterparts – were stuffed mainly with textiles, small articles of apparel, trimmings, and notions.[82]

Like market sellers, many peddlers did not focus on fashion items apart from ribbons and suchlike ornamentation. But all were crucial for the wide distribution of the quotidian textiles that, the merchant stocks have demonstrated, were consequential for the diffusion of similar goods. At the same time, they had to address the specific needs of their customers. Their offerings demonstrate the combination of the general and the particular. For the Indians and modest planters he visited in backwoods Louisiana in 1765, Joseph Dupré or Beaupré carried mainly inexpensive coarse hempen St.-Jean linen, as well as small amounts of only slightly more expensive *siamoise*, flannel, and cotton handkerchiefs.[83] Françoise, called "Fanchon Signore," also sold lengths of cheap linens and handkerchiefs in and around Aquin in the Southern District of Saint-Domingue in the early 1770s, but she also had ready-made apparel, including black hats, some intended for enslaved men and women, others for all comers.[84] In prosperous Lancaster County, Pennsylvania, where inexpensive locally woven linens and woolens were often readily available, fine holland, sheer plain-weave lawn, and shirting linen, together with middling-priced muslin and variously colored stamped (printed) cottons, predominated in John Caroll's 1767 stock, and he also found space for fine cambric and silk handkerchiefs.[85]

Auctions played a similar dual role. Supplementing – and at times rivaling – other forms of retailing, auctions were increasingly popular and regular sources of both new and second-hand consumer goods as well as transfers among merchants in many settler colonies.[86] Variously termed "vendu(e)s," "*ventes*," "*encans*," "outcrys," "public auctions," "public sales," or "*tiendas públicas*," they were favored by merchants and shopkeepers to top up shortages in their stocks or move excess goods, as well as to dump damaged, outdated, or otherwise difficult-to-sell merchandise, or simply to wind up a business.[87] In Buenos Aires, contraband goods were often laundered through authorized auctions announced by the public crier and held in the town's main plaza, in shops, and in private houses; some were wholesale, intended for local as well as inland merchants, while others were retail.[88] Around the Atlantic, private individuals could likewise find useful items at bankruptcy or business cessation sales, but more regularly at probate or post-mortem auctions, which often featured modestly priced lengths of fabric and used garments.

While these types of auctions were held in city and countryside alike in most colonies, from the late seventeenth century more formal public auctions became institutionalized in some urban centers, complete with municipal regulations, designated auctioneers, and fixed sites, sometimes specially constructed for that purpose; in some places, too, private "vendue masters" (as they were termed in the British Atlantic) opened their own auction establishments.[89] Retailers might bemoan what they depicted as auctions' unfair competition, and critics might denounce them for "the Uncertainty whether such Goods as Housekeepers happen to want will be sold," not to mention "the Hazard of buying when there is not Time to examine" the items on offer, and the fact that "goods of the worst fabric are imported, on purpose to be sold in that Way, with which the Ignorant and Unwary, who are generally the least able to bear it, are egregiously gulled."[90] But advocates praised auctions for pushing down prices; as one crowed, "if some Importers are satisfied with smaller Profits than have been customary, so much the better for the Consumers," who did indeed flock to them.[91] Auctions and retail shops functioned as both complementary and competing ways of distributing both standard goods and those specific to their localities.

Finally, textiles and garments were transferred by non-market means. Inheritance and post-mortem donations were sources of mainly second-hand items of every type and quality; the quantities involved, though doubtless substantial, are difficult to gauge with any precision because probate inventories generally ignored such items or did not distinguish them from other listings. Individuals were also gifted fabric and apparel during their lifetimes; female slaves might be thus favored for sexual services (so their presents might better be considered earnings), but other enslaved men and women were beneficiaries as well, as were servants.[92] Self-gifting – theft – also transferred cloth and clothing both new and old among individuals across and within cultural frontiers. Amerindians stripped garments from raid victims, donning the apparel for symbolic as much as utilitarian reasons.[93] Settlers, too, found textile goods – particularly high-priced fashionable items, quickly taken, easily carried, and much in demand – irresistible targets for stealing.[94]

Allies and trade partners in West Africa were gifted with textile items; descriptions of the procedures and ceremonies that sought to ensure that rank and honor were properly observed were staples of contemporary accounts. Presents were likewise a considerable and consistent source of textile goods for Native North Americans. Distributions of lengths of cloth, of blankets, and of ready-made garments were a regular and organized component of religious evangelization as well as diplomatic and trade relations.[95] Alcoholic beverages and all manner of manufactures also served as gifts, but cloth and clothing nearly always ranked among the leading items that Europeans distributed.[96] So central were textile items, in fact, that Europeans commonly employed "cloth," "clothing," "clothed," and "to clothe" as synonyms for both the act of conferring goods and the concomitant gifts.[97]

Valued for the symbolic properties and messages it could convey and for the material, behavioral, or attitudinal responses it could evoke, gift-giving held an essential place within pre-contact African, Amerindian, and European cultures and, very quickly, within their intercultural transactions.[98] Bestowing presents was at once a cordial gesture and a purposeful, interested, and polysemous act that helped generate the trust vital for commercial and diplomatic relationships in cross-cultural situations lacking the "shared cognitive frameworks and rules" that typically undergird such transactions.[99] Indeed, as several scholars have suggested, rather than sharply contrasting forms of transaction, gifting and commodity exchange share characteristics of reciprocity, sociability, and calculation; though analytically distinguishable, they overlap in practice.[100] Some of the textiles and apparel transferred as gifts were expensive and showy, but others were ordinary in price and quality. Either way, they fostered the distribution of imported styles and materials across ethnic, social, and geographic borders.

The largest and most widespread non-market transfers of cloth and clothing involved slaves. Statute and practice directed masters to provide apparel (or sufficient fabric to make clothing) for the women and men they held in bondage. The prescribed dress was cheap and minimal, not to say inadequate, and even then many owners failed to comply. Slaves therefore frequently had to self-provision, at least in part, usually through some sort of market transaction, and often, too, they acquired garments and lengths of cloth in return for labor for which a free person would have received a wage. Indentured servants – half of all European immigrants to North America before the early nineteenth century – likewise typically received clothing, both during their term of service and as part of the "freedom dues" delivered upon its expiration; these might be considered deferred wages, indicating yet again the blurriness of the market/non-market distinction at the level of the individual.[101] Given the general unwillingness of both slaveowners and employers of indentured servants to spend much on the maintenance of their workforce, and the laborers' own meager resources, most of their textiles were likely to be cheap and standard. Yet even when provided with dress, as we shall see, many bondsmen and bondswomen in particular sought to obtain additional better attire, and in this way fashion ideas and items could circulate among the most deprived – and largest – Atlantic populations.

The multiple modes of textile distribution – wholesale and retail, market and non-market, new and second-hand – meant that virtually every location and social group around the Atlantic had more than one way to gain access to textiles and clothing from more than one area of production, distant or local. If the same modes of diffusion did not exist everywhere, some sort did, and almost always more than one.

Should a particular type of cloth or garment not be produced within a given empire, moreover, it might well be available through contraband. As this chapter has shown, these factors tended to make textile supplies more uniform.

Other circumstances complicated this development. Mercantilism and empire operated with various levels of efficacy and impact on textile stocks: The Navigation Acts were much more effective at excluding foreign goods and merchants from the British empire than were the laws designed to fence off the Spanish colonies. Commercial innovations and thus the possibilities for distribution of fabrics and fashions spread widely but unevenly. Most important, the Atlantic comprised diverse socioeconomic and natural ecologies, individuals of multiple ethnicities, statuses, occupations, and identifications, and groups with specific sartorial habits and demands, differential access to materials, and disparate degrees of legal and economic autonomy regarding decisions about dress. From the encounter of increasingly similar yet unavoidably different textile supplies with distinctive yet imbricated personal and collective consumer demands materialized the dress regimes of the shared Atlantic world.

3 REDRESSING THE INDIGENOUS AMERICAS

In 1730, an otherwise unknown English artist named Markham painted a group portrait of a Cherokee delegation currently in London for treaty negotiations. The original picture seems to have been lost, but at some point the printmaker Isaac Basire engraved a widely circulated version known as *The Cherokee Embassy to England* (Figure 3.1).[1] Images of the indigenous peoples of the Americas had become popular among Europeans from the time of initial contact, and within that genre portraits of Amerindian visitors proliferated in the eighteenth century, particularly in Britain, in prints, engravings, and paintings not just by obscure artists such as Markham but by luminaries such as Sir Joshua Reynolds and George Romney.[2]

Like all portraits, "The Cherokee Embassy" was carefully staged by subjects and artist alike; as in all portraits, therefore, multiple and perhaps conflicting purposes governed the image's creation, and all of these conditions were magnified in this case by cultural distance between subjects and artist. On one level, the engraving depicts the incorporation of Attakullakulla, Oukah Ulah Moytoy, Clogoittah, Kallannah, Tahtowe, Kitegista Skalilosken, and Ounaconoa into the norms of European civility.[3] A number of pictorial elements manifest the process of assimilation: the classicizing configuration and poses of the seven men's bodies, the overt designation of a "King" and a "Prince," the rapiers, musket, halberd, and small bow that they carry, and, most obviously, the fashionable "*Habits*" – breeches, fitted jackets, and shirts – with which they had been "*Cloath'd … out of ye Royal Wardrobe*" with subtle yet real distinctions of rank, notably mantles for "King" and "Prince." At the same time, the image depicts objects that

3.1 *The Cherokee Embassy to England* (*c.* 1740–60), by Isaac Basire.
Engraving after painting by Markham. Basire, best known for his map engravings,
came from a famous family of printmakers. Why he did this piece and its relation
to the original painting are unknown, but the men shown definitely did visit
England in 1730, accompanied by Sir Alexander Cuming, a former Scots lawyer,
then intermediary, and future adventurer and alchemist, to negotiate a renewed
treaty of Cherokee–English alliance.

many earlier depictions had made signs of savagery: moccasins, an
Amerindian ball-headed club, facial tattoos ("*NB,*" concludes the
accompanying caption, "*The marks on their faces & bodys are tokens
of Victory*"), and distinctive hairstyles (including the plume worn by the
"King" in the center). For good measure, the men are visually situated
within a presumably primeval, if fanciful, forest.[4]

It is impossible to determine who, among all those who had a
hand in the production of this image, was responsible for its specific
features, or what precise message they intended to convey. Yet in its very
amalgam of items, materials, and styles, "The Cherokee Embassy"
illustrates nicely both the manifold and not always congruent purposes
of dressing in the early modern Atlantic world and the array of elements

that sartorial initiatives entailed. Many inhabitants of the Atlantic redressed during the seventeenth and eighteenth centuries. The act of redressing lies, of course, at the heart of the venerable human practice of corporeal adaptation to mark and to help effect transitions to new life stages, occupations, and statuses. It is the final stage in a classic rite of passage entailing separation (symbolized by removal of previous garb), transition (cleansing), and reincorporation (denoted by investiture with new apparel).[5] In many cultures, including Amerindian, redressing, like dressing, involves not simply clothing but modifications of the body: scarification, painting, and other signs inscribed directly on the skin, and shaving, braiding, knotting, or otherwise grooming hair. Beyond its specific somatic content, moreover, dress renovation conspicuously signifies change in status: It testifies to sexual maturity, adulthood, personal or professional mobility (including downward), rebirth, social or even literal death. But as an initiation or socialization ritual, it is focused on determinate individuals or groups and occurs within a given culture and dress regime.

In the early modern Atlantic, redressing occurred on a much larger scale than these individual or communal rituals. Its proponents often had impressive, even grandiose sociopolitical ambitions, but it also – and increasingly – occurred as a largely unintended by-product of the expansive globalizing merchant economy with its new consumer goods and tastes. When accomplished by Europeans and settlers of European background, Atlantic redressing emphasized garments, preeminently those shaped from woven fabrics supplied by European and colonial merchant networks; relegated fur and skin to the extremities (head, feet, hands); and ignored, concealed, or denigrated tattooing, body painting, and other epidermal alterations. The most calculated examples of redressing involved cross-cultural interventions not simply to reclothe individuals but to transform utterly the dress regimes of entire populations of "savages" and of newly enslaved women and men. Initially, redressing might be involuntary, but over time, the people who had at first been the objects of these initiatives blended elements from several cultures to create their own dress regimes and thus to participate in the contemporaneous "democratization of fashion" along with settlers and metropolitan Europeans, who also reappareled, albeit in forms that required less cultural and material adaptation. The general availability of global textiles left very few people untouched, as redressing provided sites for displaying various forms of identification, drawing and crossing sociocultural borders, and inventing hybrid dress regimes.

Increasingly similar fabrics were to be found throughout the Atlantic, and broadly shared European colonial, economic, and ideological projects were at work across that world. But these materials and interests had to operate within a variety of geographic, cultural, and political ecologies. Global textiles were appropriated for a large variety of reasons and in many different ways. This chapter initiates analysis of the appropriative process by examining what transpired among indigenous populations in Brazil and eastern North America. Generally deemed "naked savages" in dire need of civility, as we have seen in Chapter 1, inhabitants of these regions received substantial attention from missionaries and colonial officials, and most were subject as well to long-term acculturating pressures of economic exchanges with Europeans and of acquaintance with imported cloth, fabric, and styles. The outcomes, however, were various.

Brazil and Río de la Plata: from "stark naked" to undress

Native Brazilians had virtually no pre-contact experience with the use of fabrics of any type in apparel, much less, Léry and other early observers reported, with the belief that garments were necessary elements of dress. The advent of Europeans did not necessarily make any difference in either of those circumstances, for in many areas, existing dress practices continued for generations with little if any alteration. The many Native peoples living in the vast interior had little contact with missionaries or with the colonial economy, focused as it was on plantation agriculture and mining. It is hardly surprising, therefore, that the Dutchman Johan Nieuhof, who lived in Brazil for nine years during the period (1639–54) that Holland controlled much of the northeast, described the clothing habits of the inland Tapuia or Tapuya in terms little changed from those Léry applied many decades earlier to the Tupinambá. "Men as well as women go stark naked ... without any shame," Nieuhof declared; at most, women covered their genitalia with "tree leaves worn as a kind of sash," men with a net penis sheath. But all bedecked themselves with ample decorations, including brilliantly colored feather headpieces for the men, ear and lip piercings, small feathers attached to the trunk.[6] Though shown in conventionalized settings and poses

Map 3.1 Indigenous South Americans

(and presented as cannibals), images of Tapuia men and women by Frans Post and Albert Eckhout, painted in Europe from sketches and other materials gathered when both lived in "New Holland" between 1637 and 1644, confirm the essentials of their contemporary Nieuhof's textual claim.[7]

Near the coast, in contrast, the Tupí lived in proximity to the settler population and often participated in the colonial economy, notably as casual or enslaved laborers, as suggested by the background to Plate 3. In that capacity, they often received lengths of fabric and clothing. For example, Indian men (*indios*) employed from the early 1620s through the mid-1640s on the Engenho de Sergipe, a Jesuit-operated sugar plantation in the captaincy of Bahia, acquired linen (and perhaps woolen) cloth and, on occasion, shirts and breeches made of those fabrics.[8] Contemporary accounts recorded the new costume. Though he deemed them scandalously underdressed, Nieuhof did note that native Brazilians who dwelt in the vicinity of the Dutch or Portuguese wore linen or cotton attire. An accompanying image depicted both a man and a woman in a short wrapped garment extending from waist to mid-thigh, much like the attire in Eckhout's contemporaneous paintings (Plates 3 and 4).[9]

Those indigenous Brazilians who became Christians may have altered their dress a little more in order to demonstrate their new identification. In a print by Carlos Julião entitled "Couple of new native converts " (*Casal de nativos já catequizados*) from the late eighteenth century, the man wears just a pair of knee-length loose breeches, but the woman has on a long, loose, short-sleeved white shift that covers her torso from neck to mid-calf, her arms almost to her elbows.[10] Moreover, according to this image as well as earlier sources, change extended to other aspects of dress as well. Nieuhof does not mention any body markings, nor does the image that accompanies his text, of a man and a woman both wearing versions of a skirt or waistcloth, show any. Similarly, there are no indications of epidermal decoration in either Julião's print or Eckhout's paintings; more striking, apart from the braided cord on the woman and smaller one around the child's head in Plate 3, the many additional adornments and hair arrangements that Léry had described in great detail and which Fernão Cardim likewise emphasized in the late sixteenth century, have wholly vanished as well.[11]

The extent of these changes should not be discounted, implying as they did a new definition of appropriate dress as apparel rather than body decoration. That imported cloth and garment styles were involved were effects of the new conception of dress, not its cause. Putting on such apparel did not prove, however, the first step in an ongoing transformation of Brazilian Indian dress. In fact, it is not certain how securely the new dress regime and the new identifications that it implied got implanted. Observers continued to comment disapprovingly on Brazilian Indians' minimal attire, easily visible when native villages adjoined settler communities. Though the few Indians living in Salvador da Bahia wore knee-length skirts, those in the interior went wholly naked, an Italian visitor claimed. Hence missionary priests working there lent Indians pieces of cloth to cover their genitalia before participating at Mass, then took them back for reuse once the ceremony was over.[12] Again, in 1752 a Brazilian governor denounced Jesuits for tolerating Indian nakedness (by which he meant undress above the waist) in their missions. Laboring alongside enslaved Africans, who typically stripped to the waist in the fields, may have helped entrench the new style among the Tupí.[13] But whatever its origins, the dress regime of Tupí men and women manifested their subordinate status within colonial social and economic structures.[14]

On large Jesuit mission plantations in interior Río de la Plata, the Guaraní encountered a singular form of European colonialism that at once separated them from and integrated them into Atlantic fabric and dress regimes.[15] Like all missionaries, the Jesuits believed clothing the previously uncovered Guaraní integral to the civilizing project, and they also employed differential dressing both to secure the allegiance of Native leaders and to establish an appropriately hierarchic Christian community. Indigenous women spun wool from mission ranches and cotton cultivated in family and communal plots, while men as well as women, assisted in the eighteenth century by professional weavers, wove the thread into coarse, heavy fabrics destined for family use and for communal stocks that were redistributed or sold. Each year, the distributions were to supply all adults with about 8 meters of cotton cloth that the women would tailor into long trousers and shirts for men, and for themselves long tunic-like gowns similar to those worn by female Tupí converts. All Guaraní were likewise to be given 2 meters or more of woolen cloth for ponchos (striped for the elite, plain for the rest), and, at least by the later eighteenth century, underwear, hats, and sandals for wear on special occasions such as religious feasts.

Thus the Guaraní were clothed in fabrics produced and distributed outside merchant-controlled networks; however, the style of their garments and of the austere dress regime that left no place for corporeal adornment were firmly based on imported notions of somatic modesty and simplicity and uniformity for subordinate groups' attire. As with the Tupí, however, it is unclear how much impact the new dress regime had on the day-to-day sartorial habits of most Guaraní. Even in the mid-eighteenth century, colonial officials decried the undress that in their eyes characterized mission Guaraní as well as Tupí, while after the expulsion of the Jesuits in 1768 and resulting disruption of estate management, fabric production and distributions dropped drastically, leaving commoners with insufficient material for basic outfits. Elite Guaraní may have more fully assimilated imported fashions. The Jesuits had sought to acculturate them by gifts of luxury materials and elaborate apparel: coats, cloaks, and breeches tailored from damasks, velvets, and other expensive silks and woolens. These items were, to be sure, intended for special occasions, but in the post-Jesuit period distributions by authorities competing for their allegiance allowed Guaraní to acquire European-style garments that they henceforth could wear more regularly.

Settler notions, styles, and goods intended to constitute a new dress regime among Tupí and Guaraní engaged with the colonial society and economy. Redressing in Brazil and Río de la Plata did mean the end of what Europeans understood as the most extreme case of savage nakedness. The process did not eventuate, however, in broad European-style appareling but in what observers often regarded as a new form of indigenous undress.

"Old rags" to "compleat suits of clouts": Atlantic North American dress projects and products

If the pre-contact indigenous inhabitants of Atlantic North America used few woven fabrics in clothing and for many garb included directly applied corporeal ornamentation, the great majority did wear some sort of garment as an integral part of their dress. Hence redressing in Native North America, while subject to similar ideological and economic forces

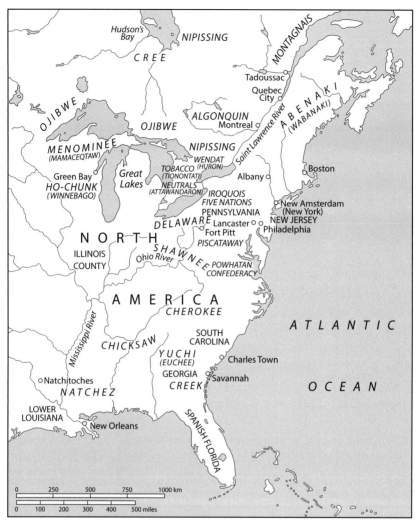

Map 3.2 Indigenous peoples and European settlements in the Eastern Woodlands of North America

visited upon "naked savages" elsewhere, involved distinctive combinations of cultural processes, material objects, and both European and indigenous projects.

Thanks both to the spatial and temporal unevenness of contact and to the extensive Native trade route systems, imported wares often appeared ahead of Native North Americans' first sightings of Europeans. But most Amerindians' initial experience of woven textiles, the garments made from them, and redressing occurred at their earliest meeting with these new arrivals. The introduction might be abrupt. After planting a cross and banner along the Saint Lawrence River in 1534, Jacques Cartier sailed off with two sons of an unnamed headman (*cappitaine*). Before weighing anchor, "we dressed each son in a shirt, red livery garments [*livrées*], and a red cap, and put a brass chain around each one's neck, which pleased them very much," Cartier smugly reported, so "they gave their old rags to those going ashore."[16] Cartier's was a bold but ambiguous gesture. The men received clothing of a color honorable in Native and European societies – yet the inclusion of servants' livery coded the recipients of the gift subordinate in status to the donor.

As in the Río de la Plata, missionaries engaged more systematically in redressing, which they believed to be a necessary step in the joint process of spiritual conversion and cultural rehabilitation of Amerindians; imposing new external fashion would accompany, even initiate, approved internal refashioning. Novel styles would, it was hoped, not simply mark acolytes but motivate them, not only distinguish them from the unconverted and uncivilized but establish a positive new identity and new inclusionary relationships. In the Ursuline school of Marie de l'Incarnation in Quebec City, for instance, newly arrived Amerindian girls were stripped of their protective coating of bear grease and then dressed in *linge blanc*, "*simarres*," and imported French leather shoes; they also had their hair arranged "*à la française.*"[17] Boys were similarly reappareled and educated both in Christian doctrine and in artisan crafts: Tailoring and shoemaking were explicitly cited at the mission at Lac des Deux Montagnes outside Montreal. Presumably these skills would help disseminate and maintain the attire needed for their new lives and those of their fellows.[18]

Though all Christian missionaries sought to promote civility by conversion, Catholics in particular were strongly committed to the program of redressing. Optimistic proponents of educating peoples long immersed in pagan darkness, the Catholics believed that new external fashions brought about both mental and spiritual reorientation.[19] Writing about young Amerindians "given" to his order by their parents in the 1630s, the Jesuit missionary and chronicler Paul Le Jeune boasted, "these little girls are dressed in the French fashion; they care no more for the Savages than if they did not belong to their Nation."[20] Indeed, redressing was thought essential to retrieve for civility and Christianity

European youths who had passed time in native areas. So when two French boys who had been sent to live among the Wendat for four years returned to the French settlement at Quebec in October 1645, they were at once clothed "decently" in European-style outfits to efface any residual traces of naked savagery.[21] More than simply displaying their renewed Christian identity, European-style dress would promote and sustain it.

Adults were also targeted, though more subtly, by the example of missionary apparel as well as by images employed in evangelization that depicted properly attired Christians.[22] But from an early date, many more were redressed thanks to official and merchant gifts focused on strategic and commercial advantage, as well as acquisition or use of land, rather than on religious objectives. On occasion – particularly during periods of war or threatened war – whole bands would be garbed; in six months (June 18–December 10, 1759) during the French and Indian War, the Pennsylvania colony's Indian agent George Croghan outfitted more than 1,500 Indians from half a dozen nations in order to secure their identification with the British side.[23] Even in more peaceful eras, allies and trading partners were sent a steady flow of standard items – virtually an outfit – or (especially, but not only, when women were recipients) lengths of fabric with which to make clothes: a breechclout (or "flap"); an outer garment, sometimes a coat or (in French-oriented areas) a *capot* (a long, loose, usually hooded cloak), but more often a blanket worn by men and women draped over the body in the form often referred to as a "matchcoat"; and a shirt or shift (typically a chemise or knee-length tunic), always sent ready-made. From time to time, other garments were offered, and a few, like caps and leggings, became more regularly gifted items. But shirts, flaps, and heavy, typically draped, outer garments remained central to the largely linen and woolen apparel that from the mid-seventeenth to the late eighteenth century Europeans and settlers made widely available to Amerindians to convince them to identify their diplomatic and material interests with one or another colonial power.

Amerindian leaders – notably those who dealt with Europeans as speakers or emissaries – often received more impressive presents. Though formal sumptuary laws were falling into disuse, both the long-running debate about "luxury" and the incessant commentary about dress practices in other cultures demonstrate that settlers as well as metropolitans remained attentive to and anxious about dress as marker of social distinctions. As might be expected, then, they consciously deployed fashionable items to recognize and consolidate what they perceived as existing hierarchies of prestige and power within Native societies, or even to create or recast them into a more familiar idiom.

Apparently first practiced by the Spanish in the sixteenth century throughout the Americas, differential gifting was later adopted by both the French and British, most notably when dealing with headmen in the stratified societies found in southeastern North America.[24] Thus when the first royal governor-to-be Francis Nicholson was about to set off for his posting in South Carolina in 1720, he was advised that the "usuall presents made to the head men of the Indians" comprised "Compleat suits of clouts [clothes] from head to foot," while their "attendants" should receive "shirts, flaps, and stroud matchcoats."[25] Even finer distinctions were drawn as imperial rivalries heated up. The July 1753 "List of Presents given to the Cherokee Indians now in Charles Town," to take just one example, sartorially demarcated four categories. Individually designated "Head Men" of Indian towns each received "a Suit of scarlet Cloaths, a ruffled Shirt, laced Hat ... stroud Blanket, Shoes, Stockings, Garters, Buckles, silk [Handkerchiefs], Ribbon, Buttons"; unnamed "Head Men of inferiour Rank ... a cloth Coat, white [plain] Shirt, Hat, ... Stroud Blanket, Pair of Boots, and Flaps [breechclouts]"; a larger group of "common Men" just "a white Shirt, Hat ... Stroud Blanket, Pair of Boots and Flap"; while each woman had to be content with "6 Yards of Calico, 3 Yards embossed Searge, 3 Yeards of Ribbond, a Shirt, Pair of Ear Bobs, [and] Stroud Blanket."[26]

In northeastern North America, where indigenous cultures were relatively egalitarian, gifts were generally granted en bloc to nations, tribes, or bands so that they could be, as one Native orator expressed it, "divided into the smallest parts," in order to "reach all the Indians every where and be read as a Letter."[27] The echo of Kitegusta's quoted words, cited above, underlines the communicative role of dress in intercultural transactions. On occasion, nevertheless, grants of special items singled out leaders alone, as for example in 1722, when Pennsylvania Governor Keith sent to "the Sachims [sic] of the [Iroquois] Five Nations" one each of "the finest Calico Shirts," "fine silk Stockings," pair of silk garters, and silk handkerchief to assure them of the colony's continuing friendship, and presumably perpetuate theirs toward it.[28] And even in mass distributions, subtle distinctions – a handful of coats together with a larger number of *capots*, fewer pieces of expensive stroud than of cheaper duffel – make clear that colonial officials intended dress to respect and sustain vertical rank-based distinctions that Europeans not only recognized and valorized but assumed to influence Indians' diplomatic and commercial transactions.[29]

Redressing projects also typically sought to promote proper sartorial gendering, another project shared by missionaries and colonial officials alike. As noted in Chapter 1, Europeans criticized the lack of clear male–female differentiation in Native dress. Admittedly, men wore breechclouts and women short skirts, and some observers discerned usages specific to one or the other gender. But many commentators were upset that both sexes wore robes, leggings, and moccasins and that all garments were tailored from the same kinds of skins and furs. Some settlers and officials therefore considered it a priority to organize Amerindian gender difference through fashion. Besides introducing a fitting spiritual regimen and proper physical comportment, for instance, Marie de l'Incarnation's redressing initiatives were designed to inaugurate the correct gender order. It was only "adoption of the gown," she claimed, that allowed one to "tell a man and a woman apart," because otherwise all Indians appeared the same.[30]

This was an ongoing and expansive enterprise.[31] Reflecting, as we shall see repeatedly, a growing trend in much of the eighteenth-century Atlantic world, Europeans also took steps to ensure that not only articles of clothing but types and qualities of cloth would demarcate sexual as well as status boundaries in Native North America. Sometimes the distinction was enunciated as explicit policy: In the 1720 gifting instructions for Governor Nicholson, only woolens and linens were suitable for presents for Amerindian men, whereas "course [*sic*] calico gowns and petticoats" could be offered to women.[32] Gendered textile difference held true even in the absence of any formal directive. Not only did British gifts generally identify cottons with Indian women, but cheaper woolens as well, while expensive woolens were presented to Indian men; in New France, where Indians were not granted cottons, female shirts were typically tailored of morlaix linen, male of more expensive Lyon.[33]

Though presents introduced many Native North Americans to examples of fabrics and garments made from them, neither elaborate gifts nor the more pedestrian items received by less exalted Indians were sufficient for the purposes of ordinary life. Amerindians acquired much larger, more varied, and more regular supplies through commercial transactions, most prominently for furs and skins but also for food-stuffs, not to mention as in-kind payments for all sorts of skilled and unskilled labor they provided to settlers. Contemporary merchant records indicate that an ever-greater variety of fabrics and apparel became available for these kinds of transfers. The documents show as well that stocks of textiles destined for Native North Americans at once shared in and stood somewhat apart from wider Atlantic trends.

Table 3.1 illustrates developments in eighteenth-century Pennsylvania. Between 1722 and 1728, the Philadelphia merchant James Bonsall sold Indian traders mainly woolens with a smattering of other types. He offered an assortment of textiles in each major fiber group, but only a few colors – red and blue woolens, red check, and "colored" (dyed) South Asian cottons – and some striped woolens, most listed as "blanket-ing" but likely stroud, duffel, or both. In the early 1760s, the selection that David Franks purchased for sale at Fort Pitt remained heavily tilted toward woolens – led as before by stroud, duffel, and blanketing – but the proportions of both cottons and linens in the mix had grown signally, and new types had become popular. More varieties of all the main fiber categories were likewise available. The growth of colors was particularly striking. In addition to the hues found in the 1720s, Amerindians supplied through Philadelphia in the early 1760s could acquire cottons that were red, blue, white, red and white, and purple as well as printed and figured, not to mention woolens in all the cottons colors plus black, crimson, green, scarlet, and embossed. And whereas Bonsall's clients only acquired ribbons, Franks offered an array of textile ornamentation including lace, ribbon, gartering, ferret, orrice, and others.[34] Ready-made apparel and accessories, though a much smaller part of each merchant's transactions, likewise became more varied in type and fiber. Whereas Bonsall sold Indian traders just silk handkerchiefs and hats (some noted as felt), Franks selected linen and silk handkerchiefs, worsted and cotton caps, and thread (linen), cotton, silk, and worsted hose.

Similar trends emerge from invoices for Amerindian trade cargoes sent from Montreal to the long-established French trading post among the Menominee and Ho-Chunk (Winnebago) at Green

Table 3.1 *Pennsylvania Amerindian trade textiles, 1722–28 and 1760–63*

Fiber	Percent cloth 1720s	Percent cloth 1760s	Number of types 1720s	Number of types 1760s	Top types 1720s†	Top types 1760s†	Number of colors 1720s	Number of colors 1760s
Cottons	2	8	6	9	Mulmul	Calico	1	5
Linens	6	25	9	11	Garlix	Irish Linen	–	1
Mixed	1	1	2	2	Poplin	Check	1	–
Silks	1	1	1	2	Persian	Alamode	–	2
Woolens	90	66	10	17	Duffel, Stroud	Duffel, Stroud	2	7
Total	100	101	28	41			2	8

† Mulmul (malmul) was a plain white, usually fine-quality, Indian cotton muslin; garlix an unbleached coarse European linen; persian and alamode both thin, light, glossy silks, both imported from Asia and woven in England.

Sources: James Bonsall Account book, 1722–28, HSP, Ms. Am. 909; David Franks Account Book, 1760–1822, HSP, Ms. Am. 684. The two books are somewhat different. Bonsall's covers nearly seven years of sales in Philadelphia to five merchants, whereas Franks's comprises three years of purchases from more than a dozen Philadelphia merchants for Franks to sell on the frontier. In both cases the goods were destined for the Amerindian trade.

Table 3.2 *Fabrics and garments in Montreal trade cargoes to Green Bay, 1724–25 and 1740–48*

Fiber*	Percent cloth 1720s	Percent cloth 1740s	Number of types 1720s	Number of types 1740s	Top types 1720s†	Top types 1740s†	Number of colors 1720s	Number of colors 1740s
Cotton	0	6	0	2	–	*Coton*	–	–
Linen	5	10	2	4	–	Trade	–	–
Woolen	95	84	4	8	*Drap*	*Molleton*	4	9
Total	100	100	6	14			4	9

* Only woolens were sold by the piece as well as in garments, cottons and linens only as apparel.
† *Drap* was broadcloth; *coton* probably plain cottons or cotton-linens; trade linen the equivalent of the English garlix; *molleton* thick and flannel-like.
Source: AndD.

Bay on upper Lake Michigan (in today's Wisconsin) in the mid-1720s and the 1740s.

In Green Bay as in Pennsylvania, by the mid-eighteenth century Amerindians were offered both a greater variety of fabrics and apparel and a different mix of types (Table 3.2). *Drap* gave ground (from three-fourths to less than one-third of all woolens) to *molleton*, which grew from a fifth to at least a half. Unavailable in the 1720s, cottons were tailored mainly into shirts but also into breeches and handkerchiefs a quarter-century later. In the 1740s, about a quarter each of woolen garments (no colors were specified for other sorts of fabrics) were blue and red, but blue had declined sharply from its 60 percent share in the 1720s, and was surpassed by purple (30 percent). Textile adornment offerings, however, changed little: edging silk added to the ribbon, tape, and gartering already dispatched in the 1720s.

Apparel stocks also changed at Green Bay.[35] Admittedly, blankets – typically made of *molleton* and employed as draped outerwear, as we have seen – continued to account for a fifth of garments shipped. But Montreal merchants also dispatched shirts (up from a fifth to a third of all apparel), about a tenth of them made of cotton; perhaps a growing Amerindian taste for shirts also underlay the rise of cottons and linens in Franks's Fort Pitt assortment. The hooded greatcoats known as *capots*, in contrast, experienced a sharp reversal, dropping from a third to a tenth of total garments available. *Mantelets* (probably not a short cape but a woman's hip-length jacket, usually made of *calamande*, which was glossy on one side, and lined with a woolen) emerged to become 5 percent of all garments in the 1740s, and sleeves (worn with *mantelets*) increased from a tenth to a sixth. Yet the gains registered by *mantelets* and sleeves would not have been sufficient to offset the decline in *capots*, suggesting a shift in demand. Headgear was also subject to a sharp decline: Caps virtually disappeared (11 percent to 1 percent), and the addition of a few Caudebec felt hats (1 percent of the 1740s total) did little to right the balance.[36] Equally striking was the appearance of cloth leggings: Not mentioned in the 1720s, they were an eighth of all garments in the 1740s.

That expansion and change in fabric and garment offerings were not limited to the Northeast is indicated by price lists of goods available in the trading posts operated by the South Carolina colony in Cherokee towns. The documents do not provide information about amounts stocked, so quantitative shifts cannot be tracked. But they do show that between 1718 and 1762 the number of cotton textiles grew from one to three, linens one to four, and woolens five to seven.[37] Diversification of colors was limited, however: purple joined red, blue, and white. Changes in garments were likewise restrained. Silk, linen, and patterned cotton handkerchiefs were now available along with coats, shirts, and blankets; hats disappeared. Styles on offer altered, but the presence of mainly the same or similar fabrics and apparel in 1762 as in 1718 indicates continuity, though now garments were tailored in the Cherokee towns rather than in Charles Town or England. Coarse shirts, all that were available in 1718, had been replaced by checked, striped, and plain white varieties, and they could be had unadorned or with ruffles; but two kinds of coarse linen remained available. Again, coats became simpler: just a heavy surtout (overcoat) model in 1762 rather than the choice of lace or plain offered in 1718, but bed lace, gartering, and silk and cotton ribbons were also on offer at the later date. From all evidence, the Cherokee had developed preferences for selected imported fabrics, attire, and adornments that British traders and officials sought to accommodate, while also continuing to try out novelties that they hoped would please these clients and allies.

"Dressed deer skin" to "Christian apparrell": from undress to dress in Atlantic North America

Albeit with local variations, then, the cloth, clothing, and adornments stocked by Indian traders expanded in variety and changed somewhat in composition across the eighteenth century. That increasing amounts of cottons and decreasing quantities of woolens, together with greater variety of fabric types, were to be found in frontier zones at and after mid-century shows that textile supplies intended for Amerindians followed the same stocking trends as the Atlantic world as a whole (see Tables 2.1 and 2.3). At the same time, woolens' continued heavy predominance distinguished the Amerindian stocks even from those found in the colonial ports that supplied Indian traders. Taken together, these findings suggest at least partial Amerindian participation in broad Atlantic dress fashions, though not which textiles, attire, and styles were accepted, how, or to what degree.

Many historians have argued that Amerindians quickly adopted cloth garments – more comfortable and easier to dry, clean, and otherwise maintain than furs and skins – by an essentially utilitarian calculus.[38] European and settler contemporaries often made the same claim, pointing to, for example, "capes ... bed-blankets ... hats, shoes, caps, woolens and shirts" that, according to the Jesuit Pierre Baird, the indigenous inhabitants of Acadia already were "quite willing to make use of" in 1616.[39] There were also good practical reasons for Natives to don imported apparel for intercultural communication. Commenting on a visit to Quebec City in June 1646 by the Christian Indians Et8et and Iabmets (together with a canoeload of bandsmen), the Jesuit chronicler Jérôme Lalemant observed that the two spokesmen dressed "mainly, Est8et [*sic*] entirely, in the French style – a shirt of white Holland linen, a lace band [sash], and a scarlet jacket." By his garb, Lalemant asserted, Et8et "attempted to be on an equal footing with the governor, and in every way to act like a king": to behave, that is, so as to be perceived as a valid interlocutor as he complained of a French trader's prices and behavior to the colony's highest civil official.[40]

Among some Natives, in fact, attraction is said to have become complete identification, indeed obsession. According to the Chicksaw chief warrior Oboystabee, the South Carolina Indian agent Thomas Nairne wrote, around 1700, that this nation had changed allegiance to the French after "they presented [gave presents to] our Chief men very liberally." But by 1708 it had returned to the English side for good. Why? Not simply because of receiving good prices for slaves and skins, but because the beauties and fine women who are the warriors wives and mistresses, are altogether of your [the English] party, for these ladies are so pleased to look sparkling in the dances, with the Cloaths bought from the English, that they would be very loath any difference [conflict] should happen, least they again be reduced to their old wear of painted Buffeloe Calf skins.[41]

Thirty-five years later, James Isham related a cross-gender echo of that statement. "Give us Good measure, in cloth," the Cree "Ukemaw" (trading captain) orated at the Hudson Bay Company's York Factory, for "the young men ... Love to Dress and be fine."[42]

Closer examination suggests, however, that the Amerindian appropriation of European fashions was uneven, protracted, and incomplete. For one thing, as in Brazil so in North America some Native groups lived at or beyond what might be termed the "fabric frontier" even in the 1760s, and thus had little or no regular access to woven textiles and cloth garments. The fur trader Alexander Henry encountered some at Chagouemigon, an Ojibwe settlement on western Lake Superior: "the clothing, in which I found them, both men and women, was chiefly of dressed deer-skin, European manufactures having been for some time out of their reach."[43] Well before that date, however, woven-fabric textiles and apparel were obtainable by most of the indigenous peoples living in the Eastern Woodlands. In the Southeast, early Spanish exploration and later abortive French and English settlement had brought the novel goods to a few groups during the sixteenth century.[44] But along most of the North American Atlantic seaboard and its major tributaries, commerce and gifts were to do so only from the early seventeenth century, when trade and settlement began in earnest. Thereafter, the ongoing search for furs and skins for European markets, the establishment of sustained missionary efforts, increased colonization, and eventually heightened imperial rivalries brought imported cloth and clothing progressively further into the North American interior.

The result, according to many reports and images, fell well short of textile triumph. It is very probable, to begin, that in addition to his shirt, sash, and jacket, Et8et also wore a breechclout, moccasins, and perhaps leggings, not to mention forms of corporeal decoration. Rather than an entire outfit, dressing "in the French style" would have been a matter of presenting the body above the waist suitably appareled; Native items, materials, and conventions dressed the rest. More specifically, Louis Hennepin wrote that those Amerindians who "Trade with the *Europeans*" in the early 1680s, put on cloth apparel "over and above" their traditional fur garments.[45] This pattern – not the wholesale adoption of imported styles but the formation of hybrid peltry-textile fashions – was repeated elsewhere right through the eighteenth century. The Yuchi (Euchee) "King" in the 1736 drawing made on the spot in Georgia by the German visitor Philip Georg Friedrich von Reck is wearing what the accompanying notes described as "a shaggy buffalo skin" as well as a woolen breechclout and leggings (Plate 5).[46] Among "tribes in contact with the Europeans," the anonymous French traveler "J. C. B." asserted in the 1750s, breechclouts and matchcoats were fashioned either "of deerskin or of cloth," leggings from woolen "cloth," "milton [*molleton*]," or "deer or elk skin."[47] According to these and many other sources, the central attribute of late seventeenth- and eighteenth-century Amerindian fashion was its composite character – composite in garments but also in materials and inspiration.

The dress of Native converts to Christianity indicates the complexity of the finished artifact and its effects. Not only were acolytes subjected to redressing projects, but many eagerly embraced a fresh style of dress that accompanied and symbolized their novel faith and accompanying way of life. In the mid-seventeenth century, the English Jesuit Father White affirmed (perhaps too hopefully) that the Piscataway Indians whom he sought to evangelize in lower Maryland "exceedingly desire civill life and Christian apparrell."[48] By the 1680s, the Jesuit missionary at Sault Saint-François-Xavier outside Montreal reported with assurance that both male and female Indians wore "fine white chemises" and the women red or blue cloth petticoats whenever going to church.[49] And by the mid-eighteenth century, according to the Swedish naturalist and traveler Pehr Kalm, the spiritual-cum-sartorial transformation was virtually complete, at least among males. "I've seen, among the various [Amerindians] whom the French have converted, a large number of men who are starting to dress exactly like them, so it's nearly impossible to tell [Indians] and French apart."[50]

For proselytes like these, adopting a new style demonstrated identification with fellow Christians and conformity with their manner of self-presentation. But the "Christian apparrell" that allowed Amerindians to "dress exactly like" settlers was in fact their own fashion. Just as Native American Christianity was a *sui generis* formation of beliefs and practices, so were the fashions of Native converts. This is strikingly revealed in a widely circulated (and apparently accurate) image of the Iroquois saint Catherine Takakoüita or Tekakwitha (1656–80), whose dress was said to be the model for other convert women at Sault Saint-Louis (Caughnawaga or Kahnawake), the village for Christian Iroquois outside Montreal where Tekakwitha lived (Figure 3.2).[51] At first sight, she seems enveloped in a version of a European nun's costume: a somber external garment over a long white chemise, both evidently made of imported fabric, which conceal everything but her hands, face, lower legs, and feet. Together with the clerically derived color scheme, this apparel enables the image to sum up Tekakwitha's much touted modesty, humility, and faith, which the text sharply contrasts with pagan Indians' evil brutishness.

Yet the elements derived from Indian women's dress are if anything more pronounced. Tekakwitha's over-garment is not a tailored vestment but a draped blanket or piece of cloth, and her skirt is worn Indian length – mid-calf – and possibly made of deerskin; in any event, the decoration along the hem is an emblematic Native feature, as are her (admittedly hard to see) leggings and moccasins. Her rearrangement of materials and apparel from two cultures permitted Tekakwitha at once to cross and to draw boundaries, to identify with her new faith and with her ancestral group, and to be both a follower of an imported fashion and the leader of a new indigenous style.[52] As a message, the image was equally multivalent. While it visually distinguished between believer and non-believer, it also suggested that becoming a Christian did not involve a total break with one's culture of origin.

Breechclouts and breeches: an Amerindian wardrobe

Europeans noted and depicted cloth and clothing with this level of attention because of both their interest in the state of civility of their Amerindian interlocutors and their knowledge of trade goods. Still, these valuable testimonies are all artistic or literary representations, and most refer in vague, general terms to those people whose dress was under consideration or offer a composite if not fanciful portrait. Fortunately, while probate inventories were very rarely drawn up by or for Amerindians, one was drafted for the estate of the Delaware

Catherine tekakoüita Iroquoise du Saut
S. Louis de Montreal en Canada morte
en odeur de Sainteté.

3.2 *Catherine Tekakoüita Iroquoise du Saut S. Louis de Montreal en Canada morte en odeur de Sainteté / Catherine Tekakoüita, Iroquois woman from Saut St. Louis de* headman Koquethagechton (White Eyes), a signatory of the controversial 1778 Treaty of Fort Pitt, after his apparent murder by frontiersmen during the American Revolution.[53] Given his social and political prominence as an intermediary between Indians and both the British and insurgent colonials, his inventoried wardrobe cannot be regarded as representative of Native Americans. But it does reveal the fashions current among one elite Amerindian in the late eighteenth century and, by comparison with other testimony, shows some styles more broadly present in Native America.

Koquethagechton's clothing stock was both substantial and syncretic. Peltry and textiles were both significant elements, and both types of garment material were found in long-customary items as well as in those introduced by Europeans. His more traditional attire included two breechclouts, an old one of blue cloth, another, "fully trim'd," likely of skin; a matchcoat almost certainly of fabric; and both buckskin and white (probably woolen duffel) leggings. Of garments of imported style, Koquethagechton had four jackets, all made from textiles (one old and one new of scarlet, both "plain," one of printed linen, and one spectacular "Scarlet Silk Jacket Trim'd with Gold Lace"); two probably woolen green coats (an old cutaway and one faced with red); two pairs of breeches (buckskin and scarlet); two pieces of headgear, both of peltry (a fur cap and a beaver hat); and three pairs of undoubtedly leather shoes. Equally striking is the amount and variety of ornamentation for Koquethagechton's clothing and person: a "Bundle of blue & Red Ferreting," "paint" (probably vermilion, used for body decoration), a "Silver Medal Effigee of Geo. The 3d of Great Britain," a large (11-row) wampum band, 3 yards of gartering, a "Broach & Ear Ring," and knee and shoe buckles.

Caption for 3.2 (cont.)

Montreal in Canada, who died redolent of holiness, from Claude-Charles Le Roy, Bacqueville de La Potherie, *Histoire de l'Amérique septentrionale...*, 4 vols. (Paris: Jean-Luc Nion et François Didot, 1722), I, following 350.

A French-born naval official, La Potherie lived in New France for a few years at the turn of the eighteenth century and from 1701 to his death in 1736 in Guadeloupe in the West Indies. His *Histoire de l'Amérique septentrionale*, apparently composed during or immediately after his years in Canada, was based on his own observations as well as extensive reading of earlier sources and conversations with knowledgeable informants in the colony. Nothing is known about the artist who produced this image.

Koquethagechton's inventory tells much about Amerindian fashion besides the persistence of peltry as a material for customary garments and the parallel incorporations of peltry into items adopted from Europeans and of textiles into traditional apparel – all significant, and all, as we have seen, well attested by multiple sources. In particular, his wardrobe suggests that even among the late eighteenth-century Native North American elite, apparel remained grounded in a long-standing basic outfit of breechclout, draped outerwear, and protective leggings; at the same time, novel objects had been added to this ensemble. Some had been urged on Indians from the beginning of European contact and, from all evidence, had been quickly, even enthusiastically accepted. Often, like coats and jackets, the new clothing supplemented items, such as Koquethagechton's matchcoat, which were themselves composites of customary and new garments.

Derived from an Algonquian word signifying mantles fashioned from skins, whose use long predated Euro–Native contact, the term "matchcoat" was initially used by Europeans to refer to peltry or feathered draped capes made by Amerindians; when elaborate or ornamented, they were expensive labor-intensive items probably restricted to elite use and/or to special occasions.[54] In the course of the seventeenth century, however, matchcoat came to refer to a garment made from imported woolen fabric and thus much cheaper and available to a much larger group of Amerindians; textile matchcoats became fundamental to a large proportion of market and non-market exchanges in French and English North American colonies across the entire period. Made usually of stroud, duffel, or *molleton*, a fabric matchcoat might take the form of a length of woolen cloth worn wrapped around the body as a mantle by both men and women; on occasion, women draped it like a skirt. Likely to be ornamented with stripes, ribbons, or paint, a matchcoat could be virtually indistinguishable from a blanket, a use to which it was also put and a term frequently used synonymously.[55] A matchcoat could also be a loose tailored coat, ready-made by European or Euroamerican tailors and decorated with lace rather than beads, copper, or an indigenous dyestuff. Though occasionally found in seventeenth-century settler inventories,[56] use of matchcoats remained essentially limited to Native America, but the garment was modified substantively and socially as it became a European and settler manufacture. As Koquethagechton's inventory also shows, Amerindians owned both matchcoats and other outerwear; which they chose to wear presumably depended on the self-presentation desired in a particular situation.

Some pieces of introduced attire in Koquethagechton's wardrobe are notable because they often met determined Amerindian opposition. Breeches were chief among them. To be sure, in the eighteenth century important Amerindians often received them as gifts (sometimes separately but typically as part of suits), and Koquethagechton was nothing if not a Native leader, so his scarlet breeches may have come to him as part of a gifted suit, together with one of his scarlet jackets and perhaps a coat.[57] Yet breeches passed partially and grudgingly at best into Amerindian costume. Not one of the five Indian men portrayed in the top row of Plate 6, created by an anonymous German immigrant to Canada about 1780, wears breeches, even though their outfits incorporate other imported garments. Even Christianized Native Americans disregarded scandalized missionaries' "earnest entreaties" to substitute breeches for the (to Europeans) too revealing breechclout or flap; and as late as 1752, the French visitor Louis Franquet mentioned that the "rich" Indians of the missionary village of Kahnawake near Montreal (where Tekakwitha had lived in the later seventeenth century), garbed in shirts, woolen blankets, and leggings, nevertheless "all were without breeches [*culottes*]."[58]

Some commentators detected a utilitarian calculus in this refusal (breeches, Kalm wrote, "would greatly hinder their walking"), others a moral position: According to von Reck, Indians in the Southeast thought breeches "indecent."[59] Others emphasized symbolic considerations: Breeches denoted gender disparagement ("helplessness" and "effeminancy") or improper cultural border-crossing, as with "a Nipissing Indian, dishonored in the eyes of his brothers and of the Canadians because he wore breeches, covered his head, ate, dressed, and slept like a Frenchman."[60] Among the stratified and rank-conscious Natchez and Tunica, according to the usually well-informed one-time Louisiana settler Jean-François-Benjamin Dumont de Montigny, only chiefs wore breeches; he also noted that whereas Frenchmen acquired "magnificent" painted deerskins, a Natchez specialty, to fashion into "very handsome" *culottes*, the Natchez used them for leggings.[61] Little wonder, then, that though the Hudson's Bay Company initially offered breeches for trade and long included them among gifts to trading captains, Native demand was apparently so weak that they were withdrawn from sale in the early eighteenth century.[62] And though French traders occasionally offered breeches at western Great Lakes posts from the mid-1730s until records end in the late 1740s, the quantities were always small, so there, too, demand must not have been substantial.[63] Whatever the reason, in sum, breeches were garments that did not readily make their way into Native fashion. Wearing breeches at least some of the time therefore would have marked Koquethagechton off from many of his fellows. Most likely, he put them on, together with one of his tailored coats and jackets, when meeting with colonists and perhaps on other ceremonial occasions; they seem less apt to have been included in his everyday attire. As he had an equal number of breechclouts, his breeches allowed him to participate in two dress regimes when he wished to do so, or to fashion his own.

Indians regarded ready-made headgear with only slightly less ambivalence: Recall the testimony cited above that among the acts that disgraced a Nipissing was covering his head. Though gifted by officials, caps and hats do not loom large either in traders' records or in narrative accounts (often they are entirely absent), lending credence to the numerous commentators who even in the mid-eighteenth century insisted that Amerindians normally went bareheaded, at most covering themselves with their blankets if need arose.[64] Still, as we have seen, Pennsylvania traders offered caps and hats, and Plate 6 indicates that both could be worn by Natives, often in combination with customary items such as feathers. Koquethagechton could have done the same, though his inventory mentions no feather, that emblem – or cliché – of Indianness and particularly of Native leadership (cf. Figure 3.1). More incongruous is the fact that his cap was fur, his hat beaver. When Indian caps were recorded, they were typically made out of felt or fabric, as seen in Plate 6 or in cargo manifests.[65] Most likely, the peltry headgear indicates gifts suitable to Koquethagechton's high rank, but it might signal his individual taste or an attempt to assert status, whether among Indians or vis-à-vis settlers, or both.

His apparent exchange of moccasins for shoes also would have distinguished Koquethagechton from many Indians. Even in the second half of the eighteenth century, Henry Timberlake declared that Cherokees did not wear shoes; David Jones, writing of Shawnees, who in apparel "differ nothing from most of other Indians," noted that they wear "mockesons"; when James Smith was captured in western Pennsylvania in 1755, he was redressed Indian-style, which meant moccasins on his feet.[66] Moreover, as Plate 6 illustrates, some

Amerindians wore no footgear whatever, even when donning hat and shirt or blouse and skirt. For all that, Koquethagechton would not necessarily have been regarded as exceptional or eccentric for incorporating shoes into his wardrobe. Even in the opening decades of the seventeenth century, Jesuit missionaries were reporting the willing adoption of shoes,[67] and along with boots they became regular components of gift packages, as we have noted. Among Amerindians, that is, footwear seems to have become a matter of individual style, perhaps based on wealth and status or a specific religious identification: In 1735, some converts residing in Kahnawake wore moccasins made of "smoke-dried deerskin," others, "silk Stockings and shoes of French make and silver buckles."[68]

Rather more singular was the lack of shirts in Koquethagechton's inventory. This may have been the result of an oversight by the compiler of the document, but shirts were not usually omitted from inventories and this one seems remarkably detailed with regard to its subject's wardrobe. Not all Indians wore shirts, of course. The well-informed early eighteenth-century French Jesuit Joseph-François Lafitau, for instance, wrote that while the tunic ("a kind of sleeveless shirt") was part of the usual dress of Wendat and Iroquois, it was, "of all their garments, the one that they consider the least necessary, and many of them – especially the men – easily dispense with it." Still, he was speaking of traditional skin tunics, and two pages later he added that Indians who traded with Europeans "wear linen shirts instead of tunics."[69]

Many other sources lend support to that last statement. Not only were shirts included in nearly all seventeenth- and eighteenth-century French and British gift packages and cargo manifests, but numerous Indian leaders of the time were depicted wearing them.[70] In fact, shirts may have been more widely adopted, as virtually every account of typical Indian dress mentions them. Both women and men portrayed on the top row of Plate 6 suggest, moreover, that Indians who, like Koquethagechton, had other items of settler-styled apparel wore shirts as well. Even more intriguing are two pieces of information relating more directly to the Delaware. In the first, the Scot Peter Williamson, who claimed to have been abducted by and lived among the Delaware, declared that "The better Sort have Shirts of the finest Linen they can get, and to [with] those some wear Ruffles."[71] Koquethagechton was certainly of "the better Sort" of Delaware. Second, the Moravian missionary John Heckewelder, who spent years in Ohio with the Delaware – where he became acquainted with Koquethagechton – wrote, in a book based on his experience, that among men "plain or ruffled shirts" were constituent elements of "the present dress of the Indians."[72] Though circumstantial at best, the evidence suggests that the absence of shirt citations was another token of Koquethagechton's personal style, his way of marking his individuality and perhaps an indigenous identity within a larger fashion system.

Perhaps he found one of his jackets a more than adequate substitute. If so, he would often have sported the color particularly associated with Amerindian males, scarlet or some other tone of red; note the jacket on the second man from the left in Plate 6, top row. Scarlet was also the hue of one of his pairs of breeches, the decoration of one of his coats (and perhaps the entirety of the other coat though the inventory is unclear), while half a bundle of ferreting for ornamenting garments was red; red, too, was the "small Pocket Book" in which Koquethagechton carried papers (even though he was not literate) and needles. And a red – vivid vermilion – was most likely the color of his "paint." In all these ways, Koquethagechton would have associated himself and his self-presentation with the characteristics denoting power that many Amerindians attributed to red, particularly when worn by influential men.[73]

Koquethagechton also had items – a breechclout and the rest of his ferreting – dyed blue, the other color widely (and accurately) said to be a Native favorite, but fewer.[74] This disparity was not unusual. Whereas blue was considered appropriate for both genders, red was often more closely associated with men.[75] Yet in his color palette, too, Koquethagechton did not limit himself to standard issue fashion, and he must have looked particularly dashing in his green cutaway coat, not to mention his jacket of printed linen, a fabric much resembling calico. Embellishing his garments with paint would have added yet more drama. According to Peter Williamson, Delawares inscribed a kind of leafy camouflage on white blankets during wartime and at all times delighted in painting shirts; using red, brown, black, and other pigments on skin garments was noted by numerous commentators, and illustrated by others.[76] Like Koquethagechton's garments, Amerindian paint was a hybrid: Though originally made by Indians from indigenous dyes, by the eighteenth century paints had become stock, often imported, trade goods.

The paint may (also) have been intended for Koquethagechton's body, perhaps in a manner like von Reck's Yuchi king (Plate 5) – or, indeed, like many Amerindian men and some women. Observers never tired of emphasizing how Native Americans "paint their faces in various styles, and on sundry occasions; and many, their whole bodies," as a Jesuit missionary wrote in 1653; "The Indians paint their Bodies, legs, & head &C," reiterated the British visitor Warren Johnson more than a century later.[77] Observers differed on the specifics of the practice. The artist who created Plate 6, for example, depicted only men with red face markings. Alexander Henry declared that Ojibwe "men paint as well their whole body as their face," but whereas both male and female Cree painted their faces, only the men painted their bodies.[78] The variety probably derived from the habits of discrete Indian groups as much as from commentators' acuity or lack thereof.

"Both men and women paint with Vermillion and other colours" in the Ohio country, the Briton Nicholas Cresswell affirmed.[79] We have no contemporary image of Koquethagechton, so it is impossible to know whether he, who spent much of his adulthood in Ohio, used body paint. But John Heckewelder, who would have known as well as anyone, stated that "wealthy" Delaware men were fond of "the painting of themselves, their head and face principally."[80] If Heckewelder was correct, a man of Koquethagechton's status would likely have followed the collective fashion, but we have also seen instances where he diverged from the expected style.

The fact that inventories ignore the person of the deceased also makes it impossible to learn about Koquethagechton's hairstyle. But it was probably distinctive, since cutting the hair in ways specific to each nation, gender, even individual was a meaningful Native American fashion, as is visible even with the redressed Cherokees in Figure 3.1.[81] Nor do we know whether Koquethagechton was tattooed. It would not be surprising if he were, for as we have seen in Chapter 1, tattooing was widely reported among many Amerindian nations.[82] From John White's 1585–86 watercolors of Algonquians to mid-eighteenth century descriptions of Cree, some Amerindian women were depicted as being tattooed.[83] Most often, however, tattooing was limited to men. Among the Iroquoian Tobacco (Tionontati) and Neutrals (Attawandaron), wrote the mid-seventeenth-century Jesuit missionary Francesco-Giuseppe Bressani, "I know not whether a single individual [male] was found, who was not painted in this manner, on some part of the body" with designs of "some animal or monster ... or any other figure which they prefer."[84] A century later, all male Creeks and Cherokees painted their heads and breasts with vermilion, but tattooing was a privilege of warriors, some of whom "have the skin of the breast, and muscular parts of the body, very curiously inscribed, or adorned with hieroglphick scroles [sic], flowers, figures of animals, stars, crescents, and the sun in the centre of the breast."[85] Across the seventeenth and eighteenth centuries, images like Plate 1 vividly illustrated the designs, variety, and extent of North Amerindian tattooing; as they demonstrated, paint and tattoos could combine to produce striking personae.

Among Delaware, according to Heckewelder, tattooing was a habit "especially with those who had distinguished themselves by their valour, and acquired celebrity," so Koquethagechton would seem to have been a prime candidate for such adornment.[86] But maybe not: Heckewelder qualified his comment, characterizing tattooing as "a custom formerly much in use among" Indians, but now much less practiced.[87] Regrettably, Heckewelder did not specify what era he meant by "formerly." Yet since he wrote his book in the second decade of the nineteenth century, tattooing might have been current among the Delaware during Koquethagechton's lifetime nearly forty years earlier. If so, Koquethagechton's body would have displayed another instance of the hybrid nature of his fashion.

We can be much more assured that Koquethagechton wore his silver medallion, wampum band, brooch, earring, and buckles. Perhaps they were reserved, along with some of his other apparel, for special occasions, since they would seem to have complicated many quotidian tasks such as farming, hunting, trading, and warring. Still, many commentators mention Indians wearing adornments as part of their usual costume.[88] Though even a selection would have made for an impressive appearance, Koquethagechton may have donned many at once, for observers claimed that Amerindians delighted in profuse decorative elements both attached to clothing and worn directly on the body or in the hair. In the early seventeenth century, the explorer Samuel de Champlain described Montagnais and Algonquin men as going to great trouble to decorate their clothing and women of these nations as "laden with quantities of wampum, both necklaces and chains, which they allow to hang in front of their robes and attached to their belts, and also with bracelets and ear-rings."[89] At their ceremonies, the Recollet missionary Sagard claimed in these same years, Wendat often wore nothing but a breechclout, no matter how cold the weather, but "never" would they neglect to put on "wampum bands [*colliers*], earrings, and bracelets," not to mention feathers and other hair ornaments.[90]

If anything, ornamentation became more profuse over the following years, thanks to the addition of imported goods, already reported by Sagard, to rich indigenous supplies of porcupine quills, bird feathers, worked animal skins, local copper, and yet more.[91] "Most" male Iroquois outside Montreal, Franquet was astonished to note in 1752, hung "silver medals around their necks" and trimmed their clothes with gold and silver braid, while Wendat women at Lorette, another convert village, were as richly adorned.[92] Cresswell could not get over the "great number of small silver brooches" Ohio Indian men attached to their linen shirts, together with "silver plates about three inches broad round the wrists of their arms, silver wheels in their ears ... silver rings in their noses," not to mention the "silver plates" women wore in their hair ("if they can afford it, if not [their hair is] tied in a club with red gartering"). "No rings in the nose [of a woman] but plenty in the ears," he added.[93] Black and white wampum neckpieces, together with other adornments, are likewise portrayed in the top row of Plate 6.

Things were much the same in the Southeast. The words "ornamented" and "decorated" recur repeatedly in the naturalist William Bartram's mid-1770s delineation of Creek and Cherokee dress: "silver crescents, or gorgets," "silver bands, or bracelets," "silver and gold chains," beads, quills, silver plates, wampum, tinsel lace, silver and brass bells, fringe, "an incredible quantity of silk ribbands, of various colours," feathers of scarlet or "the gayest color" – all these embellishments of both Native and European origin were used to create a style most conspicuously displayed by youths at dances, festivities, and other "particular occasions."[94]

Delawares, announced Peter Williamson, did not lag behind. "They take great delight in wearing Trinkets; such as Silver Plates round their Wrists and necks, with several Strings of *Wampum* (which is made of Cotton, interwove with Pebbles, Cockle-Shells, &c.) down to their Breasts; and from their Ears and Noses they have Rings and Beads, which hang dangling an Inch or two." Men, he went on, often wove "Wampum and Feathers of various Colours" into a lock of hair hanging from the center of the head, while women twisted "Beads, Feathers, and Wampum" into their hair and crowned their heads with "little Coronets of Brass or Copper."[95] While agreeing that Delaware wore various silver ornaments, wampum, and beads, Heckewelder also emphasized the prominence of imported "choice ribands of various colours" and gartering, sometimes worn as sashes decorated with brooches or buckles, for both women's and men's costumes, concluding, "the women . . . as well as the men, know how to dress themselves in style."[96] On the basis of his inventory, Koquethagechton surely deserves inclusion in this encomium to Native elegance. His hybrid wardrobe materially, visually, and symbolically sustained the variety of positions he occupied during his lifetime, from "savage" to "civilized," from headman to ally, from Amerindian interlocutor to initially valued but eventually, and fatally, distrusted intercultural intermediary.

"Look large" and "tight-fitting": Amerindian and European fashions

Koquethagechton's inventory reveals the contours of the male wardrobe shared widely over eastern Native North America and the variations in apparel, adornments, materials, and occasions that could be rung on it. The items in the document also reflect – and in a small way perhaps helped shape – both gift packages and merchant stocks, notably the centrality of woolens and the substantial presence of objects for apparel and corporeal ornamentation. It is necessary to examine other evidence, however, to get a sense of development over time in Amerindian dress regimes and how they compared with those of Europeans and Euroamericans living nearby. Of course, Amerindian dress, like every other, varied for all sorts of reasons, among them climate, accessibility to traders, group convention, personal tastes and identifications. But several pieces of evidence indicate that Koquethagechton's inventory exemplified several broad trends in Amerindian dress: After Native North Americans began to engage with imported fabrics and apparel, their dress demonstrated at once a strong continuity in basic materials and garments, and the progressive addition of new textiles and (to a lesser extent) novel items, particularly adornments.

    As merchant stocks and cargoes reveal, Amerindian dress regimes – garment, fabric, color preferences, and more – were hardly static. But much persisted, too, notably a lack of interest in shaped and tailored apparel. Breeches, gowns, and dresses were offered at one time or another in Green Bay, for instance, but never more than two or three per year; and whether blankets or *capots* were favored, they were equally loose, draped outerwear; coats and jackets held little interest when Amerindians bought garments rather than received them as gifts. The growing use of shirts and cloth leggings demonstrates nicely the pattern of continuity with slow change: Both were new iterations, now in textiles, of customary items, tunics and *mitasses*. But like the other items that Indians bought from traders, shirts and cloth leggings reveal not simply that textiles had become intrinsic to Amerindian dress but also that Natives were increasingly caught up in the evolution of the larger Atlantic textile regime – in their own way. As we have seen, the proportions of cottons in stocks of textiles for Native American use rose, but less than in stocks in North American ports that also served Euroamericans, while percentages of woolens remained higher.[97] At the same time, all textile stocks participated in trends and fashions that favored lighter fabrics and brighter hues.

Participation in broad textile trends did not translate into matching dress regimes. Early observers were as impressed by the fashion differences between Native North Americans and Europeans and settlers as by the similarity of basic wardrobe among Indians. In 1657, the French Jesuit Paul Ragueneau provided one of the most detailed accounts, based on his experience in the Saint Lawrence valley.[98] Significantly, he began his commentary with a comparison of facial ornamentation. In his telling, a well-scrubbed, unadorned visage was a mark of beauty in France, whereas Amerindians "anoint and grease [the face] as much as they can," then paint it. Once a male Indian "has been well bedaubed, he is looked upon as a handsome man, whereas in Europe he would be taken for a demon." Amerindians' "fancy is their fashion," Ragueneau declared, because hair "is not dressed according to fashion" but according to individual taste. The placement of jewelry both in the body (piercings) and on it (bracelets, necklaces, and the like) likewise demarcated Indian *mode* from French; so did cutting fingernails – or not.

Head coverings, too, marked stylistic divergence. Frenchwomen considered it "indecorous ... to appear bare headed," whereas Native women commonly did so, but they greased their hair and decorated it with small porcelain beads. More startling, whereas "the head-dress distinguishes men from women" in France, Natives made no such distinction, judging headgear solely by the criteria of warmth and comfort. And though Amerindians were beginning to adopt French-style gender-appropriate hats and caps, "they are not so particular that a woman will not use a riding-cap, and a man a nightcap, in the very middle of the day." Indeed, Indian unawareness of gendered fashion was such that "a woman's dress is not improper for a man," and Ragueneau presented several instances in which Indians showed, to his mind, their utter incomprehension of proper fashion – or, we might say, in which they showed their own fashion sense.

Garment conventions were no more similar, even though many of the items were much the same. The French preferred "rather tight-fitting" clothes, Indians sought to "look large"; Frenchwomen preferred very long dresses, "but Savage women would make fun of a dress that came down much below the knees"; Europeans wore their stocking seams in the back, with little decoration, Indians on the side (inside for men, outside for women), covered with porcupine quills, dyed bits of fabric, fringes, and tinkling spangles. Footwear styles told the same tale of disparate tastes. "In France, pattens and raised shoes are considered the most beautiful; but among those [Amerindian] peoples the ugliest." Shirt fashions were a matter of particularly sharp divergence. Europeans wore them "next to the skin, under the other garments," Indians "over their dress"; whereas Europeans washed them, Natives wanted them greasy and water-resistant; Europeans always tucked in shirts, but Indians let them hang out. "That fashion seems all the more tasteful in their eyes because they regard our breeches as an encumbrance, although they sometimes wear these as a bit of finery, or in fun."

Accessories drove home difference. Amerindians slung pouches over their backs, whereas the French "put their purses in their pockets." Handkerchiefs were thought a matter of "politeness and propriety" among Europeans, but Indians scorned them as "unclean" repositories of "filthiness." And even the dead proclaimed the contrast of fashions.

> In Europe, we unclothe the dead as much as we can, leaving them only what is necessary to veil them and hide them from our eyes. The Savages, however, give them all that they can, anointing and attiring them as if for their wedding, and burying them with all their favorite belongings.

"I do not profess to observe much order in this medley; it comes from my pen as the items occur to my mind," Ragueneau claimed, but his is obviously a rhetorical piece based on emphatic strategies of comparison and contrast. Still, his careful and detailed remarks, largely confirmed by other sources, capture an early confrontation of fashions, at a time when Native Americans were formulating new styles out of innovative and traditional fabrics and items according to both collective socio-cultural needs and attitudes and individual desires. Later documents reveal that clear differences continued to obtain between Amerindian and settler styles and attitudes as the dress of both groups evolved across the eighteenth century. To be sure, many records attest that both Indians and frontier settlers regularly acquired textiles like heavy woolen *mazamet* and flannel, ozenbrig and garlix linen, calico, and striped cottons. Yet at the same time, certain textiles gained a kind of Amerindian ethnic association – woolen duffel and strouds prominent among them for British-supplied groups, *limbourg* woolens and St.-Jean linen (and for a while cheap but allegedly poor-quality woolen "*Iroquoise*") among French allies – as did specific colors, patterns, and finishes of more widely used fabrics, such as purple halfthicks and flowered and embossed serge.[99] Moreover, even though the array of garments and of fabric varieties, colors, and finishes broadened in Native North America, it never came close to matching the profusion that settlers could count on.

Native disregard of gender-defined and gender-defining Euroamerican styles, and of the apparel that materialized them, likewise continued to evoke surprise and some dismay throughout the eighteenth century. When in 1716 South Carolina's Indian Commissioners chose "to gratifie" the Cherokee "Indian Peggy" with "a Suit of Calicoe Cloaths" for turning over a captive Frenchman, she adamantly refused the gift, eventually receiving what she had initially demanded: lengths of strouds, which Indians of both sexes throughout British-oriented Native North America wore as draped matchcoats rather than tailored garments.[100] On the eve of the American Revolution, Cresswell noted that Amerindian "women wear the same sort of shirts as the men … leggings and Mockeysons, the same as the men"; like earlier observers, the only clear distinction Cresswell saw was that between the female "short petticoat" and the male breechclout.[101]

The "List of a Large Assortment of Indian Goods suitable at this time at Pittsburg Nov 24th 1761" and the "List of an Assortment of

Table 3.3 *Goods to be made available at Fort Pitt, November 1761*

	"Indian Goods"	"Goods to Suit the white People"
I. Lengths of fabric		
Cottons	Calico (30 pieces)	Chintz (4 pieces)
		Cotton (1 piece)
Linens	Stamped (15 pieces)	Cambric (2 pieces)
	Irish (30 pieces)*	Lawn (5 pieces)
	Garlix (30 pieces)*	
	Check (10 pieces)	
	Striped holland (10 pieces)	
Mixed		Hairbine (1 piece)
		Poplin (2 pieces)
Silks		Alamode (1 piece)
Woolens/worsteds	Stroud (*c.* 60 pieces)	Broadcloth (4 pieces)
	Matchcoating (*c.* 385 pieces)	Shaloon (5 pieces)
	Blanketing (*c.* 20 pieces)	Durant (2 pieces)
	Halfthicks (*c.* 45 pieces)	Hair shag (*c.* 1 piece)
		Worsted shag (*c.* 1 piece)
		Calimanco (3 pieces)
		Camlet (1 piece)
II. Garments		
Breeches patterns		Knit (6 scarlet, 1 buff)
Caps		Cotton (1 dozen)
Hats		Newest fashion (1 dozen black)
Bonnets		(half dozen)
Stockings		Women's fine (2 dozen)
III. Accessories		
Handkerchiefs	Silk (5 dozen largest)^	Gauze (1 dozen)
	Silk (4 dozen common)†	
Ribbon	Plain (100 pieces plain)#	Satin (8 pieces black)
	Flowered (50 pieces)	Padusoy (8 pieces black)

* "(it would be Best to get them made into shirts in the inhabitants [by settlers])"
^ "Dublin Manufactory of the largest Sort & of Several Collours but few of them dark collours"
† "several sorts"
# "of several deep collours viz mostly green, dark and light blue, yellow & some pink collour"
Source: derived from HSP, Etting Collection, vol. 40, Ohio Company, vol. I, doss. 36

Goods to Suit the white People about the fort [Pitt]" (drawn up on the same day), summarized in Table 3.3, nicely encapsulate some of the chief contrasts in fashion ecologies as they existed in the second half of the eighteenth century – at least as perceived by Euroamericans. Neither

Indians nor colonists nor merchants felt constrained to abide by the suggested material boundaries; Philadelphia-based Indian traders looted by French allies in the late 1740s and 1750s, for instance, reported losing cambric and calimanco.[102] Still, the rest of the despoiled traders' losses agree remarkably well with the "Assortment of Indian Goods" list, suggesting that the merchants who composed it were surely cognizant of their customers' preferences, and that those preferences changed but slowly.[103]

The Native–settler disparity is marked first of all at both the categorical and varietal levels of fabrics. The Indian list proposed that 80 percent by length of textiles should be woolens, about 15 percent linens, and 5 percent cottons, while that for settlers suggested some 50 percent woolens, 20 percent linens, and 15 percent cottons, along with more luxurious poplin (a wool and silk mixture), hairbine (silk and worsted), and alamode (a thin, glossy silk). Second, it is striking that there is no overlap in the specific types of fabrics listed in each category, though in Pennsylvania "chintz" was the term employed for an expensive type of calico.

Vermilion and beads are also mentioned for Indians; shoes for settlers. Though most "Indian Goods" linens were intended for shirts, no other garments are cited for Natives. To be sure, a contemporary list of "proper" gifts for Indians includes caps, women's stockings, laced hats, and "Made up Cloathing such as laced Coats [and] laced jackets," but this hints strongly that tailored apparel was not something that Indians sought to purchase.[104] Comparing colors is also instructive. All three lists propose a variety of red/scarlet, blue, white, and black woolens. But silver and striped poplins are reserved for whites, "brightest flourishing" calicoes for Indians. Similarly different are the colors proposed for ribbons.

The distinctiveness of Amerindian fashion – both including aspects of contemporary European and settler costume and diverging substantially from it – also emerges from a comparison that can be derived from Alexander Henry's journal, which dates from the same years as the Fort Pitt data. In pursuit of fur-trading opportunities, Henry found it prudent to change his apparel thoroughly on three separate occasions when switching identity: from English colonial to (French) "Canadian" trader, from trader to Amerindian, and then back to Canadian; he also purchased additional garments when disguised as an Indian.[105] Table 3.4 charts Henry's iterations of fashions on the Upper Great Lakes at the beginning of the 1760s.

Table 3.4 *Alexander Henry's fashions*

(French) Canadian trader	"Indian" (Ojibwe?)	"Indian" (Purchases)	(French) Canadian
"a cloth, passed about the middle"	Shirt, painted with vermilion and grease	Shirt	Shirt
Shirt, hanging loose	Blanket, scarlet	Blanket	Molton (*molleton*) blanket coat
Molton (*molleton*) blanket coat	Leggings, scarlet cloth	Leggings, scarlet cloth	Handkerchief, "hats being very little worn in this country"
Red worsted cap [*toque?*]	Head shaved, except spot on crown; large bunch of feathers		
Smear face & hands with dirt and grease	Paint face red, black, and other colors		
	Wampum bands (neck and breast)	Ribbon to garnish leggings "fashionably"	
	Silver arm bands		

Source: Henry 1809/1969, 34–35, 111–12, 147, 154

The originality of Henry's iteration of Amerindian fashion lay to some extent in a different display of color. Though as both a Eurocanadian and an Indian he wore red items, he would have been much more thoroughly enveloped in that color as a Native, and only in the latter role did he put on other colors. His sartorial Nativeness lay somewhat, too, in different kinds of garments: leggings were specific to his Indian identity, a cap or kerchief to his colonial self or selves. Still, shirts and some sort of heavy outerwear were common to all Alexander's roles (and probably his quasi-breechclout), though the coats of his Canadian personae may have been loosely tailored. But the main contrast among his dress identities consisted in ornamentation of body and apparel. Just as in Ragueneau's account a century earlier, so in the mid-eighteenth century Indian fashion comprised abundant adornment that tightly associated the somatic and the sartorial.

All these examples testify not just to the existence of unique Amerindian styles. They also reveal that even in the later eighteenth century, fashion continued both to traverse and to delineate interethnic boundaries, to promote identification as well as differentiation between Indians and Europeans. Images teach the same lesson more vividly. The anonymous drawing (Plate 6), for instance, suggests that some Amerindians, both male and female, adopted shirts and shifts, outerwear, skirts and breeches, and even caps and hats, much like those worn by Euroamericans. It reveals, too, that insofar as Amerindians began to put on these imported garments, they inevitably participated in a semiotics of gendering visible at least to Europeans: The European-inflected dress of the Natives depicted on the top row identifies them by gender as clearly as does the apparel of the settlers below.

Plate 6 illustrates as well distinctive Native styles: shorter skirts among women and the absence of breeches among men (long shirts serving instead); the wearing of leggings by both men and women; the persistence of breechclouts, of moccasins rather than shoes, and of male facial painting; distinctive headgear (including, on the two women, load-bearing headbands, and on men flat red woolen caps that were not at all like the habitant's characteristic "*toque*" or "*bonnet rouge*"); and even one man clad only in a breechclout and another in a blanket.[106] Though a couple of the free settlers shown on the lower row had adopted Indian items (moccasins, leggings, decorated sash, and snowshoes), the arrangements of their clothing and accessories – not to mention their neglect of the Native habit of incorporating the surface of the body into the overall fashion effect – were certainly dissimilar to those of the Amerindians, and vice versa: Even the one Native man in European-style hat and coat is not wearing breeches (though perhaps a breechclout under his long shirt), is barefooted, and boasts red face paint. The two dress regimes overlap at points and – if asymmetrically – borrow from each other. But each comprises a style of its own, with the Amerindian being much more interculturally hybrid.

This partial overlap and both the dangerous and beneficial possibilities that it opened up were at times painfully obvious. In September 1763, a time of great interethnic tension on the long Appalachian frontier, a self-described group of "peaceable Indians" (Moravian converts) published a remarkable "Notice" that they "may be known" by their different appearance from hostile or "wild Indians" and thus, they pled, ought not to be shot at or "spitefully treated" (as many already had been).

> The wild Indians generally go only in a shirt, whereas these [the peaceful] are always cloathed with something.
> A wild Indian is generally painted and weareth a Feather, or some other Indian Ornaments, these are never painted and wear no feather, but they wear Hats or Caps.
> The wild Indians get their Heads shaved but these let their Hair grow naturally.[107]

The petitioners acknowledged that both groups engaged with imported textiles and garments, but the peaceful more fully. Neither, however, unconditionally participated: The peaceful did not claim to dress like settlers but only to wear "something," perhaps a blanket or matchcoat, perhaps only a breechclout, but implicitly more than a shirt alone. Still, the critical weight of the appeal rested on things that still defined "Indian style" to Europeans – including, notably, captives in the recently concluded French and Indian War that had much to do with the current antagonisms – but also to many Indians: direct bodily adornment and hair arrangement, including feathers.[108] Even if Indians were no longer "naked" in European eyes, these attributes of Native attire still defined Native savagery – and the converts, cognizant of that perception, desperately sought to mobilize it to deflect aggression away from themselves. In their broadside, Amerindian style was not a sinister monolith of total corporeal modification but included a garmented variant that, if dissimilar to Euroamerican fashion, was nonetheless self-depicted as innocuous.

"No cloth" but a "flannel peticoat": resistance and syncretism

Not every Amerindian was a fan of the new dress regime. The German visitor Gottlieb Mittelberger claimed that "savages that live on the borders of the Europeans" he encountered in Philadelphia in the early 1750s disdained the accoutrements of Euroamerican urban life as "quite unnecessary" due to the toil and cost they demanded. "Still more they wonder at the garments of the Europeans and their costly finery; they will even spit out when they see it," preferring "instead of clothes, blankets … hanging uncut and unsewed about their bare bodies," with "neither shirts, nor breeches, nor coats beneath."[109] Mittelberger's assertion, which evoked contemporary luxury debates and "noble savage" ideology, may be overly dramatic. But the attitudes he reports testify to the consequential symbolic, aesthetic, and practical work that imported textile goods had come to perform in woodland North America: After all, the scornful Natives donned blankets (probably matchcoats), not furs, to set themselves apart, and they were fully conversant with the styles they disparaged. The same held true among a more comprehensive opponent of the new ways. Neolin, an influential Delaware revitalization prophet in the early 1760s, cited woven fabrics and dress made from them as emblematic of the corrupting practices that Amerindians seeking moral, spiritual, and worldly regeneration had to spurn in favor of living "without any Trade or Connections with ye White people, Clothing & Supporting themselves as their forefathers did." Indians should, he proclaimed, "Clothe themselves with Skins."[110] But as Neolin tacitly admitted, imported fabrics and garments had become ubiquitous not only in Native American dress but in their imaginary as well, so much so that when rejected they still supplied the discursive stuff for protesting settler behavior.

Those same goods, it turned out, also provided the means for resolving such challenges. When in late 1756 the Tellico Town (Cherokee) headman Kenoteta wanted to communicate his anger at slights by colonial officials and mistreatment by English traders, he declared (as narrated by Captain Raymond Demere, officer at Fort

Loudon on the South Carolina frontier) "that he would then go to Warr, that he was going with some Horses into the Woods to fetch some Skins that he had, and that he would make with them all Kind of Clothing for himself and his Family, and that he wanted no Cloth ..." After conciliatory talk by Demere, however, Kenoteta asked for (and received) shirts, several yards of stroud, blankets, and a "flannel Peticoat [sic]" for his wife.[111] The request, and its fulfillment, under-lined the critical role of woven textiles and apparel in intercultural relations and the well-established place of standard fabrics and garments in eighteenth-century Native North America. They show as well the ongoing inclusion of new items into Amerindian dress regimes, notably those continuous with existing styles: Just as Kenoteta most likely wanted strouds and blankets for matchcoats, so a flannel petticoat would be worn in the same way that Native women often wrapped woolen matchcoats around the waist.

So not all indigenous Americans were enthusiastic proponents of redressing, and some did not participate at all. Yet most Native people in the Atlantic Americas wove into their dress regimes textile goods and modes that involvement in the merchant economy and the political and ideological programs that accompanied European evangelization and colonial settlement introduced into their communities. Observing this development, James Axtell postulated that Native North Americans underwent "the first consumer revolution."[112] In fact, Native Americans' fashioning of new dress regimes was more far-reaching. Unlike other denizens of the early modern Atlantic, they simultaneously encountered wholly new materials, garments, styles of constructing and of wearing apparel – and active emissaries of all of these novelties.

No single Native dress regime was born from this engagement, however, not even in Atlantic North America. Besides the kind of creative individual variation evident from Koquethagechton's inven-tory, or the differences between nations that can be discerned in Great Lakes cargo manifests, Native dress might take on distinctive regional configurations. Indians in southeastern continental North America, for instance, integrated imported materials and styles into already elaborate ways of accoutrement.[113] And as everywhere, Native dress regimes involved both general and particular omissions as well as inclusions. Items, materials, and tastes failed to be adopted (like waistcoats), were no longer maintained (like deerskin tunics), or were tried but then disregarded (like *capots* around Green Bay).[114]

The results were syncretic but recognizably both Native and, as Ragueneau (if reluctantly) acknowledged, fashions rather than misunderstood attempts to copy random aspects of European modes. And like those styles, albeit at a somewhat different pace and with somewhat different content, Native dress regimes continued to change, adding and deleting apparel, fabrics, colors, patterns, and adornments in response both to evolving supplies of consumption goods provided by the globalizing merchant economy and to their own evolving sociocultural needs and resources. As such, they participated in the commercial and colonial dynamics that were concomitantly redressing the enslaved settler majority.

4 DRESS UNDER CONSTRAINT

RUN away from the Subscriber, living in Donegall, Lancaster county, an Irish servant man, named JOHN ROBESON, about 22 years of age, about 5 feet 6 inches high, of a fresh complexion, red hair, and commonly wears it tied behind, and cued; had on, when he went away, a shirt and trowsers, a linen jacket, with 4 rows of buttons on the breast, and a pair of old shoes; he is a good scholar, and perhaps may pass for a Doctor. There went off with him, a Negroe man, named NED, well set, and strong, but not very tall, aged about 28 years, born in the Jerseys, speaks very good English, and can read and write, of a down look, and thick lips; had on, when he went away, a coarse shirt and trowsers, a hat, bound round the edge, and a hood worked in it; he may be taken for a Mulattoe, by his colour, and probably both may have provided other clothes. Likewise ran away in company with them, a likely Negroe man, belonging to Joseph Chambers in York town, named JAMES JONES, about 28 years of age, about 5 feet 11 inches high, slim made, born in this country, and has a good countenance; he took with him a blue broadcloth coat, black velvet jacket, and breeches, a pair of leather ditto, two fine shirts, one of them ruffled, 2 coarse ditto, two pair of coarse trowsers, a pair of pumps, with silver shoe buckles, a pair of strong shoes, a blanket, and a gun, with a splint in the stock, near the butt. It is likely they may have forged passes, as the white man writes a good hand. Whoever takes up and secures the said servants, so that their masters may have them again, shall have SIX POUNDS reward for the three, or Forty Shillings for either, if taken separate, and reasonable charges, paid by us, ALEXANDER LOWRY, JOSEPH CHAMBERS.

This highly circumstantial advertisement was one of three concerning runaway laborers published in the *Pennsylvania Gazette* dated August

17, 1769.[1] Most such listings were briefer, and it was rare for both enslaved persons and indentured servants to appear together, so this one is in effect a compendium of the types of information proffered by (and the preoccupations of) masters seeking the return of valuable human property. By virtue of its detail, the notice not only tells much about Robeson, Ned, and Jones, but also suggests lines of inquiry about the material lives of the great number of men and women who lived and labored under constraint around the Atlantic world.

The announcement is particularly valuable for revealing the range of apparel worn by those in permanent or temporary bondage, even if it cautions that its catalogue is likely incomplete. The differences did not fall neatly along a slave–servant continuum, indicating that a wider array of determinants was at work. Whereas Ned had on garb minimal in quantity and quality and apparently went unshod, John Robeson was somewhat better attired despite well-worn shoes, yet it was James Jones who boasted a wardrobe much richer in every respect, including some fancy footwear. Were the differences in apparel between Ned and Robeson, both from a rural township, typical of disparities obtaining between the enslaved and the indentured? What accounts for the dress discrepancies of Ned and Jones, equally enslaved? How representative of their gender and status was the attire worn by each of the men? What did enslaved women or female indentured servants put on? By what means did any or all of them acquire their dress? Would individuals like them have dressed differently had they lived in the Cape Colony, the Caribbean, or Brazil, or in the seventeenth century? And did they – any of them – have a say in the making of the dress regimes they inhabited?

Dress and redressing were matters of particular moment for those held in permanent bondage in settler colonies around the early modern Atlantic, and for those who held them. Enslavement had existed throughout the Atlantic basin long before it became "the Atlantic," of course. But as David Eltis remarks, the striking expansion of export-oriented plantation agriculture in the Americas "gave the institution a new scale and intensity,"[2] and slavery took root as well in non-American colonies like the Cape. In most parts of the Atlantic, permanent, heritable chattel slavery supplanted looser systems in which bondspeople had been less ethnically, legally, and socially distinct from the larger cultural environments in which they were embedded. Not surprisingly, then, their redressing differed qualitatively from that experienced by other Atlantic peoples.

Defined as chattel, enslaved men and women lost virtually all autonomy, and as personal, movable property themselves they had no right independently to acquire or legally own possessions. As human beings, however, they needed food, shelter, and clothing, which law and convention mandated that masters supply. Indentured servants, too, though not chattel, found their ability to provide for themselves sharply reduced during their terms of service. In the populace at large, many free adults occasionally acquired articles of clothing that others had chosen for them as gifts, bequests, incentives, and truck pay, while children, apprentices, household servants, inmates of workhouses and hospitals, and some military personnel regularly had the bulk of their dress imposed upon them. Across the early modern Atlantic as a whole, however, it was above all those in bondage who routinely received – or were supposed to receive – apparel that someone else selected. Subject to what John Styles has termed "involuntary consumption," their dress was to be "provided by others by means of non-market or semi-market mechanisms, on terms which offered little choice."[3] Slaveowners and masters of indentured servants were not interested in redressing per se: what mattered to them was acquiring, marking, and profitably exploiting bonded labor. In contrast to the experience of those "naked savages" whom missionaries and officials intended to reclothe and civilize, the redressing of the enslaved was a side effect of their transformation into labor units. Similarly, whereas free people could purchase clothing and fabrics through market exchange, masters' bestowal of apparel on the enslaved and indentured was an act of unilateral power.

In principle, laws and conventions accorded both slaves and indentured servants regular clothing allotments. How adequate the required provisions were, or whether they were fulfilled even in part, was hotly disputed among contemporaries, particularly with respect to the dress of the enslaved; even defenders of slavery who wanted to make the institution more "humane" voiced criticisms. Adequately exploring dress under constraint also requires attention to the differences among those subject to it, and not only in terms of slaves as compared to indentured servants. For one thing, neither the enslaved nor masters formed homogeneous groups across space and time. For another, the societies in which slaves lived differed, notably between "slave societies," in which a great part or even the majority of the colonist population was held in bondage and "the order of the plantation shaped every relationship," and "societies with slaves," where economic structures were more varied and the enslaved comprised a minority of settlers.[4] Moreover, slaveowners were not necessarily the sole source of necessities of life: Some bondsmen and bondswomen developed various forms of self-provisioning, best known in terms of food but also for apparel, and they might acquire not only basic necessities but also additional items, leading, paradoxical as it may seem, to complaints about "slave luxury."

So what, given all this, did slaves and indentured servants actually wear? The sources do not make that question, the subject of this chapter, particularly easy to answer. Slaves could not legally bequeath property, no matter how acquired.[5] So probate inventories were not prepared after they died. Very seldom, too, did slaves leave the letters, journals, reports, and other types of first-person documents that free colonists abundantly produced. Notices for runaways can, as we have seen, furnish a great deal of information, but newspapers were only published in some places for some of our period, and not all even of those have survived. Rarity of plantation records and gaps in commercial documents likewise compromise research, and contemporary observers, including those who produced visual images, had their own particular conventions, commitments, and objectives. Yet if it would be ill-advised to accept their representations at face value, nonetheless each of these sources provides valuable and indicative details. By collating the evidence that does exist, it is possible to uncover at least the outlines of the dress cultures of the enslaved, and in a few places a surprisingly detailed picture can be drawn.

"Good and sufficient" apparel: the limits of redressing

Constrained dressing began with forced undressing. In fact, the enslaved often had to endure the indignity of repeated strippings: At the time of initial enslavement in Africa, during transport to the coast, in the course of examination on shore, or even before being ferried out to a waiting ship.[6] Figure 4.1 – which portrays stages in the process from display in a rudimentary market at water's edge (1), through inspection (2) and the tagging of an enslaved man after purchase (4), to loading slaves on a longboat (6) for transfer to the slaver offshore (5) and the distress this caused onlookers (7) – indicates the disrobed or near-naked state of the

Marché D'esclaves   *Pl:xi·*

4.1 *Marché d'esclaves / Slave market*, from M. Chambon, *Le commerce de l'Amérique par Marseille*, 2 vols. (Avignon and Marseille: Marc-Michel Rey & Jean Mossy, 1783), II, pl. XI, following p.400.

A treatise on trade that included much information on how and what to trade with slaving areas in West and west Central Africa, on how to transport captives to the Americas, and how to set them to work on plantations, Chambon's work included numerous illustrations to supplement textual descriptions.

enslaved even before they left Africa, particularly in contrast to the European slave trader (3).

Disrobing served pragmatic ends: It facilitated inspection of bodies for disease or infirmity, removed potential implements of suicide, prevented the hiding of weapons, and controlled vermin.[7] The literal act was also a classic instance of the first or separation stage in a rite of passage leading to the terrible transition of the Middle Passage.[8] It was a symbolic measure as well. Not only did coercive disrobing break enslaved individuals' principal material link to their families, communities, and cultures of origin. It also demonstrated their powerlessness in a particularly humiliating way, marking their entry into captivity and even more into a new status as, in the words of the French slaver Jean Barbot, "a commodity in this country."[9] Incised scarification and tattoos, of course, could not be effaced, and these "country marks" survived to be cited in runaway advertisements, serving as a kind of ghost presence of the bearer's life preceding the social death of enslavement.[10]

Redressing completed the process, materially integrating the enslaved into their new status while conspicuously manifesting proprietors' acquisition and authority as well as bondspeople's dispossession and subordination. Like stripping, redressing was likely to occur several times as individuals passed from owner to owner between Africa and the Americas, or between Native and settler Americas, or between the Indian Ocean and South Africa, thereby re-enacting subjection and loss. At least by the late seventeenth century, reports suggest, on some ships the enslaved received a minimal garment once boarded, though it seems likely that many men, women, and children traversed the Atlantic wholly or largely naked.[11] Even summary garb, moreover, was likely to be destroyed before the enslaved were allowed on shore, lest "the least Infection" arrive with them.[12] As a result, newly arrived slaves typically experienced another re-appareling in the Americas, at times something meager to prepare them for sale ("Pieces of Cotton to serve as fig leafs, " as one observer tartly put it) but almost always when their new owners took possession.[13] Indeed, visual signaling of proprietorship by attire – and often by branding on the skin – frequently preceded the act of verbal proprietorship denoted by renaming.[14]

Branding and renaming are ostensibly permanent; dress is not. Though owners' responsibility for unwaged laborers' subsistence may seem obvious, imperial authorities wanted to ensure that this obligation would be honored. Hence minimum obligations were statutorily established soon after Africans began to be imported to the Spanish "Indies."[15] As early as 1528, Madrid directed masters to provide "at least" breeches (*calzones*) and long smock-like shirts (*camisoles*); later enactments used slightly different terms but followed the same template.[16]

A usually two-piece outfit comprising garments worn both above and below the waist, made most often of some type of rough linen and distributed annually, became the legal norm in slave colonies. For French colonies, the so-called *Code Noir* (1685) specified "two suits [*habits* of tunic-like jackets and breeches or skirts] of linen clothing or four ells of linen, as the master wishes," while a Jamaican statute of 1696 called for "Jackets and Drawers" for men, "Jackets and Petticoats, or Frocks [one-piece gowns]" for women, though without designating a fabric.[17] By the early eighteenth century, the conventions were so well known that dress edicts enacted in or for other slave societies could be even more cursory: "the quality of clothing that masters ought to supply to their slaves" each year was stipulated for Louisiana, for example, "sufficient" dress in South Carolina, "good and sufficient" at the Cape of Good Hope.[18] Throughout the Atlantic world, in short, authorities intended slave status to be materialized in a remarkably consistent costume consisting of two loose-fitting, formless garments of cheap, coarse, often uncomfortable fabric, usually linen and/or, occasionally, woolen. Reflecting Europeans' concerns about nakedness, the outfits mandated for both men and women were supposed to cover their torsos above as well as below the waist, if rudimentarily. Enslavement was also to be sartorially signaled by omissions: by what fully dressed slave bodies would lack – footwear, shaped headgear, accessories, and adornment – as well as by what garbed them.[19] As a visitor to Saint-Domingue wrote, though "all commonly wear a handkerchief on their heads," slaves "always go barefoot: … in town as in the countryside, it's one of the attributes of slavery."[20]

Sometimes slaves received ready-to-wear garments. Masters and mistresses might hand out their own cast-off clothing, or – as in rural areas of the Cape Colony – second-hand attire bought in town.[21] Alternatively, they purchased new, specially made slave apparel in European metropoles or colonial towns, or had it fashioned on the plantation, whether by slaves or by free women in their overseers' or even in their own families.[22] But most slaveholders provided lengths of fabric, leaving it up to slaves to fashion their own apparel or find enslaved seamstresses and tailors. In backcountry Brazil, planters trained slaves to manufacture rough fabrics using cotton grown on the estate,[23] but the great majority of the textiles that clothed slaves was imported.[24]

Many contemporaries insisted that masters in the main dutifully distributed apparel sufficient to discharge their obligations.[25] In Brazil, reported a well-informed Bahia resident, "the ordinary clothing, given to each laboring slave" comprised "a pair of shirts, and skirts, or trousers"; in South Carolina, avowed the pastor of a backcountry congregation, the norm was a coat and breeches for men, a gown or petticoat and a "camisole" (a fitted waist-length shift with sleeves) for women; and at Cape Town – at least when conscientious officials were in charge – female VOC slaves received cloth sufficient for several dresses or skirts and shifts, while each male got several jackets and pairs of trousers.[26] In some places, planters were said to exceed the minimum requirements, for example by endowing the enslaved with light summer apparel or with woolen fabric for winter garments in addition to the usual linen garb.[27]

There is no evidence that slaveholders who followed the laws did so because they feared punishment for infractions. Every code established mechanisms for enforcing slaves' dress entitlement, but none of the individuals or state officials thereby empowered to act on slaves' behalf seems to have done so.[28] Yet even without the threat of penalties, there were good reasons for masters to apparel their slaves. One was simple convention, legitimated by law but not directly reliant upon it, which made provisioning part of masters' habitus. Contemporaries cited other considerations. Proposing that provision of good material conditions, including sufficient dress, was central to creating "trustworthy and peaceful" slaves, the 1528 Spanish ordinance voiced a belief that continued to be echoed for centuries. In mid-eighteenth-century Jamaica, for example, the overseer Thomas Thistlewood expressed no surprise at a neighboring plantation's recurrent problem with runaways: "These Negroes have never had Cloaths or any other encouragement."[29]

More amply developed paternalistic thinking likewise contended that properly deployed material benefits could elicit consent or at least passivity among the enslaved. According to seventeenth-century Portuguese writers and royal decrees, servitude involved mutual obligations: The enslaved owed labor and obedience, while masters had to supply clothing as well as other forms of physical and spiritual sustenance.[30] Versions of this creed that emphasized sartorial provisioning were articulated and acted upon around the Atlantic. Bondsmen, the South Carolina merchant-cum-planter Henry Laurens informed one of his plantation managers, earn "no Wages being my property as Slaves, except Cloathing and provision from me and good usage from you." Laurens also made sure that the slaves were told of his efforts to clothe them on time and in good-quality fabrics.[31]

But even where force was more continuously in evidence than beneficence, dressing policies had much to recommend them to slaveholders as a way to advance their goal of slave acquiescence, or at least quiescence.[32] In particular, masters sought to exhibit and strengthen distinctions and hierarchies among the enslaved so as to pursue divide-and-conquer strategies or other forms of manipulation. Masters therefore offered desirable items as status markers or as incentives or rewards for what they deemed meritorious effort. The owner of one Saint-Domingue plantation gave slave drivers an additional outfit of Vimoutier (a fine linen that was two or more times as expensive as the coarse varieties that other slaves received), together with a tailored, metropolitan-style "redingote" (lapeled frockcoat), further singling out the head driver with a blue coat while the others had to be content with grey. The planter also reserved calico petticoats for the nurse and chief housekeeper, a vest and a hat for the coachman; and if indigo makers "performed their duty well," they, too, would get a Vimoutier ensemble.[33] Similarly, the enslaved officers who helped manage the VOC slave lodge in Cape Town received more apparel than other slaves, along with pieces of cotton and of linen fabric; and the Jamaican Thistlewood's differential grants of garments and lengths of cloth – cheap hempen ozenbrig linen for field hands, more expensive and varied fabrics for a select group – followed the same rationale of awarding or withholding garments in order to enhance masters' power and slaves' dependency.[34]

Nevertheless, despite widely known conventions, countless laws, bold affirmations, and manipulative possibilities, masters' commitment to either the letter or the spirit of slave appareling, other observers contended, was indifferently honored at best. Both from self-interest and as Christians, the Dominican Jean-Baptiste Labat wrote in the 1690s, slaveholders are obliged to supply their slaves with "everything necessary for their subsistence." But only a minority did so satisfactorily. "There are fair (*raisonnables*) masters," he acknowledged, who bestowed on each man two jackets and two pairs of breeches, on each woman two jackets and two skirts – who complied, that is, though Labat did not say so, with the *Code Noir*'s directive. But they were badly outnumbered. Another group of masters, "less fair," eliminated one of each gender's jackets; yet others furnished only one outfit (a jacket and breeches or skirt) per person. The remaining masters, finally,

> who are not at all fair, give [slaves] only enough linen to make a single jacket and pair of breeches or a skirt, with a few needlefuls of thread, not caring who makes their clothing or how they make it, nor how they are supposed to pay for the tailoring. As a result, they have to sell their linen and their thread, and go around nearly naked the whole year.[35]

Across the period, and throughout the Atlantic, visitors, officials, missionaries, and even – on rare occasions when their testimony was recorded – slaves themselves voiced similar complaints.[36] "Because of getting no clothes, nor tobacco," the Cape Colony slave Cinna absconded in 1705, while in 1753 Neptunus van Bengalen explained at his murder trial that at the time of the deed he had been "almost stark naked and without clothes" in the "severe cold."[37] In Louisiana, where supply problems were legion, officials of the Compagnie des Indes in New Orleans lamented in 1727 that "the want of ... cloth to apparel [slaves] causes the death of many of them," and again two years later, "there is no cloth for a third" of the enslaved people in Louisiana.[38] According to a 1782 letter from the resident manager of a Saint-Domingue indigo plantation to its absentee owner, he had "handed out enough linen to clothe" the slaves (a gesture that "gave them great pleasure") after learning that "some years" (*quelques années*) had gone by since the last distribution: In fact, thirteen years had passed.[39]

Louisiana's supply troubles were beyond planters' control.[40] But most blame for appareling problems, observers agreed, should be laid squarely at owners' feet. Many pointed to simple greed, others to poor management.[41] Immoral and irresponsible spending was also said to play a role. According to one critic, a Brazilian planter would lavish silks, fine woolen *serafina*, and "other fineries" on "women who cause his downfall" while denying his slaves "four or five *varas* of cottons and a few more of rough woolens."[42] Not all planters prospered, moreover, and skimping on slave dress was an obvious way to minimize costs. Judging from plantation accounts, supplying textiles and apparel for the enslaved could amount to as much as 8.27 percent of annual operating expenses, though often the figure was lower; little wonder, then, that even successful planters like Laurens who discharged their obligations were hawkeyed about expenditures on slave attire.[43] No matter what the specific cause cited, a chorus of complaints about masters' appareling failures resounded all across the era with enough force and specificity to suggest that these claims contained a good deal of truth.[44] And even when masters obeyed the laws, it is hard to disagree with contemporaries who believed that the stipulated dress allowances were themselves inadequate. In 1760, the manager of Jamaica's Island Estate advised its owner, "the customary allowance as I have found it before me" of five yards of ozenbrig should be raised to six, along with some woolen "flannell or Bays [baize]" because more and warmer garments "would be a great Preservation for their [slaves'] health."[45] That even the higher figure virtually guaranteed that the few garments made from them would be in rags at the end of the year – and that the coarse fabrics rendered them uncomfortable – went unsaid.

"Some decent as well as necessary cloaths": slave self-dressing

Masters' supply left an unknown but probably substantial portion of slaves poorly dressed. Some enslaved women and men, however, had access to other sources of apparel. Atlantic slavery was violent, oppressive, and restrictive, but at times it contained – partly by intent and partly by default – possibilities for self-provisioning. Autonomous home manufacture was not among them. Slaveholders organized and controlled the rare instances of plantation textile production; in Brazil, masters sold the output – including to slaves on the same plantation – to bolster their bottom line. If slaves needed or wanted to attire themselves, they had to acquire already fabricated cloth or clothing.

One way was by theft, from the free population or, more likely, given both propinquity and sheer numbers, fellow slaves.[46] The eighteenth-century Louisiana plantation manager Antoine Le Page du Pratz considered such "larceny" the inevitable and excusable result of masters' neglect of the enslaved's basic needs; the modern historian

Trevor Burnard sees it as an instance of "general conditions of law-lessness in a lawless society."[47] Surely it was both. Fabrics and garments were not only useful in themselves – whether in their original form or suitably altered to complicate discovery – they could also be bartered or exchanged for money. It is hardly surprising that clothing led the list of goods that a 1700 placard forbade free Cape Colony residents to trade with slaves.[48] The very prohibition suggests that such trade was proceeding apace.

Sundry types of work also provided the means to acquire dress, or the items themselves. Wages earned by enslaved artisans often went for clothes, food, and housing as well as fees to owners.[49] Less skilled slaves relied on expedients, ranging from porterage, hunting, and fishing to local specialties like beachcombing in the wake of shipwrecks near Cape Town.[50] All too commonly, female slaves were forced to barter sexual services for clothing. In late seventeenth-century Cape Town, bondswomen were so wretchedly dressed that they sold their bodies "for an old jacket or blanket," and during his decades of predation the Jamaican overseer and later planter Thistlewood often paid his sexual partners with new and old garments as well as lengths of fabric.[51]

The most remarked-upon slave self-employment was petty mar-keting: both Sunday markets and itinerant peddling.[52] Particularly in the Caribbean, enslaved hawkers and hucksters mainly sold produce grown in personal provision grounds – from which they often had to feed themselves as well – and at times pigs and chickens raised around their dwellings. One Saint-Domingue sugar planter thought it advisable that even slaves employed in domestic service have garden plots to work so that they "could earn a little to help clothe themselves."[53] Slaves also offered goods like ceramics, baskets, and brushes that they had made, along with imported manufactures, notably fabrics and garments, sup-plied by their masters, with whom they split the proceeds.[54]

Contemporaries often spoke of the "troops" of slave hawkers and hucksters.[55] Still, for a number of reasons, including plantation location, commercial food production on neighboring farms, lack of spare time, personal characteristics, and master's fiat, slaves might have little or no access to provision grounds, marketing, or other forms of remunerated labor.[56] At least one planter, convinced that slaves' ability to sell in markets and to buy dress items on their own bred "corruption" and disturbance (we might say autonomous desires and independence), prevented slaves on his remote estate from participating. Instead, he created a pseudo-market of his own: After purchasing in town those "articles" he would allow, he bartered them for "fowls, eggs, or other productions, at stated or market prices."[57] Whatever the venue, those enslaved men and women who did manage to sell their labor or the products of their labor "to enable them to purchase some decent as well as necessary cloaths for their wives and themselves," did so by taking on a yet more excessive workload, by foregoing some of their own food supplies, and/or by enduring still harsher and more degrading exploitation of their bodies.[58]

The "masters thank": enslaved dress in slave societies

Through various combinations of imposition and self-provision, bondsmen and bondswomen in slave colonies throughout the Atlantic were, for better or worse, dressed both by others and by their own initiatives. Much of what they obtained was ordinary, "necessary," quotidian garb, but some acquired additional items, the "decent cloaths" to which Browne also referred. What did the resulting wardrobes comprise? Of the slave societies considered here, South Carolina runaway advertisements provide the best data over time, so it makes sense to begin by examining slave attire in that colony.

More than two-fifths of runaway advertisements in the colony's first and most prominent newspaper described the garments of the absconded, a large and apparently random sample.[59] Like all descriptions of apparel, some listings may be incomplete, though masters had every reason to offer as thorough a portrayal as possible to aid in the identification of escapees. Table 4.1 summarizes the most significant findings.

The information in Table 4.1 indicates not only that the convention of a two-piece outfit was embodied in the daily dress of nearly all enslaved men but also that it had a much weaker influence on the costume of enslaved women, nearly half of whom were dressed in just a single garment, typically a gown. In principle at least, this alternative convention did assure that slave women's bodies, like men's, would be covered above as well as below the waist. Still, the dress of the South Carolina enslaved exhibited a stronger gender asymmetry, a much more evident sense of gender difference, than what the norm proposed. The table also shows the stability of the conventions; if anything, they

Table 4.1 *Garments of South Carolina runaways, 1730s and 1760s (percentages)*

	1730s	1760s
Leading outfits: men†		
Jacket/waistcoat/shirt/frock and breeches/trousers	61	83
(Suit of) clothes	18	7
Both above	79	90
Jacket/waistcoat/coat/shirt/frock but NO breeches/trousers	16	9
Leading outfits: women†		
Gown/wrapper/frock/jacket and petticoat	29	30
Habit/clothes	21	19
Both above	50	49
Gown/wrapper/frock/jacket/coat only (mainly gown only)	46	49
Leading fiber category^		
Woolens	64¶	75
Linens	16	20
Leading fabric#		
Woolen plains ("Negro cloth")	72 (47)	81 (61)
Ozenbrig linen	74 (12)	68 (13)
Total fabrics named	22	25
Leading colors		
Whites	49	45
Blues	25	33
Total colors named	10	14

† Percentage of all garments.

^ Percentage of all garments with fabric listed; 1730s: 191 of 244 (78 percent); 1760s: 377 of 497 (76 percent).

¶ Probably above 70 percent, because much of the 11 percent listed as "cotton" is likely "Welsh cotton," "kendal cotton," or plains/Negro cloth (all names for the same woolen fabric); cf. 1760s data, where "cotton" has disappeared and nearly the only "cotton" is fustian, usually a mixed cotton-linen.

Percentage of garments with specified fabric in each fiber category; in parentheses, percentage all garments with listed fabrics.

Source: S. C. Gaz., 1732–39, 1760–69, transcribed by Windley 1983, III: 1–39, 179–284.

became more firmly rooted over time. Admittedly, some changes did occur: additional fabrics and colors were in evidence, as well as some additional items. Between the 1730s and the 1760s, aprons, pea jackets, robins or robbins (sleeveless vest-like under-jackets), knee-length surt-out coats, and wrappers (short gowns) appeared and drawers and undercoats disappeared, while frocks (long, loose, gown-like garments, not frockcoats), greatcoats, and waistcoats became more common. Still, none of these accounted for more than 3 percent of garments, and most were cited a handful of times. More often, some items occasionally cited in the 1730s were more regularly mentioned three decades later: jackets and coats among women, among men shirts (21 percent of enslaved male runaways had them in the 1760s, as against just 3 percent in the 1730s), and trousers, found on about ten percent of fugitive male slaves in the 1730s, double that in the 1760s. In some cases, the advertisements may have used the terms interchangeably, but it seems probable that over time a larger minority of enslaved men came to wear longer trousers in place of, or in a few cases explicitly over, shorter breeches.

Yet these were marginal changes that did not affect the existence or the persistence of the norms. Both headgear (worn by 6 percent in the 1730s, 7 percent in the 1760s) and footwear, an entirely male prerogative (respectively 4 and 3 percent), remained atypical, suggesting that the customary identification of the barefoot, bareheaded slave held sway even in the absence of legislation explicitly prohibiting shoes and headgear.[60] Some composite of male jackets and breeches/ trousers, and female gowns or jackets and petticoats continued to define slave outfits. So did woolen and linen fabrics, and among these plains and ozenbrig: Decade in and decade out, the enslaved continued overwhelmingly to wear the same rough and durable fabrics.[61] And in the same colors, most often in single-color outfits: 49 percent of all listings were either all white or all blue in the 1730s, 43 percent thirty years later. Though white remained dominant, the enslaved did partake in the growing popularity of blue in the eighteenth century.[62] Beyond these two colors, slave garments did become a bit brighter, as dark hues (black, brown, grey, drab, and "dingy") fell from 14 to 4 percent, brighter (green, red, yellow, and "light") rose from 10 to 17 percent, and two-colored garments (notably, red and white and blue and white) began to appear. For all that, there is no doubt that slave outfits in the 1760s appeared very much the same as in the 1730s. Stability rather than change was their hallmark, and this held true for the apparel omitted as well as for that included.

In South Carolina, in other words, enslaved men and women had uniforms across the eighteenth century. Standardization arrived early and persisted.[63] Though the garb of some became more varied in garments, colors, and fabrics, the majority of slaves experienced virtually no change in attire. What is more, the colors and fabrics of the quotidian outfits of bondspeople clearly distinguished them from free persons, who were cognizant of this from an early date. In a September 1738 list of "Goods proper for So Carolina" that the factor Robert Pringle sent to his English supplier, he distinguished between "low pric'd" fabrics such as "3/4 and 7/8 Garlix ... Brown Osnaburggs, Dowlas, & Russia Linnen," and items explicitly identified for the enslaved: "White, Bleue, & Green plains for Negro Cloathing ... Ruggs for negroes Beds ... Course Worsted stockings For negroes ... Womens Course Worsted stockings For Negroes."[64] As we have seen, the one fabric that had a race-specific name dressed most enslaved women and men; little wonder, then, that Pringle named it first, as did a 1735 South Carolina law itemizing fabrics acceptable for slave apparel.[65] Nor did the enslaved participate much in the growing Atlantic market for cottons, most likely, as with indigenous Americans, due to their higher price and inferior durability compared with linens. This fact goes far to explain the slow rise in cottons, the continued strong presence of woolens, and the notable predominance of linens in Charles Town area merchant stocks (Tables 2.1, 2.3). In South Carolina, at least, dressing the enslaved manifested and then perpetuated subordination in a stable visual semiotics.

Outside continental North America, newspapers and thus runaway advertisements were fewer, and in those that do exist absconded slaves were often described not by dress but by branded marks, considered a surer means by which owners could recognize and prove ownership of runaways.[66] A variety of other sources, however, attest that similar outfits, and a similar gender asymmetry, dominated throughout the slave societies of the Atlantic, though varied climates, merchant networks, and textile traditions resulted in different specific garments and fabrics.

During the second quarter of the seventeenth century, a Jesuit estate near Bahia distributed a male outfit of breeches (*calcões* or *ceroulas*) and shirt (*camisa*) or doublet (*jibão* or *gibão*), mainly using cheap rough linens and woolens, but in about a fifth of the cases cottons.[67] The account book rarely mentions variations in dress, though a "boy" (*mosso* or *moço*) employed as a house servant might wear shoes and a hat along with the regular outfit; more favored male mulattoes (*mulatos*) regularly got black hats. The one enslaved female mentioned wore a woolen skirt (*saia*); perhaps she got a shift or vest when the men got shirts, or perhaps she went unclothed above the waist.

According to a discomfited early eighteenth-century French visitor, in Bahia slaves of both genders went "entirely naked, apart from those parts that modesty obliges us to cover"; as a near-contemporary Italian missionary put it, they wore just "a very simple rag" or "a dirty set of drawers" to cover their "shame."[68] Paintings and engravings confirm but nuance the documentary evidence. They suggest that when engaged in physical labor, enslaved men typically wore only knee-length or shorter white breeches or wrapped skirts, as seen on the hammock porters in Figure 4.2. Occasionally depicted wearing just short skirts, bondswomen are most often shown with skirts and sleeve-less vests or jackets – usually dark – over white shifts, often with puffy sleeves, or in mid-calf, typically light-colored gowns. Both genders went barefoot, men without headgear, women at times with a simple white headband.[69] Little changed thereafter. In the later eighteenth century, the same outfits of breeches or skirts and shirts were said to be "the ordinary clothing given to each laboring slave," made out of "rough cotton cloth," though some planters gave them "their own baize apparel [*vestes*]."[70]

In mid-seventeenth-century Río de la Plata, which obtained many of its slaves from Brazil, adult and child enslaved males were dressed the same: breeches (*calzón*) and doublet or waistcoat (*jubón*). Made up at planters' expense from a coarse woolen (*cordellate, sayal*, or *sayalete*, all of which came from Córdoba, 450 kilometers inland from Buenos Aires, or from Andean producers), outfits were apparently dis-tributed biennially.[71] As in Brazil, the costume persisted over time though fabrics changed; unlike Brazil, however, the shift was not toward cottons but within woolens, to imported as well as colonial varieties like the blue baize listed in a 1760 inventory.[72] None of the textiles was produced solely for the enslaved, but the garments made from them were skimpier than those worn by free people, including laborers. Whereas 2.5–3.5 *varas* (about 2–3 m) of cloth sufficed for slave outfits, ranchers used 6 *varas* (5 m) for their own dress and those of their servants and helpers.[73]

Just as they copied Brazil's plantation slavery system, so Caribbean colonies copied its ordinary slave outfit of shirts (occasion-ally jackets or sleeveless vests) and breeches or skirts (occasionally petticoats), though headgear – caps or kerchiefs – was more common in the West Indies.[74] Some slaves – both men and women – wore only the long tunic-like frock, which Thistlewood, at least, called a "sacca"

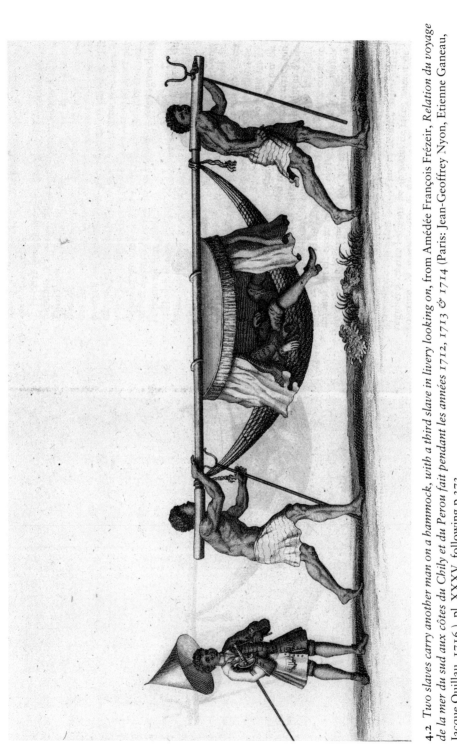

4.2 *Two slaves carry another man on a hammock, with a third slave in livery looking on*, from Amédée François Frézeir, *Relation du voyage de la mer du sud aux côtes du Chily et du Perou fait pendant les années 1712, 1713 & 1714* (Paris: Jean-Geoffrey Nyon, Etienne Ganeau, Jacque Ouillau, 1716), pl. XXXV, following p.272.

This image appeared in the book that the French military engineer and artist Frézier wrote to report on his reconnaissance trip to Iberian America; the work includes a great deal of information about the natural environment as well as the human in Chile, Peru, and coastal Brazil.

(zacca, saccha) when for a woman.[75] Besides the frock, the sartorial regime of the enslaved in the British Caribbean shared other significant characteristics with their counterparts in the British North American plantation colonies. Woolens (notably baize and plains) and linsey-woolsey comprised a significant part of slave garb, to the surprise of some contemporaries. "Who would believe that woollens constitute an article of great consumption in the torrid zone?" exclaimed one Jamaican. "Such, however, is the fact. Of the coarser kinds especially, for the use of the negroes, the export [from Britain] is prodigious."[76] Blue and white ozenbrig and other inexpensive, often hemp, linens were of equal importance. In contrast, cottons were insignificant, though from the mid-eighteenth century mainly mixed linen-cotton check that showed up in merchant stocks became slave shirting too.[77]

By the end of the century, according to Bryan Edwards, "oznaburg-linen, woollen baize," and linen-cotton check were the main kinds of fabric that slaves got as their "yearly allowance."[78] Distributing fabric rather than garments violated the explicit provisions of Jamaican statute, but the amounts disbursed for "their years clothes, or masters thank" – at least 4.5 yards (4 m) and generally 5.5 yards (5 m) or more – would have been more than sufficient for the items that the law prescribed.[79] Slave garments on French islands and in Louisiana were much the same in terms of apparel and colors, though woolens may have been less in evidence. In runaway advertisements from Saint-Domingue between 1766 and 1775, the great majority of men and women had on just two garments: among women, a skirt and shift or short jacket combination (sometimes grouped together as a *rechange*), for men breeches and a shirt; about a half of both genders wore a headscarf, cap, or hat, while none had shoes.[80] About a tenth of fugitives absconded garbed only in a skirt or breeches, about a fifth of men in just a long cassock (*casaque)* or knee-length *veste*. More than half of all garments were made of cheap, rough hempen *brin* and particularly *gingas* linen that closely resembled ozenbrig, a tenth each of coarse woolens and cottons and cotton-linen mixtures. More than three-quarters of garments were blue, white, and blue and white stripes (the usual color of *gingas*), the rest green, red, grey, brown, and black.[81]

Painters and other image producers largely averted their gaze from the field labor that was both the lot of the enslaved majority and the foundation of great wealth in plantation colonies and mother countries. Yet if displaced from its proper centrality, the physical labor

4.3 *Ménagerie / Workplaces in plantation courtyard*, from Jean Baptiste Du Terre, *Histoire générale des Antilles habitées par les François*, 4 vols. (Paris : T. Jolly, 1667–71), II, following p.418.

P. 417

MÉNAGERIE

1. *Café a Petun.*
2. *Nègre qui s'jambe le petun.*
3. *Nègre qui le torque · 1.35.*
4. *Nègre qui le monte.*
5. *N. qui raisfont le Manioc.*
6. *Moulin a greger le Manioc.*
7. *Ancienne maniere de greger le Manioc. 11a.*
8. *La Presse.*
9. *Negresse, rassant la farine.*
10. *Negresse, qui cuit la cassaue.*
11. *la Caise du maytre.*
12. *La Cuisine.*
13. *Cassaue qui seiche.*
14. *Corassole p.171.*

In front of the planter's house (11) enslaved workers on the right side of the image strip tobacco leaves (2), then twist (3) and roll them (4), while those on the left and center scrape manioc (5) after it has dried in the sun (13), grate it in a machine (6) or by hand (7, "the old way"), press (8) and grind it into flour (9), then cook the cassava (10). The missionary's book was as much a practical guide for would-be colonists as it was a description of the enslaved was often revealed at the margins of images, whether of bustling markets, panoramic views of estates, title-page vistas, or even maps, and on occasion – particularly in manuals or sections about plantation management – depictions as well as text focused on working slaves.[82] Together with other documentary evidence,[83] these sources disclose that on the job – rather than on the run, in codes, or in apparel distributions – enslaved men usually and women often wore only a single garment: breeches, skirts, or even wraps, leaving the upper torso exposed, as with the tobacco (2–4) and manioc (5–10) processers depicted in Figure 4.3.

This informal work outfit may reflect ongoing African influence. Texts and images such as Figures 1.1 and 1.3 concur that Atlantic Africans of the time dressed in this way when working,[84] and the constant expansion of plantation agriculture, as well as horrifically high slave mortality and low reproduction rates, assured that the African-born component of most slave populations would remain substantial. Masters also might command slaves to strip down at work, whether to minimize wear (and thus costs) or from a popular belief that African bodies, because of their "savagery," demanded less dress, disregarding condemnations of slave "indecency," calls by religious leaders for proper dress that would curb the temptation to lust, and steps such as the ban by the bishop of Pernambuco, Brazil, on half-clothed slaves entering church.[85] Doffing the top garment was also a reasonable response on the part of the enslaved to hard labor in hot weather, the discomfort of the rough fabrics of their ordinary dress, and the strong smells consequent on the infrequent washing or changes that their scanty allowances permitted; perhaps, too, they wanted to show off distinctive country marks. Equally if not more importantly, slaves' undress noticeably manifested their subordinate status, particularly if the exposed skin was covered with lash marks.[86] In formal markets, however, and when employed as domestic servants, a one-piece or two-piece slave "uniform" that fully covered the body, along with a head-wrap, seems to have been the female norm, as shown, for example, in Plate 2; males, however, might dress only in breeches and some form of head cover, as in the right foreground and background of the same scene.

The slave uniform was found not only in plantation colonies in the Americas but in an only slightly modified form on farms in the slave society of the VOC Cape Colony as well, though the enslaved there came mainly from East Africa and Asia. Enforcement was often lax, but VOC rules called for women to receive woolen winter attire consisting of two skirts (*rokken*) and jackets (*baatjes* or *kabaaien* based on an East Indies prototype), plus an unlined coat (*rok*), with two probably cotton skirts and jackets for the summer. Men were to get a woolen jacket or waistcoat (*hemdrok*) or coat lined with sailcloth (probably a cotton) and two pairs of sailcloth breeches (*broeken*) for winter; a coat and a pair of breeches made of a cheap fabric such as gingham (a striped or checked cotton or linen) for summer.[87] Visitors in the 1730s elaborated that women's "smocks" might be imported from Batavia, that longer trousers made of coarse woolen were worn by some slaves, and that blue linen was now in use; on the whole, however, they confirmed that the same outfit still garbed the colony's slaves.[88] Private owners seem to have followed the same template of garments and fabrics, often adding a shirt or shift (*hembd*) or vest (*camisool*) under blue woolen jackets.

  All this garb – along with bare feet and what one observer called "a twisted handkerchief" under presumably illegal hats – is evident on the enslaved men leading and driving the ox-team in Plate 7a, as well as on the slave accompanying his master on horseback (Plate 7b).[89] Enslaved males in the Cape Colony also might wear leather breeches, though not necessarily willingly.[90] Upon being asked what was wrong during his 1739 trial for violent crimes including murder, the slave Cupido van Mallabaar "took off his jacket and shirt and threw them down on the ground," then went on, "pointing to his leather trousers: 'I am not used to wearing trousers like these …'"[91] Going barefoot was enforced as a badge of enslavement, but prohibitions on Dutch-style hats were evaded with caps and kerchiefs or simply ignored.[92] These variants notwithstanding, the costume of enslaved men and women in the Cape was legibly that of their counterparts around the Atlantic.

"Suffitient and convenien[t] cloathing": servant dress in slave societies

Were free workers, who labored under similar conditions in similar jobs, and often alongside the enslaved, also their sartorial counterparts? Formally free indigenous people and indentured European servants were found on plantations in slave societies, albeit in diminishing numbers across our period. Was their dress distinguished in any meaningful way from that of enslaved men and women? The answer to both questions is a qualified yes. At least legally, the divergences were greatest when whites were involved – as between white indentured servants and non-white slaves – and smallest when other ethnic differences were in play: when, say, Amerindian or Khoikhoi wage laborers worked with African or Indian Ocean slaves. Distinctions did not lie in basic garments – the standard ordinary outfit – but in the number and assortment of items, the inclusion or not of the most widely recognized sartorial mark of the free – footwear – and at times in the quality of fabrics. In practice, however, dress disparities may well have been minimal: When laboring together on the same tasks, slaves, indentured servants, and waged employees likely dressed, or undressed, in the same way.

In the Cape Colony, the indigenous Khoikhoi were noted for retaining their traditional animal-skin dress within their own communities. It comprised "the skins of beasts quite undressed, one they tie over their shoulders, and another round their waste [sic] by way of apron," as an Englishwoman put it after a 1764–65 visit; other visitors noted sheepskin caps, and small bags hung around the neck.[93] When employed on farms, where their knowledge of animal husbandry was particularly valued, some may have worn this garb, if sometimes with the addition of a European hat; the two men walking in the right foreground of Plate 7b illustrate both the original and the modified styles.[94] But for the most part they dressed just like the slaves who performed the same tasks – so much so, indeed, that modern scholars often find it almost impossible to distinguish them – and they often received items of apparel as part of their pay package.[95] Khoikhoi insisted on hats, but if contemporary images are any guide, slaves wore them as well, despite prohibitions; neither group of laborers, however, wore shoes, though Khoikhoi might wear sandals of their own manufacture.[96] Similarly, in the Río de la Plata and Brazil, Indians employed for wages on plantations received as pay precisely the same items (shirts and breeches), made of the same fabrics (linens and perhaps woolens), as enslaved laborers.[97]

Though essentially unknown in Iberian America, indentured servants (engagés) supplied a critical European labor force in the British and French Caribbean as well as in their North American mainland colonies.[98] Service under indenture, which drew on a venerable Old World lineage of contractual service, involved presumably negotiated relationships with stipulated rules, duration, and final payment ("freedom dues"). Yet if indentured servants never lost their legal personhood, their contracts were longer and more restrictive than most in Europe: For three to seven years they toiled under the control and discipline of employers who were in return responsible for paying some combination of wages, food, lodging, and clothing.[99]

Anxious to attract immigrants, British Caribbean colonies legislated clothing (and food) provision for indentured servants. In Jamaica, from some point prior to 1681 "the lawes of the island" mandated for men four each of hats or caps, white or blue ozenbrig shirts, neckcloths, pairs of white or blue ozenbrig breeches, and pairs of ozenbrig or cotton stockings, and twelve pairs of English shoes; for women, four each of calico "hoods," "coiffes" (close-fitting caps), white or blue ozenbrig "smocks," white or blue ozenbrig petticoats, and pairs of ozenbrig or cotton stockings, along with six pairs of English shoes and one coarse woolen gown or waistcoat, obviously intended as an outer garment. For both genders, the garments were to be distributed quarterly "every year during their servitude."[100] The statute claimed that this was "suffitient and convenien[t] cloathing according to the custome of this island," though from 1681 the allowance was cut down to three of each item for men (and just one hat or cap), "and to the Woman proportionably."[101]

Even in its reduced form, the provision was far superior to slaves' statutory entitlement: not so much in color or fabric – where despite the marginal (and optional) presence of a few cotton items, blue and white ozenbrig linens reigned supreme – as in variety and quantity of garments, notably including European-style footwear and headgear, and perhaps ankle-length rather than knee breeches. With these costumes, indentured servants would have stood out from slaves both by the the state of their dress – which could have been washed and renewed regularly – and by visible symbols of freedom, literally from head to toe.[102]

How closely practice resembled legislation is debatable. Already in 1687 an English visitor deemed the garb "pore," adding that it was "seldom given 'em [servants]"; in his opinion, this was part of the reason that "English servants labouriously weare out their fouer years' servitude, or rather slavarey."[103] Nearly a century later, the planter Edward Long, who detested indentured servants – "the very dregs of the three [united] kingdoms" – and was pleased that their numbers had fallen steeply, nonetheless also questioned whether employers regularly provided the dress allotment. Yet he outlined the same outfit as prescribed in the 1681 law, suggesting that at least in the

Jamaican imaginary, indentured men and women should be sartorially distinguished from their enslaved counterparts.[104]

In what is ostensibly a more empirical report, Charles Leslie wrote in 1739 that servants dressed simply, women in gowns and "plain headclothes," men without stockings. Still, servant men did wear "frocks" (jackets or coats) with buttons over speckled shirts and long trousers; and both genders were sharply differentiated from male and female slaves who "go mostly naked" (most likely meaning clothed only below the waist).[105] A smattering of runaway advertisements from 1718–30 supports Leslie's depiction, even though the dress listings were clearly incomplete. Seven of the ten indentured male servants described had at least breeches and jacket, six had woolen coats (for three, it was the only garment cited), others had speckled shirts, shoes and stockings, a waistcoat, a hat.[106] Though none had abundant apparel, they all had more than enslaved men, and their outfits included items rarely cited in descriptions of bondsmen. Just as important, indentured servants received finished garments, in contrast to slaves who often had to fashion their own as best they could. In the Caribbean heat, of course, indentured servants, like slaves, probably removed some apparel when at work.

Though initially important for overcoming labor shortages in South Carolina as in other continental plantation colonies, indentured service waned from the later seventeenth century as the number of enslaved laborers surged.[107] Just four (all men in 1732) can be found in runaway advertisements, and the dress information is minimal. Still, the citation of red, blue, and cinnamon-colored coats, of a brown double-breasted pea jacket, and of blue stockings does suggest that indentured servants' outfits comprised some different garments than those of slaves.[108] Bolzius's attudinally revealing calculation of what it cost "if one wants to keep the white servants in a Christian way and not like Negroes [slaves]" – which not all employers did, he conceded – also points to a dichotomy at least of quantity and probably variety, since annual food and clothing costs for servants were four times those of slaves (£8 as against £2).[109] South Carolina's freedom dues, initially promulgated in 1717 and reiterated in 1744, indicate that indentured servants were presumed both to have basic garments that, as runaway advertisements reveal, slaves regularly wore – for men, breeches and shirt; for women, petticoat and shift – but also to receive some lengths of fabric: coarse woolen kersey, halfthicks, and even (optionally for women from 1744) plains. In addition, all indentured servants were to be given coats, and women "waistcoats" (probably short jackets), shoes, stockings, hats or caps, and aprons; their linen was to be "white" (which ruled out most varieties used for slaves) and men might receive broadcloth; all the items were to be "new" or "good"; and, in contrast to slave appareling, where laws left it to masters to decide what was "sufficient" dress, the precise dress items were carefully spelled out.[110]

For French indentured servants, attire, like other provisioning arrangements, was a matter of contractual negotiation rather than statutory requirement. Men bound for the Caribbean were commonly outfitted either at embarkation in France or upon disembarkation in the Antilles; those headed to Canada were clothed upon arrival in the New World. In the West Indies, they received inexpensive woolen or linen suits (*habits* comprising jackets, breeches, and perhaps coats), three or four linen shirts, cravats, stockings, new or remade shoes, and a cap or, after about 1670, a hat. As in British slave colonies, the provision of ready-made items meant that indentured servants in French colonies did not have to tailor their own apparel. Female servants were many fewer in number but much sought, so they could negotiate for better and more distinctive wardrobes: a good-quality woolen or linen skirt, several handkerchiefs (of cotton or even silk rather than linen), a silk cap, gloves, ribbons, some lace decorations.[111] Notably, indentured servants bargained not only for different items and much more expensive fabrics than enslaved women or men, but also for adornments, never mentioned in slaves' dress allotments.

Though some French colonial masters did provide a yearly outfit or even two during *engagés'* terms of service, most servants received wages with which to provide for themselves, according to their own tastes.[112] If French servants' choices followed the template of the initial dress rations, they, like their counterparts in British colonies, would have had some garb that slaves also wore, and at labor they might well have been dressed much the same. But they would have had larger wardrobes and more diverse types of garments, and very likely would purchase different qualities of linens than slaves, perhaps including cottons, not to mention ornamentation.[113] Quotidian dress differences among European indentured servants and African or Amerindian slaves were not dramatic, but they were real and easily visible.

"Better cloaths for holiday-wear": slave special-occasion self-dressing

While a ubiquitous and persistent uniform was central to the daily material life of bondsmen and bondswomen in slave societies around the
Atlantic, contemporaries and historians have devoted more attention to
instances where slaves had more abundant or distinctive dress. The
frequent placement of enslaved individuals dressed this way in the center
of images visually symbolized this state of affairs. Such apparel might take
the form of a special costume designed to exhibit the domination of the
free donor and the subordination of the enslaved recipient. The expensive
dress of slave mistresses – "splendid muslins, calicoes, and [light, brightly
colored silk] persians," in one telling – and the elaborate and often
painfully uncomfortable livery imposed on personal servants so that
their masters could publicly manifest social standing, were widely noted
instances.[114] "Planters who want to have proper lackeys," Labat
contended, "dress them in *candales* and colored doublets, with braid on
their livery, with a turban instead of a hat, with earrings, and a silver
carquant with their arms." However, "only a few people of quality . . .
have their lackeys shod" ("that is, having stockings & shoes"), eloquent
testimony to the tenacious hold on free colonists' mentality of one of the
central symbols of enslavement, even in a moment of ostentatious settler
self-promotion.[115] In a late eighteenth-century print from Brazil, the
livery worn by two sedan-chair-carrying slaves – breeches and coats of
rich deep blue woolen fabric decorated with gilt buttons, as well as
brilliant yellow silk waistcoats, shirts ruffled at the neck, and black
hats – is only subtly distinguished from the dress of the white man
accompanying them by the slaves' smaller and undecorated hats, absence
of ruffles at the wrist, shorter coats, but much more evidently by the
slaves' lack of shoes and stockings (Plate 8).

  Though usually less lavishly garbed than the liveried, regular
house servants were likely to receive better and often more clothing
than field laborers, and unlike the latter they usually received finished
garments rather than lengths of fabric that they themselves had to
tailor.[116] Female domestics in Brunias's paintings, such as Plate 9, for
instance, typically wear a plain white shift and single-color skirt,
together with a headwrap, the whole forming a less colorful, less costly,
little adorned, and explicitly unshod version of the attire worn by the
women whom they serve.

More often, however, it was slaves' showy self-dressing that excited commentary. Urban slaves, particularly artisans, who lived and worked apart from their owners, typically provided their own apparel, and thus were able to dress more as they pleased. "The skilled Negroes in Charlestown," Bolzius asserted, "are very well dressed," though he did not elaborate.[117] In comparison with field hands, his claim was apt. Nevertheless, South Carolina runaway advertisements indicate that urban slaves' ordinary outfits were characterized by greater abundance and variety more than by lavishness: When Tom, "used to the house carpenter's trade," ran away, he had on a surtout coat made of blanketing, ozenbrig shirt and breeches, and a green jacket.[118] In Saint-Domingue, too, the creole wigmaker and violin player Baptiste ran off in a pair of black velvet breeches (he "ordinarily wears them," his master assured readers), but otherwise only a *veste*.[119]

Much more impressive was the dress intended for special occasions that even field hands could purportedly assemble through additional labor or marketing. "Not only in towns" was slave sartorial *"coquetterie"* apparent, exclaimed the creole and perhaps mulatto French West Indian lawyer, colonial official, and slaveowner Médéric Louis Élie Moreau de Saint-Méry; on Sundays, "the man who has handled a hoe or other tools all the week long" dressed up so stylishly that "you'd be hard pressed to recognize him under his fine apparel."[120]

At the end of the seventeenth century, Labat had enumerated what slaves in the French Caribbean "who work enough on their own account to be able to buy all these things at their own expense" donned "when they dress themselves on Sundays and holidays." Men boasted "a handsome shirt with narrow drawers of white linen," together with a *"candale"* made of "colored linen or light woolen." If "prosperous enough," they wore silver or jeweled shirt cuff and collar buttons ("otherwise, they put ribbons in the same places"), while "over their shirts, they wear a little doublet without tails." When young, they wore earrings in both ears, "like women," but when married "just one." Only "rarely" did they wear "cravats and fitted coats [*justaucorps*]," but "when their heads are covered with a hat, they're good looking, and usually they're well turned out." The "festive dress" of enslaved women typically included two skirts, a colored one underneath, and above it another of "fine white cotton or muslin." To them was added "a *corset* [a sleeveless fitted but stayless garment for the upper torso] with small tails that's white or of the same color as their under-skirt," decorated with a cascading beribboned ornament called an *"échelle"* (ladder), all set off with gold and silver jewelry. Lace adorned their shifts, "and their headdress is made of very fine, very white linen with lace." As they, too, "are usually very well put together, if they only be well dressed they look very good."[121]

A century later, Moreau de Saint-Méry rendered an equally effusive description that revealed change as well as continuity in slave fancy self-dressing. In his account, as in Labat's, the basic outfit (shirt or shift, trousers or skirt) is the implicit starting point of slaves' special dress. In each account, too, upgraded fabrics and distinctive ways of forming and wearing ensembles were as important as supplementary garments, and festive dress was as notable for its adornments as for its apparel: The difference must have been particularly striking in comparison with the dull plainness of ordinary dress. But special wardrobes were not static. Woolens and lace were absent from Moreau de Saint-Méry's scenario, over-garments had become fewer, and cottons played a new role in the form of handkerchiefs deployed over the body, most spectacularly as elaborate headgear. This style may have drawn on African models, and on the contemporary European craze for the turban – but it also made excellent sense as a form of protection in a hot climate.[122]

Enslaved men acquired "a better quality of linen," often white, for some outfits; added "more or less fine" hats, jackets, shoes, and "kerchiefs, more or less expensive," to their conventional shirts and breeches; and donned breeches of one variety of linen and shirt of another ("a kind of affectation" (*recherche*) in Moreau de Saint-Méry's opinion), or special shirt collars, cuffs, and shoulder-straps. Though less dazzling than those in Labat's telling, unique items did feature in Moreau de Saint-Méry's: hats with folded brims, long trousers ("because the *culotte* of the field laborer is always short"), and multiple handkerchiefs "on the head, around the throat, and in the pockets." While pursuing the same strategies, slave women effected a greater transformation of their "ordinary dress." Diverse qualities of linen permitted "many nuances," and even more striking possibilities were realized with expensive cottons and silks for skirts, not to mention richly dyed Indian cotton handkerchiefs, gold and garnet jewelry, "beautiful white or black felt hats" beribboned with silk or gold, hip-length jackets (*casaquins*), leather mules, "and sometimes even stockings." But it was expensive headscarves – "ten or twelve handkerchiefs one on top of the other to form an enormous cap (*bonnet*)" and that required not simply matching neck and pocket kerchiefs but a particular manner of walking and self-presentation – that to Moreau de Saint-Méry defined the specificity of enslaved women's sartorial deployment.[123]

These enthusiastic depictions of slave festive magnificence are partisan and exaggerated, of course. Even apart from Moreau de Saint-Méry's constant insistence throughout his two-volume text on the benign nature of slavery, it is hard to credit his assertion that ordinary male slaves "often" had wardrobes worth more than half an overseer's annual salary or that slave women had up to one hundred outfits, valued at more than twice that salary.[124] But Labat and Moreau de Saint-Méry do point to important features that other contemporary sources confirm. Most immediately striking was slaves' ability to obtain at least some fashionable fabrics and garments, "to furnish themselves with a wardrobe of better cloaths for holiday-wear," as one Jamaican put it.[125] It was items like these – good-quality dimity *veste* and breeches, two fashionable cotton *gilet*-style waistcoats – that Apollon carefully wrapped in a Cholet handkerchief before taking off, or that distinguished Victoire in her deep-colored calico skirt and multicolored neck and headscarves.[126] And not only better. As all the sources make clear, their acquisitions also included items like long pants, footwear, headgear, and adornments that were normally out of reach or out of bounds. The resulting raiment thus stood out from slaves' quotidian dress by its coverage of the body. Moreau de Saint-Méry understood this as a kind of disguise; even more it was at once a sharp alternative to the exposure enforced by even the most complete iteration of the work outfit and an appropriation of key symbols of freedom.

The possibilities for fancier dressing may have been particularly expansive in the Caribbean, where slave marketing was highly developed.[127] But special slave garb was deployed, and evoked anxieties, throughout the Atlantic: Such apparel on the enslaved was understood as both an overt and a tacit challenge to the social ordering that dress expressed and consolidated. In light of its role as a summary symbol of enslavement, footwear was particularly noted when it appeared in bondspeople's self-chosen dress – thus Moreau de Saint-Méry expressly contrasted the shoes of slave "luxury" (*luxe*) with the quotidian fact that "slaves have bare feet" – and at least in the VOC colonies footwear was forbidden to the enslaved by law.[128]

More generally, slave fancy self-dressing threatened status and gender distinctions that dress was traditionally mobilized to display and that sumptuary laws had long been instituted to guarantee.[129] If such laws were of waning significance in metropolitan Europe, the concerns they encapsulated continued to perturb European colonies, taking on additional urgency in the context of chattel slavery. Thus statutes forbidding the enslaved to wear expensive fabrics (notably silks), costly jewelry, and sometimes specific articles of clothing, began to appear as early as the mid-sixteenth century in Spanish Peru. Eventually they spread to many other slave societies in which the unfree had managed to secure resources enabling them to acquire goods and thus to construct appearances that violated dress conventions designed to proclaim their subordinate status.[130]

Many such statutes justified dress prohibitions by reference to threats to public order posed by slaves who allegedly stole fancy apparel or bought it with ill-gotten gains from other crimes.[131] Two other concerns appeared more insistently from the late seventeenth century. One pertained to "luxury" (luxe, luxo, lujo) as that concept became central to early modern debates about morality, social rank, consumer behavior, and economic growth.[132] In eighteenth-century Europe, luxury underwent a gradual if incomplete redefinition from social and individual sin to positive economic benefit and manifestation of sociability, while the cultural capital embodied by "taste" supplanted officially ordered consumption as the key manifestation of hierarchic distinction. Together, these trends toward informal ways of drawing sartorial borders doomed sumptuary regulations.

Moreau de Saint-Méry's account shows the effects of this development. Though his tone is somewhat condescending, he invokes "luxe" neutrally or even positively to mean something much like fashion (mode), involving "degrees" of elaboration and expense and producing striking effects.[133] But to colonial officials, luxury retained its negative meaning. In an echo of Europe's long correlation of the female gender with luxury – whether traditionally understood as vice or newly as virtue – bondswomen were said to be especially prone to ostentation and were often alleged or implied to engage in prostitution in order to be able to buy expensive fabrics and adornments, though slave men might also be denounced for "excess and luxury."[134] By that metric, sumptuary laws remained an appropriate way to protect (or, in the colonial context, to create) a hierarchic social order with the unfree as the bottom rank defined by exclusion from "fine fabrics" and jewels and thus from the dress possibilities of the free.[135]

In societies where entrepreneurial marketing by slaves was especially well established and where individual emancipations gave rise to a sizeable group of free blacks or free persons of color, thus complicating visual recognition of freedom and unfreedom, luxury was increasingly deemed a danger that overspilled the unfree–free boundary, to be, that is, a matter of race *tout court*. Attempts were accordingly made to adjust sumptuary laws: Free persons of color were grouped together with slaves. All were forbidden to wear certain fabrics and/or attire – sometimes, as in Brazil, the prohibition was cast only in terms of race (blacks and mulattoes); elsewhere, as in the Cape Colony, emancipated slave women were assigned specific fabrics, slaves others. But no matter what the details, dress was to correlate with skin color instead of legal status, and the ability to wear garments perceived as excessively fancy was sharply restricted for non-whites. As Silvia Hunold Lara has pointed out, henceforth luxury was to be reserved for whites.[136]

Illustrations of the kind of very fancy dress that Labat and Moreau de Saint-Méry described and sumptuary laws decried are found in the works by or based on Agostino Brunias. For example, the female spectator on the extreme right in Figure 4.4 gives a good sense of this fashion, and the women on the far left and behind the male dancer manifest variations.[137] However, the central female dancer in the image shows – and other sources, including the bulk of Brunias's work and Labat's and Moreau de Saint-Méry's texts, corroborate – something less spectacular but no less impressive: By dint of their own efforts, an indeterminable but not insignificant number of slaves managed to obtain and don for special occasions some apparel that was cleaner, more capacious, and more abundant than their daily outfit. Compared with their quotidian costume, the stylish self-fashioning enslaved woman or man acquired finer, more colorful, and more varied fabrics – dazzling white linens, colorful cottons, and printed linens – and supplementary and distinctive items, not only apparel but adornments: ribbons, trim, lace, rings, bracelets, glass bead necklaces, fancy buttons.[138]

Images from late eighteenth-century Brazil suggest, too, that a multiplicity of garments, the presence of footwear, and brighter-colored fabrics differentiated fancier garb from ordinary.[139] What is more, the sources agree that bondsmen and bondswomen deployed this apparel in unique ways. Fancy dress and normal outfits shared garments and fibers.

DANSE DE NÉGRES.

4.4 *Danse de Négres / Slaves dancing,* from Nicolas Ponce, *Recueil de vues des lieux principaux de la colonie françoise de Saint-Domingue* (Paris : Moreau de Saint-Méry, Ponce, Phélipeau, 1791), pl. 26.

Although there is no evidence that Agostino Brunias ever visited Saint-Domingue, the engraving, derived from a Brunias painting, was intended for Moreau de Saint-Méry 1784–90, a compilation of French Caribbean colonial laws.

But the synthesis of upgrades, additions, and bearing – the hybrid fashion, in short – that they forged was transformative. No wonder Moreau de Saint-Méry marveled at (and rued) the "affectation" and the "many nuances," resulting in "metamorphosis," that unfolded before his eyes.

This kind of transformation – subtle but tangible – obtained in other slave societies for which we have evidence, though slave fancy dress outside the Caribbean and Brazil seems to have been more subdued. A few runaway advertisements in South Carolina provide glimpses of fashionable slaves, such as Othello, who boasted a fustian frock, purple halfthicks breeches and jacket, blue cloth coat, and old silver laced hat.[140] Similarly, supplementary pieces, along with more varied and brighter colors, appear in "The Old Plantation" (Plate 10), tentatively identified as having been painted near Beaufort, South Carolina, in the late eighteenth century, and thus likely contemporary with Brunias's paintings.[141] The overall palette, the absence of patterned-fabric female garments apart from handkerchiefs, the cut of the women's dress, the probably woolen outerwear on nearly all men, the less intricate headwraps, the minimal jewelry (apart from male earrings) – all this demarcates the enslaved individuals shown in the South Carolina image from their fellows in the Caribbean. But the same process of syncretic material culture formation is at work, creating a distinctive special-occasion dress regime of the enslaved.[142] Significantly, however, the difference between Carolinian and Caribbean fancy dress is more marked than in the variations in the workaday outfits of each. A substantially similar enslaved daily uniform came to characterize plantation colonies in the Atlantic, based mainly on masters' decisions to identify the enslaved as definitively such. But when the enslaved had control, they crafted more locally distinctive dress that incorporated identifications with the free.

The connections between the Caribbean and New Orleans suggest that "finery" of the enslaved in Louisiana shared some characteristics with their Antillean counterparts; tenuous economic conditions and recurrent supply problems, however, may have curbed the emergence of abundant or lavish slave wardrobes along the lower Mississippi. When the eleven-year-old Babete stole some cash in 1765, the four ells of calico and two ells of more expensive cotton cloth that she bought, and the red linen that she unsuccessfully sought, would certainly have created skirts that stood out in quality and probably color from those that masters distributed. Babete also purchased several items denotative of "luxury": a short over-jacket, a silk handkerchief, and a cheap gold ring.[143] In the course of the many burglaries in which he was involved in 1764–66, the "thief and runaway" Louis acquired a mixture of cloth, clothing, and related items: velvet and blue woolen breeches, ruffled shirts, vests, silk stockings, a hat banded with gold braid, a silver buckle, and red ribbons; but also cheap cotton, wool, and linen breeches, linen thread stockings, unbleached linen shirts and others of hempen striped *gingas* linen, lengths of rough, inexpensive varieties of hempen *brin*, Breton, and blue and white checked or striped *fil d'épreuve* linen and, of coarse, heavy *cotonade*. It is unclear which items Louis intended to keep for himself (or for gifts) and which were to be fenced.[144] But he definitely had at hand stylish garments, fabrics, accessories, and decorations that would at the least have enabled him (or those he made gifts to) to embellish a familiar outfit, at most to construct a strikingly new one.

With special-occasion dress, enslaved men and women distinguished themselves from their workaday personae, asserting thereby not the inexistence of bondage but their dignity within it. Their deployments of such dress exploited dominant conventions of the time. Opting for brilliant white linens, for instance, associated bondsmen and bondswomen with a growing orientation to cleanliness-as-civility.[145] At the same time, fashionable slave dress signaled autonomous sartorial styles and modes of behavior, as contemporary observers recognized, whether grudgingly or respectfully. According to Moreau de Saint-Méry, "a great pleasure" was the "*assortiment*," which involved, "on certain important holidays," two or more enslaved women "dressing exactly the same" before "going for a walk or to dance."[146] Assembling the resources needed to dress in these ways required a great deal of effort and could not erase distinctions between the unfree and the free. But within the limits of a harsh system, fancy attiring enabled the enslaved to innovate dress regimes that expressed their own fashion preferences, endowing them with some measure of control, however temporary, over their self-presentation.

"Had on, when he went away": slave and servant dress in societies-with-slaves

In contrast to slave societies, societies-with-slaves had no explicit laws to set provisioning norms and obligations; the socioeconomic, political, and legal systems that ordered the material life of the minority of permanent bondsmen and bondswomen were more informal, local, and ad hoc than in slave colonies. At the same time, all colonies shared prevailing attitudes toward the enslaved and knowledge of dress conventions, and all were served by merchants from the same metropoles. Thus it is unsurprising that in the Philadelphia area, where slaves formed a small minority of the population, jackets, breeches, gowns, and frocks were widely worn by the enslaved, nor that most of their garments were made out of cheap linens and woolens.[147] Ned's apparel (described in the runaway advertisement with which this chapter began) would not have been out of place in South Carolina or other slave colonies. But whereas most slaves in those societies had just a basic outfit, around Philadelphia they typically had more varied and greater amounts of ordinary apparel, and that gap widened as time went on.[148]

The ruder mid-Atlantic climate explains some of the difference. More important, bondspeople in societies-with-slaves mostly labored individually or in small groups alongside indentured and free persons rather than in tasks that were exclusively the domain of the enslaved, and they typically lived in close proximity to their employers and fellow workers. In the rare instances where a big estate was predominantly staffed by slaves, however, such as the Penn family's country seat outside Philadelphia, enslaved men wore a typical slave outfit of a jacket, waistcoat, or vest with breeches, enslaved women jackets, coats, and some sort of gown or frock.[149] The majority of slaves, though, wore apparel that differed little if at all from that of their workmates, although as Ned's case shows, shoes or their absence might well be among the few distinctions, and as James Jones's example likewise demonstrates, a slave might well have a substantial wardrobe.

Normally, men of both groups wore hats or caps (often both), shoes, and stockings, as well as both coats and jackets over shirts and breeches.[150] All regularly dressed mainly in cheap fabrics, but chose from a wider range than in slave colonies (thirty-five types for Pennsylvania slaves in the 1760s, as against twenty-five in South Carolina advertisements). By the 1760s, mixed-fiber cloth (largely linen-cotton check) and cottons each accounted for about a tenth of garments among both groups of Pennsylvania laborers, both shares far above what was found in South Carolina; correlatively, woolens lost ground among slaves and indentured servants alike, as both – again in contrast to their counterparts in slave societies – shared in Atlantic-wide trends. In addition, the choices of garment fabric for both groups were dispersed much more evenly across a spectrum that was also broader than in plantation colonies: No single type dominated as plains did in South Carolina, kersey in Jamaica, *brin* in Saint-Domingue.[151] Slaves in and around Philadelphia were also less demarcated by the color of their clothing. While some garments were tailored of white and blue fabrics, shades of gray and brown were more conspicuous, and lively hues like greens, yellows, and reds became increasingly common as time went on.

Precisely the same lightening trend occurred in the clothing of indentured males, aided, as among slaves, by the greater popularity of cottons, which in general were livelier and more varied in color than the linens that they supplanted.

To be sure, the apparel of the two groups did exhibit some differences. Indentured servants' garments drew on a larger variety of fabrics (sixty-six in the 1760s as against thirty-five for slaves), they had slightly more basic items on average (just over four as against just under four among slaves), and they were a bit more likely to have things like silk handkerchiefs or velvet or plush jackets. But these were marginal divergences (and in some part may be due to the much larger number of indentured servants in the notices); what is more, slave dress was becoming more like that of the indentured, with a bigger growth in number of garments (a rise of one-third between the 1730s and 1760s as against one tenth among the indentured), larger increase in fabric varieties, more pronounced lightening of both individual garments and overall wardrobes. With very few exceptions, it would be an exaggeration to characterize either the enslaved or the indentured Philadelphia-area runaways as elaborately clothed. But not only did the Pennsylvania runaway advertisements regularly list considerably more apparel than that described for any free or enslaved runaway South Carolinian of the time, but in most instances they described the same costumes for indentured servants and the permanently enslaved.

The numbers, working conditions, and dress situation of slaves in the Montreal area were much the same as around Philadelphia, though in New France most were Amerindians rather than Africans. Employed in the fur trades, as domestic servants, on farms, and in many other jobs, Native American bondspeople comprised up to 5 percent of New France's population in the eighteenth century.[152] Our knowledge about these individuals is minimal, and scantier yet about their appearance. Scraps of information strongly suggest, however, that enslaved individuals in New France dressed no differently than, and in many cases as well as, the free persons among whom they lived: wearing a draped blanket and leggings like other Native American males at Michilimacinac, European-style tailored garments like hemp linen shirts and shifts, cotton aprons, flannel petticoats, *mantelets* (the New France term for *casaquins*), double-breasted twilled woolen *mazamet* vests, bonnets, caps, stockings, and gloves in Montreal.[153] Amerindians (at least those allied with the French) also seem to have dressed the people whom they enslaved in the same way as themselves. In a 1735 watercolor of individuals from the Illinois, Fox, and Atakapa nations, a figure labeled "Fox Indian slave" (*Renarde sauvagesse esclave*) wears a short red skirt or matchcoat, exactly the same apparel as a clearly free Native woman. The image also depicts an African boy, who, like all the Indian males shown, wears a breechclout, though unlike virtually all the others he has no red body paint, instead sporting a distinctive red cap.[154]

In short, enslaved people living in societies-with-slaves where they formed only a minority of the population were incorporated into the majority textile culture rather than being segregated into distinctive, easily identifiable garb. Few dressed or were clothed in racially marked fabrics or singular work uniforms; no specific garments or fabrics were differentially named, mandated, or furnished to them; and they wore shoes, stockings, and hats like others of their occupational and socioeconomic level. By the same token, however, they did not develop their own special dress regimes. Participation in the dominant material culture meant that slaves in predominantly non-slave societies did not have to engage in self-fashioning, but it also meant that they had less occasion to do so. Bondsmen and bondswomen in slave societies were less favored in dress than their counterparts in societies-with-slaves, yet they might enjoy more ability to self-fashion sartorially.

The irony of slave dress

Dress regimes did not escape the distorting power of slavery. Though imposed apparel did not necessarily occupy the entire sartorial space of the enslaved, it always set the parameters of their dress. The particulars of fabric, mode of provision, and details such as color and pattern varied by climatic zone, commercial orientation, imperial policy, and colonial statute, as well as by individual master, and specific conditions of labor modified the ways in which bondsmen and bondswomen actually dressed. But the basic outfit was remarkably similar, and remarkably simple, around the Atlantic. This was not the result of a scheme to redress and thus to "civilize" slaves, but an expedient to exploit them as cheaply as possible. Yet the same drive for efficiency frequently, if usually unintentionally, gave many slaves some scope for self-fashioning. This was hardly a planters' gift, since it demanded additional self-exploitation – or, through theft, the exploitation of others, often inside slaves' own communities – within an already highly exploitative system. The self-fashioning it permitted, moreover, was restricted save, perhaps, in a few exceptional situations. One Saint-Domingue commentator pointedly noted that silks were off-limits: "only white men and women wear them," and the same held true for other expensive fabrics and items, whether or not enforced by sumptuary laws.[155] Yet the creation of their own dress was not simply a material thing. Fearfully or with sneaking admiration, observers remarked on the transformation that enslaved men and women wrought upon themselves as they dressed themselves in distinctive styles.

Ironically, the greatest possibility for such activity was found in colonies – most of all in the Caribbean – where slaves were most neglected, where indifferent or ignorant owners kept the greatest distance from slaves, and where the violence of a violent system was most apparent.[156] To be sure, in colonies with slaves, bondspeople enjoyed superior opportunities to acquire material goods and to integrate into the larger consumer society – on its terms.[157] But the price was foreclosure of the possibility of developing a distinctive – if isolated – dress culture like that which appeared in slave societies. Where dress constraint was weakest, so was slave self-fashioning.

5 DRESSING FREE SETTLERS IN THE "TORRID ZONE"

There is great luxury in the Antilles. People are especially desirous of fine linen, and because most don't wear a doublet they have very beautiful Holland linen shirts with neckcloths more than an ell and a half long. Breeches are made from handsome broadcloth or beautiful serge embroidered with gold and silver braid, or covered with lots of trim ... Cloaks are only worn when it's raining, or for travel.[1]

Our English belles in Jamaica ... do not scruple to wear the thickest winter silks and sattins; and are sometimes ready to sink under the weight of rich gold or silver brocades. Their headdress varies with the *ton* at home; the winter fashions of *London* arrive here at the setting in of hot weather ... Nothing surely can be more preposterous, and absurd, than for persons residing in the West-Indies, to adhere rigidly to all the European customs and manners; which, though perhaps not inconvenient in a cold Northern air, are certainly improper, ridiculous, and detrimental, in a hot climate.[2]

European settlers in the Atlantic colonies brought dress regimes with them, and they retained commercial, political, cultural, and personal links with their homelands that could serve to perpetuate styles, habits, even garments. Yet in the colonies they encountered diverse geoclimatic conditions and socioeconomic ecologies, disposed of dissimilar resources, and developed novel ambitions and identifications. How they adapted sartorially to their new environments is the subject of the next two chapters. Employing sources concerned particularly with Jamaica, Saint-Domingue, and Salvador da Bahia, Chapter 5 investigates free settler dress regimes in tropical Atlantic colonies. It begins with contemporary accounts that identified but disparately evaluated a cluster of issues defining torrid-zone free settler dress, then establishes the general sartorial profile of the three colonies, before focusing on the role of some specific social groups in promoting or resisting sartorial change.

"Colonial livery" in the eyes of contemporaries

As the excerpts from the French missionary and botanist Jean-Baptiste Du Tertre and the Anglo-Jamaican planter Edward Long indicate, seventeenth- and eighteenth-century commentators often remarked on the allegedly ostentatious dress of settlers in tropical American colonies.[3] By some accounts, virtually all colonists indulged a taste for luxury, even to excess. In 1686, according to a clergyman in Port Royal, Jamaica's bustling slave, contraband, and privateering port, "even a cooper's wife could 'go forth in the best flowered silk and the richest silver and gold lace.'"[4] The French Dominican Jean-Baptiste Labat assured his readers that when it came to "the upkeep of settlers" in the Antilles, merchants could never ship "too many" or "too well chosen" goods, nor those that were "too fashionable, too luxurious, and too expensive," since "the finest linens, the most beautiful & most elabo-rately worked muslins . . . every kind of broadcloth, silk, gold, and silver stuffs, gold braid . . . the finest laces," and yet other adornments and accessories would "sell very well, and [at] a high price and quickly."[5] Other observers identified those particularly prone to excessive sartorial display. "The merchants and gentrey live here [Port Royal] to the hights of splendor, in full ease and plenty, being sumptuously arrayed," declared the visitor John Taylor in 1687.[6] A century later, Michel Réné Hilliard d'Auberteuil, lawyer of Saint-Domingue, contended that colonial townspeople, civilian and military officials, and men engaged in commerce dressed in an especially lavish manner, "covered with jewels, embroidery, and ribbons."[7]

As in the European metropoles, luxury in attire was frequently described as a notably female attribute. The indictment might denounce all settler women or pick out specific categories, such as officers' wives, whom Du Tertre claimed dressed in "*des-habilles* of taffeta or colored satin" embellished with ribbon and lace.[8] The purported habits of free women of color received most emphasis. Already in 1709, the Salvador municipal government petitioned the Portuguese crown to forbid the supposedly lavish dress of free mulattas as well as enslaved women,

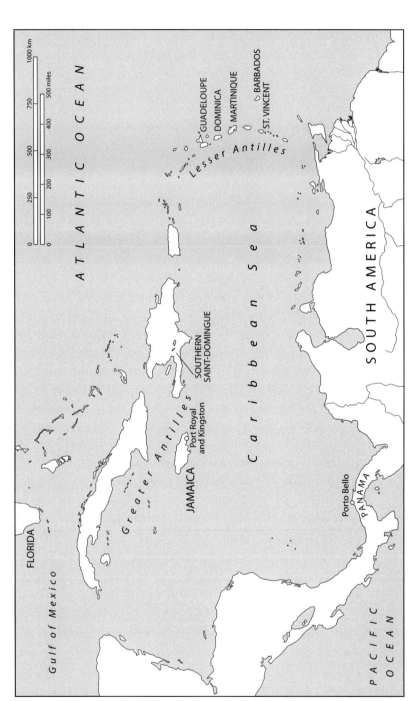

Map 5.1 The early modern West Indies

while Moreau de Saint-Méry insisted that for *mulâtresses*, "luxury consists, almost entirely, in a single object, dress," so "everything is devoted to clothing."[9]

No matter what their attitude to luxury or to its alleged proponents, contemporaries took it as axiomatic that settlers in the "torrid zone" should redress themselves in a manner appropriate to dwelling under "an always scorching sun."[10] Some were said to have done so out of economic necessity. In Jamaica "you shall see," Taylor averred, "a common woman only in her smock ore linnen peticote, barefooted, without shoo or stockins, with a strawn hatt and a red tobacco pipe in their mouths."[11] A century later, according to Hilliard d'Auberteuil, "humbler people, estate stewards, peddlers" in Saint-Domingue had the habit, "so suitable for hot climes," of wearing "only light jackets" rather than the "velvet suits" that the elite donned to show off.[12]

But luxury and light apparel were not necessarily incompatible. Just before castigating Jamaican clothing, Long himself had penned a rhapsodic sketch of the dress of "our Spanish neighbours," which he praised for "richness" as well as simplicity, "loose" fit, "light" materials, and avoidance of excess attire.[13] Perhaps not only the Spanish got it right. Du Tertre's "great luxury," after all, highlights not only a preference for linen but the absence of jackets and outerwear. After describing the correct "colonial livery" as "fashionable luxury" that "requires not rich fabrics but light ones; expensive, delicately woven linens, their simplicity set off by striking jewels," Moreau de Saint-Méry avowed that white women born in Saint-Domingue usually "dressed in the light style that the climate demands."[14]

These divergent, when not contradictory, reports suggest important issues about the appareling habits of free settlers: the degree to which they relied on metropolitan fashions, the definition and significance of "luxury" in colonial attire, the content and reach of a common "torrid zone" settler dress regime or "colonial livery," the influence of empire, occupation, gender, and race on settler sartorial practices. Analysis of probate inventories can help elucidate these topics.

"Abundance of finery" or "abundance of comfort"?[15]

In their actual luggage or in their minds, free male European settlers of the later seventeenth century carried breeches, doublets (or, increasingly, waistcoats or vests), coats (sometimes the three first garments were summed up as a "suit"), shoes or boots and stockings, some type of hat, and usually shirts. Their female counterparts arrived with long skirts, short jackets or bodices (and/or gowns with underskirts or petticoats), aprons, shoes and stockings, caps of some sort, cloak or mantle, and, like men, more and more often they had smocks or shifts. Both genders sought as full body coverage as possible, though the dress of the laboring population tended to be looser and shorter than that of the leisured.[16] Despite some variation – just as in Europe – these free settler outfits were as widely worn, or at least as widely owned, as the basic outfit of enslaved men and women.

To judge by Jamaican inventories, the only ones extant from the period, wardrobes bore a strong metropolitan imprint but were starting to accommodate warmer weather; in addition, they had luxurious items but overall were modest.[17] Basic and outer garments were tailored mainly from woolens (37 percent), and linens (28 percent), though silks (18 percent) and cottons (16 percent) together accounted for a third.[18] Comparison with merchant stocks (Table 2.1) suggests that the exiguous amounts of cottons in shops were likely destined in the main for the dress of the island's free settlers, along with a substantial share of the woolens, and that while many silks may have been destined for Spanish consumers, many likewise remained in Jamaica.

Taylor's remarks about the "sumptuousness" of Port Royal merchant and gentry attire of the period contain a partial truth. Some boasted broadcloth and silk coats and breeches, more had expensive white holland linen shirts. But rather than being lavishly dressed, such men owned but a handful of fine garments – which were not necessarily in good condition – and dressed mainly in common workaday cloth: strong, coarse ozenbrig linen, generally plain, inexpensive worsted camlet and similar woolens. In his January 1683 inventory, for example, the merchant Joshua Spenser left two pairs of breeches (one of camlet, the other of crape) and four coats (one of black silk ferrandine, one of camlet, and two of broadcloth). But the inventory described as "very old" his crape breeches, ferrandine coat, and one of his broadcloth coats.[19] The "gentleman" Thomas Gregory left more clothing, but its magnificence was equally restrained: one pair each of broadcloth, blue knit, and lined scarlet knit breeches; a blue probably woolen coat that had been "turned" (i.e., refashioned) and another of thick, strong, generally cheap woolen drugget; and ten waistcoats, four of them knit, three strong ribbbed cotton dimity, one each of drugget, broadcloth, and holland. His main luxury apparel comprised four small fine holland linen sleeves, a single silk stomacher (probably worn for show more than warmth), and three satin handkerchiefs.[20] The planter Nicholas Hickes left two pairs each of white dimity and of silk breeches, a broadcloth coat with silver buttons, three expensive holland coats, along with two silk coats and five holland shirts. Still, all his silk garments were marked "old," as were his three camlet coats, and while he boasted two complete suits, both were of plain-weave, unbleached brown holland, light and particularly appropriate for summer clothing.[21]

Taylor characterized more accurately the simpler dress of "common people."[22] The minimal clothing listed for a handful of ordinary men inventoried comprised an ozenbrig suit and one of woolen stuff; a pair of stuff breeches and a stuff coat; two pairs of unspecified (so likely cheap) linen breeches, though also two holland shirts.[23] The only two inventories of women's dress suggest that it too combined a few expensive, showy pieces with lighter and usually less costly everyday apparel.[24] These free female Jamaicans owned flowered and striped satin and silk gowns and petticoats, and soft, thin, fine white sarcenet silk "hoods" (caps) from Avignon: That perhaps apocryphal cooper's wife could have put on an item of flowered silk attire – though just one. In the main, she and her peers had calico, cotton-linen fustian, and holland petticoats and jackets, ozenbrig smocks, and muslin aprons.

By the 1730s, the outfit of Jamaican males had not changed, even if most men now wore caps or, much less often, hats (often trimmed with gold or silver lace), while about half had handkerchiefs and one-third dressing gowns or "banyans." Most men did own one or more garments not previously cited: outerwear such as cloaks or informal, loose-fitting, single-breasted frockcoats or longer, heavier greatcoats; neckwear (long, narrow cravats, scarf-like neckatees, close-fitting stocks or neckcloths); nightgowns and nightshirts; gloves; socks, slippers, and boots. The profusion of apparel items was not, however, accompanied by a growing taste for luxurious or sumptuous fabrics: In fact, the proportion of silks had fallen to 13 percent. Perhaps reflecting restrictions on English cotton manufacture, cottons also dropped to a tenth, whereas linens had risen to just under two-fifths (38 percent), and woolens remained stable.

Expensive holland and broadcloth did continue to predominate among linens and woolens respectively. Nevertheless, cheaper and lighter varieties made inroads, suggesting a growing attention to the demands of tropical climate as well as metropolitan fashion. Fustian was employed as a coat fabric; thinner worsted duroy replaced broad-cloth in some breeches and coats; linen and cotton check challenged holland for shirting; and most silks were plain varieties or thin taffetas. At the same time, new items, more shops, and growing colonial wealth allowed some Jamaican men to put on a more spectacular sartorial show than earlier, and many to acquire a few showy garments. Isaac Allyn, cooper become planter and gentleman, could choose from among 18 pairs of breeches (two were velvet including one with gold buttons), 16 waistcoats (among them a velvet and two other silk pieces with gold buttons and trim), 35 shirts (31 holland), 6 jackets, 10 coats (some broadcloth, others silk), silk stockings, laced hat, and yet more. Still, half or more of his garments were noted as "old" or "much worn"; even he, moreover, had often to be content with a plain linen shirt or prosaic cheap ticking linen or coarse duroy breeches.[25] More representative were the wardrobes of humbler men like the bookkeeper William Dreier, whose inventory was valued at one-fortieth of Allyn's. Though he owned a pair of silver-trimmed silk breeches and a matching coat, four pairs of fine holland stockings, and five silk handkerchiefs, the bulk of his apparel had been fashioned from less exalted linens and woolens.[26]

As before, some items in Jamaican women's dress were showier than men's: silk gowns, often flowered; figured damask coats, silk and lustrous; scarlet camlet cloaks; along with a quilted purple calico coat and another of quilted green calimanco (a glazed, patterned worsted that competed with calico). As before, too, women owned numerous linen and inexpensive woolen garments. Like the male, so the female outfit added some items, including shift and wrapped or rolled headcloth, and aprons and handkerchiefs became typical rather than optional acces-sories; at the same time, coats replaced jackets. The spinster Ann Scott boasted nearly all these new pieces, and she also had some showy items: silk gown, coat, cap, handkerchiefs, shoes, and stockings. But she would have dressed most often in the linens and woolens that dominated her wardrobe.[27] Continuity in basic attire and fabrics, and a mix of a few striking pieces amid mostly plainer quotidian apparel, were the watch-words among women as among men in Jamaica.

Dress in 1720s to 1730s Saint-Domingue equally showed the influence of metropolitan models, with particular touches: At least half the men boasted caps (hats being much less worn) as well as neck and pocket handkerchiefs. Free Saint-Domingue males had supplementary or alternative attire very similar to their Jamaican counterparts: large overcoats (*surtouts* and *volants*), redingotes (the French iteration of the frockcoat), cloaks (*manteaux*), nightshirts, cravats, socks (*chaussettes*), sashes. Though variations existed, they were slight. Fewer men on the French than on the British island (a sixth as against a third) owned a *robe de chambre* (dressing gown or banyan), but a fifth reported having drawers (*calçons* or *caleçons*), found in just a handful of contemporary Jamaican inventories.

The common West Indian male free settler outfit also exhibited some shared textile preferences. Like Jamaican men, males in Saint-Domingue favored linens for two-fifths (41 percent) of their attire, notably for breeches and waistcoats. In both colonies, too, dimity (French *bazin*) was the leading cotton, taffeta the premier silk (and velvet and other heavy silks rare), broadcloth the first choice among woolens. Nevertheless, empire – more precisely, imperial trade and industrial policies – did cause some divergence. Nearly two-fifths (37 percent) of men's garments in the French colony – including at least a fifth of their coats – were tailored from cottons, notably *bazin* that was imported from both the metropole and Holland. In the British colony the corresponding figure was just 10 percent, with coats accounting for a very small fraction.[28] Conversely, Saint-Domingue males chose silks (5 percent) and woolens (18 percent) appreciably less often than their counterparts in Jamaica, perhaps testimony to the excellence of British woolens, particularly lighter varieties suitable for hot climates. It is hardly surprising that of the dozen garments that the poor mason Jean-Jacques Vuan left at his death, all but a pair of cotton breeches were made of inexpensive linens.[29] But it is noteworthy that the wealthy planter Gaspard Berty also dressed wholly in cottons and linens save for a matching pair of grey woolen breeches and coat and another black coat.[30]

A trans-imperial but European-inflected free settler women's dress regime had also taken shape. Like their sisters in Jamaica, females in Saint-Domingue seem to have worn more silks than their male counterparts; as in Jamaica, both genders preferred taffeta to richer varieties. On both islands, too, the greater part of women's wardrobes comprised linen blouses or shifts, aprons, and caps; along with cotton (on Saint-Domingue, *bazin* [dimity] and calico) skirts, petticoats, gowns, and coats.[31] The planter's widow Marie Naval thus boasted twenty calico skirts, two calico gowns, and one of white cotton, whereas inventoried Jamaican women had at most a single calico gown or coat.[32] But otherwise their wardrobes did not differ much. In sum, Labat's portrayal of French Antillean sartorial luxury, even excess, seems as one-sided as those focused on Jamaica. Du Tertre's was more accurate, but still exaggerated. If silk garments were likely to be adorned with embroidery, lace, or gold trim, and men's woolen coats might sport gold or gilt buttons, the daily practice of most settlers seems to have been rather more mundane. Yet there is no evidence of a sartorial break with the metropoles: If lighter fabrics were coming into vogue in the eighteenth century, the overall dress inspiration was still clearly European in origin.

Garments in Bahia resembled those in the French and British Caribbean. About a third of inventoried men and women owned a *timão* (usually translated as "tunic" or "kimono," but probably much like the banyan). In contrast to the Caribbean, however, women donned a frequently elaborate cloak-like veil (*manto*), and some members of both genders had a cloak or cape (*capa* or *capote*) instead of or in addition to a coat. Some third of male inventories mention drawers and hats, and handkerchiefs crop up in inventories of both genders, indicating that these items appeared in Brazil in about the same proportions and at about the same time as in the Caribbean. Nevertheless, it appears that some Bahia inventories – women's most of all – list only a decedent's best garments, obscuring the full extent of wardrobes and skewing reported fabric preferences. Compared with free settlers in the other tropical colonies, Bahians had few cotton and linen pieces in their attire (respectively 4 and 23 percent for men, 0 and 4 percent for women), while the proportions of silks (17 percent for men, 56 for women), and woolens (56 percent for men, 41 for women) are considerably higher. It is striking, too, that few fine linens and no fine cottons make an appearance in the Bahia listings. Both were features of the dress regimes of the tropical plantation colonies of Jamaica and Saint-Domingue; moreover, Bahians could find such fabrics in local shops and did use britannia linen for shirts and blouses, and men and women alike in Brazil owned cotton stockings and handkerchiefs.

Yet it may well be that Bahians of the time simply did not consider cottons and linens appropriate for the most visible garments, perhaps because of the strong association of these fabrics with the work outfits of slaves and Indians. Or, as contemporaries and historians have argued, colonial Brazilians may have valued public displays of sartorial opulence based particularly on wearing expensive imported fabrics as well as showy adornments.[33] For well-to-do women, who were subject to a strong degree of seclusion,[34] such occasions focused on attendance at church; as one recent writer has remarked, "Sunday Mass was the main social forum in which to see and be seen," beginning with progress through town borne in a sedan chair (cf. the seated woman in Plate 8).[35] Men likewise seem not to have been immune to the allure of a splendid sartorial presence (see Figure 4.2). A 1703 price list of apparel deemed appropriate for a free Brazilian man included two woolen coats (one of moderate-priced baize, the other of expensive broadcloth), silk waistcoat, fine broadcloth and silk breeches, silk stockings, linen shirt and drawers, beaver hat, and distinctive cone-shaped silk or silk-lined broadcloth cap (*carapuça*).[36] Actual dress might correspond: Witness the prosperous Salvador shopkeeper Leonardo da Costa's "fine" broadcloth and black silk suits of breeches, waistcoat, and coat, not to mention his expensive best-quality cambric shirts and linen drawers, "fine" hat, muslin cravats, and silk or cambric (some laced) handkerchiefs.[37]

Among affluent people at home, however, or on most occasions among the less prosperous, Bahian dress was likely closer to the Caribbean model. Francisco Gonçalves Dantas, a well-to-do Salvador merchant, had some apparel comparable to da Costa's, including a fine broadcloth suit lined with blue silk, a damask waistcoat, and silk stockings. But his wardrobe consisted mainly of less good woolen and linen garments.[38] The less well-off Bartolomeu de Barros Freitas, for his part, had only inexpensive woolen attire (including a "very old" cloak), though he did own a pair of silk stockings and his one coat was lined with silk embroidered with taffeta.[39] As already stated, women's inventories are less revealing of daily wear. But the linen blouses, *droguete* woolen skirts, and light, durable serge suits found scattered through them suggest that, like their male counterparts, many Bahian women dressed more simply than inventory data suggest, at least at home, in keeping with the sharp difference between female public ostentation and private informality reported by visitors from abroad.[40] What does seem established, in any event, is that the garments that comprised Bahian dress differed little from those worn in the Caribbean – and in European metropoles – though its fancy iterations included a considerably larger component of silk and woolen fabrics.

"Preposterous" or "proper" attire

All three tropical colonies experienced increasing demographic and economic growth as the eighteenth century went on.[41] From the mid-1760s, the resulting wealth led some commentators to decry what they saw as the growth of inordinate luxury and ostentation, particularly evident in "preposterous" dress that took its cues from the metropoles.[42] As we have seen, this was not a new complaint: In fact, it had been voiced since the earliest days of French and British settlement in the Caribbean and may have gone back further in Brazil. Recurrence does not necessarily mean that it was incorrect in this period, however, when "prodigious riches" characterized not just Jamaica but Saint-Domingue and Brazil as well.[43] After all, colonial newspaper advertisements for specialized apparel shops and services, fancy fabrics and garments, and costly accessories proliferated during these years. Jamaicans could patronize Hollister and Hill's vendue store with its enticing array of striped or solid-color silks or Christopher Wynn's shop offering "superfine broad cloths of the most fashionable colours" and sixty or more other fabric varieties "of the newest patterns."[44] In Saint-Domingue, tailors and seamstresses promised clothing "in the latest taste and every fashion" and had all sorts of attire made in Paris for those who spurned colonial products. In these colonies, too, many a shopkeeper boasted of a "magnificent assortment of the most fashionable merchandise" from lace to silk stockings, gold jewelry to hats with silver trim, while "well versed" dyers, hatters, pressers, and staymakers all promised to clean, repair, and update existing items so that their owners could appear "in the style now in vogue."[45]

In Jamaica, inventories nuance the story of intensifying sartorial splendor. To be sure, the garment listings lend some support to Long's description of a settler taste for heavy, rich fabrics. Women wore brocaded silk gowns, jackets, and coats, while in contrast to earlier decades, velvet became one of the leading silks among men – notably for breeches – and men were also attracted to cotton "thickset" for its velvety finish that often came in flowered patterns. Men's laced jackets remained popular, as did ruffled shirts. While outfits remained largely the same overall, both genders did accept a few new garment styles. Women took up sack gowns and increasingly replaced their coats with cloaks; men fully adopted the frockcoat. All these were fashions both luxurious and metropolitan.

1 *La pesche des Sauvages /Indians fishing* (*c.* 1700), by Louis Nicolas.

Nicolas had seen images of Amerindians published by François Du Creux, *Historiae Canadensis, sev Novae-Franciae* (Paris: Sebastian Cramoisy, 1664), who in turn was influenced by conventions in the engravings of Theodore de Bry (de Bry 1590–1634). But Nicolas had been a missionary in the Great Lakes region and had seen the diverse forms of tattooing depicted in his images of Amerindians. For a modern critical edition, see Nicolas 2011.

2 *Linen Market, Dominica* or *Linen Day, Roseau, Dominica – A Market Scene* (c.1780), by Agostino Brunias.

The titles are not Brunias's but later additions. Brunias painted numerous scenes of markets, focusing on textile vendors, their wares, and their customers. For more information about his life, work, and context, see Bagneris 2010, Kriz 2008, Honychurch 2004, Tobin 1999.

4 *Tupí Man / Tupinambá Man / Brazilian Man* (c. 1641), by Albert Eckhout.

The still-life artist Eckhout went to then-Dutch Brazil in 1636–44 with his fellow artist Frans Post under commission from Count John Maurice to paint the natural landscape and human portraits. For more extended discussion, see Brienen 2007; Buvelot 2004; Post 1990.

3 *Tupí Woman / Tupinambá Woman / Brazilian Woman* (c. 1641), by Albert Eckhout.

This is one of eight portraits of indigenous and enslaved men and women that Eckhout painted, along with a large depiction of a Tapuya dance. All are in the National Museum of Denmark.

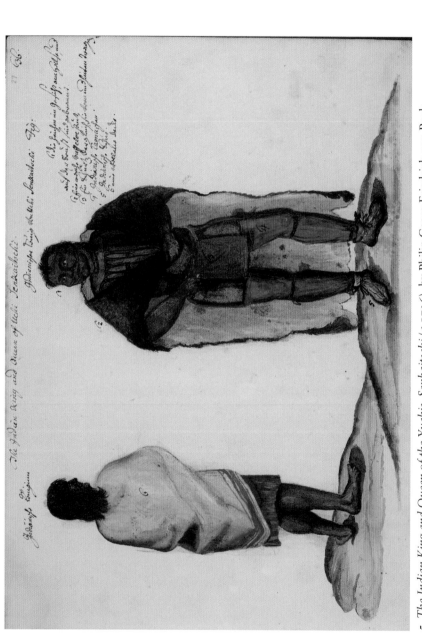

5 *The Indian King and Queen of the Yuchis, Senkaitschi* (c.1736), by Philip Georg Friedrich von Reck.

An able artist and careful observer, von Reck made about 50 pencil drawings and watercolors of Amerindians, plants, and animals he saw in Georgia, along with explanatory notes. Dating from the early days of settlement in the new colony, his images are the best visual evidence available of Native dress and folkways in the early days of European settlement. Additional images and information are in Hvidt 1980.

6 *Genre Studies of Habitants and Indians* (c. 1780), Anonymous.

Little is known about this work, but the inscriptions at the bottom ("peasants of Canada" on the left, "Canadians travel on snowshoes in winter" on the right) indicate that it was created by a German visitor or perhaps resident.

7 *Side view of Table Mountain and the Devil's Peak* (1786–87), by Jan Brandes outside Cape Town, Cape Colony, southern Africa. Brandes, a Lutheran clergyman, depicted natural and human life in the Dutch East Indies, the Cape Colony, and aboard VOC ships. Nearly 200 of his works are reproduced and discussed in de Bruijn and Raben 2004.

8 *Woman being carried in a sedan chair* (c.1776), by Carlos Julião.

An Italian-born artist and military engineer, Julião left at least two paintings and numerous watercolors featuring people and objects in the Portuguese global empire. The best known are 43 images of the dress and activities of Brazilian indigenous, enslaved, and free colonial inhabitants. See Lara 2002.

9 *West Indian Creole woman, with her Black Servant* (*c.* 1780), by Agostino Brunias.

Brunias reused the Creole woman's image in his *Market Day, Roseau, Dominica*, which has also been dated to 1780, again to depict an affluent free person of color.

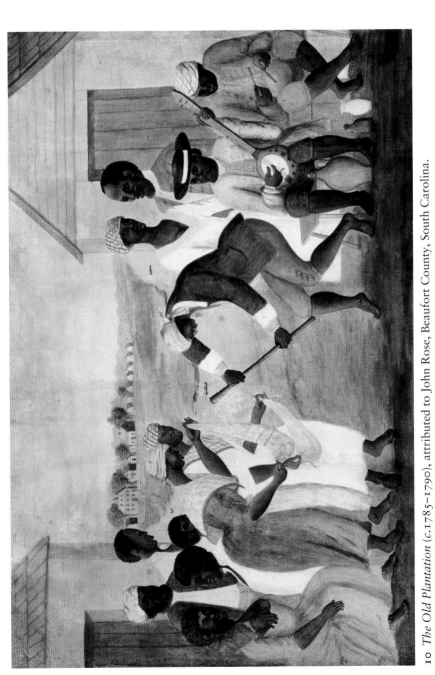

10 *The Old Plantation* (c.1785–1790), attributed to John Rose, Beaufort County, South Carolina. Only in recent years has the likely location and date of composition of this unique work been identified. See Handler 2010 and Shames 2010.

11 *Free West Indian Dominicans* or *A West Indian Dandy and Two Ladies* (*c.* 1770), by Agostino Brunias.

The titles, added at an unknown later date, suggest how Brunias's scenes were not specific to a single Caribbean island (see also Fig 4.4).

12 *A West Indian Flower Girl and Two other Free Women of Color* (*c.*1769), by Agostino Brunias.

Once again, the title is a later addition. Like many of Brunias's works, this painting includes figures seen elsewhere.

13 *Nicholas Boylston (1716–1771), (1767)*, by John Singleton Copley.

The ship safely entering harbor in the background emphasizes that Boylston was a successful merchant, as does the thick account book with its spine toward the viewer; the other volume suggests that he was a man of learning as well as wealth.

14 *Sir John Caldwell* (*c.* 1774–80), Anonymous.

A British army officer in the Lake Erie border region, Caldwell participated in councils with Amerindians. Many of items that he donned for this portrait were in his impressive personal collection of Native objects.

Pl. VI.

Corn.ᵉ Buys, del.   J. le F. v. B. inv.   Corn.ᵉ Brouwer, fec.

15 *Dress of Dutch Countryfolk* (*c.* 1775), by Cornelis Buys.

For Francq van Berkhij's volumes, Buys also produced several similar images
showing the dress of court and elite persons.

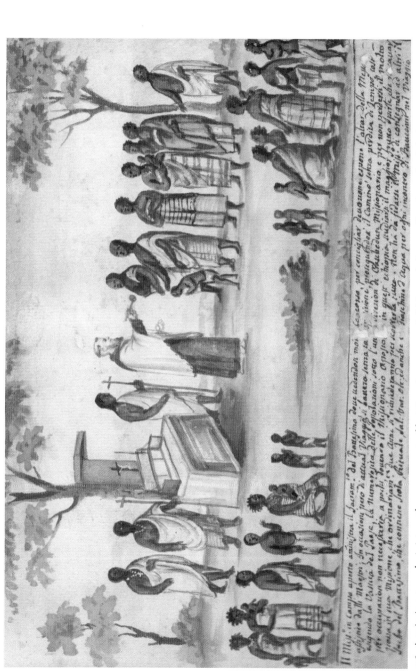

16 *A missionary administers the sacrament of baptism in an open field* (1747), Bernardino Ignazio d'Asti.

From the only illustrated copy of Asti's manuscript *Missione in prattica de Padri Cappuccini ne Regni di Congo, Angola, et adiacenti*. Asti was a Capuchin Franciscan missionary in Sogno during the 1740s and author and illustrator of the manual from which this image is taken.

17 *Portrait of a Haitian woman* (1786), Francois Malépart Beaucourt.
The first Canadian known to have studied in France, Beaucourt lived in Saint-
Domingue in the late 1780s, though where this work was composed is not known.

On the whole, however, Jamaicans chose lighter fabrics. In the 1730s, about a tenth of the attire left by Jamaican males had been fashioned from cottons; in 1760–74 a fifth (21 percent). Linens maintained their primacy (35 percent), and male Jamaicans developed a taste for check trousers: not available earlier, this textile (which could be a pure linen, pure cotton, or linen-cotton mixture) comprised 6 percent of apparel in 1760–74. Thus linens, cottons, and mixtures of the two rose from less than half (48 percent) to nearly two-thirds (64 percent) of men's basic and outerwear. Checks also became the dominant shirt fabric, accounting for nearly three-fifths (57 percent) of men's shirts in 1760–74, linens falling to 37 percent. Woolens lost ground (from 38 to 28 percent), and among woolens light worsteds and flannels rather than broadcloth became the fabric of choice for breeches, jackets, and waistcoats. Though broadcloth remained the dominant woolen coat fabric, ozenbrig linen, tailored into the increasingly fashionable frockcoat, had become about as popular for outerwear. Silks, used mainly in jackets and breeches, also declined in popularity, from 13 to 8 percent, as even for these garments Jamaican men were more and more likely to choose a cotton such as calico, thickset, or fustian. Though the few women's inventories do not cite cotton garments, they do list considerable quantities of linen gowns, aprons, caps, and even coats, not to mention blouses.

Along with harsh criticisms, Long offered apparel recommendations. He deemed the "loose, cool, easy" Asian banyan "much easier and better fitted for use in a hot climate, than the English dress, which is close and tight," but conceded that the "tyranny of custom" had largely ruled it out "in other hot countries." Closer to home, Jamaicans could learn from Spanish America, where men wore linen waistcoats and breeches, and coats "of some other thin stuff," while women donned a *pollera* (petticoat or skirt) of "thin silk," white linen jackets in cold weather, and "when they go abroad . . . a mantelet or short cloak." Like Moreau de Saint-Méry, Long was no opponent of luxury, but he preferred "the finest linen, laces, and jewels," simply but artfully arranged, of Spanish female dress to the English style of "a multitude of things piled one upon another." And rather than male Jamaicans' "ponderous coat and waistcoat, richly bedaubed with gold lace and embroidery" and "complete suits of thick broadcloth, laced from top to bottom," he recommended unlined, unadorned, loose coats tailored from the light broadcloth known as "kerseymeres" (cassimere); waistcoats, breeches, and stockings made of cotton rather than linen; and clothing that was all "light-coloured."[46]

Judging by inventories, free Jamaicans' dress did not closely correspond to Long's specific sartorial pronouncements – dimity, which he named as the best cotton, was tailored into only a minority of cotton garments, and cassimere was never cited – and in some cases went against them. Velvet or velvet-like fabrics were gaining a limited popularity, and a minority of attire continued to be brocaded, embroidered, and otherwise adorned. But the movement away from woolens and silks; the growing taste for cottons and, when woolens were selected, for lighter varieties; the adoption of the frockcoat by men and of the cloak by women – all of these larger trends are signs that in the most important respects Long was preaching to the choir. While still taking cues from England, Jamaican settlers had accepted that simpler attire and lighter fabrics were most appropriate for the torrid zone and were beginning to dress in accordance to this new understanding.[47]

Bahians were moving in the same direction. To be sure, Bahian and Jamaican developments were not identical. While silks were losing ground on the Caribbean island, they were gaining in Brazil (to 22 percent from 17), and linens, while gaining marginally (23 to 25 percent) were still employed far less often in Brazilian attire than in Jamaican. Moreover, the fashion for the *timão*, the Brazilian form of the banyan that Long so admired, and whose absence from late eighteenth-century Jamaica he so rued, endured in Bahia, and some form of cloak remained an essential part of outerwear, now enriched by the long, wide, often hooded *capote* style.

Nevertheless, the major trends were remarkably similar. Though the proportion of cottons in Bahian free settler male apparel did not approach Jamaica's, their presence had more than doubled (4 to 10 percent); similarly, while woolens retained their primacy, use had fallen substantially (56 to 43 percent), proportionally the same as in Jamaica. In the Portuguese colony, too, lighter types of woolens had appeared, notably lustrous *brilhante* and *gala*, and *droguete* (which often combined flax or silk with wool) became much more popular. If *paño* (broadcloth) continued to be important, many garments tailored from it were described as "old," while items made from the recently popular varieties were termed "good" or even "new," suggesting an ongoing switch from heavier kinds of woolens in Brazil that resembled the one underway in Jamaica. Even the contrary trend was alike in the two places. In Bahia as in Jamaica, velvet had become a popular clothing material, in particular for velvet suits and for separate velvet breeches, waistcoats, and coats.

As in Jamaica, too, Bahians' wardrobes remained a mixture of mainly middling or cheaper fabrics, enlivened with a special item or two. A moderately prosperous Salvadoran male like João Cardoso, for instance, owned two pairs of blue linen breeches, three linen and two cotton shirts, three pairs of linen drawers, two woolen (burgundy-colored *droguete* and black *gala)* and one linen waistcoat, burgundy *paño* and black *gala* woolen coats, two pairs of cotton stockings, topped off by a pair of black velvet breeches and a blue and red baize *timão*.[48] His contemporary, the Salvador widow Maria do Carmo Gomes, could dress partly in apparel made of silk, the material of her *timão*, two of her skirts (one of black velvet), a cloak decorated with polished silver rings, and two belts, one crimson and embroidered with gold thread. But Gomes would mainly have donned a linen blouse (or perhaps muslin), and one of her four linen or one calico skirts and short woolen cloak.[49]

Many dress developments in Saint-Domingue tracked those seen in the other two tropical colonies. For one thing, a few new items were integrated into ordinary outfits without these undergoing any significant change. Thus half the men inventoried in 1760–74 had added wide breeches (*grandes culottes*) for riding while retaining regular breeches for other activities. As elsewhere, a third now had linen drawers, and an equal proportion boasted *gilet*-style waistcoats that were supplanting the *veste* (jerkin) type, while an eighth now used longer redingotes instead of or in addition to the *habit*. While not disappearing, the *robe de chambre* was clearly of waning interest: Not only did less than an eighth of men own one, but many were "very bad," "worn out," or "torn," just two "new." As elsewhere, too, a variety of linens took the once central place of fine holland, lighter woolens appeared alongside *drap* – and men joined their counterparts in the other colonies in adopting rich velvets, particularly for breeches. Women likewise proved amenable to novelties without giving up their accustomed dress. The hip-length *pet-en-l'air* variant joined the *casaquin* jacket, and, like their sisters in Jamaica and Bahia, female Saint-Dominicans began to favor the cloak in its short hooded *mantelet* version. Long partial to cottons, they welcomed chintz and other printed varieties manufactured legally in France after 1759 as well as imported from India or elsewhere in Europe.

In contrast to Jamaica and Bahia, however, overall fabric choices in Saint-Domingue did not increasingly tend to cottons and linens. In fact, the proportion of male garments made of cottons fell slightly to 33 percent, those of linens to 30 percent.[50] Conversely, men's use of silks rose from 5 to 14 percent, and of woolens from 18 to 23 percent. Still, cottons and linens comprised nearly two-thirds of attire materials. Thus the wardrobe of the wealthy planter Claude Mariot held waistcoats of black linen with gold braid, black, silver-trimmed yellow, and blue woolen, along with 14 pairs of breeches (11 of broadcloth, and one each of black silver-trimmed velvet, red velvet, and green camlet) and 7 coats (6 of woolens including scarlet broadcloth, green camlet, two others with gold braid, and one of black silver-trimmed velvet). Nevertheless, Mariot relied on linens and cottons: 64 trimmed and plain linen shirts, 12 white dimity waistcoats and 11 more of white linen, 20 pairs of linen drawers, 94 pairs of cotton, thread, and silk stockings, 8 cotton caps.[51] Even the more modest Pierre Pouget, a mason, boasted two pairs of silk velvet breeches and a silk drugget *veste*, though he, too, owned mainly linen attire (3 pairs of *grandes culottes*, 9 shirts, 5 *vestes*, 5 pairs of stockings), along with a pair of regular cotton breeches and a pair of cotton stockings, and mid-range blue woolen camlet breeches and coat.[52]

These examples might suggest that free settler dress in Saint-Domingue was becoming unlike what was worn in the other tropical societies. In fact, the rising consumption of silks and woolens in that colony, as well as the declining use of cottons and linens, was evidence of an emerging tropical free settler dress regime. Despite their different paths, across the eighteenth century the textile cultures of Jamaica, Bahia, and Saint-Domingue were converging. Admittedly, in terms of fabric choices, the Caribbean colonies together differed significantly from Brazil, as summarized in Table 5.1. By 1760–74, about two-thirds of attire in Jamaica and Saint-Domingue was tailored from cottons and linens, the remaining third from silks and woolens; Bahia's profile was the mirror image.

Dress differences were, however, less stark than these figures suggest. For one thing, Bahians wore much the same ordinary outfit as their peers in the Caribbean, and remaining distinctions were being eroded. Thus many Jamaicans and Saint-Dominicans added cloaks, long a staple of Bahia dress, to their wardrobes, and men in all three colonies participated in the fad for velvet attire that emerged in the

Table 5.1 *Free male settler garment fabric choices in three tropical colonies*

Percentages of basic and outer garments

Jamaica, 1730–39	S. Distr. St-Domingue, 1722–39	Bahia District, 1715–39	Type of fabric	Jamaica, 1760–74	S. Distr. St-Domingue, 1760–74	Bahia District, 1760–74
10	37	4	Cottons	21	30	10
38	41	23	Linens	35	33	25
0	0	0	Mixed	6	0	0
13	5	17	Silks	8	14	22
38	18	56	Woolens	28	23	43
1	0	0	Other	2	0	0
100	101	100	Total	100	100	100

Sources: See Appendix 2.

mid-eighteenth century. Most important, free residents in all these tropical societies increasingly clothed themselves in textiles that were lighter in fabric and, so far as can be told, in color as well; even Bahians were moving in that direction.[53] Such dress fabric convergence demonstrates that the growing similarity of merchant stocks around the Atlantic, outlined in Chapter 2, was translated by free settlers onto their bodies as well as onto those of enslaved and indigenous men and women. It shows as well how fashions for specific garments and fabrics circulated across boundaries to help create regional styles. At the same time, however, the clear disparities among colonies reveal that creating "proper" dress and avoiding the "preposterous" in any location was not a matter simply of appropriating global goods and styles but also depended on specific trade patterns, imperial policies, and cultural imperatives.

Sumptuous array, suitable dress, light style: occupation, wealth, gender

Inventories, then, show the dress of free settlers in the late seventeenth- and eighteenth-century tropical Americas to have been on the whole a sober affair that over time was becoming more closely attuned to these colonies' specific climate. But if these documents do not sustain the broadest charges about out-of-place sartorial display that contemporaries leveled, what about those statements that rebuked or praised the dress practices of specific groups?

Already in 1687, John Taylor had identified merchants as exemplars of elaborate clothing, and nearly a century on Hilliard d'Auberteuil echoed the assertion. Was this indictment true? Compared with other males, Saint-Domingue evidence suggests, it often was.[54] Merchants did not dress in an extreme manner. Linens and cottons outnumbered silks and woolens in their wardrobes as in those of all Saint-Domingue males. Yet men of commerce exhibited much less partiality for linens, and a greater preference for silks and woolens, than other men. The disparities date back at least to the early eighteenth century, when merchants chose silks three times as often as other men (13 percent of garments as against 4 percent), nearly twice as many woolens (20 rather than 12 percent), and far fewer linens (28 vs. 44 percent). Within fiber categories, however, all men favored the same varieties, and though inventory listings of adornments are rather hit-or-miss, they do not suggest that merchants' attire was any more often festooned with braid or ribbon, gold or silver buttons, embroidery or brocade, than that of other Saint-Domingue men – or that it was any less adorned.

While becoming less sharply etched, the fabric differences persisted. Merchants had 19 percent of their attire fashioned from silks in 1760–74, other men 12 percent; among woolens the gap was 28 to 22 percent respectively, and among linens 23 percent for men of commerce as against 31 percent for other Saint-Domingue males. In contrast to earlier, in 1760–74 merchants also used cottons less than other men (28 percent of their garments vs. 33 percent). Among cottons, moreover, merchants favored more ornate calicoes to cheaper, coarser varieties like checked or striped *siamoise* by a ratio of about three to one. Finally, only merchants (and their wives and widows) owned lustrous, patterned damask apparel. As observers claimed, in short, merchants exemplified a fashion for heavier and/or showier dress fabrics than other male Saint-Dominicans.

A similar pattern obtained among Jamaican merchants, at least in the 1760s and 1770s; gaps in fabric listings do not allow analysis of earlier periods.[55] To be sure, their attire favored cottons even less than their counterparts' on Saint-Domingue and woolens more. But Jamaican men of commerce were more committed to luxurious fabrics than other men in their colony: not only silks (20 percent as compared with 8) but also woolens (36 as against 27 percent). Correlatively, they showed less interest in cotton clothing (16 rather than 33 percent) and, though less dramatically, in linen as well (23 for men of commerce, 27 for other free Jamaican males). Only with respect to mixed-fiber fabrics (4 percent, in both cases almost entirely checks) did their tastes converge. Distinctions obtained as well on the level of individual fabrics. Compared to broadcloth, for example, lighter worsted held little attraction for merchants, though they carried both the fabric and ready-made worsted breeches in their shops; similarly, they attended more to selling fustian garments than to donning them.

Lack of sufficient information about occupation makes conclusions about specifically merchant dress in Bahia tentative at best. It is nevertheless noteworthy that in the later eighteenth century the handful of identifiable men of commerce wore even more silk and woolen garments than their peers – and, it seems, more than their predecessors – and very few cottons. Manoel Ferreira de Oliveira, trader with West Africa, had a pair of ordinary linen breeches and waistcoats, lined with expensive holland, but otherwise he dressed in rich green, blue, and black silk and woolen garb, most lined with colorful holland, taffeta, or another "magnificent" cloth.[56] Thus he could make an even richer display than his 1730 precursor, the Mina (Gold) Coast merchant Manoel Ferreira dos Santos, the bulk of whose apparel was made of durable linens, though he, too, sported some blue and blue striped woolen items.[57] Merchants may have sought to project an image of successful businessmen, to advertise their most profitable wares, or to identify with metropolitan fashions. Whatever the reason, their dress emphasized expensive and showy fabrics and pieces of apparel that were somewhat out of tune both with their setting and with their fellows' apparel.

As on average the wealthiest men in their societies, planters might be expected to epitomize sartorial magnificence.[58] Some most surely did. The Jamaican Nicholas Hickes's late seventeenth-century apparel has already been mentioned; it was far outshone by Isaac Allyn's finery in the mid-1730s. On Saint-Domingue, Allyn could be matched by Louis Étienne Calquier's fine white pekin silk breeches, waistcoat, and coat (the coat with gold buttons, the waistcoat trimmed with gold braid), new velvet breeches, silk serge waistcoat adorned with gold gauze, coat of costly Indian bark cloth (écorce d'arbre was often mixed with silk) lined with scarlet taffeta, shirts with very fine linen batiste and muslin ruffles, and cotton-lined taffeta-like striped pekin robe de chambre.[59] Surely, too, the Brazilian sugar planter Francisco

Teles Barreto was resplendent in either his blue satin suit with vest of blue satin, with all its (unfortunately undefined) trim, or his pure silk suit, both among the most expensive pieces of attire listed in early eighteenth-century Bahian inventories.[60]

The majority of planters did not dress anything like these men. In early eighteenth-century Saint-Domingue, their garments comprised mainly sturdy, mid-range or cheaper linens (51 percent) and similar kinds of cottons (31 percent).[61] Though also favoring lighter fabrics, other Saint-Domingue males chose linens for 23 percent, cottons for 46 percent. Again, whereas silks comprised just 3 percent of planters' apparel and woolens 14 percent, the figures for other men were 8 and 23 percent respectively, and whereas planters selected plain woolen serge, their non-farm peers preferred broadcloth. For their shirts and shifts, too, planters used inexpensive hempen *brin* linen while other men wore a good deal of fine, bright white flax *royale*.

Planters were not immune to fashion trends: Like all Saint-Domingue men, across the eighteenth century they chose increasing amounts of silks and woolens (11 and 19 percent respectively in 1760–74), and decreasing if still substantial quantities of cottons and linens (39 and 31 percent).[62] But these figures continued to differ appreciably from those of other men, a sixth of whose basic and outer-wear was fashioned from silks (15 percent), a quarter each from woolens (26 percent) and cottons (28 percent). Consumption of linens, however, always the most similar among all men, was now essentially the same (29 percent for non-planters), as Saint-Domingue males switched their light fabric preference to cottons, which now became the favored material for breeches and waistcoats. Besides their greater commitment to light textiles in general, planters also continued dispro-portionately to select more durable varieties: *siamoise, coutil, brin, fil d'épreuve* (a waterproof striped hempen linen much like *gingas*). Dress distinctions also obtained between planters' wives and widows and other women. Like their spouses, plantation women in Saint-Domingue were more likely to possess linen attire (19 percent as against 11 percent) and less likely to own silks (7 vs. 14 percent) than other free settler women; at the same time, all women favored cottons in the same very substantial proportion (nearly three-fourths) and owned virtually no woolens (1 percent).[63]

By this period, the fabric composition of planters' wardrobes in Jamaica resembled that of their counterparts in Saint-Domingue in some respects while differing substantially on all accounts from other men's in their own society.[64] Two-fifths (39 percent) of their clothes were tailored from cottons as against just one-fifth (19 percent) among other male Jamaicans: Planters seem to have recognized, as one of their number wrote from Saint-Domingue, "of all materials, cotton is the most suitable for appareling us: that's the result of climate."[65] Again like their French peers, Jamaican planters had a lower quotient of silk garments than other men in the British colony (6 percent as against 13) and a greater taste for light worsteds rather than broadcloth. Whereas about a third of their French colleagues' attire in addition to shirts was made of linen, however, Jamaicans had less than a fifth (18 percent, compared with 41 percent among other male Jamaicans); Jamaican planters also wore considerably more woolens (35 percent) than either Saint-Domingue planters (19 percent) or other Jamaicans (23 percent).

Caribbean planters hardly eschewed some showy pieces: As a matter of fact, half of them in both Jamaica and Saint-Domingue acquired velvet breeches. Despite this nod to fashion, however, and despite differences between empires, all West Indian planters developed a dress regime, focused on newer, lighter, and brighter fabrics, that more closely resembled Moreau de Saint-Méry's appropriate "colonial livery" than Long's "sweltering load of garments."[66] It did not, moreover, distinguish them only from other free settlers. It set them apart even more sharply from the mass of their enslaved laborers, not only the rough linens and woolens of slave work clothing but also slave fancy dress, so heavily based as it was on linens.

"Common" and "humbler" folk purportedly avoided the excesses that marred the dress of many wealthier, elite free settlers. Relative or absolute poverty had much to do with this. Recent research has shown that impoverishment affected the great majority of Brazil's eighteenth-century population.[67] Though the poor were rarely inventoried, the widower Manoel Gomes, whose only listed garment was a worn cloth suit, and whose entire estate was valued at less than the clothing alone of his more affluent neighbors, was surely among them.[68]

Individuals like Gomes are more visible in the Caribbean records. Ten poorer men left usable inventories in early eighteenth-century Saint-Domingue, among them masons, carpenters, and plantation employees. Their wardrobes were small, on average containing just ten basic and outer garments, as compared with sixteen for merchants of the time, twenty-two for planters. Their wardrobes were more narrowly focused as well: a quarter (23 percent) cottons, a sixth (15 percent) woolens, no silks, and two-thirds (62 percent) linens, virtually all of them coarse hempen *brin* and *halle*; their shirts were also tailored from these and similar coarse varieties. As such men lacked even a silk hand-kerchief or pair of stockings, their only touches of luxury were the taffeta linings of a vest and two old coats, and a few muslin and batiste collars. A handful of artisans – a joiner, a shoemaker, a staymaker, and a couple more whose occupation is not mentioned – were also inventoried in 1730s Jamaica. Unfortunately, it is just their listings that most often lack speci-ficity about fabrics, though it seems probable that fancy items would have caught the enumerator's eye. When materials are cited, in any case, they are durable linens like garlix and check; woolen flannel; worsteds such as duroy and coarse, thin tammy; and cotton dimity, enlivened at most with a pair of silk stockings or a holland vest.[69]

Perceptible disparities in dress remained thereafter: In 1760–74 Saint-Domingue, for instance, poorer free settlers had on average four-teen outer and basic garments, as against the male mean of thirty-three. But the differences had eroded. Along with their more prosperous fellows, less affluent residents increasingly wore woolen attire (the proportion having doubled to 29 percent), while reducing their consumption of linen, now two-fifths (39 percent). Breeches, waistcoats, and coats of broadcloth appeared alongside more workaday fabrics, as did *cala-mande*, a glossy, colorful worsted alternative to calico or pricy woolens. Though use of cotton did not change overall, calico supplanted some *bazin* (dimity). And, albeit at a lower level than other Saint-Domingue males, poorer men even acquired silk items (6 percent), not only less costly silk drugget and silk *coutil* waistcoats but also faddish velvet breeches. Though much of their apparel continued to be labeled "old," "bad," "used," and "coarse," some was now characterized as "new" and fine, and festive touches such as embroidery, garlands, velvet trim, and silver and gold buttons became noticeable, along with ruffled shirts.

Though still employing linen for a greater part of their outfits than other men in their colony, in sum, by the 1760s "humbler people, estate stewards, peddlers" participated more fully in the dominant colonial livery. Increasingly, it was the quality rather than the kind of the fabrics they donned that defined their dress, as is indicated by the plain yet substantial workaday attire of the steward (*économe*) depicted in Figure 5.1 (no. 15).[70] Improvement in the dress of "humbler people" reflects the increasing wealth of Caribbean plantation colonies after the

5.1 *Indigotérie / Indigo manufactory*, from Élie Monnereau, *Le parfait indigotier on description de l'indigo* (Amsterdam and Marseille: Jean Mossy, 1765), frontispiece.

Indigo preparation, with plantation and drying shed (numbered 12, in the background). Most letters and numbers name the tools and infrastructure. The two figures labeled "10" are "slaves carrying sacks" of indigo; number 15 is the steward ("économe").

Seven Years' War; its growing similarity to wealthier colonists' apparel was also a material demonstration of the greater reciprocity among all Caribbean whites in the face of the black majority that all free settlers exploited, a contrast clearly visible in Figure 5.1.[71]

Wealth and occupational dress distinctions had a gendered dimension, as we have seen, but gender also cut across these lines. It appears, in fact, that gender affected free settler dress more strongly than did either resource level or profession. This was true first of all in lower-body garments, where in the colonies as at home Europeans generally distinguished male breeches from female skirts or gowns. On males, in fact, skirt-like lower garments denoted specific occupational moments – or, if commonly worn and short, enslavement.

Gender operated as well on other, equally visible aspects of dress. In late eighteenth-century Saint-Domingue, all women showed a much greater propensity for cottons, all men for linens and woolens, while both genders equally favored silks.[72] As cottons became strongly identified with women, they lost favor among men.[73] Gender also shaped individuals' specific fabric choices. Men were likely to have *gingas* linen shirts in their wardrobes, while that material was never used for women's shifts, and whereas men employed *coutil* in waistcoats and breeches, it never appeared in a female inventory, where dimity, another male favorite, likewise was an infrequent presence. Many men, too, had a good selection of cotton stockings, whereas women preferred silk. Further, men used mainly striped mixed cotton and linen *siamoise* and *cotonade* (often the terms were used synonymously) for outer garments, while women avoided these fabrics for more colorful patterned pure cotton calico and chintz; again, when silks were involved, men preferred heavier velvet, which women avoided for lighter taffeta. And as women's dress increasingly favored cottons, it tended to be lighter in color and livelier in design. So as tropical free settler dress converged across boundaries of empire and wealth, sartorial difference became marked by occupation, but even more by gender.

"Aux vêtemens tout est réservé": race and tropical settler dress[74]

Besides Europeans and their descendants, free people of color of many ethnic origins and combinations formed a significant part of settler populations throughout the Atlantic world; they were particularly numerous and prominent in Brazil, Jamaica, and Saint-Domingue.[75] Some were emancipated slaves or their descendants, others the offspring of relations between individuals of diverse ethno-racial backgrounds, including indigenous peoples as well as settlers.[76] In the West Indies, manumitted slaves or *affranchis* (including those who purchased their freedom) and free people of color (individuals of mixed ancestry, known in French as *gens de couleur libres, mulâtres, or mulâtresses*) formed a particularly substantial part of the total free population.[77] By the later eighteenth century, the two groups comprised nearly half Saint-Domingue's free people, and their numbers were increasing at a faster pace than whites'.[78] As elsewhere, most were domestic servants, artisans, and petty retailers, many of them women; however, some became prosperous property owners, interisland shippers, planters, and wives or mistresses of affluent males.[79]

According to Article 59 of the 1685 *Code Noir*, free people of color in French colonies were to enjoy the same rights and privileges as whites. As elsewhere in the Atlantic, however, they encountered increasing informal discrimination, declining rates of exogamy, and legal restrictions across the eighteenth century, particularly from the late 1750s, as sharper distinctions were drawn between groups now imagined in racialized terms.[80] Severe limits on carrying weapons were followed by compulsory separate registration in religious and notarial documents, exclusion from judicial office and from the practice of many professions, and yet more. Together, the discriminatory acts consciously demarcated persons of color, whether born free or manumitted, as belonging to a separate and inferior caste. Decreeing that no such person could register letters of nobility, irrespective of parentage, a 1767 ministerial decision summed up the thinking that lay behind this policy: Because blacks had been brought to French colonies "to be and remain in a state of slavery," their descendants always retained "that first stain" that "the gift of freedom could not efface."[81] A 1774 ruling on estate succession drove home the point: "public opinion has established an insurmountable barrier between whites and people of color that the wisdom of the Government maintains."[82]

In light of their varied socioeconomic roles, more rapid increase in numbers, and the parallel growth of racialized thinking, it was probably inevitable that *gens de couleur* would figure prominently, sometimes obsessively, in contemporary representations. A mulatto, according to Moreau de Saint-Méry, "loves finery," so he wore a waistcoat, trousers (*pantalon*) "of fine linen," "touched up" hat, and costly head and neckerchiefs, "always with grace and elegance"; on special days, he added stockings and a coat.[83] As previously noted, free women of color received particular scrutiny.[84] If Thomas Atwood, chief judge on the formerly French island of Dominica, is to be believed, they attended dances "usually dressed in silks, silk stockings and shoes; buckles, bracelets, and rings of gold and silver, to a considerable value."[85] The "luxury" of *mulâtresses* – whose "being is entirely given over to *volupté* (sexual pleasure)" – likewise focused on clothing and jewelry, gifted them by lovers, mainly white men with whom "most" mulattas lived as de facto wives.[86] In this way, Moreau de Saint-Méry claimed, *mulâtresses* acquired multiple outfits comprising every kind of garment, all fashioned from "the most beautiful and most precious products of India": handkerchiefs, muslins, linens, "rich laces," and other fabrics. Some mulattas could wear an entirely new ensemble "every day of the year"; and as none ever repaired or otherwise cared for garments, their wardrobes were constantly renewed.[87]

To such contemporaries, race was a powerful determinant of dress among non-enslaved settlers of color as well as among the enslaved. In fact, Moreau de Saint-Méry subtly, and surely knowingly, sartorially assimilated the two groups. Though he himself did not point out the likeness, both the male and the female mulatto outfits that he sketched resembled nothing so much as the slave fancy dress he had described earlier in his book. At the same time, growing discrimination and separation, whether legally prescribed or privately initiated, created conditions that might have led to the development of a distinctive dress regime among free people of color, whether as conscious signal of a clear and conclusive "specific identity," or as unconscious sartorial acknowledgement of difference.[88] Contemporary images, together with inventories, shed light both on Moreau de Saint-Méry's insinuation of dress similarity between free people of color and the enslaved and on possible contrasts in attire between free people of color and whites.[89]

Agostino Brunias placed free persons of color at the center of his West Indian *oeuvre*, which was set in colonies recently under French dominion.[90] Fashionably attired and depicted with lighter skin tones, free women of color are often the focus of his portrayals. They may be posed alone or with a woman friend with enslaved female personal servants, as in Plate 9; as observers of dances (like the woman with the hat in Figure 4.4); promenading with their husbands or in a family group. Or, as in Plate 11, they appear in a tropical version of the "conversation piece," an informal group portrait in realistic setting that was a popular eighteenth-century genre.[91] In a commercial variant (Plate 12), they are consumers as well as sellers. Most famously, they are the central characters in Brunias's many market scenes, typically accompanied by suitors or paramours: In Plate 2, three such couples can be discerned.

In all these depictions of leisured free people of color – who best correspond to the group whose costume Moreau discussed – the women are thoroughly garbed in colorful (perhaps with multicolored stripes) or dazzling white garments that are clean and in excellent condition, well cut and tailored, trimmed with lace or *manchettes* (ruffle-like ornaments basted onto or worn under sleeves), and accompanied with a full range of accessories and jewelry. Over their flared-sleeve shifts and skirts or floor-length gowns, they usually wear shawl-like neckerchiefs, trimmed with lace, or some type of short jacket (*casaque, casaquin*, or *pet-en-l'air*), or both, and a very tall headwrap fashioned of multiple handkerchiefs, occasionally enriched with lace, and often topped with a hat banded by a ribbon and set at a rakish angle. Such clearly well-to-do women always sport earrings; many have necklaces as well and some carry a (usually bright red) handkerchief in one hand. Often, a petticoat is worn under and an apron over the skirt; less often, a gown that opens to reveal a petticoat replaces skirt and shift. Sometimes, too, the gown incorporates an embroidered stomacher or stayless corset and is finished off with an apron. Headdresses likewise may be single-color or multihued; at times, they incorporate a kind of tightly wrapped turban, at times are fashioned of more loosely tied handkerchiefs. Women in these depictions are shod, if often in a very subtle manner, with just the toe of a pink or a blue slipper barely peeking out from under their skirts, as in Plate 11.

Only handsomely appareled free men of color appear in Brunias's images, and only in relation to elite free women of color. Their dress usually includes white shirt, often with simple lace at the wrists and sometimes subdued ruffles on the chest; breeches with knee buckles and often some sort of costly-appearing trim; white stockings and leather shoes with silver buckles; fitted jacket or coat that may have a lively striped pattern, brass or gold buttons; and some type of black hat. As among the women, men's outfits display a degree of variation, in their case apparently indicative of occupational difference. A planter, for instance, wears a black cravat, a round black hat, and ankle-length pantaloons; the putative plantation overseer in Plate 11 a striking white cap as well as a small tricorne that denotes authority. All, however, are well dressed and all their garments, like those worn by Brunias's free women of color, contrast visibly with the clearly unfree laborers who are often portrayed at the margins of Brunias's scenes, unshod and often only partially clothed in apparel that is typically torn as well.[92] To Brunias, at least, free people of color and enslaved men and women inhabited different dress worlds.

Probate inventories of free people of color reveal garments that could well have been fashioned into the ensembles that Moreau de Saint-Méry described and Brunias depicted; the inventories also indicate that while Moreau de Saint-Méry surely exaggerated the number of outfits that Saint-Domingue's free women of color held, they did own multiples of most garments.[93] The wardrobe of Cecile Bouchonne counted 16 white linen shifts, 23 calico and other cotton skirts and matching *pets-en-l'air* (together skirts and tops formed *rechanges*, as worn by several of the women in Plates 11 and 12), 5 linen *casaques*, 14 linen petticoats, 8 linen caps, 9 white handkerchiefs; she also owned 6 ells each of chintz and printed *siamoise* that could be made into additional garments.[94] The prosperous planter's wife Marie, *dite* Boudrüe, boasted more varied apparel, including matching cherry-colored silk skirt and *casaquin*, another *rechange* of patterned silk, an expensive holland linen corset, and multiple colored and white handkerchiefs.[95]

Brunias also depicted free women of color engaged in retailing. Not as elaborately appareled as their leisured sisters to whom they are selling, nonetheless they are shown fully garbed, and often have aprons over skirts, large headwraps requiring multiple handkerchiefs, shawls, and jewelry (Plate 12).[96] This kind of attire likewise appears in probate inventories. The inventory of Marie Françoise, *dite* Fanchon Signore, a "marchande," listed 8 shifts, 16 *casaquins*, 25 skirts, and 22 handkerchiefs – all of "various fabrics" and "various colors" – and also credited her with a necklace of precious stones and gold strung on silk, worth 50 livres.[97] Other free working women of color likewise had impressive numbers of basic garments, though few additional items. The laundress Françoise had the smallest inventory value of all free women of color and unlike virtually all her peers did not own a slave. Nevertheless, at her death she had accumulated nine shifts, seven cotton and three linen *casaquins*, eleven calico and chintz skirts and three of linen, eight *rechanges* of calico and chintz, eight handkerchiefs, and a petticoat; apparently, however, she had no shoes or stockings.[98]

Yet if some free women of color acquired some unusual items or fabrics, these and the other inventories reveal that most of the alleged "luxury" of their apparel was defined by quantity and color or pattern, and occasionally by expensive linen or cotton fabric rather than the cheaper types out of which the rest of their clothing was tailored. Despite Atwood's declaration, only rarely did that "luxury" result from a rich silk or a large variety of diverse garments. The inventories, which recorded the condition of 42 percent of garments of free people of color, also show that Moreau de Saint-Méry's claim about the constant renewal and newness of mulattas' wardrobes was far-fetched. No piece was listed as "new," just 7 percent as "good," another 35 percent as "half worn" or "partly used," 39 percent as "more or less worn," and 19 percent as "old," "worn," "bad," or "very bad."

Some free men of color, too, could dress up in the style outlined by commentators and illustrated in Brunias's paintings. More than women, indeed, it was male planters who were the clotheshorses among free people of color. The well-to-do planter Ambroise Collard, *dit* Namur, for example, had workaday outfits built from numerous thread and cotton stockings, simple cotton breeches, plain linen shirts, cotton and linen jackets, cotton and linen handkerchiefs. But he also boasted silk stockings, two pairs of silk breeches (one blue, the other crimson), a new pair of black velvet breeches and another of red broadcloth, long linen pantaloons, and trimmed shirts, not to mention the uniform that he wore as a brigadier in the mounted constabulary (*maréchaussée*).[99] In contrast to free women of color, moreover, well-to-do male planter *gens de couleur* were more likely to have new or good clothing (between them, a third of all those individuals' garments that have specific conditions attributed to them). Other *gens de couleur* planters, however, would have made less of a show. Yet even though they could boast just a handful of breeches, shirts, and jackets – and much of the apparel was described as "very used" or barely wearable – such men did manage to secure a red worsted *calamande* jacket with black trim or a pair of sky blue velvet breeches.[100] At the same time, surely there were many *gens de couleur* like Pierrot, a *valet* (manservant) who counted just three coarse linen shirts and four equally coarse (and old) linen breeches, and who therefore could have dressed himself little differently from a slave.[101] The resemblance would have appeared, however, not when the two men dressed up – as Moreau de Saint-Méry implied – but in their workaday attire.

If Saint-Domingue probate inventories reveal a stratum of stylish *gens de couleur* – and also others with simple utilitarian dress – did their clothing set them apart from whites? In some respects it did, but not according to any neat pattern. Overall, free people of color and whites of the same occupation and wealth level wore essentially the same outfits, and women and men of both groups typically owned enough clothes to allow for frequent changes and washing. The similarities obtained across types of attire: All women and men wore white linen shifts or shirts, had a majority of thread stockings as well as significant numbers of cotton and silk stockings, and – when they had them – had acquired bright Cholet as well as plain linen handkerchiefs.

Still, some differences can be discerned. Free women of color wore skirts and short jackets (whether *casaquins* or *pets-en-l'air*), in some cases defined as *rechanges*. White women also dressed in skirts and jackets, but nine of thirteen also owned single-piece *robes* (gowns), not one of which was to be found in the wardrobe of an inventoried free woman of color. Again, the short cloak or *mantelet* that was becoming popular was specified only in wardrobes of white women – more specifically, of wives and widows of merchants (a group not represented among inventoried female *gens de couleur*) – whereas free women of color apparently owned very few outer garments of any sort. At the same time, the inventories confirm the emphasis in both written and pictorial depictions on the proclivity among free women of color for numerous handkerchiefs – but nearly all white females showed the same fervor, both groups of women probably using most of them for headwraps that would be attractive as well as protective.[102]

For their part, a few white men's wardrobes also held items not mentioned in those of free men of color – dressing gowns (*robes de chambre*), nightshirts, *capots* for outerwear – though the differences may result from the much greater number of inventoried white men as compared to free men of color. Both, in any case, were attuned to some ascendant styles, such as redingotes and velvet breeches; moreover, free men of color and white men were about as likely to forego handkerchiefs as have them.[103]

Gendered fabric choices complicated but did not alter the mosaic. Though all women showed a much greater propensity for cottons than men, four-fifths of the apparel of free women of color was tailored from cottons, as against two-thirds (63 percent) among white women; among men of both groups, in contrast, the figures were very similar (36 percent for *gens de couleur*, 33 for whites). Linens were male, but for two-fifths (39 percent) of the garb of free men of color, less than a third (30 percent) of whites. Men also more heavily favored woolens – indeed nearly monopolized them – but whereas whites favored them for a quarter (23 percent) of their garments, that proportion dropped to a sixth (17 percent) among free men of color (among white females and free women of color, the percentages were 2 and 0 respectively). Overall, silks were not gendered. But whereas they comprised nearly a quarter of white women's attire, they were found in just 1 percent of garments of female *gens de couleur*; and if less sharp, the same racial division obtained among men (14 percent among whites, 8 among free men of color). The comment by a former colonist, "we use silks a great deal, but here only white men and women wear them," was not entirely correct, but he did put his finger on an important nuance of dress habits in Saint-Domingue.[104] Still, while damask turns out to have been not only a specifically merchant pattern but a white one as well, choices of particular fabrics within each fiber category were not racialized. However, as we have learned, they were gendered: Indeed, Moreau de Saint-Méry's emphasis on the partiality of *gens de couleur* for white linens and muslins overlooked the marked preference shared by all women for multicolored calico and chintz.

The inventories indicate, then, that there were some sartorial distinctions between free people of color and whites in Saint-Domingue, but also that these differences were subtle and often barely perceptible. The situation seems to have been much the same in Jamaica, though inventories (and other evidence) are lacking.[105] In Brazil, too, inventories of wealthy free women of color in Minas Gerais (the central mining region) indicate that they, like affluent white women, dressed in "rich and colorful" silk, satin, and woolen attire when in public – so much so, indeed, as to earn rebukes from the provincial governor and repeated (and repeatedly ignored) royal ordinances intended to curb their behavior.[106] Gender was most often salient; dress was a relatively weak marker of racial identity, but a much stronger signal of gender across racial lines. So was occupation, to judge by the inventories of three *gens de couleur* who were planters.[107] Not only was the attire of these men identical to what their white peers wore, but their fabric preferences were also the same.[108] A 1766 law may have forbidden free people of color throughout the French West Indies to wear "shoes, stockings, ornaments, or any dress after the fashion of white people." But the inventories indicate that if the law was promulgated (which is uncertain) it had no immediate effect, and Moreau de Saint-Méry's account suggests that it was largely ignored in subsequent decades as well.[109] Rather than reflecting practices on the island or even influencing them, the discriminatory law would have put an official seal of approval on an ideology of stark, even unbridgeable racial difference. At a time when barriers were rising to limit if not end their participation in many public activities, clothing enabled free people of color visibly to declare their membership in the social class commensurate with their economic position. Though whites increasingly discriminated against free people of color in ways large and petty, dress stubbornly continued to associate them across racialized boundaries.

Colonial livery in the American tropics

Writing in 1766 to advise French merchants who complained about poor colonial sales even after the disruptive Seven Years' War had ended, a resident outlined the proper apparel fabrics to ship to Saint-Domingue. Woolens, he began, are simply not suitable in "our always hot climate," so only "a little" would ever be sold there. "We use a great deal of silk," he went on, but such fabrics cannot be worn constantly, as sweat discolors them and when washed, silks' luster vanishes. Linens are much more appropriate: coarse hemp for dressing slaves and "many other uses," but also finer flax, except closely woven varieties. "Due to the climate," he concluded,

> cotton is best for clothing us. It's light, it washes like linen without losing its beauty; it dyes readily and doesn't fade despite frequent washings; it keeps its shape, not wrinkling quickly like linen, which to boot dyes badly and fades easily. For all these reasons, we consume a prodigious amount of cotton cloth.[110]

Though not wholly accurate, the anonymous account does provide a good guide to both contemporary ideas about the correct colonial livery in the tropical Americas and the dress regime that had developed there. As we have seen, of course, while sartorial trends were convergent, they were far from uniform among places and social groups. Despite representations that announced – and often deprecated – characteristic mulatto fashions, *gens de couleur* appear to have dressed much like their peers: Sometimes these were enslaved laborers, more conspicuously they were other free settlers of like occupations and wealth levels. Thus race, which observers of the time often invoked as a key marker of appareling difference, held a more prominent place in the colonial imaginary than in settler sartorial experience.

Occupation, gender, and local culture proved more salient. Though acquiring some heavy and luxurious items, planters stood out for dressing in the lighter-colored and lighter-fiber linen and cotton garb that observers repeatedly recommended for tropical colonies, whereas merchants identified with heavier and darker traditional metropolitan materials. Women, too, created dress regimes defined by characteristic fabrics and finishes. For their part, Bahians wore much the same attire as free residents of the Antilles, and by some accounts many Brazilians dressed informally.[111] Yet on the whole they remained more committed to rich – if often lightweight – fabrics than their Caribbean counterparts. Even the modestly wealthy Felix de Sousa Vasconcelos, resident of the town of Cachoeira in the Recôncavo, boasted a pair of yellow satin breeches, a pearl-colored satin waistcoat and matching silk stockings, and his cambric linen suit was lined with blue taffeta, while the same material was embroidered on the front of his stylish *timão*.[112]

Despite these inflections of style, nevertheless, free settlers in the western Atlantic torrid zone wore attire similar in structure and content, close to European dress styles, and distinct from that worn by other tropical residents, including the great majority of their fellow colonists. Heedful of metropolitan conventions, influenced as well by widely held fears of degeneracy that the white body would suffer if exposed to the tropical sun,[113] and seeking to distinguish themselves visibly from less clothed indigenous and enslaved men and women, free settlers wore apparel that covered them nearly completely. And if slaves dressed up in ways that also involved substantially concealing their bodies, free settler attire remained different in fabrics and style. Ironically, perhaps, free settlers creolized their dress less successfully than slaves did.

Trevor Burnard has argued that settlers in the British West Indies sought to model their colonies on home-country norms but were thwarted by their colonies' increasingly singular social and demographic structures.[114] Though focused on Jamaica, "a very bizarre imitation of

British society,"[115] his interpretation provides a fruitful way of thinking about the tropical Americas as a whole. Dress – or at least elements of dress – allowed many of the free residents of the torrid zones to try to maintain some link with the metropoles: Velvet breeches were more than just pairs of pants. Tropical "luxury" was not slavish adherence to metropolitan fashion for its own sake, however, but an element of a syncretic colonial livery by which free settlers sought – in varying degrees according to individual and group preferences – at once to identify with European conventions, to accommodate local climatic conditions, and to set themselves apart from the unfree and indigenous. Free settlers in temperate colonies felt many of the same pressures, along with others posed by their distinctive environments. The dress regimes that emerged are the subject of Chapter 6.

6 FREE SETTLER DRESS IN TEMPERATE ZONES

> The French men of Canada ... are very well dressed. ... They have
> the custom of putting ribbons on their clothes, especially the *gilet*.
> Most of all they wear silk stockings ... On Sundays, the women
> dress in a refined manner, just like our Swedish wives ... During the
> week, they don't dress so elegantly ...[1]

> The country [white] women of Africa [Cape Colony] do not need
> many clothes; rarely does a wife or maiden have more than a long
> dress for Sundays which, made of East Indian chintz, costs little more
> than four or five rixdollars.[2]

Like their fellows who colonized the tropical Americas, free settlers in
the more temperate zones of the Atlantic were accustomed to European
clothing, imported textiles, and metropolitan standards. The climatic
conditions they faced, socioeconomic ecologies they constructed, and
relations with indigenous people they developed were individually more
disparate and collectively quite different from those obtaining in the
tropics. Yet the dress regimes they created were less syncretic and more
oriented to European norms than those found in warmer areas.[3]

South Atlantic singularities

At the edges of both the Atlantic basin and European Atlantic empires,
the colonies centered on Cape Town and Buenos Aires developed dress
regimes that always stood somewhat apart from Atlantic trends. Yet to
express sartorially their specific geoclimatic environments and their

distinctive development trajectories, both increasingly employed metropolitan European textiles, garments, and styles.

The dress of Cape Town residents in the late seventeenth and
early eighteenth centuries was shaped by their mixed demographic
origins, cultural orientations at once to Europe and to the East Indies,
and the VOC's ready access to Asian textiles and monopoly control of
imports to its nascent provisioning station and settlement. Two-fifths of
all inventoried attire was tailored from cottons and another fifth from
silks, as against just over a third from Dutch woolens and linens combined. The Cape's population was, in fact, precocious among colonists
not merely in wearing large amounts of varied cotton garments but in
the pronounced gendering that came to characterize apparel fabrics in
the eighteenth-century Atlantic. Whereas Cape women preferred cottons for about half their items, and silks for another third, men's favorite
textiles were woolens (half, as against less than ten percent among
women), followed by cottons (a third), while silks were just a tenth.

Acquaintanceship with Asian culture may also have promoted
integration of a modicum of Eastern attire into Cape residents' dress,
notably the *kabaai*, a banyan-style gown or cassock based on the kimono
but usually named after the Indian port of Cambay (today's Khambat),
source of the chintz from which so many were tailored. Adoption of the
banyan was not unique to the Cape, as we have already seen, but who
preferred it and how they wore it were. In Europe, as in many colonies,
the banyan was pre-eminently male and mercantile, a sign of luxurious
and leisured cosmopolitanism, as illustrated by the costly silk damask
version in which the extremely wealthy Boston merchant Nicholas
Boylston posed, the gown's richness (and his) emphasized by his other
splendid garments and the showy textiles that help define the sitter's space
(Plate 13).[4] At the Cape, however, women of all backgrounds much more
readily adopted *kabaaien* than men: Two-thirds of women inventoried in
the late seventeenth and early eighteenth centuries owned at least one, and
most owned multiple examples, commonly tailored from colorful flowered chintz. Some women may only have donned the *kabaai* at home or in
informal settings, but most apparently wore it as outerwear in place of a
coat or cloak, and among poor women it was the single most important
garment they owned. Yet the banyan usually stood as the sole Asian-
inspired item in a female wardrobe that otherwise epitomized the Atlantic
free settler woman's outfit: shift (*hembd*), skirt (*rok*), cap and/or bonnet,
and for about half, a bodice or vest (*borstrok*). Though willing to adopt

fabrics and a fashionable item of attire from another culture, female Capetonians' sartorial identification was European.

The garb of Cape men likewise hewed closely to the free colonist model. Only five of the forty males inventoried had a *kabaai* (and none more than one), and they had no other Asian items. Instead, the typical male wore a shirt (*hembd*), breeches (*broek*), coat (*rok*), shoes or boots and stockings, and headgear, typically a hat though often with a cap underneath, to which some added a waistcoat or vest: an outfit, that is, like the one worn by the horseman in the faded red coat in Plate 7b. Rural male settlers proved slightly less reluctant to learn from their Khoikhoi neighbors, at least according to the VOC employee O. F. Mentzel, who lived at the Cape during the 1730s, for they did wear "little *veldschoens* [field shoes] of raw hide" that were (although Mentzel does not say so) of indigenous origin.[5] Overall, however, male style was as thoroughly European as female, and there is no evidence that free settlers wore native-style leather capes or caps, even though these served the Khoikhoi well in the Cape with its cool if not cold winters, warm – often hot – summers, and varied microclimates.

In the colony's early years, urban Capetonians shared a common sartorial core with their fellows who had begun to settle inland, but their complete wardrobes differed in significant ways. For one thing, townspeople boasted more types of garments. Whereas all women, town and country, owned caps, for instance, most urban women also had another kind of headgear – and many had several kinds, such as hats or hoods. In addition, many wardrobes had items specific to their urban or rural milieu. In Cape Town, these included the one-piece *japon* and *samaar* gowns, short jacket (*jakje*), and distinctive "horned" *cornetmuts* style of cap; in the countryside, breeches designed and designated for women and large *sonnehoetjes* to protect against the sun. Among men, the tie or scarf (*das*) and the fitted *camisool*-style waistcoat were essentially urban fashions, found even among farmers living in town; looser *hemdrok* waistcoats and leather breeches were rural.

Some of the distinctive wear resulted from occupational differences. Like the great majority of the inventoried rural populace, the men who wore leather breeches, for example, were agriculturists who favored apparel that prioritized durability over display. But other sartorial dissimilarities attested to differential development that marked the Cape Colony in its early period. Though by 1717 four-fifths of the colony's 2,000 free residents lived on farms, the countryside was

isolated and economically stagnant, as strict VOC price controls, ineffi-
cient farming techniques, and extremely poor roads hampered commercialization and communications.[6] In addition, most mobile rural wealth
was tied up in equipment, stock, and, increasingly, slaves, which curbed
expenditure on material culture, including garments. So if the principal
clothing of urban and rural residents was the same, a visible minority of
country folk stood out for the skimpiness of their dress, another sizeable
rural group dressed in garments specific to their milieu, the rest – apart
from a handful – lacked several of the items that Capetonians wore as a
matter of course, and all tended to stand out by virtue of the plainness of
their sturdy yet often thin-fabric dress.

Across the eighteenth century, as maritime and internal demand
stimulated farm output and specialized urban crafts and services, living
standards rose steadily and the Cape Colony became "an affluent, market-
integrated settler society."[7] Residents of the interior regularly traveled to
Cape Town to sell produce and buy imported and local manufactures.
Noting the long journeys that farmers from the far interior took to trade at
the port city, Anders Sparrman wrote in the early 1770s that "the whole
colony," including not only merchants but also "the country people," had
common economic interests and commercial orientations.[8] The benefits of
economic growth were not, however, evenly distributed. The colony
experienced "growing disparities of wealth and capital" between a small
wealthy elite of VOC officials, traders, and substantial slaveholding farmers in and around Cape Town, and a mass of increasingly poor, largely
subsistence, and often landless agriculturists who often had to do without
imported manufactures.[9]

Across the eighteenth century, too, imported textile stocks
underwent some change in provenance and composition (Table 2.3).
Suggesting greater attention to local climate conditions, linens' share
fell, a decline more than compensated for by the rising presence of
European woolens and mixed-fiber fabrics such as silk and worsted
alapeen and bombazine, which combined silk and cotton, linen, or
worsted. Though retaining their pronounced dominance, cottons, too,
betokened cultural reorientation, since an ever-increasing percentage
was of European manufacture. The admixture of both generally advancing living standards and rising inequality, together with growing internal market integration and changing textile supplies, had complex
effects on the colony's dress regimes. To begin, a growing concentration
and polarization of clothing ownership occurred both in Cape Town as

against the countryside and within colonial society as a whole. These dual processes were manifested in, respectively, some very sizeable urban wardrobes, much larger than any rural resident had, and some very small ones in both town and, especially, country. Four Cape Town women boasted more than 100 articles of clothing, while a quarter of urban women and men had 50 or more garments in their inventories. In sharp contrast to the urban situation, just one countryman (a farmer) had more than 40 garments (42, to be precise), and no rural female more than 27.

At the other extreme of the sartorial spectrum, between 1689 and 1717 no inventoried Capetonian of either gender had fewer than six items of clothing – enough for two changes and thus regular washing – but a fifth of those listed in 1760–74 did, at a time when mean urban garment holdings had increased markedly.[10] The proportion of very small wardrobes also grew markedly in the countryside: Less than a fifth of males had half a dozen or fewer garments in the earlier period, a third in the later.[11] Overall, VOC officials, merchants, a handful of farmers, and their spouses had the largest wardrobes, whereas the smallest belonged to artisans and day laborers and their spouses in Cape Town together with artisans and poor farmers in rural areas.

In contrast to the earlier period, however, these quantitative disparities did not denote significant apparel and fabric differences between dress cultures of town and country. Not only, as before, did rural and urban residents share some basic garments – now virtually their entire dress regimes were very much the same. Expansion of specialized commercial grain, wine, and livestock farms in the interior knit town and country into a single market for attire as well as for other goods, with Cape Town as its cultural and commercial hub. As a result, rural folk may have had fewer garments than their counterparts in town, but they followed the same styles. This uniformity was evident first of all in the sharp decline everywhere of items like the *kabaai* that had been popular among women in the early eighteenth century, or the *borstrok*-style vest among men. It was equally visible in the general adoption of new garments, such as the sack gown or the petticoat (*gon*), or, among men, the more cloak-like *jas* style of coat.[12] Sartorial homogeneity was manifest, too, in the adoption in both areas of styles previously associated with the town, such as the *borstrok* among women or the *camisool* among men. And finally, it was seen in apparel fabric choices: Though townspeople showed a slightly greater taste for silks, and slightly less interest in woolens, this reflects the fact that a higher proportion of wealthy individuals lived in Cape Town than in the countryside.

As city–country differences eroded, free settlers' apparel in the Cape Colony as in tropical colonies more forcefully expressed occupational differences and socioeconomic stratification. No matter where they lived, top civil and military officials, merchants, and a minority of wealthy farmers owned on average about three times as many garments as artisans, lower VOC employees, and most farmers; among women, the gap grew to about 4:1. Not only did members of this composite elite own the most garments, they also owned distinctive pieces that would set them apart from their contemporaries: a black velvet cloak with blue pelang silk lining, a brilliant gold belt, a suit of expensive brilliant red woolen broadcloth (*laaken*).[13] Recalling conditions nearly half a century earlier as he composed his *Description of the Cape of Good Hope* in the 1780s, Mentzel may have correctly lumped all "country women" together as having skimpy garb, but by the 1760s an individual's dress announced not where she or he lived but her or his social status and well-being.

Ever-greater divergence between men and women likewise marked not only the garments that Cape Colony settlers wore but styles and fabrics as well. Thus the *borstrok*, once also worn by males, became strictly female, with the *camisool* (and *hemdrok*) waistcoats making the opposite move. The same strengthening of gender identifications seems evident as well in fabric preferences, as cottons became much more female (two-thirds of identifiable women's garments, as against less than a twentieth of men's). In contrast, woolens now accounted for three-quarters of identifiable men's clothing (up from two-fifths), whereas among women they still remained a distinctly minority taste at 13 percent of attire. As we have already observed in torrid-zone colonies, and will see again in the temperate zone, among free settlers the triad of occupation, wealth, and gender increasingly defined appropriate attire.[14]

As in tropical colonies, so in the Cape the dress of free people of color faced growing scrutiny. Free blacks (the Cape terminology for free people of color) were a smaller proportion of the settler population than in the contemporary tropical Americas, forming about five percent of the total free population, though up to three times as much in Cape Town itself.[15] Also in contrast to the Americas, no substantial planter or commercial elite emerged among free blacks; lacking the capital or connections to engage in wholesale trade or large-scale farming, most were artisans, petty retailers, gardeners, and fishers. Nevertheless, VOC officials, like their New World counterparts, considered free blacks – particularly, as always, women – sartorially unruly and similarly sought to implement sumptuary rules to control their dress. Accusing free black women of conduct "unseemly and vexing to the public," since by their clothing they allegedly put "themselves not only on a par with other respectable burghers' wives, but often pushed themselves above them," a 1765 law limited them to chintz and striped cotton apparel fabrics and forbade them "to appear in public in colored silk clothing, hoop skirts, fine laces, adorned bonnets, curled hair, or even earrings."[16]

It is possible that free black women owned and flaunted the prohibited items. Yet whereas Cape Colony inventories of men and women among the (white) propertied and high officialdom over and over again list costly, ornamented garments – damask petticoats, silk skirts, satin coats, velvet breeches, and on and on – the only hints of sartorial opulence in inventories of free blacks are a handful of chintz skirts, velvet caps, and printed cotton handkerchiefs, none of which the law saw fit to enjoin. Two inventoried free black women did own gold ear ornaments (*oorcrabben*); one of them, the prosperous owner of fishing boats and slaves Tjojingjo, had a couple of other pieces of jewelry, including two with diamonds. But these items were unexceptional among even mildly affluent Cape residents rather than specific to free women of color.

The inventory evidence indicates, in fact, that like their counterparts in the Americas free black Capetonians did not set themselves apart sartorially from those of European descent of the same socioeconomic status; nor was their dress inflected by Asian or African influences. On the contrary, black or white, all wore the basic outfit and, significantly (symbolically as well as in terms of comfort), stockings and footwear for both genders. Variations did mark individuals' apparel: jacket rather than vest, gown rather than shift and petticoat or skirt, type of hat or cap. But these idiosyncrasies followed no pattern among either free blacks or their European-descent counterparts; rather, they were indexes of personal fashion that betray no desire on the part of either group to mark itself off from the other.[17]

As in the Americas, in short, growing official attention to and disapproval of the dress of free people of color reflected not actual dress regimes but attitudes and ideologies. At least in the eyes of those with power to legislate, a traditional hierarchic gender and wider social order was under attack by daily practice, an alarming situation that the new laws sought to reverse by inaugurating sartorial markers and privileges of rank. Whereas no specific free black style had heretofore existed, the directives of officialdom would create one. That the dress of free blacks inventoried after 1765 shows no differences whatsoever from that catalogued before that date – and continued to resemble nothing so much as the dress of socially if not pigmentally similar free whites – suggests, however, that the law's exercise in racial sartorial classification arrived as a dead letter, at least for the moment.[18] Just as in torrid-zone colonies, free blacks were targeted for sartorial censure, and just as in the tropical Americas their dress practices ignored or sought to overcome rising racialization.

So while market integration and the increasing overall prosperity of the Cape Colony promoted forms of sartorial similarity across city and country, at the same time occupation, wealth, and gender drew unmistakeable distinctions of fabric and fanciness, and these identifications overrode color and former status, not to mention climatic adaptation and earlier cultural orientation. You dressed much alike whether you were an official in Cape Town or in the interior, and you also dressed much alike – but choosing from a much smaller and plainer assortment of garments than the affluent – whether you were a port city or a rural shoemaker. Changing textile regimes penetrated widely across the Cape Colony, and climate as well as commerce promoted a greater European orientation. Still, the easing of city–country contrasts yielded not a single colony-wide dress standard – not a common colonial livery – but new criteria of difference.

The kind of integrated commercial and sartorial space that developed in the Cape Colony during the eighteenth century was by then more than a century old in Buenos Aires and its hinterland. Attracted both by the region's livestock, hides, foodstuffs, and other agricultural products, and its position as terminus of overland routes to the great mining center of Potosí and the colonial administrative center at Lima, official trade, semi-legal schemes, and outright smuggling distributed a wide array of goods that allowed residents of the interior to wear the same garments tailored from the same fabrics as Porteños.[19] By the second half of the seventeenth century, if not earlier, these tightly linked interregional and international trade relations delivered not only imported textiles and fashions but cottons and woolens from *obrajes* and workshops (*chorrillos*) located in some interior Argentine towns, on Jesuit estates in Paraguay, and especially in upland Andean communities.[20] Most of the coarse inland cloth was destined for Indians and slaves. But free settlers did wear fine Andean broadcloth (*paño de Quito*) and baize as well as Spanish and other European silks and woolens and, in very limited quantities, linens and cottons.

Between 1652 and 1697, inventories reveal, men and women in both Buenos Aires and the interior dressed in the basic Atlantic free settler outfits with Río de la Plata nuances: shawl-like veils (*mantellinas*, *gabachas*, or *dengues*) for women; the poncho, apparently a seventeenth-century Araucanian Indian innovation from the earlier indigenous tunic, for both genders; virtually no cottons and relatively few linens for anyone.[21] Some slight occupational distinctions did mark dress: In particular, farmers and ranchers wore more durable linen garments and fewer of silk and other showy fabrics like *lama* (a popular jacket material woven from gold and silver threads). But all men and women wore a heavy preponderance of silk, woolen, and rich mixed-fiber garments, and all enlivened some of their garments with colorful ribbon, braid, lace, and other trim.[22] As elsewhere in Iberian America, silks and fine woolens served to distinguish free settlers from the indigenous and the enslaved, who were dressed, as we have seen, in rough cheap cottons and woolens of local or Andean manufacture, as well as in imported linens.[23]

Thanks to continued expansion of both the hinterland's export-oriented agriculture and trade licit and illicit along the commercial networks that converged at Buenos Aires, the port city became the largest settlement on the Atlantic façade of the Viceroyalty of Peru.[24] As in Cape Town, with increased commercial activity came a textile profile more closely resembling that of other Atlantic colonies (compare Tables 2.1 and 2.3). Once virtually absent from merchant stocks, and wholly so from settlers' wardrobes, cottons of European manufacture became available. In contrast to other Atlantic ports, however, Asian cottons were not in evidence; apparently, the Río de la Plata remained outside relevant trade circuits. Linens recorded a more striking success. Much of the linen available for purchase was unbleached *crudo* that with other cheap varieties was likely to end up on the backs of the rapidly growing throngs of enslaved and indigenous laborers in town and country alike, in a domestic setting, or in a workshop. But a substantial part was medium-quality mid-price linens from Brittany such as *crea, pontevi* (named for the central town of its area of production), and particularly semifine narrow and fine wide *bretaña*, so highly prized for the excellence of its tightly regulated and highly standardized flax, spun thread, and bleaching that it was widely imitated (e.g., platilla) and counterfeited (including by French rivals).[25]

Yet if Río de la Plata merchant stocks followed the Atlantic trend to lighter-weight fabrics, the change was not evident in inventoried apparel. As many scholars have noted, cottons and linens are less durable than silks and woolens; this may have made cotton and linen attire less present in wardrobes than in actual garb, though if they had truly won consumers' fancy they ought to have been replaced as they wore out, as happened elsewhere. Cottons' presence did increase from essentially nul in the seventeenth century to 5 percent in both female and male attire in 1760–74, mainly in skirts, waistcoats, and jackets; additionally, cotton cloth was fashioned into handkerchiefs and caps. Despite this gain, cottons for apparel did not win the same favor in Argentina as elsewhere. In addition, linens actually lost ground as a fabric for attire. To be sure, among free settlers linens retained a near-monopoly position as shirting material and thus benefited from increased holdings of shirts and blouses: an average of 3.5 among women in 1760–74, as against 2.8 in the later seventeenth century; a more impressive 13.5 among men, up from 7.9. Linens were also found in attire such as aprons, drawers, and caps that more men and women wore. But overall, they were employed less in garb than in the later seventeenth century and indeed declined more sharply than cottons advanced: from a tenth to only a few percent in women's attire, a sixth to 6 percent in men's.[26] In sharp contrast, silks and woolens remained the overwhelming preferences for both male and female free settlers' garments in the Río de la Plata region and indeed marginally increased their hold.[27]

The lack of colorful calicoes may have contributed to free Argentines' relative indifference to cotton clothing even in the later eighteenth century, since the arrival of these fabrics is often credited with sparking a rage for such attire in New Spain; similar reasons may explain why the banyan-like dressing gown (*peinador* or *bata*) was so rarely found in Río de la Plata inventories.[28] But it appears that in Argentina, as in Brazil and throughout much of Iberian America, cottons and linens remained so strongly associated with indigenous and enslaved populations that they long made little headway among free colonists' basic and outerwear, whereas silks and woolens retained their status as a badge of free settler identity. Spanish government policies encouraged such attitudes. Repeated reissuance suggests that the numerous sumptuary laws decreed by the Viceroyalty in Lima explicitly forbidding blacks and mulattoes from using silks and woolens failed to achieve their objective. But they did cement the association of rich, mainly imported fabrics with free settlers of European descent.[29] At the same time, both tacit and actual identification of cottons and linens with the enslaved and the uncivil curbed their appeal to free settlers. In the 1780s, the government did an abrupt about-face and began to encourage cottons consumption, a move designed equally to support the Barcelona cotton industry, reduce costly imports, and promote unity among restive colonists of Indian and European descent. But only then did Spanish manufacturers make headway in American markets.[30]

Free settlers in the Río de la Plata did adopt new varieties and give up some old favorites, a trend that cemented European fabric dominance. Andean fabrics suffered badly from increased imports of English, Spanish, Dutch, and French woolens and the failure of manufacturers in the kingdom of Quito to adjust prices and quality of their textiles in the face of this competition.[31] *Paño de Quito*, often tailored into breeches and outerwear in the late seventeenth century, virtually disappeared by 1760–74, as did cheap, coarse Andean woolens such as *cordellate* and *pañete*, while *bayeta de la tierra* (baize) lost favor among better-off settlers to become firmly identified with the poor and particularly with the enslaved.[32] Still, Andean products were not the only losers. Some once-popular European types also vanished: *lama*, satin (*ormesí*), woolens such as coarse camlet-like *barragán* and *estameña*, baize-like but thicker *serafina*, and better-quality vivid scarlet *escarlatilla*.

The new imports considerably broadened the range of appareling fabrics employed in the Río de la Plata: The most important among them were silk and worsted *princesa*, luxurious textured brocade (*brocato*), flowered silk *griseta*, lutestring (*lustrina*) that often included gold and silver threads to enhance its silken brilliance, silk *persiana* with its large flower designs and multitude of colors, thick woolen and silk *tercianela* (grogram), heavy woolen *tripe* that resembled velvet, and velvet itself (*terciopelo*), which became the leading silk for men's attire and attracted considerable female custom as well. Some lighter-weight varieties were used for apparel beyond shirts and shifts: printed and plain cottons and Breton and copycat linens. In the main, however, the new favorites, like the old, perpetuated Argentines' preference for heavier textiles.

In the free settler Atlantic world as a whole, lighter fabrics – most notably cottons – became identified as female in the eighteenth century, heavier textiles – woolens in the lead – as male. The tepid enthusiasm for cottons and tilt toward thicker cloth among all free residents of the Río de la Plata sharply limited those possibilities for fabric gendering. To be sure, a degree of dimorphic taste did exist with respect to specific fabric varieties: dimity (*cotonía*), grogram, *tripe*, and broadcloth were much more popular among men than among women, who disproportionately favored *persiana*, baize, and camlet (*camellón*). But two silks, velvet and taffeta, which in many places exemplified the gender divide with respect to showy textiles, indicate that such divergence was much weaker in and around Buenos Aires. The Atlantic-wide enthusiasm for velvet breeches and jackets also swept up men in the Río de la Plata – yet women there likewise tailored velvet into skirts, jackets, and coats. Similarly, whereas in most colonies taffeta became increasingly identified with female attire, in Argentina it was fashioned into male apparel as well.[33] The gendering that innovative fabric choices promoted elsewhere in the Atlantic was limited by the tastes of free settlers in the Río de la Plata: The oft-noted rich-fabric splendor of Spanish Americans involved men as well as women.[34] Indeed, the silk- and woolen-based ostentation decried among torrid-zone colonists was exhibited much more conspicuously – and, given the climate, much more appropriately – in the temperate Río de la Plata.

Garment styles also changed, but again rather modestly. In the second half of the seventeenth century, the tight-fitting doublet-like *jubón* with short skirts had been worn by both men and women, in both port and hinterland, on the farm and in the shop; a century later, it was a distinctly minority taste among women, and entirely absent from men's wardrobes. In the seventeenth century, too, men had worn several types of jacket over the *jubón*, such as the *ropilla* that might or might not have sleeves, yet all were supplanted thereafter by the *chupa* variant, long-sleeved with skirts extending below the waist, and many men also had a sleeveless waistcoat (*chaleco*) that might replace the *chupa* or be worn under it. In overall composition, however, settler outfits, like fabric preferences, remained much as they had been; indeed, they became even more strongly oriented toward European fashions that they copied.

Argentine free settlers did, however, participate in the wider Atlantic trend toward more forcefully expressing occupation and social stratification in their dress regimes. Already in the seventeenth century, the garb of farm and ranch men and women had shown some differences from men of commerce and their wives and widows: Agriculturists of both genders wore more linen garb, merchants and their families more silks, *lama*, and other showy items. The discrepancies were minor at that point (a quarter to a fifth in each case); they became much more pronounced by the later eighteenth century. Apart from shirts and shifts, the little linen attire worn had become almost entirely associated with agricultural pursuits, while merchant men and women were more than twice as likely as farmers and ranchers to boast silk garments; as for woolens, they were two-thirds or more of farm men's and women's attire but barely half among merchant and shopkeeper families. Similarly, it was among men of commerce that fashions like the dressing gown and fitted frockcoat found whatever limited welcome they received.

The contrasts were circumstantially linked with place of residence, for a greater proportion of wealthy merchants lived in Buenos Aires, and most agriculturists lived outside the city, though it is a simplification to counterpose city modishness to country stodginess.[35] They were more the effect of wealth differentials: Even excluding two extravagantly rich merchants, the inventoried estates of merchants and shopkeepers were on average worth more than twice that of ranchers and farmers,[36] and they could more readily afford the materials for display. But most of all, sartorial disparities were rooted in occupation. The ranchers depicted in Figure 6.1 wore garb much the same as their peers at the Cape of Good Hope (Plate 7) that was also quite unlike that of merchants and shopkeepers in either colony. Like their counterparts elsewhere, that is – albeit in an idiom that suited their specific cultural conventions – agriculturists and merchants of the Río de la Plata learned to manifest profession and social distinction sartorially across urban–rural frontiers.[37]

Climate did not determine the evolution of dress in either the Cape Colony or the Río de la Plata. But in combination with local economic arrangements, social changes, and cultural orientations, it enabled free settlers in both colonies to elaborate dress regimes increasingly defined by and composed of Europe textiles, garments, and styles. Capetonians, Porteños, and their inland fellow free colonists were able

6.1 *Cattle Ranchers* (*c.* 1770), by Florián Paucke.

Paucke, born in Austrian Silesia, was a Jesuit missionary among the Mocoví Indians near Santa Fe in the Río de la Plata interior. His drawings and paintings included both indigenous and settler subjects.

to achieve sartorially the greater conformity to metropolitan material cultural expressions that torrid-zone settlers sought in vain.

Semitropical negotiations

British South Carolina and French Louisiana might be expected to have had dress regimes like those of the American tropics. Both were plantation slavery colonies with long hot seasons. Moreover, South Carolina, founded by planters and slaves from Barbados, maintained close demographic and commercial links with the West Indies, as did Louisiana, notably with Saint-Domingue, where most ships stopped before continuing on to New Orleans. Yet despite sharing some features of Caribbean appareling, dress regimes in the colonies of the southern mainland of North America were distinctive hybrids, neither fully tropical nor fully temperate in inspiration and material.

Inventories from late seventeenth-century South Carolina lack much information about fabrics, but they do show that free settlers in that colony wore much the same outfits as their counterparts elsewhere in the Atlantic world.[38] As elsewhere, too, by the 1730s additional items – more varieties of coats, nightgowns and nightshirts, pumps and slippers, banyans for a minority of men – had entered wardrobes without changing the original quotidian outfit of either gender. Similar as well was the emergent gendering of dress fabrics by the second third of the eighteenth century. Women preferred cottons for a third (29 percent) of their garments, men for just half that (16 percent); women avoided woolens, while they formed nearly two-fifths (37 percent) of men's attire.[39]

A more singular dress regime took shape across the next few decades. To be sure, South Carolina participated in the Atlantic-wide fashion for cottons. At least among affluent Charlestonians, these fabrics were already gaining some favor from the later seventeenth century (see Tables 2.1 and 2.2). In the two years before her marriage in June 1720, the guardians of the wealthy orphan Sarah Lindley spent more than 200 South Carolina pounds on her garments. Of the total, 37 percent each went for cottons and silks, 16 percent for linens, and 10 percent for woolens. Of various prices and qualities, the cottons were employed in sundry garments. Fine, expensive chintz was used for her Easter gown and petticoat, less costly calico for lining a gown and a quilt coat, as well as for a nightgown, a petticoat, and a winter gown (which was lined with similarly economical Dutch cotton check), and ordinary muslin for an apron.[40]

By 1760–74, these lighter, more colorful fabrics were tailored into nearly a quarter of men's apparel, virtually the same proportion as in Jamaica.[41] But unlike their West Indian peers, free Carolinians were not responding to climatic conditions by developing a dress regime grounded in lighter fabrics. Growing use of cotton garments among free settlers was matched by an equivalent decline in linens, which became increasingly identified with the growing slave population. South Carolina free colonists' linen clothing consumption lagged behind Jamaican (a quarter and a third respectively); similarly, while check caught on as a shirt material, it was not taken up for breeches and jackets, again in contrast to the Caribbean. Then, too, the favored cotton in South Carolina, nankeen, was a closely woven, heavy variety. Nor, unlike Jamaican men, did South Carolinians make use of fewer woolens or turn to lighter varieties; if anything, they reinforced their partiality for broadcloth. Similarly, lighter silk taffeta attracted less interest among South Carolina men and women than Jamaicans. And if frock-style coats (often referred to as "surtouts" in South Carolina) and complete suits appeared in both colonies, they were tailored from heavy woolens in South Carolina, as against the linens and cottons employed in Jamaica.

In some respects these developments resembled those underway in Buenos Aires. But South Carolina clothing styles and fabric choices were not associated or identifiable with specific professions: Surtouts and cottons made headway among cabinetmakers and surgeons, not to mention planters and merchants, and all these men proved equally strongly attached to woolen clothing and coats. Though wealth did influence the size of wardrobes, no city–country divisions obtained. Men of similar levels of affluence from agricultural Granville County, the small port of Georgetown, and bustling Charles Town dressed alike, illustrating notable rural–urban economic, residential, and social integration founded, as R. C. Nash has shown, on "a highly centralized and urbanized system of merchandising and distribution" that provided the same goods to consumers throughout the colony.[42] South Carolinians did acquire fashionable items: Even a moderately prosperous individual like James Fleet could sport a silk plush jacket.[43] But perhaps more telling is the inventory of the wealthy planter Henry Pagott: If it listed some silk breeches and waistcoats, it comprised mainly woolen attire, and Pagott's luxury was expensive broadcloth suits with lace-trimmed waistcoats.[44] As these examples suggest, in South Carolina free settler appareling was defined not by the innovative light attiring of Caribbean planters, nor by the silks that distinguished Iberian America, but by styles and materials that underpinned a remarkably homogeneous syncretic dress regime.

Dress developments in lower Louisiana both exhibited strong parallels to South Carolina's and stood in a relation to trends in Saint-Domingue much like that linking South Carolina and Jamaica.[45] As on the Caribbean island, drawers, *gilets*, redingotes, caps, and handkerchiefs became more regular items of male attire in Louisiana across the mid-eighteenth century. At the same time, long *pelisse* cloaks appeared more often in female wardrobes, while *robes de chambre* lost popularity among both men and women. A full participant in the growing Atlantic enthusiasm for cottons (the material for 17 percent of basic and outer garments in 1717–39, 29 percent in 1760–69), free Louisianans likewise balanced this new enthusiasm with flagging interest in linens (down from 21 to 14 percent). Both changes mirrored those occurring in the Caribbean and Carolina and reflect, as elsewhere, the growing identification of cottons with free settlers, linens with the rising populations of enslaved men and women.

Though linens retained a near-monopoly on shirts and blouses, already in the first third of the eighteenth century cottons had become significant in basic items like breeches (nearly one-third of the total), skirts (nearly three-quarters), petticoats and gowns (each half), vests (nearly half), short jackets and women's bonnets (both slightly more than half), along with a majority of cravats and handkerchiefs. Consumption of cottons was higher among women (nearly two-fifths of their garments) than among men (about one-quarter), indicating pronounced gender identification. Though the evidence is incomplete, it does suggest both urban–rural and occupational disparities. Cottons seem to have been particularly associated with merchants and planters (not infrequently the same persons) and their families, who lived both in New Orleans and on their plantations, together with government bureaucrats and professionals, whereas farmers, shopkeepers, and artisans who lived wholly in the countryside were more likely to have substantial holdings of woolen clothing.

Use of cottons continued to rise thereafter as they were tailored not only into newly popular items, notably men's *gilets* and women's cloaks, but now also into shirts and shifts, though linens remained the preferred material for that purpose. Fabric gendering became yet more pronounced. By the 1760s, women owned on average twice as many cottons as men, who owned half again as many linens and at least five times as many woolens. Indeed, woolens had all but disappeared from women's wardrobes, save the occasional heavy cloak or expensive gown. In contrast, cottons' marker as an urban good weakened, as did that of other fabrics, including silk. While that trend reveals the influence of merchant-planters, who lived in both town and country, it also suggests that a more unified settler material culture had emerged along the lower Mississippi.

From that area, moreover, the new tastes spread into the interior, carried by merchants and itinerant peddlers.[46] The gender identification of cottons seems likewise to have traveled inland. The 1767 inventory of a female farmer (*habitante*) in the Illinois country contained only cotton skirts, along with entirely woolen outerwear, whereas the listings of two male farmers (*habitants*) who died nearby in the same period included almost nothing but hard-wearing woolen and linen garments.[47] So well did preferences get rooted that when eastern merchants moved into the Illinois country following its effective transfer to British control several years after the Seven Years' War, cottons loomed large in their assortment of goods. In calendar 1769, the Philadelphia firm of Baynton, Wharton, and Morgan sold textiles worth more than 5,000 livres. Of that total, cottons accounted for 28 percent, linens 36 percent, woolens 23 percent.[48]

Unlike among West Indians, that is – though as among other free settlers in the Atlantic – silks and woolens, notably heavier varieties, remained a substantial presence in Louisiana wardrobes.[49] Louisianans continued to prefer broadcloth, for example, while adding garments made from other thick woolens like *molleton* and *couverte* (blanketing) rather than lightweight types, and among cottons heavy, coarse (and cheap) *cotonade* and *polonoise* became leading varieties, just as nankeen did among their British North American counterparts. And as in South Carolina, so in Louisiana planters did not point the way to a lighter dress regime more attuned to a hot climate. Along the lower Mississippi, as in the Lowcountry, planter fabric preferences were indistinguishable from those of other free male settlers, for, in the one as in the other, not only was there considerable overlap among planters, merchants, and other professions but planters typically spent considerable amounts of time in town, both to do business and to engage in leisure and consumption activities.[50] Status and occupation not only softened rural–urban differences but subordinated climatic considerations to socioeconomic identifications.

Still, Louisiana's dress regime was not South Carolina's with a French accent. The French colony had a much smaller population dispersed across a much larger territory than the British, with concentrations around Natchitoches in present-day northwestern Louisiana state and in the Illinois country, just south of St. Louis. These settlements housed a few military officers, professionals, and merchants whose sartorial points of reference were urban and metropolitan: men like Jean-Louis Bonnaffond, merchant and surgeon at the Natchitoches fort, whose large personal clothing supply included fashionable velvet, broadcloth, and calico breeches, waistcoats, and coats.[51] But most free settlers in these areas were small farmers and petty traders who adapted their apparel to economic and climatic conditions that resembled New

France more than the lower Mississippi. Not only did they wear hooded *capots* rather than cloaks, or rough woolen leggings (*mitasses*) instead of stockings. They also owned more cotton clothing, and just a fourth as many silks. So while a handful had a fancy item such as a pair of silk breeches, the overwhelming majority of their garb comprised cheap, coarse, durable varieties of cottons (e.g., *cotonade, polonoise*), linens (*gingas*), and woolens and worsteds (*cadis, couverte, ratine*) in contrast to colonists in or close to New Orleans.[52]

In lower Louisiana, in contrast, where a 1752 banquet was, according to a participant, graced by one hundred "most richly dressed women," there emerged a degree of "opulence and splendor."[53] In some of its manifestations – heavy, showy apparel like velvet breeches and waistcoats, or beribboned scarlet broadcloth coats, for instance, markers reminiscent respectively of Caribbean and South Carolinian *luxe* – lower Louisiana clothing gave priority to fashion over comfort.[54] But the thin striped cotton or cotton-silk *sirsaca* and brightly colored taffeta apparel also found in men's wardrobes (not to mention the gowns and skirts of the same materials worn by their wives or widows) indicate a simultaneous attempt to apparel more suitably when the weather turned semitropical. Taken together, they denote a dress regime that, like its South Carolina counterpart, resulted from negotiations at once among climate and display, Atlantic trends and local conditions, general free settler identity and occupational differentiation.

Continental distinctions

Cooler climates, substantial farm populations, and significant trade with Amerindians put large amounts of woolens and linens on the shelves of merchants in Philadelphia and Montreal from their earliest days and kept them there across the eighteenth century (Tables 2.1 and 2.3). As both towns became leading and increasingly prosperous Atlantic commercial and administrative centers, they also felt the influence of broader fashion trends. At the same time, their growing settler populations opened up new inland areas for agriculture and settlement, and some took up spinning and weaving.[55] Thus both colonies were closely linked on the one hand to farming and fur-trading hinterlands, and on the other to European, Atlantic, and global networks. However, development followed a different trajectory in each place. Pennsylvania's agriculture included a larger export component than did New France's, focused mainly on provisioning Montreal and military garrisons throughout the vast colony, while the fur trade dominated Montreal's commercial life to a greater degree than Philadelphia's.

In the late seventeenth century, the free residents of each wore variants of the basic free settler garb. Women in the Philadelphia area preferred gowns and petticoats to skirt–jacket combinations, about half wore linen aprons, and a few had shawls or neckerchiefs. In Montreal, gowns were always a minority taste, but as in Philadelphia, about half of women had shifts or blouses. Male wear was more standard and more similar, though in Canada outerwear was as likely to comprise a hooded *capot* as a tailored coat.[56] The banyan (morning gown or *robe de chambre*) had made only a timid appearance in either place. In these still small colonies, where farmers as well as most other settlers lived in or quite close to town, men and women of all professions wore the same outfit; variation demonstrated individual taste rather than occupation or geographic position.

Early fabric choices diverged only slightly more, with gender playing the strongest role. Women wore more silks, and in Pennsylvania mixed silk-woolen crape; men, though little interested in silks, were more partial to woolens.[57] A similar gender dimorphism was noticeable not only in terms of fiber categories but in terms of specific fabrics as well. Lighter textiles tended to be associated with women: less expensive thin silks like barratine (Philadelphia) or *ferrandine* (Montreal), crape in Pennsylvania, untwilled woolen *estamine* in New France, taffeta in both. Male-identified fabrics were heavier: cotton-linen fustian, silk plush, and napped woolen frieze in Pennsylvania; woolen frieze-like *ratine* and coarse *bouracan*, and linen-woolen *tiretaine* in the Saint Lawrence valley. As with garments, so with fabrics, town–country or occupational distinctions were not in evidence: In late seventeenth-century Pennsylvania and New France, a blacksmith or farmer was as likely as a merchant to wear a pair of broadcloth breeches.

Linens and woolens retained their edge well into the eighteenth century. The farmer Antoine Courtemanche spent just 8.5 percent of his textile outlays on cotton fabrics between December 1719 and March 1723, as against nearly 37 percent on linens and 55 percent on woolens. Even in 1737–47, cottons accounted for only 5 percent of textile outlays by the *habitant* Leonard Libersart, called Laviolette, while linens took a third and woolens 62 percent.[58] At the same time, pronounced economic and demographic development in both colonies promoted not only greater population dispersion and migration in search of new farmland, but greater differentiation between and within geographic location and occupation, while firming up gender distinctions.

By 1760–74, garments showed evidence of these changing conditions. Some dress developments were shared across socioeconomic and spatial frontiers. All men in New France now had the long *veste*-style waistcoat, as alternatives disappeared, at least two-fifths also had the newer, shorter, *gilet* style, and some had *robes de chambre* (often, as befit the climate, of a woolen rather than the usual calico or silk). All women now wore a *jupon* (skirt or petticoat) and the short jacket called a *mantelet* in New France though elsewhere a *casaquin*. The Swedish traveler and botanist Pehr Kalm commented on the "tight and short" skirts, which "barely reach the middle of the calf."[59] To the surveyor Louis Franquet, the artful combination of "very short" tightly belted *jupons* and waist-length jackets allowed settler women to display their shapely legs and graceful carriage with "a bit of coquetry."[60] Women also wore white caps, with the sides, Kalm observed, usually turned up,[61] as is visible on the woman on the lower right in Plate 6. Franquet claimed that Canadian women preferred two-piece ensembles, and indeed less than a third of women's inventories list gowns. As Plate 6 also suggests, and inventories confirm, aprons were less often a requisite part of female dress. Finally, the documents reveal that the use of cottons had spread widely into the countryside (albeit among women rather than men). Little wonder, then, if between November 1771 and October 1774 André Laperle of La Prairie outside Montreal devoted a quarter of his expenditures on textiles for his family to cottons; still, two-fifths did go for linens and a third for woolens.[62]

More striking were the clear sartorial and fabric distinctions in dress based on a combination of place and profession. Earlier apparel styles persisted in the countryside even as newer fashions were adopted in Montreal. About a third of rural (mainly farm) women owned a *jupe* (*de rigueur* at the end of the seventeenth century), yet less than a tenth of urban women did. Conversely, the gown, not worn earlier and still a minority taste among women in general, had become identified with the urban woman, particularly among the commercial and professional strata (about half owned one, including the woman on the lower right in Plate 6), rather than with the rural (barely a fifth), who clung to the *jupon*–jacket pairing seen on the red-cloaked woman (labeled "farmer") in the same image. And while nearly all inventoried urban residents were now credited with shifts or shirts, only two-thirds of rural men and women were.

Disparate items also now marked off country from city men. The belted, hooded *capot* has long been described as "the characteristic garment" of New France, "the first properly Canadian fashion."[63] It had been so in the seventeenth century, when it appeared in inventories of every group in all locations. By 1760–74, however, it had become a sign of agrarian rurality: Nine of ten country men – merchants, shop-keepers, and artisans as well as *habitants* – owned at least one *capot*; for nearly half, it was the only piece of outerwear they owned, and most had three or more. In Plate 6 one *capot* is shown with hood up (lower row, extreme right), while another one (third from the left in the same row) could be worn hood down because the farmer in it has on that other prototypical early Canadian garment, the *toque* or red woolen cap. In contrast, less than a third of male Montrealers owned even one *capot* (and almost always only one), and not one townsman owned just that item of outerwear. Instead, virtually every townsman wore an *habit*, a hoodless, buttoned, and often lined replacement for the *justaucorps*. The *habit* (worn both by the man on the lower far left and the man third from the lower right in Plate 6) was more elegantly cut and decoratively trimmed than the *capot* it had influenced.[64]

As much as style, fabric distinguished city and country, men engaged in physical labor (and their wives and widows) from men of commerce, government officials, military officers, landowners, and pro-fessionals, and their families. This was manifest in the lower frequency of cotton and silk garments (respectively 8 and 5 percent) among farm-ers and artisans than among other men (15 and 18 percent), and the greater use of woolens (83 percent compared with 61). Wealth-cum-occupational disparities, which mapped onto the country–city divide, caused some of the fabric differences: On average, the rural population was less affluent than the urban, the laboring population than the commercial, official, professional, and rentier.[65] This made it likely that when choosing a silk, or even a woolen, farmers, artisans, and country folk in general would opt for a less expensive variety. Thus, to take one example, in the country (and among farmers and artisans) about a third of *capots*, waistcoats, and breeches were tailored from *cadis*, a coarse to medium quality worsted, though it was used very seldom (less than 10 percent) in Montreal and among the mercantile, official, and professional strata. Among the latter groups, broadcloth, which cost on average nearly three times as much as *cadis*, was found in more than two-fifths of attire, as against just over a fifth among rural and laboring men. Similarly, nearly a third of the shirts owned by rural males were fashioned out of locally or domestically woven linen (*toile du pays*), which was entirely absent from urban men's wardrobes. At the same time, expensive velvet breeches and waistcoats set apart urban merchants, officials, and professionals, not only from country men but farmers and artisans no matter where they lived; they had to make do, for their few silk items, with *panne*, a kind of mock-velvet which cost only a fourth as much.

When he commented on the fine attire of residents of New France, Kalm was in Montreal; after visiting rural districts, his emphasis was rather on simplicity, especially of women's dress. It would appear that he was accurate in both places. Like men, urban women and mercantile-official-professional wives and widows wore twice as many silk garments as rural, mainly *habitante*, and artisan women (a fifth as against a tenth) and considerably fewer tailored from a woolen (a sixth as against more than a third). Disparities were likewise strongly evident in terms of specific fabrics. Dimity, taffeta, and kersey (just below broadcloth in quality and price) were at least twice as often used by the urban and affluent, whereas *étoffe du pays* (locally woven rough woolen cloth), drugget (also increasingly likely a locally woven woolen), and local linen (for blouses and shifts) were virtually exclusively for rural, farming, and laboring women. Kalm may have exaggerated when he wrote that "every farmer" kept sufficient sheep to yield wool for "workaday clothing," but that fiber was fashioned into a fifth of rural and peasant women's woolen garb, though much less of men's.[66] Local linen was an even more popular fabric for *habitante* shifts (more than a third), but the only urban woman who had a *toile du pays* shift was a farmer's widow. Despite remaining expensive, cottons had admittedly become by far the most popular fabric material among all women, used in half their attire (and particularly likely to be found in newer fashions like *jupons* and *mantelets*). But even it had an urban and affluent inflection: nearly three-fifths of such women's apparel, as against just over two-fifths for their rural and poorer sisters.[67]

As elsewhere in the Atlantic, particular fiber groups, and individual varieties within them, became more clearly identified as female or male across the eighteenth century. In the Montreal area, gender distinctions served to reinforce city–country and occupational divides. Cottons had made inroads into all wardrobes, yet their presence in women's apparel (49 percent of basic and outer garments) was much more substantial than in men's (12 percent). At the same time, cottons were more heavily represented among urbanites (55 percent of women's clothes, 20 percent of men's) than among country folk (respectively, 45 and 10 percent). For their part, woolens were male (71 percent as against 30 percent among women). But here, too, there was a clear rural–urban gap: 78 percent of the garments owned by men in the countryside were woolens, 65 percent for townsmen; the corresponding figures for women were 36 and 18 percent. Silks were more equally shared between the genders (women 13 percent, men 10) but they were definitively urban (16 percent to 7 among men, 22 to 9 among women). And, at the level of specific fabrics, satin, taffeta, *calamande* (the French iteration of calimanco), camlet, *toile*, and *étoffe du pays* were pronouncedly female, while velvet, broadcloth, and *cadis* were male.

Some of these distinctions were rooted in eighteenth-century economic and demographic reconfigurations. Though scholars now question the extent to which *habitants* managed to achieve their presumed goal of self-sufficiency, there was a notable increase in rural hemp and flax cultivation, in sheep herding, and in domestic weaving. These activities marked a sharp departure from the late seventeenth century, when despite repeated official urging, "few people bother to sow hemp" and "no one uses" local wool "in any significant way."[68] Recent research indicates a clear upsurge of local fabric production from the mid-eighteenth century, and by 1760–74 local linen (usually hemp but sometimes flax) comprised about a tenth of the lengths of linen found in rural non-mercantile inventories, local woolen about three percent.[69] While some country people traded at the weekly Friday market, most no longer needed to visit Montreal either to sell their produce or to buy the imported cloth that made up the bulk of their clothing, for during the 1720s shopkeepers had begun to settle in rural districts. By 1760, the twenty-five parishes around Montreal were home to forty-one shopkeepers, and thus few residents would have lived far from one.[70] Franquet, surveying fortifications in 1752, remarked that denizens of the countryside, able to fill all their needs close at hand, had no reason to go into Montreal.[71] Changes in dress thus suggest the emergence of a distinct *habitant* identity coupled with farmers' growing ability to supply themselves with some of the materials they needed.

Reflecting the situation throughout the British Atlantic, there are many fewer and much less detailed inventories with usable dress information for later eighteenth-century Philadelphia and its hinterland than for New France. Those that do exist indicate that some of the trends seen in New France were also at work in greater Philadelphia. Increasingly, fabrics were gendered as elsewhere – cottons and linens were female, woolens male – and denoted urban–rural divisions, with silks disproportionately worn by urban women, mixed linsey-woolsey and rough woolen "stuff" by rural, while urban men were much more likely to wear cottons, rural males woolen and leather garments. Fabrics likewise bore familiar inscriptions of wealth: More affluent women wore a third more cotton basic and outer items, a third fewer linen ones, and, more strikingly, three times as much silk garb, as their poorer sisters; similar disparities obtained for cottons and linens among men.[72]

Without sufficiently numerous and sufficiently detailed inventories, it is difficult to locate the genesis of changes in fabric preferences. Scattered evidence, however, allows them to be seen first among the prosperous, the urban, and the mercantile. An account book kept by trustees for the three daughters and two sons of the late merchant Thomas Coates shows that during the 101 months between November 1719 and March 1728, 12 percent of total expenditures on apparel textiles went for cottons, 14 percent for silks, 29 percent for linens, and 34 percent for woolens.[73] Women were likely in the lead. Calculations based on James Bonsall's account book indicate that his female customers spent a third of their textile purchases on cottons and another third on woolens in 1722–28, a fifth on silks, and a tenth on linens.[74] Again, between November 1759 and January 1768, Sarah Powell, member by birth and marriage of two leading Philadelphia mercantile families, disbursed a sixth of her clothing outlays on cottons, a bare quarter on linens, just an eighth on woolens – and 44 percent on silks.[75] Chintz, Powell's favorite cotton fabric, was used as well as silks for gowns; cotton check and expensive lawn linen for aprons. Powell's expenditures were doubtless peculiar to her, but her example was not singular. When describing the "very fine, neat and costly" Pennsylvania women's attire he observed, the mid-eighteenth-century German visitor Mittelberger noted that the skirts of their gowns "are made of cotton chintz, or other rich and handsome stuffs."[76] Men, however, were less committed to cottons, preferring "fine English cloth," though "in summer, on account of the great heat," they did don "light coats or jackets . . . which are neatly made of fine linen or dimity."[77]

Changes were slower to catch on outside the city. The customers of John Potts's store 60 kilometers west of Philadelphia in the late 1740s spent half of their clothing purchases on linens, a quarter on woolens, and just 6 percent on cottons; though some of the 10 percent spent on checks may have bought cotton checks, more likely they were linens or mixtures of linen and cotton.[78] Again, cottons accounted for just a tenth of sales in the two shops operated by Peter Buffington in rural Chester County in the late 1750s and early 1760s, as against more than two-fifths for linens, more than a quarter for checks, a fifth for woolens.[79]

If at a more leisurely pace, new tastes nevertheless spread throughout Philadelphia's hinterland in the course of the eighteenth century. In booming Lancaster, a farming and carting hub more than 100 kilometers west of Philadelphia, cotton textiles accounted for nearly 14 percent by value of the 1765–66 cloth sales by an unknown merchant, compared to a third each for linens and woolens and a tenth for silks.[80] The changes reached the enslaved and indentured as well. The proportion of such men's attire made from cottons doubled to about a tenth between the 1730s and 1760s, with mixed checks at the same level, while linens dropped from about a fifth to a seventh, woolens from three-fifths to half. Though many fewer in number, indentured women at least were even more substantially garbed in cottons: one-fourth of their garments, as against just a tenth in linens, a quarter in woolens, and two-fifths in linsey-woolsey.[81]

"Throughout Pennsylvania," wrote Mittelberger, men's attire "is very costly, among the farmers as well as among persons of rank; they all wear garments of fine English cloth or other materials, also fine shirts. Every one wears a wig, the peasant as well as the gentleman." Mittelberger exaggerated; perhaps he intended his remarks to describe not merely elite dress, but their dress for fancy occasions, when women might indeed wear "round their throats fine strings of beads, in their ears costly drops with fine stones, and on their heads fine white hoods embroidered with flowers and trimmed with lace and streamers," not to mention gloves "of velvet, silk and the like, usually trimmed with silver or gold lace and beautifully embroidered," "neckerchiefs" made of "velvet or of pure silk, and likewise tastefully embroidered," "blue or scarlet cloaks," and taffeta bonnets.[82] No clothing inventory has survived for the wealthy stratum on which Mittelberger's statements most likely were based. There is, however, some evidence concerning those of middling levels of affluence. Though insufficient for quantitative analysis, it indicates that divisions between country and city, between occupations, and, to a degree, between wealth cohorts were muted.

It is striking, for example, that farmers of both high and modest income wore virtually all the velvet attire inventoried, including that marker of Atlantic fashion, velvet breeches. Again, all inventoried men had thickset cottons and broadcloth, just as all inventoried women had calico, chintz, and check. Greater wealth and an urban residence put some garments and fabrics within easier reach, but there evidently remained a degree of geographic integration and social cohesion that worked against strong development of particular identifications. The runaway advertisements provide even better illustrations. They show that there were some differences in dress between runaways who fled rural employers and those absconding from Philadelphians. But the distinctions were not large: One-fourth of rural women servants' garments were fashioned from cottons, for instance, against just under a fifth of urban female servants'. Again, male servants living and working in the city had about a tenth of their garments made from linens, as against a seventh among rural servants.

More significant, as the female cottons example has already intimated, the distinctions were not those of urban fashionability and rural lag. Not only did neither group of female servants wear identifiable homespun woolen apparel, but only a fifth of rural servant women's dress was made from woolens, as against more than a third among urban indentured females. A parallel disproportion was seen among servant men: Even though an eighth of the woolens they wore were homespun (as against just 1 percent in town), in total woolens comprised under 50 percent of rural male servants' basic and outer garb, as against 56 percent among their urban counterparts, whereas urban indentured men were slightly more likely to wear leather attire than were rural. And, finally, much was shared across locations. Urban servants' shirts were as likely to be made of locally woven linen and check as rural servants', and men in both places had equivalent amounts of such popular fabrics as thickset and even (albeit limited in quantity) velvet.

Part of the reason for moderate if real dress distinctions may have been rooted in the emphasis on sartorial plainness rather than difference among the Quakers who continued to wield a good deal of

224 / Free settler dress in temperate zones

cultural authority even as their political power waned. Scholars have shown that this entailed not the eschewal of rich fabrics but simplicity in the attire into which they were tailored. As Deborah Kraak has demonstrated, "most Philadelphia-area Quaker dress ... was the conventional dress of the day, shorn of its excesses."[83] Many of the religious sects whose members had settled in the countryside similarly eschewed worldly display and the expression of social distinctions. Most important was the hegemonic role of the port of Philadelphia both in the import of a growing plethora of goods and in exporting the hinterland's rising agricultural output.[84] The result, the dress-regime evidence suggests, was not merely broad improvement in standards of living but the knitting together of town and country into an increasingly unitary material cultural zone.

* * *

Temperate and semitropical dress regimes participated in the many changes that marked the material Atlantic between the mid-seventeenth and the late eighteenth centuries. Free settlers took up a multitude of new goods, styles, and practices – from the common fashion for cottons to the male fad for black velvet breeches, from more pronounced fabric gendering to general adoption of brighter-hued apparel – and many others big and small.[85] The results were diverse, shaped by specific configurations of gender, occupation, wealth, and at times place. Some larger patterns emerge: the Iberian American partiality for silks, the even more pronounced commitment to woolen garb among men in northern North America, the impressive inroads of sturdy checks into British colonial apparel. To a degree, such patterns reveal a kind of climatic creolization or adaptation. They also indicate efforts not simply to attend to metropolitan sartorial models but to accommodate free settler dress more closely to European prototypes. Disparate colonial conditions, problematic commercial connections, and conflicting imperial policies ensured that these efforts would fall short of complete success. Still, it was in the temperate colonies that transatlantic dress uniformity came closest to being realized.

7 ATLANTIC DRESS REGIMES: FASHIONS AND MEANINGS, IMPLICATIONS AND IRONIES

The Hottentots, with their skins dressed up with grease and soot, and *bucku*-powder, are by this means in a great measure defended from the influence of the air, and may in a manner reckon themselves full dressed. In other respects, both men and women are wont to appear quite undressed; indeed, I may say naked, except a trifling covering, with which they always conceal certain parts of their bodies. With the men this covering consists of a bag or flap made of skin, hanging quite open … [T]he females of this nation cover themselves much more scrupulously than the men. They seldom content themselves with one covering, but almost always have two, and very often three. These are made of a prepared and well-greased skin, and are fastened about their bodies with a thong, almost like the aprons of our ladies.

In other respects, the garment worn by the Hottentot for covering their bodies is a sheep-skin, with the wooly side turned inwards; this pellisse, or a cloak made of some smaller fur, is tied forwards over the breast … [I]n rainy and cold weather they wrap it round them; so that the fore part of the body likewise, is in some measure covered with it as far as almost to the knees … [Men] who live nearest to the colonists, fancy the European hats, [women] a cap in the form of a short cone … Over this cap they sometimes wear another ornament, consisting of an oval wreath, or, if the reader pleases, a crown made of a buffalo's hide …

In his mid-1770s description, the Swedish naturalist and abolitionist Anders Sparrman not only acknowledges the protection that their dress affords the Khoikhoi but goes on to narrate in admiring detail women's expensive shell necklaces, glass bead "apron" adornments, and "crowns" bedecked with Indian Ocean cowries; the blue and white beaded sashes and numerous leather and metal rings both genders wore around their arms and legs; and the leather "field shoes" that they put on to traverse scorching or rugged terrain.[1]

Besides the tenacious European conflation of non-European dress with undress, what is most striking about Sparrman's report – or with images of Khoikhoi in contemporary depictions like Plate 7b – is the persistence of the dress itself. Apart from the taste for European hats, little of what Sparrman wrote about and Jan Brandes drew differed from Khoikhoi apparel described and portrayed a century earlier (Figure 1.5). Nor were the Khoikhoi the only people in the Atlantic basin whose dress regime had been minimally transformed by the late eighteenth century. In the same years, Agostino Brunias painted Carib (Kalinago) men and women in the Leeward Islands garbed in short waistcloths, thong-like pouches, or small decorated breechclouts, and adorned with feathered hair ornaments, worked leg rings, elaborate earrings and necklaces of shell and other natural materials – dress that looked much like that recounted by Jean-Baptiste Labat in the 1690s.[2] The staying power of such apparel attests to the limits of the reach of Atlantic dress regimes, at the basin's center as well as in its borderlands. Still, neither Khoikhoi nor Caribs remained wholly beyond Atlantic sartorial influences, despite their marginal position in Atlantic society and economy. After all, the Khoikhoi whom Sparrman delineated favored imported hats and beads; Brandes elsewhere depicted and described a Khoikhoi man wearing a European-style hat, white stockings, and bead breechclout; and some Caribs in Brunias's paintings fashioned their short wraps from red or white linen or cotton cloth and incorporated woven fabrics into items of adornment.[3]

In the colonized Atlantic, in sum, even the few groups that only partially engaged with globalized commodities found it impossible to remain wholly apart. More often, populations both within and outside the commercial compass of settler communities were incorporated into the colonial economy at once as producers and consumers. Native hunters, enslaved African and Amerindian laborers and artisans, free farmers, and craftsmen all produced commodities for sale in the market, and all – including those involved in some self-provisioning – supplied many of their needs and wants through market exchange. Dress-regime change thus registered the degree of European and settler ascendancy over appareling goods, practices, and discourses once labor and clothing materials were redirected toward or generated for colonist-dominated subsistence and export-oriented production. As we have seen, even the Tupinambá adopted garments made from woven textiles once they became laborers in colonial Brazil.

Fashions and meanings

The correlative extension of European and Euroamerican-dominated colonialism and commerce shaped the dress regimes of the Atlantic basin's diverse populations in distinctive ways. Native people and slaves living in or trading with colonies were most affected, experiencing something less and more than a typical European-style "consumer revolution." Less, in that while their sartorial consumption entailed some of that revolution's elite pursuit of luxurious novelties or middling-strata acquisition of "populuxe" goods (cheaper products that used alternative materials to imitate features or the appearance of costly items),[4] mainly it involved laboring women and men dressing in linens and woolens long familiar to Europeans. More, in that the new indigenous and enslaved dress regimes comprised transformations more comprehensive than those experienced by Europeans and European-descent settlers: In structure, materials, articles – often all three – the attire was wholly new to the individuals clothed in it.[5]

Powerful and often contradictory forces produced these results. The operation of European-based merchant networks and the circulation of models of apparel deemed appropriate for "savages" and bondspeople fostered uniformity of fabrics and garb. Though varied mercantilist rules and incentives, metropolitan industrial specializations, and conditions within individual colonies tended to diversify the specific fabrics mandated or offered, nonetheless the work garb imposed upon slaves and the gift apparel and conversion clothing presented to Amerindians comprised narrow selections from the panoply of cloth and clothing available to settlers. Moreover, the apparel acquired by these means was remarkably similar across imperial boundaries and trading zones.

Even within those restrictive parameters, however, slaves and Natives were rarely passive recipients of dress. In addition, many of them acquired both quotidian attire and sartorial goods of their own choosing for special and festive occasions, though here, too, law and customary restrictions, not to mention climate and cost, set limits. With these items, they assembled cross-cultural syncretic dress regimes that encompassed indigenous and imported materials, garments, and accessories, and that often involved articles repurposed into more familiar form: Handkerchiefs became headwraps, shirts were worn as jackets, blankets turned into matchcoats. The styles constructed were not more or less faithful renditions of colonial or metropolitan prototypes. Rather than the origin or use of individual pieces, the crux of sartorial syncretism was the ensemble that combined new and old materials, novel and known apparel, and, in some instances, recently introduced as well as customary corporeal adornments. Together, these expressed the aesthetic preferences, cultural imperatives, and forms of identification of their enslaved or indigenous creators.

Dress changes among free settlers were more circumscribed. These colonists were not impervious to their new surroundings or unwilling to borrow sartorial items from cultures with which they traded. Lighter fabrics appropriate to hot climates made headway among them; residents of New France put on snowshoes for winter travel (Plate 6); many Euroamericans found moccasins and leggings a comfortable supplement to their usual footwear; some free settler women in the Caribbean put on headscarves, at least at home; Cape Colony farmers might don "field shoes." But with minor exceptions, such cross-cultural appropriations involved a single addition to a wardrobe that contained few if any other novelties, were temporary and expediential gestures, or served particular purposes, whether travel, hunting, or war. Sir John Caldwell, British army officer and one-time participant in imperial–Native councils in the Great Lakes area, might affect a costume that mixed Amerindian and imported materials and attire to what is admittedly striking effect (Plate 14). From all evidence, however, this brilliant outfit was deployed for show (perhaps only for a portraitist) rather than regularly worn. Throughout the Atlantic, in fact, the most widely appreciated cross-cultural sartorial imports were, like the banyan and the turban, derived not from Atlantic but from Asian archetypes. Yet outside the Cape Colony they, too, were put on to assert distinctiveness – in their case, cosmopolitan, leisured identifications – rather than as items of workaday dress.

Thus settler dress innovation did not entail culturally syncretic ensembles but involved restrained introduction of new woven-fiber textiles, garments, and details into existing sartorial structures – and even then the borrowings were usually modified and as soon as possible produced in Europe. More generally, the components of free settler outfits varied in cut and color over time, a limited number were added or subtracted, and they were tailored out of a wider array of fabrics. Nevertheless, the dress remained consistently and identifiably that of free settlers. Not only did such settlers clothe themselves in a more complete iteration of the attire and fabrics with which they sought to redress other Atlantic peoples. They did not innovate hybrid dress regimes; nor, except superficially, did they accept apparel that would assimilate their sartorial appearance to that of the "savage" or the enslaved. Thus as the popularity of moccasins grew, for example, they were redesigned and manufactured for and by colonists who used settler-raised ox hides, added tongues, hard soles, and waterproofing, and dispensed with the decoration integral to Amerindian footwear.[6]

Settler fashions reflected developments both within colonies and their commercial hinterlands, and in their relations with European metropoles. At home, free settlers sought to inaugurate and thereafter maintain sartorially a social and cultural separation between themselves and other Atlantic populations, both Native people who were beginning to incorporate imported items into their own dress regimes and enslaved men and women whose apparel creations perforce relied on woven-fiber textiles. Equally significant were the new socio-economic divisions and group identifications appearing in colonial society, which as we have seen were increasingly objectified in real, if subtle, sartorial demarcations.

As the eighteenth century proceeded, a broad "metropolitani-zation" of settler material cultures occurred as well: a process that at once built on and amplified the flow of styles and goods from the mother countries. Free settlers had never ignored European dress: It was what had been brought initially to the colonies, and knowledge about its subsequent evolution had been transmitted thereafter by persons, correspondence, and publications as well as by imported goods. But concern with being *au courant* according to metropolitan norms – an aspiration to material rapprochement with homeland Europeans that paralleled the contemporary distancing from colonial others – intensified after the mid-eighteenth century, together with means of attaining that goal. The immigration of European tailors, dyers, and other clothing-trades artisans was one manifestation of the new situation, the appearance of clothing patterns pre-printed on lengths of imported cloth in shops and wardrobes throughout the colonial Atlantic was another. Timothy Breen has investigated the phenomenon, which he terms "anglicization," in British North America during the decades leading up to the American Revolution.[7] It occurred elsewhere as well. Hilliard d'Auberteuil, the advocate of colonial simplicity, reported unhappily that an influx of wealthy migrants from France into Saint-Domingue after 1763 had attuned the colony to luxurious metropolitan styles.[8]

Though free settlers' metropolitan identification was strong, they never completely realized the coveted sartorial congruence; climate, cost, and communications constantly threw up obstacles. Europeans on the average had more garments in their wardrobes, for instance, and if many colonists were quick to start wearing cottons, a vogue for wearing cotton garments began in Spain, for example, before it did in the Río de la Plata.[9] Particularly in an Atlantic-wide context, however, dress differences represented minor variations on common themes, whether in respect to basic apparel or the evolution of clothing regimes. By the later eighteenth century, the essentials of women's outfits in the European metropoles as among free colonists comprised a one-piece gown with petticoat or (decreasingly) skirt and bodice or jacket, cloak or other loose outerwear, headgear typically including close-fitting cap and hat, shoes and stockings; in addition, aprons decorative or practical had become normative and shifts or smocks were practically so. Among men, the equivalent transatlantic attire included breeches, vest or waistcoat, coat or similar usually tailored outer garment, hat, shoes and stockings; for males, too, shirts and drawers were becoming sartorial staples.

Changes in dress over time likewise bore a great deal of resemblance, beginning with cross-cultural apparel borrowings, which were as limited in metropoles as in colonies. Europeans, in fact, proved yet more reticent than settlers. Admittedly, in the Old World as in the New, Asian-inspired turbans and banyans became fashionable, yet "Atlantic" items like moccasins, snowshoes, and field shoes never caught on. In contrast, Europeans, like colonists, valued Atlantic raw materials, yet all used them not for novel sartorial items but as new supplies of known materials for existing apparel: furs for hats (and sometimes trim on coats), skins for footwear, and increasingly raw cotton for expanding

European cotton industries and the shirts and shifts, skirts and petti-coats, waistcoats and jackets, and other garments made from them. Changes within the shared basic dress regime were more obvious, and again very similar. As the socioeconomic differentials expressed sarto-rially widened, urban–rural disparities waned: These were general transatlantic phenomena that originated within the merchant economy before the advent of factory industrialization. Across the Euro-free-settler Atlantic basin, too, lighter and smoother fabric varieties generally supplanted heavier and coarser types, darker colors gave way to brighter shades, and multihued, pictorial, flowered, and checked patterns supplemented single colors and stripes. As the wearing of cotton clothing grew in Europe as in the colonies, increasingly such garb was gendered female, just as woolens became male.

As noted in Chapter 1, in numerous particulars dress regimes varied among the diverse states comprising Atlantic Europe; increasingly, both these distinctions and overall dress regimes were shared by mother country and colony. In Spain as in the Río de la Plata, for instance, silks were more widely employed for garments of all types than in most societies; in both places, too, the *chupa*-style jacket and *casaca* coat, notably less popular in the seventeenth century, had become features of male wardrobes by the late eighteenth century.[10] Across the British North Atlantic, developmental trend lines likewise displayed some remarkable parallels, including a prolonged partiality for durable linens. The British North Atlantic saw a rather slow turn to cottons (even mixed types like fustians and dimities, legal in Britain despite various anti-cottons laws) before the second half of the eighteenth century, or even the 1770s, when laws forbidding the wearing of pure cottons in the metropole were abolished. At the same time, despite restrictions and for some decades prohibitions on wearing imported Indian cottons in England, smuggling and other avenues of supply assured that the calico gown remained standard issue among women no matter which side of the British Atlantic they lived.[11]

Again, in Holland as in the Cape Colony, significant new apparel items were adopted on a similar schedule, whether under-trousers among men, or jackets and types of gowns (sack and *samaar*) by women, and prior rural–urban fashion differences tended to recede between the late seventeenth and late eighteenth centuries, as when country males in both places took up the waistcoat (*camisool* or *kamizool*).[12] An illustration and accompanying description from an

encyclopedic account by the Dutch naturalist, doctor, and writer
Jan le Francq van Berkhij indicate both types of convergence among
dress regimes and the ways in which clothing evinced socioeconomic
cleavages that were becoming more prominent (Plate 15).[13] The best
outfit of the prosperous peasant (1) bears a great deal of resemblance
to the merchant's attire (8), and while the dress of all peasant men had
much in common ("rich and poor, from the oldest to the youngest,
they all wear linen drawers," not to mention shiny buttons and
buckles, colorful stockings – increasingly in stripes and flower patterns –
and characteristic low-heeled shoes), there were some conspicuous contrasts, such as broadcloth or drugget overcoats and gold knee buckles
for the affluent, serge and silver clasps for the less well-off, some of
whom also wore the *camisool* in place of a coat. Occupation was also
clearly denoted: The sailor's garb (5) differs importantly from that
worn by the fisherman (6), and both from peasant attire; and wealth as
well as profession distinguish the clothing of the merchant (8) from
that of the common laborer (9). Similar overall composition combined
with significant variation in particular garments, cut and fabric, and
forms of adornment mark the dress of the four women: the church-
going peasant (2), the fishmonger (7), and the "dignified, wealthy"
woman (10) from the important industrial and commercial munici-
pality of Zaandam (seen in the background). Again, the more prosperous farm woman's attire (2) is demarcated from that of the "common"
peasant (3).

In France as in the French New World, too, city styles largely
triumphed in the course of the eighteenth century, though with an
admixture of country and new items.[14] In the late seventeenth century,
a rural man wore *hauts-de-chausse* (an early form of breeches, often
with a wide or even puffy skirt-like section around the hips), *pourpoint*
(doublet or close-fitting jacket), and an outer *casaque, manteau*, or
surtout, while his town cousin sported breeches (*culottes*), waistcoat
(*veste*), and *justaucorps* coat, and half of all men boasted a hat as well.
A century later both rural and urban men wore *culottes*, waistcoats (and
half or so had the newer *gilet* style without the *veste*'s flared skirts),
tailored coats (*habits*, or, less often, redingotes), and hats. In the early
period, rural women dressed in *jupe, jupon*, and often an apron; urban
women also regularly wore *manteaux* and aprons (particularly in the
laboring and artisanal strata).[15] By the late eighteenth century, besides
skirt and petticoat, women in both city and country had added the *robe*

(gown) and *corps de jupe* (a sleeveless close-fitted bodice) or *casaquin* (hip-length short over-blouse or jacket). Moreover, shirts and shifts were no longer optional but mandatory for both genders, as were stockings and shoes, while under-drawers, nightclothes, and handkerchiefs were becoming more common.

Already by the early seventeenth century, as we have seen in Chapter 1, Atlantic Africans employed textiles imported from and via Europe to supplement woven-fiber fabrics woven locally or imported along other channels. During the next two centuries, the accelerating expansion of the slave trade continually increased the supply of imported goods,[16] giving birth to social groups with new economic orientations that could be displayed in material as well as behavioral ways. In Portuguese Angola, for instance, linguistically skilled and well-connected black and mixed-race traders and intercultural intermediaries often donned particularly symbolic European garments. Wearing breeches in place of loincloths and going shod laid visible claim to a position in Atlantic commerce and colonialism, and local residents as well as colonial officials deemed the individuals dressed in that manner to be Portuguese, even white.[17]

At the same time, repeated if spotty missionary efforts continued both in the portions of west Central Africa that Portugal sought to colonize and in nearby autonomous kingdoms. As part of their larger campaign to introduce civility, missionaries urged converts to redress, or in their view simply to get dressed. To judge from contemporary pictorial and textual evidence, their success was partial at best, even in an area long exposed to evangelical activity though not European settlement like Sogno (Soyo), a tributary of the kingdom of Kongo. A mid-eighteenth-century manuscript by the Italian Capuchin Bernardino Ignazio d'Asti presents the results as perceived by a technically unsophisticated observer determined to reveal the situation that he experienced.[18] At least at some religious ceremonies, such as the baptism depicted in Plate 16, women did wear either a wrap around the upper torso as well as a long skirt or a single long garment from armpits to the lower legs, while men draped a mantle over the shoulder. It is unclear, however, that these changes reached far down the social hierarchy or that they affected the daily dress of the faithful. Another drawing in the same manuscript portrays an open-air Mass where the "Mani" (an aristocratic high administrator) boasts a resplendent scarlet robe over a decorated *mozzetta* (short cape) and a patterned skirt-like loincloth; yet aside from those directly assisting the priest, the rest of the men in attendance wear only loincloths.

Some missionaries explained the persistence of what they continued to deem undress by citing Africans' unwillingness to give up their pagan ways due both to moral failings and to the scarcity of clerical personnel.[19] It seems rather to indicate that established dress regimes responded most appropriately to natural, cultural, and socioeconomic realities. Even a missionary could admit that the usual fiery heat made minimal clothing desirable – though only at home in private.[20] Indifference about accumulating material goods, already mentioned by seventeenth-century missionaries (as we have seen in Chapter 1), may have continued. More important, possession of European-style garments and exhibition of costly imported textiles added a striking dimension to manifestations of power and status long demonstrated in these cultures by the quality of palm cloth or raffia fiber and by quantity of apparel.

These traditional sartorial signs did not disappear; on the contrary, European and Asian textile goods were synthesized with African into a fresh hybrid semiotics carefully calibrated to specific situations. Thus the usual outfit of the "Count" who ruled Sogno in the 1680s comprised both a palm-fiber loincloth worked in a manner exclusive to him, and a long cape (*cappa*) made of baize; unlike the attire worn by others – including the Mani, to judge from d'Asti's drawings – both garments touched the ground. On the frequent occasions when this Count heard Mass, he arrived at church with a velvet upholstered chair, one hat wrapped in a taffeta veil and a second of "the most delicate" plumage, along with a little silk embroidered white cap, a piece that only a select few were allowed to wear. On feast days the Count also donned a scarlet mantle (*manto*) apparently like that of the Mani; on "the most solemn" occasions he added a shirt "of the finest weave," yellow or crimson silk stockings, and flowered primavera silk cape; and when taking Communion, he topped it all off with a very long cape of pure white silk, the "glorious insignia" of an exclusive Christian order to which he belonged by grant from the king of Kongo, who himself had received it from the Portuguese crown.[21] In its spectacular syncretic mix of imported and indigenous shapes, styles, and materials, the garb manifested at once the Count's Christianity, political and economic power, and relations with foreigners who had presented such rich attire.

European merchants frequently gifted fancy goods to rulers and other high officials. In Sogno, for instance, Dutch and English traders provided the "prince" with his "sumptuous" silk garments, including a pair of gold-laced crimson velvet slippers.[22] They were following well-established procedure. In a representative 1763 cargo destined for west Central Africa, the slaver Pierre-Ignace-Liévin van Alstein carried one scarlet and two blue woolen cloaks with imitation gold braid, additional ellage of the same fabrics, an "old" but still costly gold ground velvet vest, and striped combed silk trim, all carefully valued and designated for presents.[23] If a taste for such goods was hardly the sole reason that African elites engaged in slaving, they were nevertheless highly prized: for example, "Textiles of Europe" headed the seven-item list of the "wealth that some lords flaunt" drawn up in the mid-seventeenth century by the Italian Capuchin Giovanni Antonio Cavazzi da Montecuccolo.[24]

Sartorial symbols of rulership retained a degree of exclusivity, even if each ruler emphasized his or her own specific combination of traditional and innovative items.[25] Yet according to one late eighteenth-century visitor, even the *canda*, a small decorative animal skin long reserved for elite men, had over time been permitted to courtiers and finally even to merchants.[26] Similarly, while elites might hope to monopolize the best palm-fiber cloth, whose weaving on narrow looms was a slow and laborious process, it was very difficult if not impossible to limit the circulation of imported textiles.[27] For one thing, leaders often redistributed prestigious items to ensure dependents' loyalty or at least good will.[28] For another, European merchants quickly learned the usefulness of velvets, silk handkerchiefs, finely woven lustrous *guingans* cotton loincloths, lengths of broadcloth, damask, and other pricey fabrics when deployed as bribes ("welcomes"), commissions, duties, or to defray other costs of doing trade.[29]

Non-elite Atlantic Africans acquired a handful of imported tailored garments by trade. But as countless cargo manifests and detailed accounts demonstrate, lengths of fabrics – cottons followed (distantly) by linens and woolens – formed the overwhelming bulk of the textiles traded. As we have seen in Chapter 1, woven-fiber textiles – and clothing made from them – were no novelty in most of Atlantic Africa, and had not been so even in the fifteenth century. European merchants were new suppliers, whose cloth mainly supplemented rather than replaced existing stocks; particularly in parts of west Central

Africa, imported cloth also likely compensated for long-standing shortages.[30] It did not, however, alter clothing styles for most people, as Plate 16 and other images and texts indicate. According to the French missionary Liévin-Bonaventure Proyart, in the important commercial but non-Christian kingdoms of Kakongo and Loango, just north of Sogno, in the 1760s inhabitants wore mid-calf-length loincloths; held in place by a wide belt "ordinarily" of red or blue woolen; these "small skirts" were fashioned from a cotton or some other light imported fabric among the "rich," from locally woven raffia or bark cloth for the "poor."[31]

In coastal Angola, the slave trader Louis de Grandpré wrote, imported textiles – cotton, calico, silk, woolen, "even velvet" – had triumphed more completely, wholly substituting for domestic fabrics. But the denizens nevertheless went about "almost naked," though "the parts of the body that they do cover are clothed with elegance [grace]." Men wore loincloths, sometimes long enough to drag on the ground, but in Grandpré's telling the distinctive aspect of Angolan dress was – just as for sixteenth-century commentators – the adornments: an ivory neckband, red coral, iron or copper leg and arm bracelets, and on special occasions body painting; wealthy individuals also sported long silver chains wrapped ostentatiously around their hips. "But most important of all their attire [toilette]" was now the canda, the animal skin decorated with little bells worn in front of the genitals as a "mark of honor," masculine power, and free status (and thus forbidden to slaves). Women's apparel – "less noble" because lacking canda or headgear – comprised a wrapped skirt and a kind of bandeau, both of cloth, as well as copious adornment: yards-long strings of glass beads, coral, bracelets.[32]

At the end of his verbal portraits of dress (enhanced by two engravings), Grandpré acknowledged that they best characterized "rich people," and that others wore simpler garb. But what is most striking in his as in Proyart's descriptions is that apart from fabric, the outfits were the same as those described several centuries earlier. For the great majority of west Central Africans, Atlantic fashion was a matter of greater availability and greater variety of materials, not of change in garments, cut, shape, or overall structure. The situation differed little on the Gold Coast. Wrapper-style garments continued to predominate, among men usually worn as loincloths; at the same time, bodily adornment remained a critical part of appropriate dress. Imported textiles were integrated into existing indigenous styles and schemata, as Europeans found again and again. In 1760, the Danish merchant Ludvig Rømer, though generally bullish on commercial prospects for textiles in particular, felt it necessary to warn prospective traders from his homeland that fabrics dyed blue "must not only be true but also dark blue," for Gold Coast consumers "do not like light blue at all," and while buyers also sought out "striped and checked linens," they would only accept thin, loosely woven varieties. As in west Central Africa, too, wealth and power were manifest in dress. One or two pieces of wrapped local or cheap imported linens or woolens had to suffice for the less well-off, whereas multiple layers of expensive silks, calicoes, or woolens garbed the affluent.[33]

Atlantic Africans involved with trade or who identified as Christians, then, modified their attire, but their novel dress regimes were syncretic rather than European, as were those of political elites with whom European missionaries, merchants, and officials dealt: Both new social groups and existing power relations had additional material means of expression. To the great majority, however, Atlantic trade supplied little more than additional materials to express existing social relations within well-known forms. Atlantic Africa was a full participant in Atlantic commerce and the enslaved labor it supplied was indispensable to colonialism. But it stood at one end of a spectrum of dress-regime change enabled by imported sartorial goods, knowledge, and models. Europe stood at the other end: There, too, the advent of new textiles brought little apparel change, much less structural innovation; indeed, even European traders in Africa wore fully metropolitan outfits.[34] Free colonists proved a bit more willing to modify their garb for utilitarian, often climatic, reasons, but they too retained the essentials of a metropolitan dress regime with additional materials. Amerindians accepted a much broader range of both new garments and new materials. But if their resulting syncretic dress regime reflected increasing incorporation into the Atlantic market economy, it also denoted only partial identification with Euroamerican culture, even, as in Atlantic Africa, among converts. Enslaved men and women experienced the greatest impact of Atlantic commerce and colonialism, symbolized by settlers' implementation and enforcement of codified slave outfits, yet even within those constraints some managed to create dress regimes of their own.

The Atlantic was an integrating system produced by ongoing exchanges and interactions, an emergent "world" exemplified by the convergence across imperial, geographic, and cultural borders of supplies of woven-fiber textiles of distant and diverse provenances. Baize and calico were available from Cape Town to the North American Great Lakes, banyans and vests from interior Río de la Plata to the Dutch countryside, ribbon and trim from the Gold Coast to upland Saint-Domingue. Yet disparate dress regimes were constructed from these similar components, shaped by specific identification, local practice, and sociocultural authority. Atlantic colonialism was a standardizing force, but commerce enabled distinction as well as homogenization.

Implications and ironies

Across the later seventeenth and eighteenth centuries, broad if uneven demographic and economic growth and increasing participation of most populations in the market economy stimulated demand for both standardized and distinctive woven-fiber textiles throughout the Atlantic, prompting producers to follow a variety of strategies that shaped specific manufactures, influenced the development of Atlantic textile production as a whole, and in the end helped assure the emergence of European industrial capitalism.

Many manufacturers relied on time-tested techniques. Often this strategy turned out well, but the nature of Atlantic markets – highly competitive, subject to mutable imperial policies, and in many places reliant on slaving and plantation agriculture – could upend that success. Focusing on low-quality goods for particular Atlantic market sectors was an attractive option. The linen industry of the Perche region, 150 kilometers west of Paris, snapped out of a prolonged decline by switching to cheap hempen goods. By the 1770s, 90 percent of Perche's output was exported to the Antilles for slave clothing or as shipping wrapper for coffee and cotton; unsurprisingly this manufacture was severely disrupted by the Haïtian revolution in particular.[35] Further west, Breton linens took the opposite route. After inexpensive flax *crées* lost the English market in the seventeenth century by ignoring quality regulations and customer preferences for narrow pieces for shirting, manufacturers turned to rigorously inspected good-quality *bretagnes* (*bretañas*) destined mainly for well-to-do free settlers in Spanish America. In this instance, equivalent Silesian platillas supplanted them after Spanish authorities slapped a 20 percent duty on French linens in 1779.[36] For its part, the Scottish linen industry owed much of its rapid eighteenth-century growth to copying already widely popular ozenbrig, long made on the Continent, but offering it at a lower price by employing cheap rural labor and securing bounties and other forms of direct and indirect government aid; thanks to a greater variety of offerings, this combination of strategies paid off even more spectacularly for Irish linens from the mid-eighteenth century on.[37]

Targeting particular markets with specialized products also happened by chance, as with medium-quality woolens known as "stroudwaters" or "strouds" after the Gloucestershire location where they were initially woven and dyed, which gained favor among Amerindians in the late seventeenth century for use whole as blankets or matchcoats or, when cut up, for coats, breechclouts, and other attire.[38] Due to the length and complexity of the commodity chain between England and the North American frontier, manufacturers may never have known much about the distant consumers of their goods. Nevertheless, merchant networks accurately transmitted Indians' insistence that strouds be dyed blue and red (occasionally green, black, or violet) and/or with stripes ("points") that denoted the gender- and age-appropriate size of pieces so they could be worn as wrapped attire (as, for instance, by the "Queen" in Plate 5). As a result, strouds remained both one of the largest-selling woolens (in fact, often the largest selling textile *tout court*) among Native North Americans and a lucrative specialty of the English West Country until the late eighteenth century.

Some manufacturers proved more innovative, taking advantage of raw materials as well as markets that Atlantic trade made available. Ashanti artisans in the Gold Coast interior unravelled imported taffeta, then combined the threads with indigenous cotton into luxurious kente cloth; weavers in the Popo region of the Bight of Benin picked apart European woolens for red thread to mix with cotton; in the Cape Verde Islands, Europeans established cotton and indigo plantations and brought laborers and skilled artisans from the nearby African mainland to cultivate the crops and make cloth sold profitably along the West African coast. Regional markets absorbed the bulk of the output, so only a small minority of any of these fabrics entered long-distance trade networks.[39]

The red Cholet handkerchief with its characteristic white stripe demonstrates at once the gains that specialization and innovation could reap, the manner in which styles and practices evolved as they traveled back and forth across the Atlantic, and the ways that integrating the raw material that became emblematic of globalization into a European manufacture altered both the resulting finished product and the organizational structure of the industry that produced it. In Europe and among settlers, the taste for handkerchiefs, initially nourished by the seventeenth-century vogue for taking snuff, was bolstered from the early eighteenth century by the rise of a new female style for kerchiefs worn around the neck. Likewise, as we have seen, enslaved women and free people of color made kerchiefs central to their sartorial regimes, notably in headwraps, as seen in François de Beaucourt's portrait of a servant in Saint-Domingue (Plate 17).

Originally, most kerchiefs came from the Levant and India. Even between 1686 and 1750, when Indian cottons were by law banned from the domestic French market, they could be re-exported and sold in the colonies. The colonial market also attracted linen merchant-manufacturers in Cholet, in western France, who abandoned their long-time but languishing mainstay, plain linen, for a new type of colorful linen or, increasingly, cotton-linen handkerchiefs, whose color and design show the influence of Palicat or Madras handkerchiefs (which Moreau de Saint-Méry cited in his description of enslaved women's special dress). These handkerchiefs quickly became signature fashion commodities in Saint-Domingue and elsewhere in the French Antilles. They were also exported to West Africa, so some Africans who became enslaved had likely already encountered Cholet wares before arriving in the New World. Building on their Atlantic successes, on the sartorial knowledge of colonists returning to the metropole (many of them accompanied by enslaved servants), and on the developing European vogue for lighter and more colorful fabrics, Cholet manufacturers subsequently turned their attention to the domestic market and made a modified version of the Cholet handkerchief part of metropolitan French sartorial usages, bearer of both implicit social signals and, at least in the nineteenth century, overt political messages.[40]

As both the African and Cholet examples indicate, Atlantic markets were significant for product innovation in mixed-fiber textiles; European manufacturers likewise profited from a growing taste for cotton-linen checks. For many years, indeed, European cottons were mainly mixed fabrics that due to shortcomings in technology, skills, knowledge, and raw materials were at a price and quality disadvantage in many markets. Overcoming these deficiencies was critical to Europe's ability to manufacture better-quality cottons and thus catch up with Asian, African, and Central and South American producers. It was also the spur that eventuated in the substitution of European cottons for those industries. As Giorgio Riello has recently elucidated, the European merchants who organized global trade were the critical agents in this momentous process, but only because of vital contributions by Atlantic populations.[41]

Across the eighteenth century, Africa and the Atlantic colonies provided the increasing quantities of raw materials, mostly cultivated by abundant, cheap enslaved labor, that Europe's cottons manufactures required. Long-term, sustained, generally growing, dissimilar but complementary, African and colonial demand for woven textiles were likewise important for the development of both trade in and production of cotton cloth. Atlantic Africans disdained most European cottons; their strong, even growing, partiality for Indian cottons (which rose, for example, from a third of RAC exports to West Africa in the early eighteenth century to two-thirds to three-quarters from the 1730s on) and the distinctive characteristics of that preference in each location, as noted in Chapter 2, compelled European merchants to learn how to satisfy specific market preferences.[42] Heavily oriented (or, in the case of the Cape Colony, increasingly so) to European products and/or cottons printed in Europe, colonists expanded the market for these goods and even more importantly supported the emergence of European finishing industries, which – rather than spinning or weaving – was the key component of eighteenth-century European cottons innovation. As a whole, moreover, overseas Atlantic consumers steadied markets during the many decades when anti-cottons laws distorted, though did not halt, European consumption. Little wonder, then, that European cotton industries developed most dramatically in places like Manchester, Liverpool, Rouen, Nantes, and Amsterdam that were closely connected to Atlantic trade.

However, Atlantic commerce and colonialism did not only contribute to industrial innovation. As we have seen, woolens/worsteds and notably linens continued to comprise a substantial proportion of both merchant stocks and individual wardrobes; furthermore, due to the remarkable growth of all textile trades, even relative decline translated into impressive absolute gains. Thus the average value of English woolens exports to the non-European Atlantic, £185,000 sterling in 1699–1701, had become £1,148,000 in 1772–74; linens exported and re-exported had risen from £157,000 at the first date to £966,000 three-quarters of a century later. Although woolens always found their largest markets in Europe, non-European Atlantic consumers took more than a quarter of those exported from England in 1772–74, as against just 6 percent in 1699–1701. In addition, those same Atlantic customers were always absolutely critical for English linens exports and re-exports, taking between 86 and 96 percent of both across the same period.[43] Because of the size of the woolen/worsted and linen industries and, with woolens, increasing exclusion from European markets, Atlantic markets were even more important for them than for cottons.

In response to these buoyant yet competitive Atlantic markets – which also compensated for rising mercantilist barriers and industrial development throughout Europe that increasingly excluded textiles made elsewhere – woolen, worsted, and linen manufacturers did create all sorts of new products, such as brightly dyed calimancoes (in French, *calamandes*), the light broadcloth called "cassimere," and printed linens, all designed to satisfy demands for lighter textiles and thus to compete with calicoes and other similarly colorful cottons. Yet before cassimere producers showed the way in the late eighteenth century, linen and woolen/worsted manufacturers did not embrace technological innovation.[44] The specific characteristics of their raw materials certainly complicated the mechanization of linens and woolens production. But the near monopoly that European manufactures enjoyed in their most important – Atlantic – markets, the lack of any competitive, much less superior, fabrics on the order of Asian cottons, their defeat of competing industries (witness the fate of Andean woolens), and the fact that even when colonists did establish linen and woolen manufactures they simply copied the rough and cheap fabrics that were the least profitable lines for European producers: All abated pressure on European linen and woolen/worsted industries to undertake technical change, the more so because they were long able to expand output by ruralizing and feminizing production.

The participation of Atlantic consumers in the growing fashion for lighter, brighter fabrics helped encourage some European manufacturers to embrace change. Yet in the aggregate, Atlantic demand served to sustain well-established industries and practices as much as – even more than – to promote new and technologically innovative products and processes. Even in 1772–74, the average sterling value of English cottons exported to the non-European Atlantic amounted to £176,000, of re-exported Asian cottons £85,000 – figures far below those of woolens and linens (as seen above),[45] even though at this point the English cotton industry was Europe's most advanced, and its Atlantic trade superior both absolutely and relatively. The fashions of Atlantic consumers both fostered and retarded Europe's capitalist factory industrialization. Yet – final irony – while every part of the Atlantic contributed crucially to the dramatic expansion of woven-fiber textile consumption and production, the structures of Atlantic commerce and colonialism assured that Europeans profited dispro-portionately. As a result, Europeans, initially incapable of making many of the goods that Atlantic consumers most desired, across the seventeenth and eighteenth centuries amassed the resources needed to initiate the textile innovations that eventually destroyed the forms of commerce, colonialism, and dress that had defined early modern globalization.

APPENDIX 1: SOURCES FOR TABLES 2.1, 2.2, 2.3

Table 2.1

Angola, 1676–93: TNA, RAC, T70/1222.

Buenos Aires, 1670–97: AGN, SL, 3857, 5671, 6248, 7146, 7261, 7369, 8127.

Cape Coast Castle, 1685–94: TNA, RAC, T70/1222.

Cape Town, 1693–1707: MOOC 8/1.8, 1.13, 1.74, 2.8.

Charles Town, SC, 1684–94: CCWB 1692–93 [*sic*], Mf. ST0500.

Kingston, 1683–99: JA, IB/11/3/2–3, 5.

Montreal, 1677–97: BANQ-M, GN, Not. A. Adhémar Mf. 4634, 4637; Basset Mf. 2038–39; Bourgine Mf. 2103; Mauge Mf. 2043.

Philadelphia, 1686–99: RWP, 1686 W30; 1687 W32; 1688 W34; 1692 W84; 1693 W97; 1694 W106, 121; 1698 W166, 182; 1699 W9, 11, 19, 199, 208, 213, 217.

Table 2.2

New Orleans: LHC, FSC1730011601, 1730033002, 1737041801, 1737081405, 1737081501, 1738012101, 1739031002, 1739070701, 1739092503.

NONA, Inventories, September 14, 1735.

Salvador da Bahia: APEB-JI, 04/1581/2050/01, 04/1601/2070/06, 08/3385/38.

Southern District, Saint-Domingue: ANOM, SDOM, Not. Delinois 471; Martin Mf. 1095759; Saunier 1567–68.

Table 2.3[1]

Angola: ZA, MCC, 20/339, 414, 512, 668, 820, 831, 838, 843, 848, 923, 943, 995, 1000, 1005; Archives départementales de la Loire Atlantique, Nantes, 8 J/10, 16 J/1, 16 J/3.

Buenos Aires jurisdiction: AGN, SL, 3861–63, 4304, 5339–40, 5560, 5672–73, 6724, 7149–50.

Cape Coast Castle: TNA, RAC, T70/927–29.

Cape Colony: MOOC 8/10.71a, 10.76, 11.28, 11.10, 12.15a, 12.59, 13.44, 13.58, 13.65–66, 14.30, 14.59, 15.15, 15.19, 16.27.

Jamaica: JA, IB/11/3/41, IB/11/3/43, 45–48, 50–55.

Louisiana (1760–69): LHC, FSC1769021303, 1769021502, 1769030201, 1769062604.

Natchitoches Parish Court House, Louisiana, Conveyance Record Book 1, 461, 596.

NONA, Inventories, January 15, 1765.

Montreal area: BANQ-M, GN, Not. Chatellier Mf. 2040; Duvernay Mf. 1509279; Foucher Mf. 2125–26; Hodiesne Mf. 1432364; Mezières Mf. 1464507–508; Mezières Mf. 2412–13; Panet Mf. 1522227–29; Panet Mf. 2736; Racicot Mf. 1430214–15; Simonet Mf. 1464537; Vautier Mf. 1562137.

Philadelphia area: CCA, WI, W1932, 1964, 1968, 2038, 2063, 2191, 2432, 2340, 2691, 2693, 2711, 2758.

Register of Wills, Cecil County, Maryland State Archives, Annapolis, Inventories 1755–, 238–42.

RWP, 1760 W13, 302, 320, 327; 1761 W35, 62, 73, 74; 1762 W148, 205, 206, 227; 1763 W28, 31, 43, 290; 1765 W115, 209; 1766 W41, 261, 265, 265½, 280; 1767 W86, 131; 1768 W173, 210; 1769 W301; 1770 W20, 362; 1771 W102; 1772 W133, 172; 1773 W168, 249, 264, 316; 1774 W23, 28, 29, 38; 1774 Admin 31.

RWSC, Burlington County, NJSLA, Mf. 0545451, #8657–66, #9094–111.

RWSC, Cumberland County, NJSLA, #261 F.

RWSC, Hunterdon County, NJSLA, Mf. 0461819 #814 J, #775 J; Mf. 0461820 #893 J.

Register of Wills, York County Archives, York, January 9, 1761; April 11, 1767; November 25, 1769; January 31, 1771.

Wills, Lancaster County Historical Society, Lancaster, PA: January 10, 1760, July 31, 1760, August 11, 1760, January 16, 1762, May 24, 1762, November 15, 1763, November 21, 1763, April 14, 1764, January 4 and February 20, 1765, May 1, 1765, October 29, 1765, February 27, 1766, June 26, 1766, October 29, 1766, January 12, 1767, September 12, 1767, September 7, 1768, December 9, 1770, ? ? [1770] (John Ashbridge), September ?, 1773 (Henry Sowder).

Salvador da Bahia and Recôncavo (1760–69): APEB-JI, 04/1582/2051/06, 07/3195/06, 08/3438/05, 03/1129/15978/07, 03/971/1440/07, 09/3926/02.

South Carolina: SCDAH, Series S213032, Inventories of Estates, Mf. 0194634, Books 2–3; Mf. 0194635, Books W, X, Z.

Charleston Public Library, Charleston, WPA 94A, 94B, 98.

Southern District, Saint-Domingue: ANOM, SDOM, Not. Beaulieu 94–96; Belin du Ressort 102, 104; Bugaret 317, 328; Daudin de Bellair 429, 431; Dupuis de Lavaux 591–92; Laroque 1194; Legendre 1214–15, 1220, 1223, 1224; Lejeune Duparnay 1261, 1264; Martigniat 1326–28.

APPENDIX 2: INVENTORY SOURCES FOR FREE SETTLER GARMENT HOLDINGS

F: number of usable women's inventories
M: number of usable men's inventories

Late seventeenth century

Buenos Aires 1652–97 (24 F, 34 M): AGN SL, 3857, 4298, 5335, 5558, 5671, 5868, 6247, 6248, 6367, 6720, 7146, 7156, 7259, 7261, 7369, 7710, 8121, 8127, 8408, 8417, 8598, 9 48-6-3, 9 48-6-4A

Cape Town 1689–1717 (25 F, 40 M): MOOC 8/1.13, 1.23, 1.26, 1.31, 1.36, 1.47, 1.52, 1.57, 1.66, 1.74–76, 1.78, 1.83, 1.85, 2.7–9, 2.11, 2.13–14, 2.20, 2.25, 2.30, 2.32–33, 2.43, 2.46, 2.60, 2.70, 2.73–75, 2.77, 2.108, 3.9, 3.15–17, 3.19, 3.24–25, 3.27, 3.31, 3.46, 3.49, 3.50–51, 3.60, 3.72–73, 13/6, 33/12; 10/1.81, 1.84–85, 1.89–90, 1.98–99; 1STB18/301/6 (2), 302/6 (2), 311/6.

Charles Town 1688–99 (7 F, 16 M): SCDAH, CCWB 1692–93 [*sic*], Mf. ST0500.

　RSP 1675–95, Mf. ST0354.

　RSP 1692–1700, Mf. ST0355.

Jamaica, 1674–1702 (2 F, 18 M): JA, IB/11/3/1–3, 5.

Montreal 1651–99 (23 F, 53 M): BANQ-M, GN, A. Adhémar Mf. 4634–38; Basset Mf. 2036–39; Bougrine Mf. 2103; Closse Mf. 2106; De Saint-Pere Mf. 3196; Gastineau-Duplessis Mf. 2132; Mauge, Mf. 2042–44; Moreau Mf. 2044–45; Pottier Mf. 2427.

Philadelphia area 1676–99 (14 F, 22 M): Register of Wills, Cecil County, Maryland State Archives, Annapolis, mf. # 0013870.

RWP, W15 1685, W18 1685, W24 1686, W38 1686 (2), W32 1687, W36 1687, W34 1688 (2), W45 1688, W47 1688 (2), W54 1688, W80 1692 (2), W103 1694, W118 1694 (2), W121 1694, W166 1698, W196 1699, W199 1699, W200 1699 (2), W201 1699, W208-9 1699, W221 1699.

RWSC, Salem County, NJSLA, mf. # 0545493.

Early eighteenth century

Jamaica 1730–39 (3 F, 44 M): JA, IB/11/3/17.

Louisiana 1717–39 (5 F, 24 M): LHC, FSC1720070201, 1724120901, 1725061801, 1725071301, 1725082303, 1725100601, 1728120402, 1730011601, 1730021001, 1730052201, 1731042801, 1731010502, 1731010801, 1731012601, 1731121401, 1731122202, 1735072501, 1735080801, 1735092701, 1735102901, 1736012301, 1736062301, 1736081301.

NONA, Inventories, September 14, 1735; April 1737.

Kask. Ms, 20:8:18:1, 21:9:13:1, 31:11:26:1, 33:6:25:1.

Salvador da Bahia 1715–39 (7 F, 12 M): APEB-JI, 02/634/1088/07, 02/635/1090/01, 02/636/1091/01, 02/687/1147A/07, 02/687/1147/08, 03/1058/1527/13, 03/1307/1776/10, 03/1351/1820/13, 03/1403/1872/09, 04/1581/2050/01–02, 04/1601/2070/02, 04/1601/2070/05, 04/1614/2083/08, 04/1695/2165/08, 04/1695/2165/18, 04/1800/2270/11, 05/1992/2463/02, 08/3396/0/11, no number Eleutéria Francisca Sousa (1717).

Southern District, Saint-Domingue 1722–39 (3 F, 34 M): ANOM, SDOM, Not. Casamajor 357; Delinois 471; Delorme de Roissy 478; Laville Mf. 1095756; Martin 1356–57, Mf. 1095759; Neys 1456; Saunier 1567–68; Vieilhomme 1710.

1760–74

Buenos Aires jurisdiction (35 F, 47 M): AGN, SL, 3860–63, 4303–305, 5338–40, 5346, 5560, 5672–73, 6724, 7149–50.

Cape Colony (39 F, 66 M): MOOC 8/10.16, 10.17 (2), 10.19b, 10.21, 10.24, 10.27, 10.43, 10.45, 10.50, 10.58, 10.69a, 10.70, 10.72a, 10.73, 10.75–76, 11 1/8, 11.10 (2), 11.11–13, 11.19, 11.23–24, 11.26–28, 11.29a (2), 11.30, 11.32a, 11.36, 11.40–42, 11.44, 11.45a, 12.9, 12.13, 12.15a, 12.16, 12.23, 12.28, 12.32 (2), 12.34, 12.52–53, 12.59–61, 12.62 (2), 12 no number 01, 13.10–11, 13.13, 13.17–18, 13.29–30, 13.42–44, 13.57–58, 13.61, 14.4, 14.13, 14.16, 14.18 (2), 14.19, 14.26, 14.28 (2), 14.29–30, 14.36 (2), 14.37–38, 14.54–57, 14.60, 15.2, 15.5 (2), 15.6, 15.14, 15.16–17, 15.19, 15.25–26, 16.27; 1STB 18/30 4/6 (2), 18/31 1/6 (2), 18/31 4/6.

Jamaica (5 F, 33 M): JA, IB/11/3/41, 43–46, 49–51, 53–54.

Louisiana 1760–69 (13 F, 68 M): LHC, FSC17620222601/032701, 1762041701/051101(2), 1762051203, 1762102001, 1763051901/102101, 1763070406, 1763070602, 1763100103, 1764020101, 1764020801, 1764022203, 1764032701, 1764050901, 1764062602, 1764080801, 1764091502, 1764101201, 1764101802, 1765010802, 1765011001, 1765012807, 1765122303, 1765020501/022602, 1765081701, 1765121102, 1766081902, 1766102301/112701, 1767031901, 1767051402, 1768053101, 1768111402, 1768120503, 1768122001, 1768122602, 1768123001/2, 1769011001, 1769020101, 1769020801, 1769021303, 1769021502/030201, 1769030102, 1769031502, 1769032501, 1769041401/042002, 1769041701, 1769051001, 1769052802, 1769062604, 1769071301-2/071701, 1769100901/101801, 1769101302/102201(2).

Kask. Mss: 63:6:19:1/20:1.

Natchitoches Parish Court House, Louisiana, Conveyance Record Book 1, 480, 552, 557, 569, 596; December 20, 1761, January 14, 1763, March 21, 1764, April 1, 1764, November 17, 1764, October 10, 1765, October 11, 1765, September 19, 1768.

NONA, Inventories, October 17, 1764 and October 25, 1765, January 15, 1765, June 11, 1765, November 10, 1766; Not. Maison 2672, 9174, 79322, 80338, 80849, 82819; Not. Garic 8927, 8930, 76750.

St. Charles Parish, LA; GS Mf. 0392503.

Montreal area (142 F, 130 M): BANQ-M, GN, Blanzy Mf. 2652; Bouvet Mf. 2104; Chatelier Mf. 2040; Cherrier Mf. 2106; Coron Mf. 2117; Courville Mf. 3200–201; Deguire Mf. 2118; Duvernay, Mf. 2723–25; Foucher Mf. 1420440–41, 1420476; Grise Mf. 2133–34; Hantraye Mf. 2696; Hodiesne Mf. 2140–42; Jehanne Mf. 2023025, 2023103; J. Lalanne Mf. 2410; P. Lalanne Mf. 5975–76, 1674289–90; Legacy Mf. 1432365; Loiseau Mf. 2738; Mezières Mf. 2412–13, 1464507–508; Panet Mf. 2735–36, 1522227–29; Racicot Mf. 1430214–15; Sanguinet Mf. 2685; Simonet Mf. 1464535–38; Soupras Mf. 2443–45, 1464539–40; Souste Mf. 2450; Vautier Mf. 1562136–37.

Philadelphia area (10 F, 12 M): CCA, WI, W1926, W1952, W1969, W2019, W2060, W2216.

RWP, W 256 1760, W 74 1761, W 169 1762, W 16 1763, W 53 1764, W 93 1764, W 36 1766, W 255 1766, W 258 1766, W 238 1769.

RWSC, Burlington County, NJSLA, Mf. 0545450 #6699, Mf. 0545452.

RWSC, Gloucester County, NJSLA, Mf. 0533154 #1033 H.

Register of Wills, York County Archives, York, November 18, 1762, October 7, 1769, October 12, 1769.

Salvador da Bahia and Recôncavo (8 F, 25 M): APEB-JI, 02/674/1133/05, 02/674/1133/08, 02/675/1134/04, 02/675/1134/08–09, 03/971/1440/05, 03/971/1440/08–09, 03/972/1441/01, 03/1089/1558/05, 03/1128/1597/08, 03/1129/15978/07, 03/1297/1766/14, 03/1309/1778/09, 04/1582/2051/03–08, 04/1594/2063/02, 04/1594/2063/04, 04/1610/2079/02–03, 04/1613/2082/05, 04/1620/2089/09, 05/2116/2585, 07/3195/06, 08/3396/06, 09/3912/12, 09/3926/02, 09/3959/26, 09/4000/08.

South Carolina (3 F, 56 M): SCDAH, Series S213032, Inventories of Estates, Mf. 0194634, Books 2–3; Mf. 0194635, Books W, X, Z.

Charleston Public Library, Charleston, WPA 94A, 94B, 98.

Alice Hanson Jones, *American Colonial Wealth: Documents and Methods*, 2nd edn., 3 vols. (New York: Arno Press, 1977), vol. III.

Southern District, Saint-Domingue (25 F, 182 M): ANOM, SDOM, Not. Beaulieu 94–97; Belin du Ressort 102–06; Berton

129–30; Bugaret 314, 316–17, 322–26, 328–31; Daudin de Bellair 428–31; Dubernes de la Greffière 539; Dupuis de Lavaux 586–92; Duval 613; Flanet 642; Guilleau 1002–03, 1005, 1007, 1010; Ladoué 1153; Laroque 1194; Legendre 1210–11, 1213–16, 1218–26, 1228–29; Lejeune Duparnay 1259–62; Mallet 1320–22; Martigniat 1325–28; Michel 1377–78; Rivet 1555–57, 1559–60; Sennebier 1575; Sibire de Morville 1604.

Notes

Introduction: Fashioning the Atlantic world

1. APEB-JI, 04/1582/2051/06.
2. Ferreira 2001; Ribeiro 2005; Verger 1968.
3. *Comerciante* could mean merchant, retailer, or someone who sold both wholesale and retail; the fact that many of the inventoried fabrics had been cut, and some were characterized as "remnants" (*retalhos*), suggests that Viana was predominantly a retailer.
4. It is possible that some of the garments, as well as the bed coverings, belonged to Viana. But the convention in Salvador inventories was to specify the condition of personal property, and no such information is given for the clothing mentioned in this paragraph.
5. Schoeser 2003; Harris et al. 1993.
6. Abu-Lughod 1989; Lemire 2009, 205–10
7. Riello 2013, 138–39; Lespagnol 1982, 333, 336.
8. Braund 1993, 122.
9. See Shammas 1990; Dessureault, Dickinson, and Wien 1994.
10. Weatherill 1988, 119, 133; Loewald, Starika, and Taylor 1958, 260–61.
11. See Ross 2008; Weiner and Schneider 1989, 1–3; Pellegrin 1993; Campbell 1997.
12. In contrast, *costume* ("dress which is donned in order to demonstrate, unambiguously, a specific identity") is less subject to ambiguity. The definitions come from Ross 2008, 6; see also Tortora 2010b.
13. See Gronow and Warde 2001.
14. Bourdieu 1972/1977.
15. Van Dantzig 1999; Daaku 1970; Kea 1982; Meuwese 2011, 310–13; Thornton 1983; Hilton 1985.
16. Gervais 2008, 465.
17. O'Reilly 2011; Hancock 2011.

18. Eltis 2000, 9.
19. My calculations are based on Davis 1962, 302–03; Léon 1970–80, 502–05.
20. Calculations based on Davis 1962, 302–03. There are no comparable data for other countries.
21. To sample the varied critical positions regarding the benefits and drawbacks of using inventories, see Main 1975; Spufford 1990; Orlin 2002; Desloges 1991, App. A.
22. Thus by using cargo listings in Montreal merchant account books, Dale Anderson's thesis (see above, List of Abbreviations: AndD) corrected interpretations that neglected the centrality of textiles and related items in European–Amerindian trade.
23. For two outstanding examples, see Jones 1990 and Marees 1987.
24. Bagneris 2010; Kriz 2008, esp. chap. 2; Tobin 1999, chap. 5.
25. Breen 1993.
26. For example, scholarly investigation of drawings in a manuscript by the author of Cavazzi 1687 show that the author, an Italian missionary in mid-seventeenth-century west Central Africa, made "accurate reproductions of [objects, including apparel] known to have belonged to specific Congolese and Angolan ethnic groups" (Bassani 1987). Unfortunately, the images are not currently available for reproduction.
27. Styles 2007, 334.
28. The quotation is from Riello 2013, 8. See also Berg 2013; Steger 2013; Pomeranz and Topik 2012.
29. See de Vries 2013, 2010; Emmer 2003; Cooper 2001.
30. For Indian Ocean globalization, see Riello 2013, 19–34; Abu-Lughod 1989.
31. Cf. Robertson 1992, 58–60; Findlay and Rourke 2003, esp. 16–17.
32. Cf. Sassatelli 2007, 177–82.
33. For an excellent case study, see Lemire 2003.
34. For influential iterations within a large and rapidly expanding scholarly literature, see Meinig 1986; Armitage 2002; Bailyn 2005; for collaborative overviews, Greene and Morgan 2009; Canny and Morgan 2011; for a textbook, Benjamin 2009.
35. Many of these criticisms are reviewed (and some are replicated) in Greene and Morgan 2009. See also Gervais 2008; Coclanis 2006; Games 2006.
36. Gervais 2008, 472.
37. See, e.g., the examples of both European- and North American-based merchant networks outlined in Gervais 2008, 471–72.
38. For influential modern works, see Baudrillard 1979/1998; Douglas and Isherwood 1979; Appadurai 1986a; Campbell 1987; McCracken 1988; Trentmann 2012.
39. Within an enormous and constantly growing scholarly literature, see McKendrick, Brewer, and Plumb 1982; Brewer and Porter 1993; Roche 1997; Smith 2002; de Vries 2008.

40. See Brubaker and Cooper 2000, esp. 14–17.
41. See Certeau 1984.
42. Cf. Lemire 2010, esp. 16, 18.
43. On fashion as new arrangements, see Howell 2010, 228–29.
44. Cf. Simmel 1904; Craik 1994.
45. On creolization, see Cohen and Toninato 2010; Stewart 2007; Buisseret and Reinhardt 2000.

1 Dress regimes at the dawn of the shared Atlantic

1. Pigafetta 1591, 67.
2. Cuvelier and Jadin 1954, 109–10.
3. See Elias 1939/1969, 1982; Becker 1988; Bryson 1998; Davetian 2009.
4. See Dickason 1984; Pagden 1982; Sayre 1997; Cohen 1980.
5. Carr-Gomm 2010; Duerr 1988/1998; Barcan 2004; Masquelier 2005; Lamp 2010.
6. For example, the custom in some German towns for families to run largely or fully naked through the streets to the bathhouse after undressing at home was dying out; Elias 1939/1969, 1982, I: 132, 138–39, 164–65. Cf. Bologne 1986.
7. Though other languages do not make the same distinction, in English, "nude tends to be applied to nakedness regarded in positive or aesthetic terms, esp. in artistic contexts" (*OED*), so this book does not use "nude" as a synonym for public undress.
8. *Dictionnaire de l'Académie française* 1694, "NUDD, nue" usage example: "les sauvages vont tout nuds."
9. Loyer 1714, 140: "ce que la pudeur veut qu'on cache."
10. Marees 1987, 11. Cf. Kupperman 1997, 199–203 for similar statements about Amerindians.
11. Hennepin 1698, 81; cf. Loyer 1714, 140; Léry, 1578/1990, 57.
12. Caplan 2000b; Gustafson 2000; Macquarrie 2000; Rosecrans 2000; Fleming 2000; Fleming 2001.
13. De Bry 1590–1634.
14. Konrad 2011, 39.
15. This section draws on Hart 1998; Harvey 1995; Hunt 1996; Jenss 2010; Kuchta 2002; Müller 2010; Pastoureau 2000/2001; Pastoureau 2009; Riello 2010a; Riello 2010b; Tarrant 2010; Ventosa and Lawton 2010; Vincent 2003; Vincent 2009; Vigarello 1988.
16. Marees 1912; Marees 1987. Evaluations: Jones 1986; Jones 1982; Iselin 1994; Sutton 2012.
17. Marees 1987, 44. In another passage, Marees claimed that women went around "entirely naked" well into adulthood before Europeans taught them about

shame – and also about using clothing for purposes of sexually attracting male Europeans (ibid., 37).

18. Blake 1941, 367.

19. Kriger 2009, 105–11, 125; Marees 1987, 51 n1; Mbow 2010; Kriger 2006, 26–30; Kriger 2005; Ballong-Wen-Mewuda 1993, 311–14, 329–30; Hopkins 1973, 48.

20. E.g., Cavazzi 1687, 172.

21. Pigafetta 1591, 15, 17–18 (first quotation), 34; Romano 1649, 84–85 (second quotation); Martin 1972, 35–37; Thornton 1998, 49; Mbow 2010.

22. Romano 1649, 85; Pigafetta 1591, 10, 36, 66–67.

23. Vogt 1975, summarized in Vogt 1978, 67–68. Blake 1941 has translations of contemporary documents that elucidate the importance of the cloth trade along the Gold Coast.

24. Pigafetta 1591, 67; Jordán Pérez 2010.

25. This paragraph draws on Marees 1987, 34–39, 51, 55, 61, and pls. 1–3 (here, Figures 1.1–1.3), 8, 9, 14, 16. For earlier partial descriptions, Crone 1937, 80 (1462); Blake 1941, 367 (1555–56).

26. Cf. Marees 1987, 175, pl. 16 A (chief's wife), B (common woman), C (fisher's wife).

27. Marees 1987, 217; cf. 36.

28. Marees 1987, 34–38.

29. This paragraph is based on Pigafetta 1591, 66–67; cf. Jordán Pérez 2010.

30. Romano 1649, 82; Cavazzi 1687, 176 (quotation).

31. Pigafetta underlined his point by adding that "poor women [dress] *al modo antico*" (1591, 67).

32. Cf. Hennepin 1698, 81 (the Louisiana country). Among the Tainos of the Greater Antilles, men apparently went naked, women with cotton loincloths or "aprons," and all wore much ornamentation (Lovén 1935/2010, 463–88).

33. Léry 1578/1990, 57; Ganson 2003, 19; Levinton 2009, 219. Brazil's initial Portuguese explorer, Pedro Álvares Cabral, had already noted the native mode of dress in 1500 (Andrade and Root 2010). The Tupinambá were a tribe within the Tupi people.

34. E.g., Staden 1557/2008; Thévet 1558; Léry 1578/1990; Montaigne 1580/2009; d'Abbeville 1614.

35. Léry 1578/1990, 56–68; on tattoos, see also Staden 1557/2008, 113. For details about dress materials, Andrade and Root 2010.

36. Elphick and Malherbe 1988.

37. For both the originals and English translations, see Schapera and Farrington 1933/1970. For very brief summaries, Davison 2010, 508; Mbow 2010, 39.

38. Smith and Pheiffer 1993.

39. Grevenbroek 1695, 255.

40. Quotation from Dapper 1668, 55.

41. For the following, Welters 2010; Jackson 2010; Bourque and Labar 2009, 45–61; Becker 2005; Paterek 1994, xii–xiv, 6–76, 432–46; Hudson 1976, 109–13, 213, 247, 260–67; Swanton 1946, 439–536; Holmes 1896. All provide copious references to contemporary sources.
42. Carocci 2010.
43. *JR* VII: 15. Cf. Samuel de Champlain, quoted in Kinietz 1940, 10: "women and girls ... are clad like the men except that they always gird up their robes."
44. Cf. Becker 2007, 66.
45. Bourque and Labar 2009, 61.
46. Vogt 1978, 67; Vogt 1975, 646–47; Miller 1988, 79–80.
47. Romano 1649, 91; Cavazzi 1687, 128 (quotation).
48. Léry 1578/1990, 66.
49. Dapper 1668, 73, 53.
50. Dapper 1668, 73.

2   Acquiring imported textiles and dress

1. Rowland, Sanders, and Galloway 1927–84, V: 228–37. I have corrected the translation of a few terms.
2. Miquelon 1978, 34, 51–52, 71. For a major West Indian merchant and real estate fortune built initially on the proceeds of *pacotilles*, see Butel 1995.
3. Cf. Bosher 1987, 68–105, who concludes (84), "it was normal rather than exceptional for French officers to trade in the colonies."
4. Daaku 1970, 5–6; Kriger 2009, 110; Hopkins 1973, 61.
5. Lopez 1976; Abu-Lughod 1989 for non-European trade networks.
6. See, most recently, de Vries 2010, 725–28.
7. Gervais 2012; Lamikiz 2010; Hancock 2009.
8. Unger 2011; van Lottum and van Zanden 2014; Menard 1991.
9. Young 1995; Bosher 1987; Hancock 1995; Lamikiz 2010; Miquelon 1975.
10. Muldrew 1998; Fontaine 2001.
11. Morgan 2000.
12. Gervais, Lemarchand, and Margairaz 2014; Gervais 2008.
13. Fisher 1971, 1–8, 32–37, 53–63; Schwartz 2007, 39–41; Tarrade 1972; Pritchard 2004, 193–94, 367; Stern and Wennerlind 2013.
14. Davis 1966, 312.
15. Dardel 1963, 109; Lamikiz 2010, 6–19, 133–34, 185–86.
16. Scammell 2000, 140–49, 165–67; Maxwell 1993.
17. Moutoukias 1988, 18, 113–14. Elsewhere Moutoukias speaks of the "mild everydayness" of smuggling in the Río de la Plata region (98).
18. Zahedieh 1986; Burnard 2002, 232–36; Geggus 1982, 6–32; Dawdy 2007, 676–84.

19. Kwass 2014; Le Gouic 2012; Cousquet 2002, 45, 65–67; Chobaut 1938, 140–41; O'Brien, Griffiths, and Hunt 1991.

20. Carreira 1983, 48–52; Ferreira 2001, 352–53.

21. Klooster 2009, 141. See also Scammell 2000; Ramos 1990; Fisher 1971, 7–8, 32; Pritchard 2004, 202–03.

22. For contemporary instructions about these matters, see, e.g., Freeman 2002, 103, 171.

23. Freeman 2002, 103 (all *sic*); cf. ibid., xxviii– xxix, 172.

24. Hanna 1917, 271.

25. Freeman 2002, 103.

26. Hanna 1917, 271.

27. Jensen 1963, 87, 135.

28. Intercolonial trade also helped balance supply and demand locally; typically it involved small shipments between merchants within the same empire. For instances, see, e.g., Hamer 1968–94.

29. Irregular and (compared with lengths of fabrics) quite small values of uncut patterns, ready-made shirts, stockings, and (yet more rarely) coats and jackets, together with handkerchiefs offered by length as well as separately, have been included in the totals in the tables below when fiber content could be determined.

30. The ell itself was not standard, ranging from 0.59 m to 1.37 m.

31. To add a further complication, the category of "cottons" had flexible boundaries. While Asian and African types were pure cottons, up until at least the mid-eighteenth century many if not most European cottons were actually mixtures of cottons with (usually) linen, wool, or silk, the proportions varying according to raw materials prices and availability; see Riello 2013, esp. 73–75, 152–57. In the tables, fabrics have been classifed according to early modern practice.

32. For the general textile price trends, see Shammas 1994.

33. Surviving colonial inventories for this period include only port merchants.

34. The data in Table 2.1 understate the store of cottons at Cape Coast Castle, notably impressive amounts of Benin cloth and lesser quantities from the Cape Verde Islands that the Royal African Company itself obtained directly rather than via London; see RAC, Cape Coast Castle Warehouse Book, June 5, 1687– March 31, 1691, TNA T70/1230. African and Arab merchants also continued to supply the Gold Coast.

35. On *annabasses*, see Savary 1742, I, part I, col. 143 (who notes that they sold "particularly" well in Angola); Riello 2013, 152; Ratelband 1953, XCVII.

36. That the Royal African Company well understood local demand patterns is clear from comparison of the inflow and outflow figures recorded in TNA T70/1230 with the detailed listings of the cargoes summarized in Table 2.1.

37. Cf. a 1706 list of goods that would sell in Cape Town (Lockyer 1711, 302).

38. Buenos Aires may have received inexpensive cottons produced in Andean *obrajes* (workshops staffed by Amerindians), as well as linens, but if so they seem to have circulated outside the inventoried merchant shops.
39. Zahedieh 1986, 582.
40. Rømer 2000, 191–92, 228–29.
41. Small samples of 1730s merchant inventories from Kingston, Philadelphia, and Montreal also disclose these trends, with proportions of cottons about doubling, those of woolens dropping by about a quarter.
42. The proportion of cottons in Salvador da Bahia and its hinterland (though not in shops) was likely greater than shown in Table 2.2, because cottons woven on plantations did not enter into the commercial circuits from which the extant inventories came.
43. The availability of cottons around Bahia was likely higher than indicated in Table 2.3, because plantation production for use thereon is again omitted.
44. Cf. Morgan 2007, 260–61, 261–62, 292–93.
45. See, e.g., "William Towerson's First Voyage to Guinea. 1555–6," in Blake 1941, 367–91.
46. Proyart 1776, 151.
47. Probate inventories and newspaper advertisements reveal the ubiquity of these dual businesses. See also Lebrero 1992; Bushman 1994, 235–36; Dechêne 1974/1992, 43; Socolow 1975, 9–10, 14–15.
48. Santos 1956, 121–22. For survivals in North America, see, e.g., *S. C. Gaz.*, August 12, 1732; LHC, FSC 1730010901. Some country shops may have evolved out of plantation sales venues, as, e.g., Dawson & Gairdner's "store at Milton, the plantation house at Monck's Corner" advertised in the *S. C. Gaz.*, July 17, 1762.
49. Surrey 1916, 169; Worden, van Heyningen, and Bickford-Smith 1998, 57–59.
50. White 2003; Worden, van Heyningen, and Bickford-Smith 1998, 59.
51. Examples of all of these are found again and again in newspaper advertisements and probate inventories.
52. For examples, see McDowell 1955, 77, 82, 131, 137, 143, 232, 237, 280, 309.
53. See, e.g., James Habersham Papers, GHS, File 337, Folder 1, November 17, 1767, Habersham to William Knox, London ("bunglers"); Morgan 2007, 189 (June 16, 1746), 191–92 (in this case, ironically, Bristol tailors badly botched the apparel of a Jamaica merchant); Laborie 1798, 184. Both Habersham and Laborie claimed that ordering from European tailors allowed them to clothe their slaves better than the norm.
54. Mui 1989; Coquery 2011; van den Heuvel and Ogilvie 2013.
55. The number 5 in the upper right display cabinet, for example, indicated rhingrave-style breeches trimmed with lace and ribbons; the letter F (on the row of fabrics hanging at waist level on the back wall), blue taffeta with small

brocaded flowers edged with black ("just a few days ago a skirt of this fabric was made for the Queen," the text helpfully notes).

56. Lebrero 1992; Socolow 1991, 249–55.

57. See, e.g., Dépatie 2003. Probate inventories best document the spread of and changes in shops in other Atlantic locations.

58. Fontaine 2008; Dépatie 2003; Muldrew 1998; Bernal 1992.

59. The grouping of shops is best revealed by newspaper advertisements, and (in Montreal) from probate inventories; see also Hornsby 2005, fig. 5.5, 186. For visual presentation of a European shopping zone, see the maps based on a 1769 survey in Coquery 2011, 331–36.

60. The most widely deployed term for goods – perhaps because it was the most broadly evocative – was "neat," which in the eighteenth century connoted "handsome," "fine," "smart," and "elegant."

61. Advertisements in virtually every British colonial newspaper reveal these developments. For the metropole, see also Walvin 1997, 155–58.

62. Coquery 2011, 302.

63. Worden, van Heyningen, and Bickford-Smith 1998, 57–59.

64. Sousa 1992, 19–20; White 2006, 529–30.

65. Allaire 1987; Standen 1994; Thomas 1989, 29–32; Dunn 1998, 15–20, 91; Barker 2001, 141–43; Socolow and Johnson 1981, 43.

66. E.g., the Saint-Domingue shop of Le Sieur Pillard, *Aff. Am.*, Supplément, July 10, 1769, 219 ("a magnificent assortment of the most fashionable merchandise").

67. E.g., the Saint-Domingue "merchant tailor" Sr Brohan, *Aff. Am.*, Supplément, March 28, 1768, 3; Lambert 2004.

68. They were less common in Brazil, however (Stols 1996, 286).

69. Hopkins 1973, 55.

70. Marees 1987, 62, for the description. For a fuller account of large weekly markets, including the rituals involved in their operation, see ibid., 63–65.

71. Apart from collections of statutes, see Mintz 1974, 197–98; Dawdy 2007, 669; Bushman 1994, 235; Joseph and Szuchman 1996, 98.

72. Olwell 1996, 98–106; Socolow 1996, 281–82; Hauser 2008, Joseph and Szuchman 1996, 98–100 (Bahia). In Saint-Domingue, to cite one instance, marketing by slaves was regulated initially by the so-called *Code Noir* of 1685, and the relevant articles were reissued at intervals thereafter, often with increased fines for violation; see Moreau de Saint-Méry 1784–90, II: 208–09, 692; IV: 228.

73. Ferreira 2012, 133.

74. Olwell 1996, 100; *Acts of assembly* 1787, I: 158; *Édit du roi* 1685/1687, Art. XIX.

75. Sousa 1992, 21–22. The text does not make it clear what women were meant nor what impediments made shops difficult of access for them, but the widely

practiced seclusion of women probably played a significant role; see Frézier 1716/1717, II: 531–32; Stols 1996, 287. See also Joseph and Szuchman 1996, 101. Cf. Worden, van Heyningen, and Bickford-Smith 1998, 61–62, and advertisements that boasted of slaves' "very good" huckstering abilities in *Aff. Am.*, no. 8, February 23, 1767, no. 10, March 11, 1767, no. 20, May 20, 1767.

76. Loyer 1714, 130.

77. Ferreira 2012, 59–60.

78. E.g., Jacques Du Verges, who traded with Amerindians in Illinois, LHC, FSC, 1739070701; or Françoise (below).

79. Stols 1996, 279.

80. For the Jamaican Alexander Walker, see JA, IB/11/3/18, fols. 148^{r}–48^{v}, December 4, 1735; for others, Alexander 1984, 160. For itinerant French and *métis* traders (in French, *coureurs de bois* and *voyageurs*) with Amerindians, Podruchny 2006; Dechêne 1974/1992, 90–96; Tanner 1994; Zimmerman 1966; Barker 2001. For peddling to other colonists, Anon. 1988; ANOM, SDOM, not. Dubernes de la Greffière no. 538, November 19, 1772.

81. John Lockhart's 1732 application, in Anon. 1988, 287 (all *sic*).

82. In the estates of five chapmen inventoried in rural Chester and Lancaster Counties, Pennsylvania, during the 1760s, between 60 and 100 percent of their stocks were textiles, sewing notions, and small garments (CCA 1932, 1968, 2038, 2063; Lancaster County Archives, Lancaster, Pennsylvania, Inventories, September 12, 1767). For a similar result for an Illinois country trader, see NONA, French document vol. 1, fols. 75128ff., January 15, 1765, Joseph Dupré or Beaupré. For Europe, Deceulaer 2006, 181; Fontaine 1996, 184. See also Brown 2000; Spufford 1984.

83. NONA, French document vol. 1, fols. 75128ff., January 15, 1765.

84. ANOM, SDOM not. Belin du Ressort no. 104, January 17, 1772.

85. Lancaster County Archives, Lancaster, Pennsylvania, Inventories, September 12, 1767.

86. Cassady 1967, 26–29. Auctions have been in existence at least since ancient Babylon and were widespread in classical Greece and Rome. During the early modern centuries, the various East India companies often auctioned imported goods in European ports and capitals.

87. For some examples from just one merchant, Hamer 1968–94, I: 101; II: 307; III: 494; IV: 108, 413–14.

88. Moutoukias 1988, 102–11.

89. Breen 2004, 140–43; Randle 2007; Hudson 1985; White 2006, 523 and n9. Elsewhere, the development of auction institutions and practices in all their forms is best seen in newspaper advertisements, statute books, merchant correspondence and account books, and probate inventories.

90. For such criticisms, see *Colonial records of Pennsylvania* 1831–40, 1852, III: 91–92 (1720); Anon. 1770; "Legion," *Pa. Gaz.*, January 30, 1772.
91. "Civis," *Pa. Gaz.*, January 30, 1772.
92. See, e.g., Hamer 1968–94, IV: 148 and n5, VI: 573; Monson 31/1–20; more generally, Mullin 1992, 131–35.
93. Cf. Kalm 1772, II: 187–88: after the revenge killing of an English farmer near Fort St. Frederic (Crown Point, New York), the Amerindians involved went off in his clothes.
94. See, e.g., Morrison 1751, the alleged pre-execution confession of a famous mid-eighteenth-century Philadelphia thief.
95. Chapter 3 below; also Jacobs 1966; White 1991, esp. 94–104; Saadani 2005; Jaenen 1985.
96. E.g., they typically accounted for a third, a half, or even more by value of gifts to Amerindians (Jacobs 1966, 49, 68; Saadani 2005, 59, table 3.1).
97. See contemporary usage in, e.g., Quaife 1947, 36; McDowell 1970, 317.
98. Mauss 1923–24/2000; Carrier 1995.
99. For the quotation, Aspers 2011, 80. Cf. Aspers 2010, 57.
100. Appadurai 1986b; Thomas 1991, 33–34.
101. These topics are treated at greater length in Chapter 4.

3   Redressing the indigenous Americas

1. For Basire, see Peltz 2007.
2. Weaver 2011; Vaughan 2006; Pratt 2005; Bickham 2005, 21–64; cf. Hamell 1987/1999.
3. The image gives their names in different forms than those now used. Colonists had given nicknames to at least three of the men: Little Carpenter (Attakullakulla), Old Warrior (Oukah Ulah Moytoy), the Conjuror or the King of Chota (Kitegista Skalilosken).
4. John Verelst had presented four Mohawk and Mahican "kings" in such moccasins when he painted them in 1710; his much copied images were reused into the 1760s, and at least one was duplicated without attribution (and transposed from an Iroquoian to an Algonquian nation) in France; see "Sauväge Nepisingue en Canada 1717," Bibliothèque nationale de France. Estampes et photographie. Gallica cliché RC-A-04362. Basire's caption underlined the purported significance of feathers in Cherokee culture: In the ceremony in which "*Articles of Friendship and Commerce*" were signed, "KETAGUSTAH" (Kitegusta, the "Prince") "*Concluded by laying down his Feathers upon ye Table & said*; This is our Way of Talking, wch. Is ye same Thing to us, as y^r Letters in ye Book are to you; and to you, *BELOVED MEN*, we deliver these Feathers in Confirmation of all that we have said."

5. Van Gennep 1909/1960; Turner 1969.
6. Nieuhof 1682, 222–24. For confirmation of Tapuia nakedness, save small covers for the genitalia fashioned from leaves (women) and bark (men), see van Baerle 1647/2011, 249; van Baerle's long, detailed description of the Tapuia and their customs (242–50) comes from Johan Rabe, who lived with them for four years as Dutch representative and translator. Cf. Piso and Markgraf 1648. The term Tapuia is a Tupí term, meaning simply non-Tupí.
7. For reproductions of the images, see Post 1990; Buvelot 2004; Chicangana-Bayona 2008, figs. 3, 4. See also Brienen 2007.
8. Anon. 1954–63, II; 15, 298, 299, 311. It is not certain what "raixeta" fabric is, but it probably was a cheap, coarse woolen resembling what in Spain was known as *rajeta*.
9. Nieuhof 1682, 218. Nieuhof calls the garment a *hemde*, which can mean shirt, vest, or undershirt, but also a knee-length shift worn directly next to the skin.
10. Housed in the Seção de Iconografia of the Biblioteca Nacional do Brasil, the image can be viewed at http://objdigital.bn.br/acervo_digital/div_iconografia/icon30306/icon30306_046.jpg (accessed September 12, 2013).
11. Cardim 1625/1939, 147–48, 153. Cardim, who also mentioned body painting, added that some men and women were beginning to go clothed below the waist for reasons of fashion and because they were ordered to do so; even so, some refused to wear anything more than a cap – an echo, perhaps, of the resistance to clothing Léry had noted earlier.
12. Zucchelli 1712, 71.
13. Stols 1996, 280–83.
14. See Chapter 4 below.
15. For what follows, Sarreal 2014, 74, 84–90, 175, 180, 185–90, 220–22; Levinton 2009, 219–22; Ganson 2003, 25–26, 41–43, 61, 73–77, 102, 111, 121–22.
16. Michelant and Ramé 1867, 42. Previously, Cartier had described Dannaconna as wearing only an "old black bearskin" (ibid., 41), and the other members of his band as "entirely naked, except for a little skin with which they covered their genitals [*nature*], and some old pelts worn as capes [*escharpes*]" (ibid., 37).
17. Oury 1971, Letter LXXX, 220, August 26, 1644. *Linge blanc* meant long undershirts worn under *simarres*, gown-like shirts or tunics, while French-style hair was short, ungreased, crimped, and given ringlets; see Gourdeau 1995, 129.
18. Saint-Vallier 1688, 72–73.
19. See, e.g., Hennepin 1698, 81.
20. *JR* IX: 102–03. Cf. Oury 1971, Letter CCXLI, 821, September 21, 1668.
21. Laverdière and Casgrain 1871/1973, 9–10.
22. White 2012, 56, 59; Gagnon 1975.

23. Croghan 1947.

24. Cf. above for Río de la Plata; see Johnson 2009, 133–34, for the southeast.

25. TNA, CO 5/358, fol. 31.

26. McDowell 1958, 453–54 (all *sic*).

27. Civility, a Conestogan, May 26, 1729, in Kent 1979, 319. Civility was referring to the previous year's "Presents," which when distributed had "pleased" Indians "of the whole Country."

28. Kent 1979, 241.

29. ANOM, 224 Mi 103, C11^A, vol. 117, fols. 282–84.

30. Oury 1971, Letter LXXX, 221.

31. It is notable, for example, that the 1753 gifts to Cherokees included boots and hats for men, earrings and ribbon for ornamentation, but no footwear for women.

32. TNA, CO 5/358, fols. 30–31.

33. TNA, CO 5/389, fols. 177–90; McDowell 1958, 376, 454; McDowell 1970, 282, 475; Robinson 2001, 174; ANOM, 224 Mi 103, C11^A, vol. 117, fol. 312. The distinctions were not always followed: for example, Pennsylvania Governor Keith gave calico shirts to chiefs (above).

34. Beads were standard offerings across the entire period as they were throughout North America.

35. Garments comprised 39 percent of cloth and clothing in cargoes by value in the 1720s, 70 percent in the 1740s; types of apparel rose from eight to twelve.

36. Caudebec hats were made of felt treated to resemble beaver.

37. McDowell 1955, 269; McDowell 1970, 566–68.

38. For representative scholarly assessments, see Axtell 1988, 153–77; Trigger 1985, 191–204; Braund 1993, 124–25.

39. *JR*, III: 74–75. Cf. Charlevoix 1722/1794, II: 657 ("nos Etoffes & nos Couvertures paroissent bien plus commodes aux Sauvages"; the word "commode" combines senses of convenience, suitability, and comfort). For a contrary view, in which late eighteenth-century Pennsylvania Indians purportedly asserted that clothing "made of the skins of animals and feathers" in "ancient times" was superior in warmth, durability, water resistance, and general comfort to "any woolen goods they have since purchased of the white people," see Heckewelder 1876, 202.

40. Laverdière and Casgrain 1871/1973, 53.

41. Moore 1988, 56–57 (all *sic*).

42. Rich 1949, 86–87. The ukemaw added that his fellow bandsmen were "great admirers of Diffent. Colour's."

43. Henry 1809/1969, 189–90; cf. 246–47, similar remarks about the Cree living further west, on the shores of Lake Winnipeg.

44. See, e.g., Axtell 1997.

45. Hennepin 1698, 79 (italics in the original). The description originally appeared in Hennepin 1683; see Hennepin 1880, 287–88. Cf. (just two of many late seventeenth- and early eighteenth-century examples) *JR* LXVII: 132–33; Rochemonteix 1904, 63–64.

46. Other images show Indians wearing a "painted leather blanket" (von Reck's inscription) and a similarly painted leather tunic; see Hvidt 1980, 126–27; cf. ibid., 46. For additional discussion of von Reck's images and careful notations, see Jackson 2010.

47. Jolicoeur 1941, 142, 43. For representative accounts, Bougainville 1757/1924, 66; Rogers 1765, 154.

48. Cited in Axtell 1988, 76. Cf. ibid., 78: part of the reform of his previous "errors" by Kittamaquund, the Piscataway leader, involved "exchang[ing] his skin garments for clothes made in the English fashion."

49. *JR* LXVII: 186.

50. Kalm 1977, 348.

51. For an excellent recent study, see Greer 2005. Greer notes that Catherine's "costume . . . corresponds to textual descriptions." For evidence of the image's diffusion and model nature, see the Jesuit Louis Nau's letter to a metropolitan French correspondent, October 2, 1735: "you've surely seen the portrait of the saintly girl Catherine Tégah-Kouita, who died in a saintly manner; all the savage women [in Sault Saint-Louis] are similarly dressed;" *JR* LXVIII: 282.

52. For other subtleties of convert dress, in the Illinois country, see White 2012, 86–87.

53. Printed in Kellogg 1916, 168–69. The treaty, the first between the nascent United States and an Amerindian nation, soon collapsed over disagreements about the provisions of the alliance it concluded, including (with what authorization is unknown) the offer of a fourteenth state for Amerindians (Richter 2001, 221). The European term "Delaware" is today often considered synonymous with and replaced by "Lenape." Yet because at least three distinct tribes (Lenape, Munsee, and Lenopi or Jersey) were grouped under the rubric, and because most contemporaries did not distinguish among them, I have retained the term "Delaware." For more discussion, see Becker 2008.

54. This paragraph draws on Becker 2005, Becker 2010, Johnson 2009, and many printed and manuscript primary sources.

55. Cresswell 1924, 121; Bourque and Labar 2009, 87.

56. E.g., SCDAH, RSP 1675–95, mf. STo354, Henry Hughes, November 28, 1688; SCDAH, CCWB 1692–93 [date *sic*], mf. STo500, Arnaud Bruneau, January 26, 1695 (ns).

57. Breeches were cited, for example, among May 1741 gifts from South Carolina to the Cherokee "Emperor" Moytoy and to Cherokee and Catawba headmen, but were not presented to "Common Men" (Robinson 2001, 171). In the 1753 South

Carolina gifting already quoted, the seven top headmen must have received breeches as part of their suits, given a contemporary definition of a "whole suit" as "Coat, Jacket, Breeches" in McDowell 1970, 413.

58. Pouchot 1781/1994, 444; Franquet 1974, 36–37.

59. Kalm 1977, 547; Hvidt 1980, 40. Cf. *JR* XLIV: 293–94: Breeches were an "encumbrance," only to be worn "as a bit of finery, or in fun."

60. Adair 1775, 7–8; Bougainville 1964, 123. For other testimonies about the avoidance of breeches, see Williamson 1758, 24 ("Breeches they never wear"); Cresswell 1924, 50.

61. Montigny 2008, 360, 359.

62. At York Factory, none were sold in the 1690s, and they had disappeared by the 1730s; Hudson's Bay Company, B239/d/1–6, B/239/d/21–30. At Fort Albany, where thirteen pairs were on hand in 1730, they remained unsold until four were traded in 1738–39, after which point breeches vanished from the accounts (Hudson's Bay Company, B/3/d/1–9, B/3/d/39–48). For trading captains' gifts, see Williams 1969, 317. Cf. Shannon 1996, 21, on Indian "disdain" for breeches.

63. AndD.

64. See, e.g., Cresswell 1924, 121; Lafitau 1724, III: 28; Mittelberger 1898, 83.

65. For the cargo manifests, which list tapabord caps (which had a brim and flaps to cover the ears and back of the head) along with Caudebec and Segovia hats – all of them made of one or another type of wool – and cotton caps, see AndD.

66. Timberlake 1765, 50; Jones 1774, 62; Smith 1799, 10–11, 36. Cf. Williamson 1758, 24 (in western New York Indians are shod in "*Mogganes*, or Shoes … made of Deer Skins").

67. *JR* III: 74–77; V: 24–25.

68. *JR* LXVIII: 265. Note that in the South Carolina 1753 gifting quoted above, only the superior headmen received shoes, the others boots.

69. Lafitau 1724, III: 26, 28.

70. E.g., the 1762 picture "Cunne Shote, Cherokee Chief," by Francis Parsons (Gilcrease Museum, Tulsa, Oklahoma); the images of the mid-eighteenth-century Mohawk leader Theyanoguin (Hendrick) discussed in Shannon 1996; the numerous paintings of the Six Nations leader Thayendanegea (Joseph Brant) by noted artists like George Romney (today at the National Gallery of Canada in Ottawa) and Gilbert Stuart, for whom see Kelsay 1984; or the Cherokee emissaries depicted above in Figure 3.1.

71. Williamson 1758, 24. Shannon (2009) has argued that Williamson fabricated his captivity narrative but that "His descriptions of the Indians' material culture" (explicitly including clothing) "are detailed and convincing and may reflect information he gathered during his residency in Pennsylvania or military service in New York" (26).

72. Heckewelder 1876, 203.

73. Hamell 1992, 456; Silverstein 2000a, 209–15.

74. For contemporary testimony, see Moore 1988, 46; Lafitau 1724, III: 28; Timberlake 1765, 133. Of lengths of woolen cloth sent to three French Upper Great Lakes posts (Green Bay, Rainy Lake, and Michilimacinac) in the 1740s, red accounted for 43 percent by value, blue for 34 percent; by length, the proportions were 36 and 30 respectively (AndD).

75. All sources on gifting show the association of red with men, which had roots in both Amerindian and European cultures. For the bi-gender relationship of blue, see Anon. 1758/1840, 16: "consumption of [dark or "blackish" blue blankets] is larger [than of red] because both women and men make use of them." In von Reck's double portrait (Plate 5) both king and queen are wearing blue, and the king has a red breechclout; in other drawings, von Reck shows a man and a woman "in their natural habit," with the woman clad in a blue skirt, the man in a blue breechclout (Hvidt 1980, 111); men performing a war dance equally dressed in red and blue breechclouts (ibid., 119); and two individual men, one wearing a deep Burgundy red blanket (ibid., 117), the other red leggings (ibid., 115). At least some Amerindian women (including slaves) did wear red garments along with men, however, as seen in Plate 6 and, e.g., Alexander de Batz's "Sauvages de plusieurs nations, Nouvelle Orleans [17]35," in the Peabody Museum, Harvard University, Cambridge, Massachusetts. For the many meanings of color among Amerindian peoples, see Feeser 2013, 33–38; Silverstein 2000a; Silverstein 2000b; Hamell 1992.

76. Williamson 1758, 24, 25. Champlain remarked that Montagnais and Algonquians painted their fur garments as well as their faces (Kinietz 1940, 9–10); see also Rochemonteix 1904, 64; Lafitau 1724, III: 30–31; Hvidt 1980, 127.

77. JR XXXVIII: 249–53; "Journal of Warren Johnson [1760–61]," in Johnson 1921–65, XIII: 194. Already in the early seventeenth century, Sagard had reported the many occasions of Ottawa and Wendat body painting (Sagard 1632/1990, 130, 198, 215, 224–25, 293). Lafitau claimed that some Amerindians wore no clothing but instead painted themselves afresh every day (Lafitau 1724, III: 50, 42).

78. Henry 1809/1969, 190, 246–48. Cf. Waselkov and Braund 1995, 122: Among Creeks and Cherokees, only men and prostitutes used body paint.

79. Cresswell 1924, 121.

80. Heckewelder 1876, 203. "The women make use of vermilion in painting themselves for dances, but they are very careful and circumspect in applying the paint, so that it does not offend or create suspicion in their husbands; there is a mode of painting which is left entirely to loose women and prostitutes" (ibid.).

81. For representative comments, see Lafitau 1724, III: 49; Waselkov and Braund 1995, 122.

82. For additional material, see Balvay 2008.

83. For White's drawings, see www.virtualjamestown.org/images/white_debry_html/introduction.html (accessed November 20, 2013); for the Cree, Henry 1809/1969, 248. Cf. Montigny 2008, 358, 366, 367, 371 (Natchez).

84. *JR* xxxviii: 251. For Ottawa tattooing earlier in the seventeenth century, see Sagard 1632/1990, 130.

85. Waselkov and Braund 1995, 122. Warren Johnson opined that tattoos, though "a great Torture" to apply, made warriors "look desperate [fierce], & besides is A Considerable Addition to their Fury" (Johnson 1921–65, xiii: 194). Lafitau 1724, iii: 34–42, went into great detail about tattooing, which he believed was most common among Indians of southeastern North America, though practiced widely, especially by men.

86. Facial tattoos are clearly visible in the 1735 portrait of the Delaware headman Lapowinsa by Gustavus Hesselius, in the Philadelphia History Museum; they are, however, difficult to discern in Hesselius's matching and contemporary portrait of the headman Tischcohan. See respectively www.philadelphiahistory.org/node/227, www.philadelphiahistory.org/node/226 (accessed May 14, 2014).

87. Heckewelder 1876, 205, 206.

88. See, e.g., Mittelberger 1898, 83–84 (long "strings of false beads" in the ears); and below.

89. Champlain in Kinietz 1940, 10.

90. Sagard 1632/1990, 191, 224–25. For Wendat practice, see also Becker 2007.

91. See, e.g., the materials reported in Rochemonteix 1904, 64. Sagard 1632/1990, 224, noted the eagerness with which Wendat acquired French jewelry and other ornamentation.

92. Franquet 1974, 36, 38, 104–05; cf. ibid., 49. See also Anon. 1758/1840, 16; Lafitau 1724, iii: 53–57.

93. Cresswell 1924, 120–21; cf. ibid., 103: "Silver Brooches and Armplates" on a calico shirt.

94. Waselkov and Braund 1995, 120–22.

95. Williamson 1758, 25.

96. Heckewelder 1876, 203. For similar praise, Jones 1774, 62–63.

97. In 1762, South Carolina fixed the price charged Cherokees for a yard of calico at twice as much as for a yard of linen, and in 1767 a British decision raised the disparity to 3:1. If such pricing was generally practiced, it may have slowed cottons' diffusion among Indians. See McDowell 1970, 566–68; TNA, CO 5/68, fol. 145.

98. The next four paragraphs summarize Ragueneau's report in *JR* xliv: 283–97, 307.

99. "*Étoffe à l'Iroquoise*" was a Dutch woolen that the French imported for exchange in New France; by 1692, however, it was described by a French official as "a very bad stuff … which the Indians are disgusted with" (Montreal

Merchants Records, microfilm edition (Minneapolis: Minnesota Historical Society, 1975), "Etoffe a l'Iroquoise," from ANOM, F^{1}A-10, fol. 211).

100. McDowell 1955, 127–31. Peggy was related to several of the 1730 Cherokee emissaries to London.

101. Cresswell 1924, 121. For similar comments, see Bougainville 1757/1924, 66; Lender and Martin 1982, 83; Adair 1775, 6–8.

102. HSP, Etting Collection, vol. 40, Ohio Company, vol. 1, doss. 7, 17, 29, 30. With those two additions, the "Indian Goods" fabrics match the same day's "List of all kinds of Goods proper for Presents to the Indians" throughout northeastern North America (ibid., doss. 37).

103. That the lists were well informed about current practice is also suggested by two August 22, 1763 documents about Indian trade items that track the "Indian Goods" list very closely: "Invoice of Sundry Goods and Merchandize brought down here [Philadelphia] from the Trading House at Fort Augusta" and "Inventory of Sundry Goods & Merchandize brought down here designed for Pittsburgh Trading House" (HSP, Gratz Collection, Box 10, Case 14).

104. HSP, Etting Collection, vol. 40, Ohio Company, vol. 1, doss. 37.

105. That Henry refers to settlers of French origin as "Canadians" signals an important change in colonial perceptions: In the seventeenth century Amerindians were designated "Canadians." The same change is seen in the label on Plate 6.

106. That all the face paint is red may be a sign of "peaceful Friendship" – "warlike Inclinations" were indicated by black (De Vorsey 1971, 109).

107. Hirsch 2004: 665.

108. See, e.g., Smith 1799, 9–11; Quaife 1958, 233.

109. Mittelberger 1898, 83–86.

110. Kenny 1761–63/1913, 171, 188. Cf. Cave 1999, and White 1991, 279–85.

111. McDowell 1970, 268, December 11, 1756.

112. "The First Consumer Revolution," in Axtell 1978, 104–21.

113. Jackson 2010.

114. For the way that fashion likewise has to do "with what one is *not* wearing" as well as with the novel things one does put on, see Svendsen 2004/2006, 14.

4 Dress under constraint

1. Rural Donegal Township is in northwestern Lancaster County, along the Susquehanna River 150 km west of Philadelphia; in the eighteenth century it was a center of flour milling. York, founded 1741 as the first town west of the Susquehanna and seat and market center of the eponymous county, is 20 km southwest of Donegal.

2. Eltis 2000, 7.

3. Styles 2007, 247–49, 257.

4. This distinction can be traced back to Finley 1980. For specific application to the early modern Atlantic, see Berlin 1996.

5. For example, the French royal edicts that regulated slavery, usually termed the *Code Noir*, declared that everything that slaves might obtain, even by their own effort or by free gifts, belonged to their masters, and for good measure forbade their children, parents, and other relatives to inherit or in any other way to claim anything that slaves might have (*Édit du roi* 1685/1687, Art. XXVIII; Louisiana Code Noir 1724, Art. XXII).

6. Bosman 1705, 364, 365; Barbot 1732, 270; Handler 2009, 2.

7. On these aspects, see Handler 2009, 2–4.

8. Cf. van Gennep 1909/1960.

9. Barbot 1732, 270.

10. Patterson 1982. An advertisement for a "new Negroe Girl" – that is, recently arrived from "Whedaw" (Ouidah) on the Gulf of Guinea in today's Benin – who was "mark'd round the Neck with three Rows like Beads," gives a vivid example of country marks (*Pa. Gaz.*, July 4, 1734).

11. Bosman 1705, 365; Barbot 1732, 326; Handler 2009, 3–4. For slavers' purchases of West African and European cloth for Middle Passage apparel, see Ryder 1969, 37, 64, 93; Donnan 1930–35, II: 119, IV: 269, 652.

12. Hamer 1968–94, II: 546–47. Labat 1722, IV: 142, stated flatly that slaves offered for sale in the Antilles were "entirely naked," including "those parts that we hide with care."

13. Stedman 1796/1988, 174; cf. illustration on 167. Cf. Labat 1722, IV: 144, who asserted that good treatment of newly purchased slaves, "along with the clothing given them," would make them "affectionate," as well as "making them forget their native land and the unhappy state to which slavery has reduced them."

14. Thus many runaway advertisements, such as the one quoted above, were for unnamed "new Negroes" (enslaved persons newly arrived from Africa).

15. Indian slaves were dressed in the same manner, but all dress regulations targeted Africans.

16. Salmoral 2001, 591; cf. 755 (Cuba, 1574). The ordinance also stipulated food and drink allowances and a day of rest on Sunday.

17. *Édit du roi* 1685/1687, Art. XXV; *Laws of Jamaica* 1716, 227. See also Sala-Molins 1993. Writing in 1696, Labat 1722, III: 443–44, defined an *habit* as a long, loose jacket (*casaque*) and either breeches or a skirt (*jupe*), depending on gender; all were made of coarse Breton linen. For other British West Indian colonies, see Dunn 1973, 238. There were probably earlier ordinances in the Caribbean, but they have been lost (Goveia 1970, 36–37).

18. Louisiana Code Noir 1724, art. XVIII: Grimke 1790, 173, Art. XXXVIII (this enactment essentially repeated provisions of a disallowed 1690 law that ordered "a convenient set of clothes" for every slave; Wood 1974, 52 n65); Schoeman 2007, 259. All the laws required annual apparel grants.

19. Slaves appreciated the symbolic meaning of these items: Participants in Tackey's 1760 revolt in Jamaica plundered stockings, shoes, and laced hats along with ruffled shirts and cravats (Monson 31/11: 104).

20. Girod de Chantrans 1785, 143. Cf. Thunberg 1986, 26: "as a token of their servile condition, [slaves] always go barefoot, and without a hat," wearing instead "a twisted handkerchief." Most exclusions were customary, but in Dutch colonies a 1642 decree forbade hats to all slaves except those who could prove by a written text that they understood Dutch (Shell 1994, 225). As noted below, apparently the prohibition was widely flouted.

21. Schoeman 2007, 217.

22. For just two examples, James Steel to Jos. Kirkbride, October 26, 1734, HSP, Logan Papers, James Steel Letterbook, 1730–41, fol. 76 (for clothing slaves at Pennsbury Manor); Santos 1956, 401.

23. Vilhena 1969, I: 187. Tellingly, when in 1775 the Portuguese crown, seeking to assist metropolitan clothmaking, prohibited colonial textile manufacture, fabrics destined for slave apparel were exempt, along with those used for packing goods (Andrade and Root 2010).

24. Even in Brazil, most planters depended on local or imported cottons (Santos 1956, 386–87).

25. Only occasionally, however, were the codes explicitly invoked; e.g., Long 1774, II: 426.

26. Vilhena 1969, I: 186; Loewald, Starika, and Taylor 1958, 256; Schoeman 2007, 144–46.

27. See, e.g., Loewald, Starika, and Taylor 1958, 236, 256; Edwards 1793, II: 135n.

28. For the Caribbean, see Goveia 1970, 48: The protective clauses of slave codes were "a dead letter," in sharp contrast to the vigorous prosecution of slaves under their policing provisions. My own searches in other colonies affirm the correctness of her conclusion.

29. Monson 31/9: 27.

30. Lara 2001, 28–29, 215–16.

31. Hamer 1968–94, VII: 232, February 15, 1770; Edelson 2006, 228–33. Cf. GHS, File 337, James Habersham Papers, Folder 1, Habersham to William Knox, London, March 9, 1764; Laborie 1798, 162–63. On many plantations, particular categories of slaves – e.g., newborns and their mothers, the ill, and the aged – benefited from special allotments that masters likewise intended as displays of paternalistic concern; see, e.g., Laborie 1798, 173–74, 188, 191.

32. For the role of force, even terror, in plantation slavery, see Burnard 2004, esp. 146–52.

33. Debien 1962, 120, 123–25. Indigo dye was notoriously difficult to make correctly. Relative prices are my calculations from inventory valuations. For similar stratagems, cf. Laborie 1798, 184, who gave hats, customarily denied slaves, to drivers and "the other chief negroes"; Labat 1722, III: 446: "hats, caps, or headdresses (coëfes)" should be given to slaves "who perform their duties well"; and Cauna 1987, 118. For attributes of the redingote or frockcoat, see White 2012, 219.

34. Shell 1994, 199; Burnard 2004, 130–33 and passim. For similar projects, Hamer 1968–94, V: 19–20, 61, VII: 329; Edelson 2006, 231; Schwartz 1985, 137; Labat 1722, III: 436–37.

35. Labat 1722, III: 443–44. Labat does not estimate the relative size of each group. "Four ells of linen suffice for men," he averred, "and five for women, to provide themselves two outfits."

36. E.g., Nicolson 1776, 52, 54; Antonil 1711/1982, Book I, chap. IX; Girod de Chantrans 1785, 143; Browne 1789, I: 25; Schoeman 2007, 76, 146, 148 (VOC officials), 131, 139, 144–46 (VOC slaves).

37. Worden and Worden 2005, 2, 3, 305, 307; cf. 344, 347.

38. Rowland, Sanders, and Galloway 1927–84, II: 559, 674.

39. Teychenie 1960, 263. The failure was destined to be repeated thereafter.

40. See Surrey 1916, 169–220.

41. Girod de Chantrans 1785, 143, listed "greed" and "poverty" (Monson 31/9: 27).

42. My slightly revised translation of Antonil 1711/1982, Book I, chap. IX, as found in Conrad 1983, 58. A Portuguese vara equaled about 1.1 m.

43. TNA, C104/8, nos. 1–5 (between 1768 and 1772, fabrics to clothe the enslaved on Chancery Hall Estate, Jamaica, cost between 1.68 and 8.27 percent of annual expenses; my calculations); Ward 1988, 46, table 2 (3.33 percent of the annual cost per slave on a sugar estate, c. 1750); Cauna 1987, 194–95 (5–7 percent on a Saint-Domingue sugar plantation from the mid-1750s to the 1770s); Stols 1996, 283 (of their total outlays, Brazilian planters spent about 8 percent on slave clothing). Labat 1722, III: 448, estimated that about 800 livres (12 percent) of yearly operating expenses of 6,610 livres on a model plantation should be spent on linen for 120 slaves, who would make their two suits of garments. For vigilance about costs, see Hamer 1968–94, IV: 598, V: 12, VII: 134; Edelson 2006, 85–86.

44. For other negative remarks by observers who had visited or lived in the areas they cited, see Du Tertre 1667–71, II: 520; Browne 1789, I: 25; du Pratz 1758, I: 340; VOC officials cited in Schoeman 2007, 143–46, 148.

45. Quoted in Ward 1988, 151. Perhaps it was from tacit agreement with such criticism that the Saint-Domingue coffee planter P. J. Laborie claimed to have

distributed quantities well above the *Code Noir* mandate: seven ells of linen to men every year, eight to women, as well as woolen jackets (Laborie 1798, 183–84).

46. See White 2003, 530, who finds that in Louisiana 82 percent of all criminal investigations and prosecutions of enslaved people in 1723–67 involved clothing and cloth; Schoeman 2007, 180–81, 219.

47. Du Pratz 1758, I: 348; Burnard 2004, 164–65. Cf. Labat 1722, IV: 171: Weak enforcement of edicts requiring slave sellers to have permits from their masters, along with dishonest regraters, encouraged slave thievery.

48. Schoeman 2007, 230.

49. Schoeman 2007, 228–29; Morgan 1984, 191–93; Boxer 1982, 138; Malheiro 1866/1976, I: 55.

50. Schoeman 2007, 227, 230, 237; cf. Debien 1962, 125; Burnard 2004, 225, 236.

51. The VOC official Van Reede, quoted in Schoeman 2007, 161; Monson, passim.

52. See also Chapter 2 above.

53. Quoted in Debien 1962, 123. Cf. Labat 1722, IV: 171–72; Girod de Chantrans 1785, 131–32. For similar practices in mainland North America, cf. Loewald, Starika, and Taylor 1958, 236; Havard and Vidal 2003, 322.

54. Garrigus 2006, 74–75; Moreau de Saint-Méry 1784–90, I: 120, 306–07, 505–06, 562–63; Monson 31/2: 61, 31/8: 184–85, 31/13: 70, 31/15: 5, 25, 48, 31/16: 59; Schoeman 2007, 227, 237; Schwartz 1992, 45; Burnard 2004, 225.

55. E.g., Schaw 1939, 107 (quotation); Long 1774, II: 492; Edwards 1793, II: 125.

56. See Sheridan 1995, 65; Barickman 1994; Schoeman 2007, 237–38.

57. Laborie 1798, 179–80.

58. Quotation from Browne 1789, I: 25.

59. Of the 279 runaways listed in the *South Carolina Gazette* between its maiden issue of January 8, 1732 and the end of 1739, 244 items of the dress belonging to 125 individuals – 101 men and 24 women – were specified (45 percent); between 1760 and 1769, 497 garments of 217 persons (180 male, 37 female), out of 535 who absconded (41 percent).

60. Bolzius asserted that both female and male slaves had shoes in winter but "none in summer" (Loewald, Starika, and Taylor 1958, 236). His claim is not borne out by the advertisements.

61. Planters' records tell the same story as runaway advertisements. See Edelson 2006, 285, table A.14: In the late 1760s to early 1770s, Henry Laurens dispatched an annual average of 4.5 yards of woolens, linens, and at times ready-made garments of these fabrics to clothe the slaves on his several plantations.

62. Across the period, planters seem to have thought white most appropriate for the enslaved. Cf. Hamer 1968–94, IV: 666; V: 19–20. See Pastoureau 2000/2001 on the growing vogue for blue.

63. For a different view, see Morgan 1998, 130 and ff. White and White 1995 argue for both the uniformity and limited nature of slave attire (154) and its "bewildering variety" (155).

64. Edgar 1972, I: 30–32 (all sic). In Pringle's as in others' parlance, "Negro" denoted "slave." Felt hats may have been another distinctive racial token: Pringle informed an English correspondent that many of his "hatts" had not sold because they were "of too Good Sorts or too high priced for Felts, being in use only for Negroes" (ibid., I: 218, June 11, 1740).

65. McCord 1840, 396.

66. Cf. Labat 1722, V: 256: Branding was "absolutely necessary" on a large island like Saint-Domingue, where runaways could easily flee into the mountains and where fugitives, if not branded, could be seized and sold by anyone claiming ownership. For Brazil, see Zucchelli 1712, 70.

67. Livro de Contas, Engenho Sergipe do Conde, 1622–53, in Anon. 1954–63, II: passim. Already in the 1570s, the inventory of a slave-worked sugar estate near Bahia revealed the presence of substantial amounts of inexpensive cotton fabrics, though garments were not mentioned: see Inventário do Engenho de Sant'Ana (1572–74), in ibid., III: 104.

68. Frézier 1716/1717, II: 532; Zucchelli 1712, 71. For similar comments, see Lara 1997, 215–16.

69. For a 1630s depiction of hammock porterage, see Ferrão and Soares 1997, 191, pl. 104. For other images of slave work dress, see Novais 1997, I; *Post* 1990; Buvelot 2004.

70. Vilhena 1969, I: 186. Cottons and woolens seem already to have been considered the norm in the early eighteenth century, as we have seen.

71. Estate accounting 1651–55, AGN SL 7145, Don Esteban de Acosta, August 25, 1655. No women are mentioned. AGN SL 6369, Juana de Heredia y Salcedo, 1649, confirms that *cordellate* and *sayal* were the typical fabrics used for slave clothing.

72. AGN SL 3860, Vicente Andino.

73. AGN SL 7145, Don Esteban de Acosta, 1655; ibid., 5558, Manuel Díaz Betancour, 1670. A Spanish *vara* equalled about 0.84 m.

74. By the 1730s, caps were common enough in enslaved male attire in Jamaica that one observer mistakenly believed them to be a part of the statutory yearly distribution (Leslie 1739, 229).

75. See, e.g., *Jam. Gaz.*, March 4 and 25, 1775, December 27, 1775; *Aff. Am.*, August 27, 1766 (an unnamed "new Negro" ran away wearing a new *brin* linen shirt, a cloth cap, but "no breeches"); Monson 31/16: 239, October 26, 1765 (frock and sacca).

76. Edwards 1793, II: 398. Cf. Long 1774, I: 493, II: 412, 426; Laborie 1798, 183; and goods ordered by the Jamaica merchant-cum-planter Nathaniel Phillips

(University of the West Indies at Mona, Jamaica, Library, West Indies Collection, Nathaniel Phillips Papers, Mf. 527, June 26, 1765, May 8, 1769).

77. The continuities and changes can be charted in Bennett 1964, 69; JA IB/11/3/1–20 (individual and merchant inventories 1674–1774); *Weekly Jamaica Courant*, July 30, 1718, June 20, 1722, October 26, 1726, November 2, 1726; *Jam. Gaz.*, May 4, 1771, March 25, 1775, December 27, 1775; TNA, C108/42, nos. 9, 11 (early 1770s plantation cloth supplies). Cf. Table 2.3.

78. Edwards 1793, II: 135n. For a longer list that agrees in substance with Edwards, while adding headgear and handkerchiefs, see Long 1774, I: 493.

79. TNA, C104/8, nos. 1–3 (distributions on three Jamaica plantations, 1754–72); Monson 31/15: 112, April 20, 1764; 31/16: 59, 79, March 20 and April 13, 1765; 31/17: 43, February 24, 1766; 31/18: 23, 90, January 18 and April 3, 1767 (quotation); Ward 1988, 154, table 19.

80. *Aff. Am.*, July 23, 1766 to November 22, 1775; 9 women, 70 men. Fabrics and colors are known for about three-fifths of garments.

81. For corroborative details from cargoes and inventories, see Cauna 1987, 118; ADG, 7 B 1449; Archives départementales de la Charente Maritime, La Rochelle, E486 and E292; ANOM, SDOM, Not., passim; FSC 1737111102; Rowland, Sanders, and Galloway 1927–84, V: 234. Cf. McDonald 1993, 112–19.

82. For markets, see Plate 2; and images in Bagneris 2010. For estate views, Higman 1988; *Post* 1990; Buvelot 2004.

83. See, e.g., Girod de Chantrans 1785, 137 (most of a hundred or more slaves digging holes for sugar canes were dressed in rags or "naked," likely meaning a summary garment below the waist); and Loewald, Starika, and Taylor 1958, 236 (when laboring in summertime South Carolina, Bolzius asserted, enslaved men wore nothing but "a cloth rag which hangs from a strap tied around the body," while women wore petticoats but "the upper body is bare").

84. Dapper 1998, 13–14; Proyart 1776, 109–10; Rømer 2000, 115; Villeneuve 1814, IV: facing 180, 181.

85. Laborie 1798, 176; Sloane 1707–25, I: xlvii; Leslie 1739.

86. Stols 1996, 280–83.

87. Schoeman 2007, 143–44, 148.

88. *Reports* 1918, 35 (112), 49 (126).

89. For the remark, see n20 above. The same garb is also shown on plowmen in de Bruijn and Raben 2004, pl. 112, "The farm owned by Mr Lochner."

90. Schoeman 2007, 217–18.

91. Worden and Worden 2005, 166 (Dutch original, 163). Van Mallabaar's surname indicates that he or an ancestor came from southwestern India, where cotton clothing was the norm.

92. Worden and Worden 2005, 261, 470, 476, 617.

93. Kindersley 1777, 69; cf. Kolb 1719/1738, I: 187–201; Sparrman 1975, II: 184–91.

94. Cf. the 1786 "Hottentot wearing a hat," in de Bruijn and Raben 2004, 381, pl. 119.

95. For an example of the difficulty of telling Khoikhoi laborers from slaves in images, see Robert Ross in de Bruijn and Raben 2004, 380, commenting on pl. 118.

96. Laura J. Mitchell, in de Bruijn and Raben 2004, 367, 368–69 (pl. 112); Elphick and Malherbe 1988, 16–30.

97. Estate accounting 1651–55, AGN SL 7145, Don Esteban de Acosta, August 25, 1655; Livro de Contas, Engenho Sergipe do Conde, 1622–53, in Anon. 1954–63, II: passim; above, Chapter 3.

98. Galenson 1984; Smith 1947; Debien 1951; Gaucher, Delafosse, and Debien 1950–60, 1960–61.

99. Gaucher, Delafosse, and Debien 1959–60, 1960–61, outline, for French colonies, five alternatives ranging from only wages to only the provision of necessities.

100. Taylor 2008, 287–88. The law also mandated freedom dues of "two sutes of new apparell" – defined as half the yearly allotment – and eight "Mexico dollars" (ibid., 288–89).

101. *Laws of Jamaica* 1683, 3; the law, which remained on the books across the eighteenth century, also converted freedom dues entirely into cash (40 s.). For other British Caribbean colonies, which had similar laws, see Smith 1947, 237.

102. Shoes were a costly as well as highly visible mark of difference. In 1670, one Jamaica planter spent as much (6 *s.*) on one pair of shoes per indentured servant as he did for the entire outfit of each slave (Bennett 1964, 63).

103. Taylor 2008, 266–67 (all *sic*).

104. Long 1774, II: 289–91. Long noted that as servants had become expensive, they had become scarce.

105. Indeed, enslaved women "go many of them quite naked" (Leslie 1739, 35–36).

106. *Weekly Jamaica Courant*, July 30, 1718, August 5, 1718, February 11, 1719, ?1721, June 20, 1722, March 22, 1726, ? 1730, June 24, 1730. The men included two bricklayers, a carpenter, a harness-maker, a medical doctor's assistant, and five unknown.

107. Galenson 1984, 1–13.

108. S. C. *Gaz.*, February 12, May 27, October 28, December 16, 1732.

109. Loewald, Starika, and Taylor 1958, 237, 257.

110. The Carolina laws can be found in Smith 1947, 117–18, 127; and, along with those from other British North American colonies, in Grubb 2000, 68–72.

111. Debien 1951, 44, 53, 71–73, 83, 180–81.

112. Debien 1951, 201–02, 224; Gaucher, Delafosse, and Debien 1959–60, 1960–61. For the same reason, freedom dues were rare.

113. Cf. B*** 1766, who claims that only slaves wore hemp linens.

114. Moreau de Saint-Méry 1797, I: 60. Significantly, "livery men or boys" were exempted from the 1735 South Carolina sumptuary law that restricted slave attire to a dozen named fabrics (McCord 1840, 396). For a similar privilege in the Cape of Good Hope, see Worden, van Heyningen, and Bickford-Smith 1998, 73.

115. Labat 1722, IV: 178–80. A *candale*, Labat specified, was a knee-length, pleated, and belted "very wide skirt." A *carquant* was a kind of bracelet. For similar accounts, see Leslie 1739, 25–26; Taylor 2008, 238; Long 1774, II: 426. Cf. Loewald, Starika, and Taylor 1958, 236.

116. *S. C. Gaz.*, March 14–21, 1761; Debien 1962, 124–25. For contemporary comments about ornately dressed and ornamented personal servants in Bahia, see Lara 1997, 214.

117. Loewald, Starika, and Taylor 1958, 236.

118. *S. C. Gaz.*, June 27, 1768. Cf. Long 1774, II: 426: in Jamaica, "tradesmen, and the better sort" of slaves are "generally supplied" with checks, handkerchiefs, hats, and caps besides the regular allotment. South Carolina runaway advertisements indicate that enslaved plantation artisans dressed in the typical uniform, their only special garment consisting at most of leather apron or breeches: see *S. C. Gaz.*, March 16–20, 1762 (the cooper Samson), July 10–17, 1762 (the "pretty good cooper" Boatswain), November 13–20, 1762 (Peter, a "shoemaker, tanner, sawyer, and jobing [*sic*] carpenter"), March 12–19, 1763 (the carpenter Limerick), October 5, 1769 (the shoemaker Scipio).

119. *Aff. Am.*, March 1, 1775. For other single special items within regular outfits, see *Aff. Am.*, May 7, 1772 (La Rose), August 9, 1775 (Marcel).

120. Moreau de Saint-Méry 1797, I: 58, 60–61.

121. Labat 1722, IV: 180–81.

122. For African influences, see Buckridge 2004, 23–24. It is notable, however, that hats, caps, and hair arrangements were much more commonly portrayed than headwraps in contemporary images of Africans; see Marees (Figures 1.1, 1.2, 1.3) or d'Asti (Plate 16). For the turban style in the metropoles, see Pointon 1993, 140–57; Rosenthal 2006, 126, 128, 143–44, 153, 158. Long 1774, II: 412–13, wrote of handkerchiefs worn on slave women's heads "in the turban form, which, they say, keeps them cool, in the hottest sunshine." Comparing the images reproduced by Pointon and Rosenthal with Brunias's indicates, however, that European turbans and Caribbean headwraps differed significantly, with headwraps more elaborate, incorporating more individual pieces of fabric, and covering all of the hair.

123. Moreau de Saint-Méry 1797, I: 58–61.

124. Moreau de Saint-Méry 1797, I: 59, 60; *Aff. Am.* 33, August 16, 1769 (salary).

125. Long 1774, I: 426. For similar comments, see Edwards 1793, II: 135; Beckford 1790, II: 386; Laborie 1798, 180. In Saint-Domingue, the anonymous "B***" declared that "the lowest slave, when he has some money buys the dearest goods, without any regard to their cost" (B*** 1766, 157).
126. *Aff. Am.*, March 25, 1774, June 13, 1768.
127. See Burnard 2004, 16, 153.
128. Moreau de Saint-Méry 1797, I: 59; Worden, van Heyningen, and Bickford-Smith 1998, 73.
129. Hunt 1996; Harte 1976.
130. For an exhaustive survey, with texts, of Spanish American legislation, see Salmoral 2001; for Brazil, Lara 2001.
131. See the 1735 South Carolina law prohibiting all slaves to wear any but a dozen enumerated inexpensive fabrics, which cited slaves' "sinister and evil methods" of "procuring" their "clothes much above the condition of slaves" (McCord 1840, 396).
132. Berg and Eger 2003; Sekora 1977; Shovlin 2006.
133. Moreau de Saint-Méry 1797, I: 59–60.
134. Cf. Lara 2000, 177–79, and the passages from a 1790 law translated in Conrad 1983, 248, which repeat language from other decrees dating back more than a century.
135. The quotation (*finos tecidos*) comes from a 1749 Brazil law in Lara 2001, 313.
136. Lara 2000, 180–81; a portion of the law is translated in Conrad 1983, 248. The sumptuary law adopted at the Cape of Good Hope in 1765 combined status differences among whites with racial distinctions between whites, the emancipated, and slaves (Ross 2007).
137. The woman with the rakish hat (second from the left) is coded by dress and skin color as a free person of color. For more discussion, see Chapter 5 below; Honychurch 2004, Bagneris 2010.
138. Du Tertre 1667–71, II: 521, had already pointed out the importance of adornments; Jamaican commentators, cited in n125 above, insisted on the bright colors, multiple garments, and superior fabric quality of slave fancy dress.
139. See the paintings by Julião printed as images 15 (garb worn by working slave women) and 17 (showing an enslaved women's fancy outfit) in Lara 2007, and discussion in Lara 2002.
140. *S. C. Gaz.*, May 22, 1762.
141. For recent discussions of the painting, see Handler 2010; Shames 2010.
142. Cf. White and White 1995, 163–65.
143. FSC 1765101001, 1765101102.
144. Louis apparently ran an organized gang that stole all manner of small objects for resale; he also hired enslaved seamstresses to manufacture clothing from both legitimately purchased and pilfered fabrics, as well as

hucksters to hawk the finished shirts, pants, and other garments. See Hall
2005, 99–100 (focusing on 1764); FSC 1764073101, 1765071301,
1765090701, 1765090703, 1765090901, 1765090902, 1765091602 for
later escapades. Louis is briefly mentioned in White 2003, 536, who
analyzes at greater length (527–29) the case of the runaway and thief
Francisque, who likewise took both utilitarian and dress clothing, in his case
from a laundress.

145. Brown 2009.
146. Moreau de Saint-Méry 1797, 1: 60.
147. Slaves were 2.4 percent of Pennsylvania's population between 1700 and 1770,
slightly more than 5 percent in Delaware, and 6 to 7 percent in New Jersey
(*Historical statistics* 1975, 1168, Series Z 10–12).
148. The following analysis is based on slave runaways described in the
Pennsylvania Gazette: 1730–39 (ten males, one female); 1760–69 (34 males,
one female). The 1730s difference was about three basic items per
Pennsylvania-area slave as against just under two in South Carolina; by the
1760s, it was respectively four and two.
149. HSP, James Steele Letterbook, 1730–1741, fol. 76.
150. In the 1730s, runaway advertisements provide usable garment information for
255 male servants and five women; for 311 men and 33 women in the sample
years of 1761, 1765, and 1769; *Pa. Gaz., sub annis*. Usable dress descriptions
exist for about four-fifths of indentured runaways. Given the gender
imbalance among both slaves and indentured servants, my slave–servant
comparison can only discuss males.
151. In fact, racially marked "Negro cloth" was absent from the wardrobes of the
enslaved and the indentured, and from merchant shelves.
152. Trudel 2004; Rushforth 2003; Rushforth 2012.
153. Collection Baby, Université de Montréal, Doc. N/7, microfiche 2535, June 10,
1698; Montreal Merchants Records, microfilm edition (Minneapolis:
Minnesota Historical Society, 1975), Monière, Livre de comptes brouillard,
1733–39, August 26, 1737, March 25, 1739; Trudel 2004, 158; Rushforth
2012, 334.
154. Alexandre de Batz, "Indians of several nations, New Orleans [17]35,"
Peabody Museum, Harvard University, Cambridge, MA, at http://pmem.
unix.fas.harvard.edu:8080/peabody/media/view/Objects/104780/334081?t:
state:flow=44877d24-8369-4c0a-b9e5-4eab80ab1d46 (accessed April 20,
2014). See also Wilson 1963.
155. B*** 1766, 157. As explained in Chapter 5, he should have written "free"
rather than "white"; that he did not was perhaps a telling conflation of race
and status on his part.
156. Cf. Burnard 2004, 17, 153.
157. Cf. Waldstreicher 1999.

5 Dressing free settlers in the "torrid zone"

1. Du Tertre 1667–71, II: 474.
2. Long 1774, II: 522.
3. See Mackie 1999, 259.
4. Quoted in Bush 1981, 249.
5. Labat 1722, III: 516–17.
6. Taylor 2008, 238 (all *sic*).
7. Hilliard d'Auberteuil 1777, II: 101. Hilliard claimed that substantial immigration from France after 1763 had introduced frivolous "luxe" to Saint-Domingue (ibid., 100), but from all indications it was a much older issue.
8. Du Tertre 1667–71, II: 475. Cf. Labat 1722, III: 516–17 n8. Long was more even-handed, for before he unflatteringly portrayed female settlers' dress, he lambasted men whose "sweltering load of garments" was testimony to "the influence of fashion and custom," not good sense (Long 1774, II: 520–21).
9. Lara 1997, 207; Moreau de Saint-Méry 1797, I: 91, 93. Cf. Antonil 1711/1982, Book I, chap. IX; Girod de Chantrans 1785, 154; Rogers 2007; Furtado 2009, 140.
10. Moreau de Saint-Méry 1797, I: 11.
11. Taylor 2008, 240 (all *sic*).
12. Hilliard d'Auberteuil 1777, II: 101.
13. Long 1774, II: 521–22.
14. Moreau de Saint-Méry 1797, I: 9–10, 18.
15. Hilliard d'Auberteuil 1777, II: 106: Counterposing "le luxe de parure" to "le luxe de commodité" that "happy people" like the Dutch enjoy, Hilliard played on the word "*luxe*," which means profusion as well as sumptuousness.
16. For more detail, see Chapter 1.
17. For all inventory sources relevant to this chapter, see Appendix 2.
18. In this and all subsequent analyses, percentages refer to the garments comprising the basic outfit, except for shirts/shifts/smocks, stockings, and headgear. Fabrics are known for between three-quarters and virtually all of the attire included, with unknowns apparently randomly distributed across garments; the figures for 1760–74 are between 90 percent and nearly 100 percent.
19. JA, IB/11/3/2, January 25, 1683.
20. JA, IB/11/3/5, March 2, 1702.
21. JA, IB/11/3/1, 1676.
22. Taylor 2008, 240.
23. JA, IB/11/3/1, October 6, 1674 (James Jordan); IB/11/3/2, May 8, 1684 (Henry Williams), August 31, 1686 (James Phelps).
24. See Appendix 2. In both Jamaica and Saint-Domingue, free settler women's inventories are much less numerous than men's, reflecting the unbalanced

gender ratios among whites: 2:1 male: female in Jamaica in 1673 and likely considerably higher as time went on (Long 1774, I: 376–77); 4:1 male: female in Saint-Domingue *c.* 1790 (McClellan 1992, 48–49), though the population of *gens de couleur* was 45 percent male, 55 female. See Burnard 1994.

25. JA, IB/11/3/17, November 17, 1735.

26. JA, IB/11/3/17, February 16, 1735. Dreier's inventory value was £62.05; Allyn's £2,593.95.

27. JA, IB/11/3/17, August 19, 1735.

28. Some of the *coutil*, traditionally a linen but increasingly woven from cotton as the eighteenth century progressed, may already have been made of cotton in the 1720s and 1730s (though context in the inventories suggests that most were linens); if so, the disproportion in cottons usage compared with Jamaica would have been even greater.

29. ANOM, SDOM, Not. Neys 1456, March 23, 1724.

30. ANOM, SDOM, Not. Saunier 1567, December 8, 1722.

31. As throughout the tropics in particular, women's inventories are few and far between. But they are consistent with evidence from men's wardrobes in Saint-Domingue in that cottons loom large (two-thirds of women's garments), while also showing a bias toward silks (one-fourth) echoing that found among women in Jamaica.

32. ANOM, SDOM, Not. Delorme de Roissy 478, 10 June 1739.

33. Frézier 1716/1717, II: 536, 538; Del Priore 1997, 286.

34. Frézier 1716/1717, II: 531; Stols 1996, 287; Lara 1997, 216.

35. Furtado 2009, 141.

36. Antonil 1711/1982, Book III, Part 3, chap. VII.

37. APEB-JI, 04/1581/2050/01, 1723.

38. APEB-JI, 04/1614/2083/08, November 10, 1738. Dantas's inventory was valued at 7,476$470, as compared with da Costa's 8,364$960.

39. APEB-JI, 04/1695/2165/18, September 16, 1739. His estate value was 1,252 $140.

40. Furtado 2009, 146.

41. Burnard 1996; Burnard 2001; Garrigus 1993; McClellan 1992; Schwartz 1985; Schwartz 2007.

42. B*** 1766; Long 1774, II: 522 (quotation); Hilliard d'Auberteuil 1777, II: 99–100.

43. The description is quoted from Burnard 2001, 506, who took it from Leslie 1739, 353.

44. Both advertisements are found in *Jam. Gaz.*, May 4, 1771.

45. For these and many similar quotations, see *Aff. Am.* 1766–69, passim; *Kingston Journal*, November 29, 1760, October 24, 1761; *The Intelligencer* (St Jago de la Vega, Jamaica), April 16, 1768; *Jam. Gaz.*, January 3, 1765, March 14 and 25, 1775, December 27, 1775.

46. Long 1774, II: 520–23.
47. Long was correct about the banyan's current lack of popularity (only two inventoried men owned one), though as we have seen it had gained a level of acceptance earlier in the eighteenth century.
48. APEB-JI, 04/1620/2089/09, 1760.
49. APEB-JI, 04/1582/2051/03, 1760.
50. The transformation of *coutil* from a linen to a cotton occurred across much of the eighteenth century, but by this period the great majority of the fabric appears to have been made of cotton.
51. ANOM, SDOM, Not. Beaulieu 96, June 14, 1763; estate valued at 161,535 liv.
52. ANOM, SDOM, Not. Legendre 1221, February 26, 1768; estate valued at 3,177 liv.
53. Though colors were typically listed for less than half of attire, and often barely a fifth, the data uniformly show a turn from black, brown, and grey hues toward white, yellow, blues, reds, and greens, not to mention floral designs, stripes, and other lively patterns.
54. In 1722–39, merchants left 17 percent of male inventories, 13 percent in 1760–74.
55. Merchants left one-third of Jamaican male inventories in 1760–74.
56. APEB-JI, 04/1613/2082/05, February 2, 1762.
57. APEB-JI, 04/1800/2270/11, 1730.
58. See, e.g., Burnard 2001.
59. ANOM, SDOM, Not. Delorme de Roissy 478, December 22, 1739.
60. APEB-JI, 03/1351/1820/13, 1716.
61. Planters left one-third of usable male inventories in Saint-Domingue from 1715–39.
62. Planters' inventories remained one-third of the male inventories in this period. Following late eighteenth-century practice, I have counted *coutil* as a cotton fabric.
63. Plantation women left one-third of the female inventories.
64. Jamaican planter inventories from 1760–74 were one quarter of all left by men. Lack of sufficient usable identifiably planter inventories makes it impossible to examine earlier periods in Jamaica, and Bahia in any period.
65. B*** 1766, 158.
66. Moreau de Saint-Méry 1797, I: 9–10; Long 1774, II: 521.
67. Stols 1996, 283.
68. APEB-JI, 04/1582/2051/07, December 19, 1760.
69. Recall that late seventeenth-century Jamaican "common people" dressed much the same.
70. Unfortunately, no "humbler" individuals left usable inventories in Jamaica during those years.

71. On the interrelations between poorer and wealthier whites, see Burnard 2004, 74–78, 85–86, 249–50.
72. In 1760–74 Saint-Domingue, some 71 percent of women's garments were fashioned of cottons, as against 30 percent of men's; 14 percent linens (men, 33 percent), 1 percent woolens (men, 23 percent). Silks, in contrast, had no gender, accounting for 13 percent of items among women, 14 percent among men. For both genders, moreover, virtually all shirts, shifts, and blouses were tailored from linen, as was underclothing. Though there are too few female inventories to permit quantitative analysis, the pattern seems already to have been established in the early eighteenth century, when women's apparel was almost exclusively tailored from cottons, followed by silks and linens, and they wholly eschewed woolen garments. Neither Jamaica nor Bahia has sufficient usable female inventories to enable calculations.
73. The share of cottons in men's attire fell from 37 percent in the early eighteenth century to 30 percent in 1760–74.
74. Moreau de Saint-Méry 1797, I: 93 (*sic*).
75. Garrigus 2006, 4–7; Andrews 2004, 40–41. A 1775 census estimated that one-fifth of urban Bahia's population of 35,000 comprised free persons of color, one-third whites, the remainder slaves and Indians (Lara 1997, 211).
76. Especially in the eighteenth century, some Europeans and settlers sought to describe or depict all possible combinations of "the different degrees of mixing"; see, e.g., Moreau de Saint-Méry 1797, I: 71–99. For equally detailed (and, as Moreau de Saint-Méry admitted, arbitrary) classifications depicted in the Spanish American genre of *casta* painting, see Katzew 2004; Carrera 2003; Katzew 1996.
77. In French colonies, they were sometimes lumped together as *affranchis*, sometimes as *gens de couleur*; I follow the latter practice here.
78. Due to a paucity of relevant information about the substantial populations of free people of color in eighteenth-century Jamaica and Bahia, this section focuses on Saint-Domingue. That colony's population *c.* 1790 was at least 560,000, of which about 90 percent, or 500,000 people, were slaves, whites some 32,000, freedmen and *gens de couleur* 28,000, with respective annual rates of population growth of 6, 4.5, and 1.5 percent (McClellan 1992, 48–49).
79. For Saint-Domingue, see Rogers and King 2012; Garrigus 2006; King 2001; Garrigus 1993. Cf. Andrews 2004, 45–46; Schwartz 1974, 635; Johnson 1979, 260.
80. For the development of racist ideas in the early modern Atlantic, see Kidd 2006; Boulle 2007; Pagden 2009; Canizares-Esguerra 2009; Bethencourt 2013.
81. Moreau de Saint-Méry 1784–90, v: 80. Garrigus 2006 charts the growth of discriminatory discourse and practices after 1763.

82. Moreau de Saint-Méry 1784–90, V: 449. Restrictions can be traced across his vols. IV and V.

83. Moreau de Saint-Méry 1797, I: 90–91. Declaring that few *affranchis* behaved any differently than their fellows who remained in bondage, his account concentrated on mulatto men and women (*"mulâtres"* and *"mulâtresses"* respectively). See Rogers 2007.

84. See Manganelli 2012, esp. 17–36; Fabella 2007.

85. Atwood 1791, 221.

86. See Girod de Chantrans 1785, 154.

87. Moreau de Saint-Méry 1797, I: 92–94.

88. Ross 2008, 6.

89. Surely reflecting, but apparently not mandated by, the growing legal and practical discrimination visited upon free people of color, such analysis is only possible in the later eighteenth century, when the status of free people of color was listed on inventories and the group became a distinct subject in colonial iconography.

90. The Paris publisher of Moreau de Saint-Méry 1784–90 illustrated it with engravings like Figure 4.4 based on Brunias's works, apparently convinced that they depicted the French Antilles.

91. For the conversation piece, see Shawe-Taylor 2009; Praz 1971. For brief discussions of this painting, de Marly 1990, 116; Powell 2008, 43.

92. See, e.g, the men at the lower right, far left and right background, and elsewhere in Plate 2.

93. The analysis is based on inventories of seventeen identifiable free people of color (twelve women, five men) documented between 1760 and 1774.

94. ANOM, SDOM, Not. Dupuis de Lavaux 589, 590, December 14, 1767 and February 6, 1768. For the very similar wardrobe of Marie Magdelaine Fraise, widow and prosperous owner of fishing boats and slaves, see ANOM, SDOM, Not. Legendre 1229, November 10, 1774. Fraise's inventory had the highest valuation of the identifiable free people of color from 1760–74.

95. ANOM, SDOM, Not. Legendre 1220, August 21, 1767.

96. In many of the market scenes that Brunias created, it is difficult to tell whether the almost uniformly female retailers are wearing shoes or not.

97. ANOM, SDOM Not. Belin du Ressort 104, January 17, 1772. For comparison, a "fine" cotton skirt was valued at 40 liv. Her commercial goods comprised "black hats, for slaves," colored handkerchiefs, and mainly inexpensive linens.

98. ANOM, SDOM Not. Bugaret 329, March 8, 1770.

99. ANOM, SDOM, Not. Legendre 1210, September 27, 1762. For a fellow planter's very similar inventory – down to the new black velvet breeches – see Pierre Mondiese, ANOM, SDOM, Not. Legendre 1210, September 10, 1767.

100. See, e.g., François Collard, *dit* Mouchiach, ANOM, SDOM, Not. Daudin de Bellair 429, April 7, 1763; Pierre, *dit* Cornet, ANOM, SDOM, Not. Martigniat 1326, July 17, 1772.

101. ANOM, SDOM, Not. Dupuis de Lavaux 586, March 12, 1764.

102. This was a trans-Caribbean style at least; see Burnard 2010, 82–83; Long 1774, II: 413.

103. The inventory of only one of twelve free women of color and of two white women (of thirteen) reported no handkerchiefs, and on average the former owned 17 handkerchiefs, the latter 21. Two of five free men of color had no handkerchiefs, 72 of 177 of white men (also 40 percent); the former owned an average of 6, the latter 12.

104. B*** 1766, 157.

105. Burnard 2010, 83.

106. Furtado 2009, 140–42.

107. ANOM, SDOM, Not. Legendre 1210, September 27, 1762 (Collard, *dit* Namur); Not. Daudin de Bellair 429, April 7, 1763 (Collard, *dit* Mouchiach); Not. Martigniat 1326, July 17, 1772 (Pierre, *dit* Cornet).

108. Cottons comprised 40 percent of the free men of color's apparel, 39 percent for white planters; linens respectively 34 and 31 percent, silks 9 and 11 percent, woolens 18 and 19 percent.

109. Kriz 2008, 58, quotes the law from Atwood 1791, 219, who claimed that it had driven free people of color to British islands. It is not, however, found in Moreau de Saint-Méry 1784–90.

110. B*** 1766, 157–58.

111. Lavradio 1972, 95. Cf. Stols 1996.

112. APEB-JI, 02/675/1134/09, October 1, 1763. His estate was valued at just 927$163.

113. Burnard 2010, 79–80.

114. Burnard 1994, esp. 77–78; Barnard 2010.

115. Burnard 1994, 78.

6 Free settler dress in temperate zones

1. Kalm 1977, 183.

2. Mentzel 1785–87/1921–44, III: 112.

3. As in Chapter 5, all fabric calculations concern basic outfits without shirts/shifts/smocks, footwear, and headgear. For inventory sources, see Appendix 2. Except in the Cape Colony and early South Carolina, fabrics are known for 80 to 95 percent of apparel.

4. Lemire 2011, 45–47.

5. Mentzel 1785–87/1921–44, III: 104.

6. Worden, van Heyningen, and Bickford-Smith 1998, 15–21; Elphick and Malherbe 1988, 12–15; Guelke 1988, 66.

7. Fourie 2012, 1. See also Van Duin and Ross 1987; Worden, van Heyningen, and Bickford-Smith 1998, 53–71; Boshoff and Fourie 2010; de Zwart 2011; Du Plessis and Du Plessis 2012. For older views emphasizing continued stagnation, see Fouché 1914/1970, 4–9, 384–87; Guelke 1988.

8. Sparrman 1975, I: 82–83, 145–46. An English traveler made a similar point in about the mid-1760s, noting that at least once a year rural folk with "farms to the distance of many hundred miles" from Cape Town brought "the produce of their farms" to trade in the port (Kindersley 1777, 60–61). For a late eighteenth-century image of oxen from the interior being driven to market through the streets of Cape Town, see de Bruijn and Raben 2004, 364–65, pl. 111.

9. Worden, van Heyningen, and Bickford-Smith 1998, 67; Fourie and von Fintel 2011, 35. See Mentzel 1785–87/1921–44, III: 98–112, who described four groups of farmers in the settler population, characterized by quite different levels of prosperity.

10. Inventoried urban women now had 43.2 basic garments, outerwear, and shifts as against 25.2 earlier; men 27.9 compared with 20.1.

11. Mean rural male holdings had grown in the meantime, from 9.6 to 12.6 garments. There are insufficient rural women's inventories for meaningful quantitative analysis.

12. For illustrations of some of these items, see Strutt 1975, 92–94, 106–07.

13. Respectively, MOOC 8/12.15, 8/13.44, 8/11.29.

14. Attire fabrics can be ascertained for only a third to two-fifths of Cape Colony garments; the omissions seem equally random across the late seventeenth and eighteenth centuries.

15. In the commonly accepted definition, "free blacks" included "all free persons wholly or partially of African (but not Khoikhoi) or Asian descent"; the term had less to do with color than with a former condition of servitude, and it also included individuals deported from the East Indies for a variety of reasons. About equally divided between women and men, the great majority of free blacks lived in Cape Town, where their numbers reached a sixth of free settlers in 1730, then slowly declined (Elphick and Shell 1988, 184n, 218–24); Worden, van Heyningen, and Bickford-Smith 1998, 64–65, 68–69.

16. Quoted from Shell 1994, 232. The law adapted a 1753 sumptuary statute from Batavia in the Dutch East Indies that had also addressed what it deemed the undue "splendour and magnificence" of some VOC officials and their wives. Ross 2007, 387–88, outlines the obsessive Batavian details.

17. These conclusions rest on ten 1760–74 inventories: MOOC 8/10.27, 10.43, 10.58, 10.73, 10.75, 12.28, 13.17, 14.28, 15.5 (two inventories); unfortunately, apparel fabrics are seldom given. They are consistent with the

very few earlier inventories (e.g., MOOC 8/1.26, 1697; and Shell 1991); with Susanna van Bougis's inventory (MOOC 8/5.144, 1737), for which see Randle 2007, 71–73; and with assertions – albeit based on material goods other than clothing – of De Wet 1981, 212, and Malan 1998/99, 66.

18. For the declining position of free blacks in later eighteenth-century Cape Town, including additional discriminatory laws and the growing salience of race, see Worden, van Heyningen, and Bickford-Smith 1998, 69–70. Possible dress changes remain to be researched.

19. Moutoukias 1988; Lebrero 2002, 67–99, 174–81; Socolow 1991, 240–46.

20. Bauer 2001, 86, 105–10; Ganson 2003, 25–26, 61, 73–74; Levinton 2009, 219–22.

21. For the poncho, see Anawalt 2010.

22. Among both women and men, silks (respectively, 39 and 31 percent) and woolens (38 and 48 percent) accounted for four-fifths of attire; another 10 percent of women's and 3 percent of men's garments were made of mixed-fiber cloth, largely *lama*; and 9 percent (women) and 16 percent (men) of linens. The only cotton garment listed is one man's fustian jacket.

23. For other Iberian colonies, see Meléndez 2005, 25–30.

24. Garavaglia and Gelman 1995; Fradkin and Gelman 2004; Romero 2006. In recognition of the area's growing importance, the Río de la Plata was erected into a viceroyalty of its own in 1779, with Buenos Aires as its capital.

25. Lespagnol 1996; Tanguy 1994.

26. Linens declined from 9 to 2 percent among women, 16 to 6 percent among men; among both genders, too, mixed-fiber fabrics fell to just 1 or 2 percent of total apparel materials.

27. Among women, silks comprised 36 percent of basic and outer attire (as against 39 percent in the later seventeenth century), woolens 54 percent (up from 38 percent). Among men, silks rose slightly (31 to 35 percent), while woolens remained stable at 48 percent.

28. Vicente 2009, 259. Only two men owned a *peinador* in the late seventeenth century, six in 1760–74.

29. Meléndez 2005, 25–27.

30. Vicente 2009; Thomson 1992, esp. 101–10, 130–32, 146–47, 162–65, 211–12.

31. See Andrien 1995, 55–59; Bauer 2001, 109–10; Fisher 1997, 53, 69–71, 88–90, 105–06.

32. This dramatic change mirrored what happened in merchant stocks. Whereas Quito *paño* had comprised 89 percent of inventoried merchant *paño* stocks in 1670–97, it had simply vanished from shelves by 1760–74; *bayeta de la tierra*, which had comprised half of merchant baize stocks in the early period, comprised barely 2 percent in 1760–74.

33. Velvet was the fabric of 35 percent of free men's silk attire in 1760–74, 20 percent of women's; taffeta formed 12 percent of men's, 17 percent of women's.

34. Earle 2001; Meléndez 2005; Bauer 2001, 111–12.

35. For a contrary perspective encompassing all Latin America, see Van Young 1996, 63–65.

36. The average for seven agriculturists was 4,995 pesos, for eight merchants and shopkeepers 10,348. The estates of Don Manuel de Escalada and Manuel del Arco were valued respectively at 101,357 and 210,368 pesos (AGN, SL, 5673, 3862).

37. Cf. Moreno 2006, 82, on the growing social, economic, and cultural differences between merchants and farmers that crystallized in the second half of the eighteenth century.

38. Men may have worn somewhat fewer waistcoats or vests, as only about half of male inventories mention them.

39. Some men also wore leather breeches, whereas women had no leather apparel; conversely, damask was found in women's clothing but not in men's. Both used silks for 15–20 percent of dress.

40. South Carolina Historical Society, Charleston, Lindley Papers, #34–355. The chintz cost 4 times as much as the calico and cotton check, 3.5 times as much as the muslin.

41. The few women's inventories from 1760–74 indicate that despite the rise in cotton's share of male attire, fabrics remained gendered, as women further increased their use of cottons and continued to ignore woolens.

42. Nash 2009, 248–50.

43. SCDAH, Mf. 0194635, 173–74, July 26, 1764. Fleet, who may have been a carpenter, left an estate valued at £104, apparently just within Nash's middle wealth group (Nash 2009, 238–39). (Confusingly, Nash, ibid., 245, classifies middling wealth as above £200.)

44. SCDAH, Mf. 0497, 167–68, July 17, 1767. Valued at £4,000, his estate was in the high wealth group.

45. The analysis only includes inventories from the 1760s because after 1769 French ships no longer visited Louisiana, officially Spanish since the 1762 Treaty of Fontainebleau, resulting in a reorientation of the colony's material culture. See Robert 1960, 22–23.

46. See the 1721 inventory of the planter, miller, and trader Louis Tessier in the Natchez country (Kask. Mss, 21:9:13:1): cottons were worth about one-third of textile totals, nearly the same as woolens (35 percent) and slightly ahead of linens (29 percent).

47. Kask. Mss, 67:10:20:1; 63:6:19:1; 63:6:20:1; 70:6:25:2.

48. Baynton, Wharton, and Morgan Papers, Pennsylvania State Archives, Harrisburg, Manuscript Group 19, mf. 2242, Journal B, Fort Chartres, 34–245.

49. Silks were 7 percent of free male Louisiana settlers' garb in 1717–39, 19 percent in 1760–69; woolens respectively 54 and 39 percent. Apart from silks, cottons – mainly calicoes – were on average the most expensive fabrics, twice as

dear as linens and 25 percent above woolens. Thus linens accounted for half of all cloth in yardage, cottons and woolens just a fifth each.

50. For South Carolina, see Nash 2009, 246; for Louisiana, inventory data and White 2004, 89.

51. Natchitoches Parish Court House, Louisiana, Conveyance Book 1, doc. 596, August 9, 1769.

52. Of rural men's attire 38 percent was tailored from cottons, 6 percent from silks, as against 28 and 22 percent respectively among urban male Louisianans; apparel made of linens (13 percent for both) and woolens (39 and 35 percent) was almost equivalent. The three rural women's inventories and eight of urban women indicate a similar pattern in female garment materials, albeit the Atlantic-wide patterns of higher use of cottons and lower of woolens among women are also evident.

53. Quoted in Surrey 1916, 281; see also Clark 1976, 100.

54. For detailed consideration of these imperatives in the dress of two individuals, see White 2004.

55. Hood 2003; Egnal 1998, 46–77, 128–40; Havard and Vidal 2003, 256–316, 367–78; Mathieu 1981; Dechêne 1974/1992; Wien and Pritchard 1987.

56. For useful illustrated guides to French Canadian garments, see Back 1991; Back 1992. For more detail about farmers' dress, Séguin 1973.

57. Women in Montreal had 62 percent of their garments tailored from woolens, 21 from linens, 11 from silks, 5 from cottons; in Philadelphia the figures were 42 percent woolens, 22 linens, 15 silks, 9 cottons, along with 8 percent crape and 3 percent other. In Montreal men's attire, woolens accounted for 67 percent, linens 13, silks just 6, cottons 9, mixed 5; among Philadelphia men, 72 percent woolens, 15 linens, 4 silks, 8 cottons, 1 mixed.

58. BANQ-M, C345. In both cases, the lower average prices of linens meant that the linens' ellages were proportionally larger than their costs, those of both cottons and woolens proportionally smaller.

59. Kalm 1977, 205, 380.

60. Franquet 1974, 57.

61. Kalm 1977, 379, 546.

62. LAC, Mf. 852, Étienne Augé, Journal E.

63. Back 1988, 99.

64. Inventories carefully distinguish among various types of outerwear, and many notaries worked in town as well as in rural areas, so differences are not due to disparate scribal conventions.

65. Mean inventoried wealth can be calculated for 79 male farmers and artisans (1,344 livres) and for 33 other male settlers (5,187 livres); for 82 rural men (1,713 livres) and 26 urban (4,666 livres).

66. Kalm 1977, 465. Of all such rural male and *habitant* garb, local woolens accounted for just 7 percent.

67. Even in the early 1770s, Laperle's cottons were twice as expensive as his linens, a third dearer than his woolens.

68. Lettre 1682/1922, 293; as a result, Canadians "are utterly dependent on everything that comes from France, such as linen, woolen cloth, serge, hats, shoes" (ibid., 292).

69. McCullough 1992, 45; Appendix 2. No fabric *du pays* was listed in seventeenth-century inventories. Though long encouraged to grow hemp, *habitants* preferred flax "for their personal use" (État présent 1754/1920–21, 22).

70. Dépatie 2003.

71. Franquet 1974, 153.

72. Affluent inventoried individuals were as likely to live in rural areas as in Philadelphia; indeed, the woman and man with highest inventoried wealth both were rural.

73. HSP, Collection of Business, Professional, and Personal Accounts, Thomas Coates Ledger. As always, cottons' higher price meant that yardage received was proportionally lower, the reverse being true for linens.

74. HSP, Ms. Am 909, James Bonsall Account Book, 1722–28.

75. HSP, Morris Papers, Deborah Morris Account Book.

76. Mittelberger 1898, 116.

77. Mittelberger 1898, 117–18.

78. Hagley Museum and Library, Winterthur, Delaware, Acc. 1338, Potts family accounts, vol. 4.

79. Chester County Historical Society, West Chester, Pennsylvania, Vault [unnumbered], Store Account Books 10 and 14. Cottons' higher cost was doubtless of some importance to their slow adoption, while checks' lower prices (as little as half of cottons') probably helped them catch on quickly.

80. Hagley Museum and Library, Winterthur, Delaware, Acc. 890, Unknown Lancaster merchant, Daybook 1765–66, vol. 3.

81. For sources, see Chapter 4, nn148, 150. Nearly four-fifths of clothing fabrics are known.

82. Mittelberger 1898, 116–17.

83. Kraak 2000, 52.

84. Egnal 1998, 58–74; Lemon 1972.

85. To cite the two places with the best-documented color listings: In the Río de la Plata, some 54 percent of men's attire was some shade of black or brown in 1650–1700, but only 28 percent in 1760–74; among women, the drop was equally marked, from 39 percent to 19 percent. In the Montreal area, nine-tenths of men's apparel was dark-hued in the second half of the seventeenth century, just half in 1760–74, while the proportions for women fell from two-fifths to one-fifth.

7 Atlantic dress regimes: fashions and meanings, implications and ironies

1. Sparrman 1975, II: 284–91. "Bucku" powder is an odiferous astringent and diuretic made from *Diosma crenata* or *Diosma odorata* leaves.
2. See, e.g., Agostino Brunias, *A Leeward Islands Carib family outside a Hut*, c. 1780, Yale University Center for British Art, Paul Mellon Collection, B1981.25.78, http://collections.britishart.yale.edu/vufind/Record/1670141 (accessed December 3, 2013); Labat 1722, I: part II, 4. Labat only visited Dominica briefly but he sought out Caribs and local settlers for information. An engraving, ibid., following 2, seeks with some success to interpret Labat's text.
3. De Bruijn and Raben 2004, 381, pl. 119; Agostino Brunias, *West Indian Man of Color, Directing Two Carib Women with a Child*, c. 1780, Yale University Center for British Art, Paul Mellon Collection, http://collections.britishart.yale.edu/vufind/Record/1670150 (accessed December 3, 2013).
4. Fairchilds 1993; Weatherill 1988; Earle 1989.
5. Hence the change was more far-reaching than the seventeenth-century English "great reclothing" that Spufford 1984 postulated.
6. Cangany 2012.
7. Breen 1986.
8. Hilliard d'Auberteuil 1777, II: 100–01.
9. Catalonia, home to a thriving cottons industry from the 1740s, showed the way; see Thomson 1992; Thomson 1996.
10. For Spain, Yun 1994; Torra 1997; Torra 1999; García 1999.
11. For England, Buck 1979; Earle 1989; Styles 2007.
12. For Holland, Kamermans 1999.
13. Francq van Berkhij 1769–1810, III: 796–809, 880–84, 944–99. The volume also contains other images by the engraver Cornelis Buys, showing the dress of courtiers and other elite men and women.
14. Roche 1989/1994; Roche 1998; Ferrières 2004; Bayard 1997; Garnot 1994. See Delpierre 1997 for details about garments.
15. As Roche 1989/1994, 121, notes, "inventories did not strictly differentiate" skirts and petticoats.
16. Miller 1988; Martin 1972; Daaku 1970.
17. Candido 2013, 81, 101; Ferreira 2012, 59–61.
18. Collo and Benso 1986 reproduce and analyze the entire manuscript, in which all the illustrations are by d'Asti himself.
19. See Zucchelli 1712, 115–22; Merolla 1726, 110–11.
20. Merolla 1726, 118.
21. Merolla 1726, 112–13.
22. Zucchelli 1712, 143; Lucca 1953, 79.
23. Rinchon 1964, 102. The gifts accounted for 1 percent of the total outlay for cargo. See Thornton 1998, 231–32.

24. Thornton 1998, 307, 50; Cavazzi 1687, 163.

25. See Zucchelli 1712, 141–43 for the variations in still-imposing ceremonial dress of the ruler of Sogno in 1704.

26. Grandpré 1801, I: 71–72. See below.

27. On the slow weaving and low output of local cloth, see, e.g., Proyart 1776, 108.

28. Miller 1988, 82.

29. See Rinchon 1964, unpaginated tables between 180–81, 284–85, 310–11.

30. Miller 1988, 79–81.

31. Proyart 1776, 107–10. Proyart does not otherwise define the wealth groups.

32. Grandpré 1801, I: 70–77.

33. Rømer 2000, 98–99, 115, 183, 229; Kriger 2006, 36–39.

34. Images like Figure 4.1 suggest this fact, and RAC records confirm it; see, e.g., TNA, T70/466, Cape Coast Castle accounts, "European stores" and "white men's pay" as compared with "black men's pay," the payments largely comprising apparel and/or fabrics.

35. Cailly 1993.

36. Lespagnol 1996; Tanguy 1994.

37. Durie 1973, 43–47; Thomas 1690, 23; Ward 1988, 151, 154; DuPlessis 2003, 136–37.

38. Willmott 2005. For stroud apparel, see McDowell 1955, 82 (breechclouts); McDowell 1958, 519–20 (matchcoats), 453–54 (blankets); Kent 1979, 266 (coats).

39. Rømer 2000, 160; Winsnes 1992, 92; Carreira 1983.

40. Berinstain 2000; Cousin 2000; Dolle 2000.

41. Riello 2013, esp. 147–51, 157, 159; Inikori 2002.

42. For the figures, see Inikori 2002, 516 (App. 9.5). Rømer 2000, 31, emphasized that Africans "much desired" Asian cottons, to which he ascribed a tenfold increase in that trade in consequence.

43. All figures are my calculations from Davis 1962, 302–03.

44. Thanks to John Styles for helping me clarify this point.

45. My calculations from Davis 1962, 302–03.

Appendix 1   Appendix 1: Sources for Tables 2.1, 2.2, 2.3

1. As the Company of Merchants Trading to Africa (the RAC's successor) no longer did business with Angola, and I have not located sufficient material regarding the cargoes of the private English merchants (mainly from Bristol) who continued to trade there, the figures in Table 2.3 are derived from fourteen voyages by the Dutch Middelburgse Commercie Compagnie between 1760 and 1772, and six by French slavers from Nantes, 1764–69. The fact that the cargoes sent by merchants from both nations were virtually identical not only fabric by fabric

but also (to within a half percent) fiber category by fiber category strengthens confidence in the Angola data presented in Table 2.3 despite the change in supplier nation as compared with Table 2.1. Still, comparison of French and Dutch cargoes to the Gold Coast in 1760–74 with RAC cargoes to Cape Coast Castle in the same period does suggest that English merchants may have shipped more woolens and somewhat fewer mixed-fiber fabrics to Atlantic Africa than other Europeans, at least in this period. If this held true for Angola, it suggests that the Angola figures in Table 2.3 should be adjusted to include more woolens and mixed-fiber textiles and fewer cottons, whereas the Cape Coast Castle figures should include fewer woolens and more mixed-fiber cloth. The adjustments in any case would have been on the order of 5 percent per fiber category at most, and likely less.

BIBLIOGRAPHY

Abu-Lughod 1989. Janet L. Abu-Lughod, *Before European hegemony: the world system A. D. 1250–1350* (New York: Oxford University Press)

Acts of assembly 1787. *Acts of assembly, passed in the island of Jamaica, from the year 1681 to the year 1769 inclusive*, 2 vols. (Kingston: Alexander Aikman)

Adair 1775. James Adair, *The history of the American Indians* (London: Edward and Charles Dilly)

Alexander 1984. Stephen Alexander, *Merchants and Jews: the struggle for British West Indian commerce, 1650–1750* (Gainesville: University Presses of Florida)

Allaire 1987. Gratien Allaire, "Officiers et marchands: les sociétés de commerce des fourrures, 1715–1760," *Revue d'histoire de l'Amérique française* 40: 409–28

Anawalt 2010. Patricia Rieff Anawalt, "Regional dress of Latin America in a European context," in Schevill 2010 (unpaginated)

Andrade and Root 2010. Rita Andrade and Regina A. Root, "Dress, body, and culture in Brazil," in Schevill 2010 (unpaginated)

Andrés-Gallego 2001. José Andrés-Gallego (ed.), *Nuevas aportaciones a la historia jurídica de Iberoamérica* (Madrid: Tavera)

Andrews 2004. George Reid Andrews, *Afro-Latin America* (Oxford University Press)

Andrien 1995. Kenneth J. Andrien, *The kingdom of Quito, 1690–1830: the state and regional development* (New York: Cambridge University Press)

Anon. 1758/1840. Anon., "Considérations sur l'Etat présent du Canada" (1758), in *Collection de mémoires et de relations* (Québec City: Literary and Historical Society of Quebec), 1–29

Anon. 1770. "We, the shopkeepers of Philadelphia" (Philadelphia: Henry Miller)

Anon. 1954–63. Anon., *Documentos para a história do açúcar*, 3 vols. (Rio de Janeiro: Instituto de Açucar e do Alcool, Serviço Especial de Documentação Histórica)

Anon. 1988. Anon., "Peddlers and Indian traders license papers, 1722–1866 Chester County, Pennsylvania," *Pennsylvania Genealogical Magazine* 35: 283–90

Antonil 1711/1982. André João Antonil, SJ, *Cultura e poulência do Brasil por suas drogas e minas*, 3rd edn. (1711; Belo Horizonte: Itatiaia/Edusp), *Biblioteca Virtual do Estudante Brasileiro* www.bibvirt.futuro.usp.br

Appadurai 1986a. Arjun Appadurai (ed.), *The social life of things: commodities in cultural perspective* (Cambridge University Press)

Appadurai 1986b. Arjun Appadurai, "Introduction: commodities and the politics of value," in Appadurai 1986a, 11–31

Armitage 2002. David Armitage, "Three concepts of Atlantic history," in David Armitage and Michael J. Braddick (eds.), *The British Atlantic world, 1500–1800* (New York: Palgrave Macmillan), 11–27

Aspers 2010. Patrik Aspers, *Orderly fashion: a sociology of markets* (Princeton University Press)

Aspers 2011. Patrik Aspers, *Markets* (Cambridge: Polity Press)

Atwood 1791. Thomas Atwood, *The history of the island of Dominica* (London: J. Johnson)

Axtell 1975. James Axtell, "The white Indians of colonial America," *WMQ* 3rd ser. 32: 55–88

Axtell 1978. James Axtell, *Natives and newcomers: the cultural origins of North America* (New York: Oxford University Press)

Axtell 1988. James Axtell, *After Columbus: essays in the ethnohistory of colonial North America* (New York: Oxford University Press)

Axtell 1997. James Axtell, *The Indians' new south: cultural change in the colonial Southeast* (Baton Rouge: Louisiana State University Press)

B*** 1766. B***, "Remarques d'un ancien Colon sur une assertion extraite du premier Mémoire de la Chambre du Commerce de S. Malo," *Aff. Am.* 18, Supplément, April 30: 157–59

Back 1988. Francis Back, "Le capot canadien: ses origines et son évolution aux XVIIe et XVIIIe siècles," *Canadian Folklore Canadien* 10: 99–128

Back 1991. Francis Back, "S'habiller à la canadienne," *Cap-aux-diamants* 24: 38–41

Back 1992. Francis Back, "La garde-robe des Montréalistes," and "À la mode du pays," in Yves Landry (ed.), *Pour le Christ et le roi: la vie au temps des premiers Montréalais* ([Montreal]: Libre Expression/Art Global), 120–23, 158–61

Bacqueville de la Potherie 1722. Claude Charles Le Roy, Sieur de Bacqueville de la Potherie, *Histoire de l'Amérique septentrionale*, 4 vols. (Paris: Nion et Didot)

Bagneris 2010. Mia L. Bagneris, *Agostino Brunias: capturing the Carribean* [sic] *(c. 1770–1800)* (London: Robilant + Voena)

Bailyn 2005. Bernard Bailyn, *Atlantic history: concept and contours* (Cambridge, Mass.: Harvard University Press)

Ballong-Wen-Mewuda 1993. J. Bato'ora Ballong-Wen-Mewuda, *São Jorge de Mina, 1482–1637: la vie d'un comptoir Portugais en Afrique occidentale* (Lisbon and Paris: Fondation Calouste Gulbenkian)

Balvay 2008. Arnaud Balvay, "Tattooing and its role in French–Native American relations in the eighteenth century," *French Colonial History* 9: 1–14

Barbot 1732. Jean Barbot, "A description of the coasts of North and South-Guinea," in Churchill 1732, V: 15–420

Barcan 2004. Ruth Barcan, *Nudity: a cultural anatomy* (Oxford: Berg)

Barickman 1994. B. J. Barickman, "'A bit of land, which they call Roça': slave provision grounds in the Bahian Recôncavo, 1780–1860," *HAHR* 74: 649–87

Barker 2001. Eirlys M. Barker, "Indian traders, Charles Town and London's vital link to the interior of North America, 1717–1755," in Jack P. Greene, Rosemary Brana-Shute, and Randy J. Sparks (eds.), *Money, trade, and power: the evolution of colonial South Carolina's plantation society* (Columbia: University of South Carolina Press), 141–65

Bassani 1987. Ezio Bassani, "I disegni dei Manoscritti Araldi del Padre Giovanni Antonio Cavazzi da Montecuccolo," *Quaderni Poro* 4: 25–87, 110.

Baudrillard 1979/1998. Jean Baudrillard, *The consumer society: myths and structures* (1979; London: SAGE)

Bauer 2001. Arnold J. Bauer, *Goods, power, history: Latin America's material culture* (Cambridge University Press)

Bayard 1997. Françoise Bayard, *Vivre à Lyon sous l'Ancien Régime* (Paris: Perrin)

Becker 1988. Marvin Becker, *Civility and society in western Europe, 1300–1600* (Bloomington: Indiana University Press)

Becker 2005. Marshall Joseph Becker, "Matchcoats: cultural conservatism and change in one aspect of Native American clothing," *Ethnohistory* 52/4: 727–87

Becker 2007. Marshall Joseph Becker, "Unique Huron ornamental bands: wampum cuffs," *Material Culture Review/Revue de la culture matérielle* 66 (Fall): 61–69

Becker 2008. Marshall Joseph Becker, "Lenopi, or, What's in a name? Interpreting the evidence for cultures and cultural boundaries in the lower

Delaware Valley," *Bulletin of the Archaeological Society of New Jersey* 63: 11–32

Becker 2010. Marshall Joseph Becker, "Match coats and the military: mass-produced clothing for Native Americans as parallel markets in the seventeenth century," *Textile History* 41 supplement: 153–81

Beckford 1790. William Beckford, *A descriptive account of the island of Jamaica*, 2 vols. (London: T. and J. Egerton)

Benjamin 2009. Thomas Benjamin, *The Atlantic world* (Cambridge University Press)

Bennett 1964. J. Harry Bennett, "Cary Helyar, merchant and planter of seventeenth-century Jamaica," *WMQ* 3rd ser. 21: 53–76

Berg 2013. Maxine Berg (ed.), *Writing the history of the global: challenges for the 21st Century* (Oxford University Press)

Berg and Eger 2003. Maxine Berg and Elizabeth Eger, "The rise and fall of the luxury debates," in Maxine Berg and Elizabeth Eger (eds.), *Luxury in the eighteenth century: debates, desires and delectable goods* (Basingstoke: Palgrave Macmillan), 7–27

Berinstain 2000. Valérie Berinstain, "Les mouchoirs à carreaux des Indes, ou madras, et la France aux XVIIe et XVIIIe siècles," in Chevalier and Loir-Mongazon 2000, 151–53

Berlin 1996. Ira Berlin, "From creole to African: Atlantic creoles and the origins of African-American society in mainland North America," *WMQ* 3rd ser. 53: 251–88

Bernal 1992. A. M. Bernal, *La financiación de la Carrera de Indias: dinero y crédito en el comercio colonial español con América* (Seville: Fundación El Monte)

Bethencourt 2013. Francisco Bethencourt, *Racisms: from the Crusades to the twentieth century* (Princeton University Press)

Bickham 2005. Troy O. Bickham, *Savages within the empire: representations of American Indians in eighteenth-century Britain* (Oxford University Press)

Blake 1941. J. W. Blake, *Europeans In West Africa 1450–1560* (London: Hakluyt Society)

Bologne 1986. Jean-Claude Bologne, *Histoire de la pudeur* (Paris: Olivier Orban)

Bosher 1987. John F. Bosher, *The Canada merchants 1713–1763* (Oxford: Clarendon Press)

Boshoff and Fourie 2010. Willem H. Boshoff and Johan Fourie, "The significance of the Cape trade route to economic activity in the Cape Colony: a medium-term business cycle analysis," *European Review of Economic History* 14: 469–503

Bosman 1705. William Bosman, *A new and accurate description of the coast of Guinea* (London: James Knapton and Dan. Midwinter)

Bottin and Pellegrin 1996. Jacques Bottin and Nicole Pellegrin (eds.), *Échanges et cultures textiles dans l'Europe pré-industrielle* (*Revue du Nord*. Hors Série. Collection Histoire. No. 12. Université Charles-de-Gaulle, Lille III)

Bougainville 1757/1924. Louis Antoine de Bougainville, "Mémoire sur l'état de la Nouvelle-France, 1757," *Rapport de l'Archiviste du Province de Québec* 4: 42–70

Bougainville 1964. Louis Antoine de Bougainville, *Adventures in the wilderness: the American journals of Louis Antoine de Bougainville, 1756–1760* (Norman: University of Oklahoma Press)

Boulle 2007. Pierre Boulle, *Race et esclavage dans la France de l'Ancien Régime* (Paris: Perrin)

Bourdieu 1972/1977. Pierre Bourdieu, *Outline of a theory of practice* (1972; Cambridge University Press)

Bourque and Labar 2009. Bruce J. Bourque and Laureen A. Labar, *Uncommon threads: Wabanaki textiles, clothing, and costume* (Seattle: University of Washington Press)

Boxer 1982. C. R. Boxer, *The golden age of Brazil, 1695–1750* (Berkeley: University of California Press)

Braund 1993. Kathryn E. Holland Braund, *Deerskins & duffels: the Creek Indian trade with Anglo-America, 1685–1815* (Lincoln: University of Nebraska Press)

Breen 1986. Timothy H. Breen, "An empire of goods: the Anglicization of colonial America, 1690–1776," *Journal of British Studies* 25: 467–99

Breen 1993. Timothy H. Breen, "The meaning of 'likeness': portrait painting in an eighteenth-century consumer society," in Ellen G. Miles (ed.), *The portrait in eighteenth-century America* (Newark: University of Delaware Press), 37–60

Breen 2004. Timothy H. Breen, *The marketplace of revolution* (New York: Oxford University Press)

Brewer and Porter 1993. John Brewer and Roy Porter (eds.), *Consumption and the world of goods* (London and New York: Routledge)

Brienen 2007. Rebecca Parker Brienen, *Visions of savage paradise: Albert Eckhout, court painter in colonial Dutch Brazil* (Amsterdam University Press)

Brown 2000. David Brown, "'Persons of infamous character': the textile pedlars and the role of peddling in industrialization," *Textile History* 31: 1–26

Brown 2009. Kathleen M. Brown, *Foul bodies: cleanliness in early America* (New Haven, Conn.: Yale University Press)

Browne 1789. Patrick Browne, *The civil and natural history of Jamaica*, 2 vols. (1759; London: B. White)

Brubaker and Cooper 2000. Rogers Brubaker and Frederick Cooper, "Beyond 'identity,'" *Theory and Society* 29: 1–47

Bryson 1998. Anna Bryson, *From courtesy to civility: changing codes of conduct in early modern England* (Oxford: Clarendon Press)

Buck 1979. Anne Buck, *Dress in eighteenth-century England* (New York: Holmes & Meier)

Buckridge 2004. Steve O. Buckridge, *Language of dress: resistance and accommodation in Jamaica, 1760–1890* (Mona: University of the West Indies Press)

Buisseret and Reinhardt 2000. David Buisseret and Steven Reinhardt (eds.), *Creolization in the Americas* (College Station: Texas A&M University Press)

Burnard 1994. Trevor Burnard, "A failed settler society: marriage and demographic failure in early Jamaica," *Journal of Social History* 28: 63–82

Burnard 1996. Trevor Burnard, "European Migration to Jamaica, 1655–1780," *WMQ* 3rd ser. 53: 769–96

Burnard 2001. Trevor Burnard, "'Prodigious riches': the wealth of Jamaica before the American Revolution," *EcHR* New ser. 54: 506–24

Burnard 2002. Trevor Burnard, "'The grand mart of the island': the economic function of Kingston, Jamaica, in the mid-eighteenth century," in Kathleen E. A. Monteith and Glen L. Richards (eds.), *Jamaica in slavery and freedom: history, heritage and culture* (Mona: University of the West Indies Press), 225–41

Burnard 2004. Trevor Burnard, *Mastery, tyranny, and desire: Thomas Thistlewood and his slaves in the Anglo-Jamaican world* (Chapel Hill: University of North Carolina Press)

Burnard 2010. Trevor Burnard, "West Indian identity in the eighteenth century," in *Assumed identities: the meanings of race in the Atlantic World* (College Station: Texas A&M University Press), 71–87

Bush 1981. Barbara Bush, "White 'ladies', coloured 'favourites' and black 'wenches': some considerations on sex, race and class factors in social relations in white creole society in the British Caribbean," *Slavery and Abolition* 2: 245–62

Bushman 1994. Richard L. Bushman, "Shopping and advertising in colonial America," in Cary Carson, Ronald Hoffman, and Peter Albert (eds.), *Of consuming interests: the style of life in the eighteenth century* (Charlottesville: University Press of Virginia), 233–51

Butel 1995. Paul Butel, "Espaces européens et antillais du négociant: l'apprentissage par les voyages: le cas bordelais," in Franco Angiolini and Daniel Roche (eds.), *Cultures et formations négociantes dans l'Europe moderne* (Paris: Éditions de l'École des Hautes Études en Sciences Sociales), 349–61

Buvelot 2004. Quentin Buvelot (ed.), *Albert Eckhout, a Dutch artist in Brazil* (Zwolle: Waanders)

Cailly 1993. Claude Cailly, *Mutations d'un espace proto-industriel: le Perche au XVIIIe–XIXe siècles*, 2 vols. ([Ceton, France]: Fédération des Amis du Perche)

Campbell 1987. Colin Campbell, *The romantic ethic and the spirit of modern consumerism* (Oxford: Blackwell)

Campbell 1997. Colin Campbell, "When the meaning is not a message: a critique of the consumption as communication thesis," in Mica Nava (ed.), *Buy this book: studies in advertising and consumption* (London: Routledge), 340–51

Candido 2013. Mariana Candido, *An African slaving port and the Atlantic world: Benguela and its hinterland* (Cambridge University Press)

Cangany 2012. Catherine Cangany, "Fashioning moccasins: Detroit, the manufacturing frontier, and the empire of consumption, 1701–1835," *WMQ* 3rd ser. 69: 265–304

Canizares-Esguerra 2009. Jorge Canizares-Esguerra, "Demons, stars, and the imagination: the early modern body in the Tropics," in Miriam Isaac, Benjamin H. Ziegler, and J. Eliav-Feldon (eds.), *The origins of racism in the West* (Cambridge University Press), 313–25

Canny and Morgan 2011. Nicholas Canny and Philip Morgan (eds.), *The Oxford handbook of the Atlantic world* (Oxford University Press)

Caplan 2000a. Jane Caplan (ed.), *Written on the body: the tattoo in European and American history* (Princeton University Press)

Caplan 2000b. Jane Caplan, "Introduction," in Caplan 2000a, xi–xviii

Cardim 1625/1939. Fernão Cardim, *Tratados da terra e gente do Brasil*, ed. Baptista Caetano, Capistrano de Abreu, and Rodolfo Garcia, 2nd edn. (1625; São Paolo: Companhia Editora Nacional)

Carocci 2010. Max Carocci, "Clad with the 'hair of trees': a history of Native American Spanish moss textile industries," *Textile History* 41: 3–27

Carreira 1983. António Carreira, *Panaria Cabo-Verdiano-Guineense*, 2nd edn (n.p.: Istituto caboverdeano do livro)

Carrera 2003. Magali Marie Carrera, *Imagining identity in New Spain: race, lineage, and the colonial body in portraiture and casta paintings* (Austin: University of Texas Press)

Carr-Gomm 2010. Philip Carr-Gomm, *A brief history of nakedness* (London: Reaktion)

Carrier 1995. James G. Carrier, *Gifts and commodities: exchange and Western capitalism since 1700* (London and New York: Routledge)

Cassady 1967. Ralph Cassady, *Auctions and auctioneering* (Berkeley: University of California Press)

Cauna 1987. Jacques Cauna, *Au temps des isles à sucre: histoire d'une planta-tion de Saint-Domingue au XVIIIe siècle* (Paris: Karthala)

Cavazzi 1687. Giovanni Antonio Cavazzi da Montecuccolo, *Istorica descrizione de' tre regni Congo, Matamba et Angola* (Bologna: Giacomo Monti)

Cave 1999. Alfred A. Cave, "The Delaware prophet Neolin: a reappraisal," *Ethnohistory* 46: 265–90

Certeau 1984. Michel de Certeau, *The practice of everyday life* (1980; Berkeley: University of California Press)

Charlevoix 1722. François-Xavier de Charlevoix, *Journal d'un voyage fait par ordre du roi dans l'Amérique septentrionale*, 2 vols. (1722/1994; Montreal: Les Presses de l'Université de Montréal)

Chevalier and Loir-Mongazon 2000. Jean-Joseph Chevalier and Élisabeth Loir-Mongazon (eds.), *Le mouchoir dans tous ses états* (Cholet: Musée du textile)

Chicangana-Bayona 2008. Yobenj Aucardo Chicangana-Bayona, "Os *Tupis* e os *Tapuias* de Eckhout: o declínio da imagem renascentista do índio," *Varia Historia* 24, online edition, www.scielo.br/scielo.php?pid=S0104-87752008000200016&script=sci_abstract (accessed November 23, 2013)

Chobaut 1938. Henri Chobaut, "L'Industrie des Indiennes à Avignon et à Orange (1677–1884)," *Mémoires de l'Académie de Vaucluse*, IIIe sér. 3: 133–58

Churchill 1732. [Awnsham and John Churchill], *A collection of voyages and travels, some now first printed from original manuscripts, others now first published in English*, 6 vols. (London: John Walthoe et al.)

Clark 1976. John G. Clark, *New Orleans 1718–1812: an economic history* (Baton Rouge: Louisiana State University Press)

Coclanis 2006. Peter Coclanis, "Atlantic world or Atlantic/world?" *WMQ* 3rd ser. 63: 725–42

Cohen 1980. William B. Cohen, *The French encounter with Africans: white response to blacks, 1530–1880* (Bloomington: Indiana University Press)

Cohen and Toninato 2010. Robin Cohen and Paola Toninato, *The creolization reader: studies in mixed identities and cultures* (London: Routledge)

Collo and Benso 1986. Paolo Collo and Silvia Benso (eds.), *Sogno: Bamba, Pemba, Ovando e altre contrade dei regni di Congo, Angola e adiacenti* (Milan: Franco Maria Ricci Editore)

Colonial records of Pennsylvania 1831–40, 1852. *Colonial records of Pennsylvania*, 16 vols. (Harrisburg: T. Fenn, 1831?–40; Philadelphia: Jo. Severns)

Conrad 1983. Robert Edgar Conrad, *Children of God's fire: a documentry history of black slavery in Brazil* (Princeton University Press)

Cooper 2001. Frederick Cooper, "What is the concept of globalization good for? An African historian's perspective," *African Affairs* 100: 189–213

Coquery 2011. Natacha Coquery, *Tenir boutique à Paris au XVIIIe siècle: luxe et demi-luxe* (Paris: Éditions du Comité des travaux historiques et scientifiques)

Cousin 2000. Françoise Cousin, "A la croisée des continents: le madras aux Antilles," in Chevalier and Loir-Mongazon 2000, 155–63

Cousquet 2002. Céline Cousquet, *Nantes, une capitale française des indiennes au XVIIIe siècle* (Nantes: Coiffard Librairie)

Craik 1994. Jennifer Craik, *The face of fashion* (London: Routledge)

Cresswell 1924. *The journal of Nicholas Cresswell* (New York: The Dial Press)

Croghan 1947. "George Croghan's Journal 1759–1763," *Pennsylvania Magazine of History and Biography* 71: 317–64

Crone 1937. G. R. Crone, trans. and ed., *The voyages of Cadamosto and other documents on western Africa in the second half of the fifteenth century* (London: Hakluyt Society)

Cuvelier and Jadin 1954. Jean Cuvelier and Louis Jadin (eds.), *L'ancien Congo d'après les archives romaines (1518–1640)* (Brussels: Académie royale des sciences coloniales)

Daaku 1970. Kwame Yeboa Daaku, *Trade and politics on the Gold Coast 1600–1720* (Oxford: Clarendon Press)

d'Abbeville 1614. Claude d'Abbeville, *Histoire de la mission des Peres Capuchins en l'Isle de Maragnan et terres circonvoisines* (Paris: François Huby)

Dapper 1668. Olfert Dapper, *Kaffrarie, of Lant der Hottentots* (Amsterdam, 1668), in Schapera and Farrington 1933/1970, 1–77

Dapper 1998. *Olfert Dapper's description of Benin (1668)*, ed. Adam Jones (Madison: African Studies Program, University of Wisconsin)

Dardel 1963. Pierre Dardel, *Navires et marchandises dans les ports de Rouen et du Havre au XVIIIe siècle* (Paris: SEVPEN)

Davetian 2009. Benet Davetian, *Civility: a cultural history* (University of Toronto Press)

Davis 1962. Ralph Davis, "English Foreign Trade, 1700–1774," *EcHR* New ser. 15: 285–303

Davis 1966. Ralph Davis, "The Rise of Protection in England, 1689–1786," *EcHR* New ser. 19: 306–17.

Davison 2010. Patricia Davison, "South Africa Overview," in Eicher and Ross 2010 (unpaginated)

Dawdy 2007. Shannon Lee Dawdy, "La Nouvelle-Orléans au XVIIIe siècle. Courants d'échange dans le monde caraïbe," *Annales. Histoire, Sciences Sociales* 62: 663–85 de Bruijn and Raben 2004. Max de Bruijn and Remco Raben (eds.), *The world of Jan Brandes, 1743–1808* (Amsterdam: Waanders)

de Bry 1590–1634. Theodore de Bry, *Collectiones peregrinationum in Indiam orientalem et Indiam occidentalem*, 13 vols. (Frankfurt: de Bry)

de Marly 1990. Diana de Marly, *Dress in North America. I. The New World 1492–1800* (New York: Holmes & Meier)

De Vorsey 1971. Louis De Vorsey, Jr. (ed.), *De Brahm's report of the general Survey in the Southern District of North America* (Columbia: University of South Carolina Press)

de Vries 2008. Jan de Vries, *The industrious revolution: consumer behavior and the household economy, 1650 to the present* (Cambridge University Press)

de Vries 2010. Jan de Vries, "The limits of globalization in the early modern world," *EcHR* New ser. 63: 710–33

de Vries 2013. Jan de Vries, "Reflections on doing global history," in Berg 2013, 32–47

De Wet 1981. G. C. De Wet, *Die vryliede en vryswartes in die kaapse nedersetting 1657–1707* (Cape Town: Historiese Publikasie-vereniging)

de Zwart 2011. Pim de Zwart, "Real wages at the Cape of Good Hope: A long-term perspective, 1652–1912," Center for Global Economic History, Universiteit Utrecht, CGEH Working Paper Series, 13 (August) http://ideas.repec.org/p/ucg/wpaper/0013.html (accessed June 4, 2013)

Debien 1951. G[abriel] Debien, *Les engagés pour les Antilles (1634–1715)* (Paris: Société de l'histoire des colonies françaises)

Debien 1962. G[abriel] Debien, *Plantations et esclaves à Saint-Domingue* (Dakar: Université de Dakar, Faculté des Lettres et Sciences Humaines, Publications de la Section d'Histoire)

Deceulaer 2006. Harald Deceulaer, "Dealing with diversity: pedlars in the Southern Netherlands in the eighteenth century," in Bruno Blondé *et al.*, *Buyers & sellers. Retail circuits and practices in medieval and early modern Europe* (Turnhout, Belgium: Brepols), 171–98

Dechêne 1974/1992. Louise Dechêne, *Habitants and merchants in seventeenth century Montreal* (1974; Montreal and Kingston: McGill-Queen's University Press)

DeJean 2005. Joan DeJean, *The essence of style: how the French invented fashion, fine food, chic cafés, style, sophistication, and glamour* (New York: Free Press)

Del Priore 1997. Mary del Priore, "Ritos da vida privada," in Novais 1997, I: 275–330.

Delpierre 1997. Madeleine Delpierre, *Dress in France in the eighteenth century* (1996; New Haven: Yale University Press)

Dépatie 2003. Sylvie Dépatie, "Commerce et crédit à l'Ile Jésus, 1734–75. Le rôle des marchands ruraux dans l'économie des campagnes montréalaises," *Canadian Historical Review* 84: 147–76

Desloges 1991. Yvon Desloges, *A tenant's town: Québec in the 18th century* (Ottawa: National Historic Sites and Parks Service)

Dessureault, Dickinson, and Wien 1994. Christian Dessureault, John A. Dickinson, and Thomas Wien, "Living standards of Norman and Canadian peasants, 1690–1835," in Schuurman and Walsh 1994, 95–112

Dickason 1984. Olive Patricia Dickason, *The myth of the savage and the beginnings of French colonialism in the Americas* (Edmonton: University of Alberta Press)

Dictionnaire de l'Académie française 1694. *Dictionnaire de l'Académie française*, 1st edn. (1694), http://artfl-project.uchicago.edu/node/17 (accessed November 13, 2013)

Dolle 2000. Pascal Dolle, "Les débuts du mouchoir dans la production de la manufacture de Cholet au XVIIIe siècle," in Chevalier and Loir-Mongazon 2000, 39–47

Donnan 1930–35. Elizabeth Donnan (ed.), *Documents illustrative of the history of the slave trade to America*, 4 vols. (Washington, DC: Carnegie Institution)

Douglas and Isherwood 1979. Mary Douglas and Baron Isherwood, *The world of goods: towards an anthropology of consumption* (New York: Basic Books)

Duerr 1988/1998. Hans Peter Duerr, *Nudité & pudeur: le mythe du processus de civilisation* (1988; Paris: Éditions de la Maison des Sciences de l'Homme)

Dunn 1973. Richard S. Dunn, *Sugar and slaves: the rise of the planter class in the English West Indies, 1624–1713* (1972; New York: W. W. Norton)

Dunn 1998. Walter S. Dunn, Jr., *Frontier profit and loss: the British army and the fur traders, 1760–1764* (Westport, Conn.: Greenwood Press)

Du Plessis and Du Plessis 2012. Sophia Du Plessis and Stan Du Plessis, "Happy in the service of the Company: the purchasing power of VOC salaries at the Cape in the 18th century," Stellenbosch Economic Working Papers 01/12, http://ideas.repec.org/p/sza/wpaper/wpapers153.html (accessed June 4, 2013)

du Pratz 1758. Antoine Simone Le Page du Pratz, *Histoire de la Louisiane*, 3 vols. (Paris: Chez De Bure, l'aîné [et al.])

Du Tertre 1667–71. Jean Baptiste Du Tertre, *Histoire générale des Antilles habitées par les François*, 4 vols. (Paris: T. Iolly)

DuPlessis 2003. Robert S. DuPlessis, "Transatlantic textiles: European linen in the cloth cultures of colonial North America," in Brenda Collins and Philip Ollerenshaw (eds.), *The European linen industry in historical perspective* (Oxford University Press), 123–37

Durie 1973. Alastair Durie, "The markets for Scottish linen, 1730–1775," *Scottish Historical Review* 52: 30–49

Earle 1989. Peter Earle, *The making of the English middle class: business, society and family life in London, 1660–1730* (Berkeley: University of California Press)

Earle 2001. Rebecca Earle, "'Two pairs of pink satin shoes!!' Race, clothing and identity in the Americas (17th–19th centuries)," *History Workshop Journal* 52: 175–95

Edelson 2006. Max Edelson, *Plantation enterprise in colonial South Carolina* (Cambridge, Mass.: Harvard University Press)

Edgar 1972. Walter B. Edgar (ed.), *The letterbook of Robert Pringle*, 2 vols. (Columbia: University of South Carolina Press)

Édit du roi 1685/1687. *Édit du roi, touchant la police des isles de l'Amérique Française* (1685; Paris: n.p.)

Edwards 1793. Bryan Edwards, *The history, civil and commercial, of the British colonies in the West Indies*, 2 vols. (London: John Stockdale)

Egnal 1998. Marc Egnal, *New World economies: the growth of the thirteen colonies and early Canada* (New York: Oxford University Press)

Eicher 2010. Joanne B. Eicher (ed.), *Berg encyclopedia of world dress and fashion*, vol. X: *Global perspectives* (Oxford: Berg), online edition

Eicher and Ross 2010. Joanne B. Eicher and Doran H. Ross (eds.), *Berg encyclopedia of world dress and fashion*, vol. I: *Africa* (Oxford: Berg), online edition

Elias 1939/1969, 1982. Norbert Elias, *The civilizing process*, 2 vols. (1939; Oxford: Blackwell)

Elphick and Giliomee 1988. Richard Elphick and Hermann Giliomee (eds.), *The shaping of South African society, 1652–1840* (Middletown, Conn.: Wesleyan University Press)

Elphick and Malherbe 1988. Richard Elphick and V. C. Malherbe, "The Khoisan to 1838," in Elphick and Giliomee 1988, 3–65

Elphick and Shell 1988. Richard Elphick and Robert Shell, "Intergroup relations: Khoikhoi, settlers, slaves and free blacks, 1652–1795," in Elphick and Giliomee 1988, 184–239

Eltis 2000. David Eltis, *The rise of African slavery in the Americas* (Cambridge University Press)

Emmer 2003. Pieter Emmer, "The myth of early globalization: the Atlantic economy, 1500–1800," *European Review* 9: 37–47

État présent 1754/1920–21. "État présent du Canada, dressé sur nombre de mémoires et connaissances acquises sur les lieux, par le Sieur Boucault (1754)," *Rapport de l'Archiviste du Province de Québec* 1: 11–50

Fabella 2007. Yvonne Fabella, "'An empire founded on libertinage': the mulatresse and colonial anxiety in Saint Domingue," in Nora E. Jaffary (ed.),

Gender, race and religion in the colonization of the Americas (Aldershot, UK, and Burlington, Vt.: Ashgate), 109–24

Fairchilds 1993. Cissie Fairchilds, "The production and marketing of populuxe goods in eighteenth-century Paris," in Brewer and Porter 1993, 228–48

Feeser 2013. Andrea Feeser, *Red, white, and black make blue: indigo in the fabric of colonial South Carolina life* (Athens: University of Georgia Press)

Ferrão and Soares 1997. Cristina Ferrão and José Paolo Monteiro Soares (eds.), *Dutch Brazil,* vol. II: *The "Thierbuch" and "Autobiography" of Zacharias Wagener* (Rio de Janeiro: Editora Index)

Ferreira 2001. Roquinaldo Ferreira, "Dinâmica do comércio intracolonial: geribitas, panos asiátios e guerra no tráfico angolano de escravos (século XVIII)," in João Fragoso, Maria Fernanda Bicalho, and Maria de Tátima Gouvêa (eds.), *O Antigo Regime nos trópicos: a dinâmica imperial portuguesa séculos XVI–XVIII)* (Rio de Janeiro: Civilização Brasileira), 339–78

Ferreira 2012. Roquinaldo Ferreira, *Cross-cultural exchange in the Atlantic world: Angola and Brazil during the era of the slave trade* (Cambridge University Press)

Ferrières 2004. Madeleine Ferrières, *Le bien des pauvres: la consommation populaire en Avignon (1600–1800)* (Seyssel: Champ Vallon)

Findlay and Rourke 2003. Ronald Findlay and Kevin Rourke, "Commodity market integration, 1500–2000," in Michael Bordo, Alan Taylor, and Jeffrey Williamson (eds.), *Globalization in historical perspective* (University of Chicago Press), 13–64

Finley 1980. Moses Finley, *Ancient slavery and modern ideology* (New York: Viking)

Fisher 1971. H. E. S. Fisher, *The Portugal trade: a study of Anglo-Portuguese commerce 1700–1770* (London: Methuen)

Fisher 1997. John R. Fisher, *The economic aspects of Spanish imperialism in America, 1492–1810* (Liverpool University Press)

Fleming 2000. Juliet Fleming, "The Renaissance tattoo," in Caplan 2000a, 61–82

Fleming 2001. Juliet Fleming, *Graffiti and the writing arts of early modern England* (London: Reaktion)

Fontaine 1996. Laurence Fontaine, *History of pedlars in Europe* (Durham, NC: Duke University Press)

Fontaine 2001. Laurence Fontaine, "Antonio and Shylock: credit and trust in France, c. 1680–c. 1780," *EcHR* New ser. 54: 39–57

Fontaine 2008. Laurence Fontaine, *L'économie morale: pauvreté, crédit et confiance dans l'Europe préindustrielle* (Paris: Gallimard)

Fouché 1914/1970. Leo Fouché (ed.), *Dagboek van Adam Tas, 1705–1706* (1914; Cape Town: Van Riebeeck Society)

Fourie 2012. Johan Fourie, "The wealth of the Cape Colony: measurements from probate inventories," Universiteit Stellenbosch Working Paper 268, February 2012

Fourie and von Fintel 2011. Johan Fourie and Dieter von Fintel, "A history with evidence: income inequality in the Dutch Cape Colony," *Economic History of Developing Regions* 26: 16–48

Fradkin and Gelman 2004. Raúl Fradkin and Jorge Gelman, "Recorridos y desafíos de una historiografía: escalas de observación y fuentes en la historia rural rioplatense," in Beatriz Bragoni (ed.), *Microanálisis: ensayos de historiografía argentina* (Buenos Aires: Prometeo Libros), 31–54

Francq van Berkhij 1769–1810. Jan le Francq van Berkhij, *Natuurlyke historie van Holland*, 9 vols. in 13 (Amsterdam: Yntema en Tiebol)

Franquet 1974. Louis Franquet, *Voyages et mémoires sur le Canada* (Montréal: Éditions Élysé)

Freeman 2002. *The letters of William Freeman, London merchant, 1678–1685*, ed. David Hancock (London Record Society)

Frézier 1716/1717. Amédée François Frézier, *Relation du voyage de la mer du Sud aux côtes du Chili, du Pérou et du Brésil pendant les années 1712, 1713 et 1714*, 2 vols. (1716; Amsterdam: Pierre Humbert)

Furtado 2009. Júnia Ferreira Furtado, *Chica da Silva: a Brazilian slave of the eighteenth century: new approaches to the Americas* (Cambridge University Press)

Gagnon 1975. François-Marc Gagnon, *La conversion par l'image: un aspect de la mission des Jésuites auprès des Indiens du Canada au XVIIe siècle* (Montreal: Éditions Bellarmin)

Galenson 1984. David W. Galenson, "The Rise and fall of indentured servitude in the Americas: an economic analysis," *Journal of Economic History* 44: 1–26

Games 2006. Alison Games, "Atlantic history: definitions, challenges, and opportunities," *American Historical Review* 111: 741–57

Ganson 2003. Barbara Ganson, *The Guaraní under Spanish rule in the Río de la Plata* (Stanford University Press)

Garavaglia and Gelman 1995. Juan Carlos Garavaglia and Jorge D. Gelman, "Rural history of the Río de la Plata, 1600–1850: results of a historiographical renaissance," *Latin American Research Review* 30:3: 75–105

García 1999. Máximo García Fernández, "Los bienes dotales en la ciudad de Valladolid, 1700–1850: el ajuar doméstico y la evolución de consumo y la demanda," in Torras and Yun Casalilla 1999, 133–58

Garnot 1994. Benoît Garnot, "La culture matérielle dans les villes françaises au XVIIIe siècle," in Schuurman and Walsh 1994, 21–29

Garrigus 1993. John Garrigus, "Blue and brown: contraband indigo and the rise of a free colored planter class in French Saint-Domingue," *The Americas* 50: 233–63

Garrigus 2006. John Garrigus, *Before Haiti: race and citizenship in French Saint-Domingue* (New York: Palgrave Macmillan)

Gaspar and Hine 1996. David Barry Gaspar and Darlene Clark Hine (eds.), *More than chattel: black women and slavery in the Americas* (Bloomington: Indiana University Press)

Gaucher, Delafosse, and Debien 1959–60, 1960–61. M. Gaucher, M. Delafosse, and G. Debien, "Les engagés pour le Canada au XVIIIe siècle," *Revue d'histoire de l'Amérique française* 13: 247–61, 402–21, 550–61; 14: 87–108, 246–58, 430–40, 583–602

Geggus 1982. David Geggus, *Slavery, war, and revolution: the British occupation of Saint Domingue, 1793–1798* (Oxford: Clarendon Press)

Gervais 2008. Pierre Gervais, "Neither imperial, nor Atlantic: a merchant perspective on international trade in the eighteenth century," *History of European Ideas* 34: 465–73

Gervais 2012. Pierre Gervais, "Crédit et filières marchandes au XVIIIe siècle," *Annales. Histoire, Sciences sociales* 67: 1011–48

Gervais, Lemarchand, and Margairaz 2014. Pierre Gervais, Yannick Lemarchand, and Dominique Margairaz (eds.), *Merchants and profit in the age of commerce 1680–1830* (London: Pickering & Chatto)

Girod de Chantrans 1785. Justin Girod de Chantrans, *Voyage d'un Suisse dans les colonies d'Amérique* (Neuchâtel: Imprimerie de la Société Typographique)

Gourdeau 1995. Claire Gourdeau, "Marie de l'Incarnation et ses pensionnaires amérindiennes (1639–1672): rencontre des cultures," *Canadian Folklore Canadien* 17: 125–38

Goveia 1970. E. V. Goveia, *The West Indian slave laws of the 18th century* (Bridgetown, Barbados: Caribbean Universities Press)

Grandpré 1801. Louis de Grandpré, *Voyage à la côte occidentale d'Afrique, fait dans les années 1786 et 1787*, 2 vols. (Paris: Dentu)

Greene and Morgan 2009. Jack P. Greene and Philip D. Morgan (eds.), *Atlantic history: a critical appraisal* (Oxford University Press)

Greer 2005. Allen Greer, *Mohawk saint: Catherine Tekakwitha and the Jesuits* (Oxford and New York: Oxford University Press)

Grevenbroek 1695. J. G. Grevenbroek, *N.N. Graevenbroeckii elegans & accurata gentis Africanae circa Promontorium Capitis Bonae spei vulgo Hottentotten nuncupatae* [*An elegant and accurate account of the African race living round the Cape of Good Hope commonly called Hottentots*] (1695 MS), in Schapera and Farrington 1933/1970, 158–299

Grimke 1790. John Faucheraud Grimke, *The public laws of the state of South-Carolina* (Philadelphia: R. Aitken & Son)

Gronow and Warde 2001. Jukka Gronow and Alan Warde (eds.), *Ordinary consumption* (London and New York: Routledge)

Grubb 2000. Farley Grubb, "The statutory regulation of colonial servitude: an incomplete contract approach," *Explorations in Economic History* 37: 42–75

Guelke 1988. Leonard Guelke, "Freehold farmers and frontier settlers, 1657–1780," in Elphick and Giliomee 1988, 66–108

Gustafson 2000. Mark Gustafson, "The tattoo in the later Roman empire and beyond," in Caplan 2000a, 17–31

Hall 2005. Gwendolyn Midlo Hall, *Slavery and African ethnicities in the Americas: restoring the links* (Chapel Hill: University of North Carolina Press)

Hamell 1987/1999. George R. Hamell, "Mohawks abroad: the 1764 Amsterdam etching of Sychnecta," in Christian Feest (ed.), *Indians and Europe: an interdisciplinary collection of essays* (1987; Lincoln: University of Nebraska Press), 175–94

Hamell 1992. George R. Hamell, "The Iroquois and the world's rim: speculations on color, culture, and contact," *American Indian Quarterly* 16: 451–69

Hamer 1968–94. Philip M. Hamer et al. (eds.), *Papers of Henry Laurens*, 14 vols. (Columbia: University of South Carolina Press)

Hancock 1995. David Hancock, *Citizens of the world: London merchants and the integration of the British Atlantic community, 1735–1785* (Cambridge University Press)

Hancock 2009. David Hancock, *Oceans of wine: Madeira and the organization of the Atlantic market, 1640–1815* (New Haven, Conn.: Yale University Press)

Hancock 2011. David Hancock, "Atlantic trade and commodities, 1402–1815," in Canny and Morgan 2011, 324–40

Handler 2009. Jerome S. Handler, "The Middle Passage and the material culture of captive Africans," *Slavery and Abolition* 30: 1–26.

Handler 2010. Jerome S. Handler, "The Old Plantation painting at colonial Williamsburg: new findings and some observations," *African Diaspora Archaeology Newsletter*, www.diaspora.uiuc.edu/news1210/news1210-3.pdf

Hanna 1917. Mary Alice Hanna, *Trade of the Delaware district before the Revolution* (Northampton, Mass.: Smith College)

Harris 1987. R. Cole Harris (ed.), *Historical atlas of Canada*, vol. I (University of Toronto Press)

Harris et al. 1993. Jennifer Harris et al., *Textiles, 5,000 years: an international history and illustrated survey* (New York: H. N. Abrams)

Hart 1998. Avril Hart, *Historical fashion in detail: the 17th and 18th centuries* (London: V&A Publications)

Harte 1976. N. B. Harte, "State control of dress and social change in pre-industrial England," in D. C. Coleman and A. H. John (eds.), *Trade, government and economy in pre-industrial England: essays presented to F. J. Fisher* (London: Weidenfeld & Nicolson), 132–65

Harvey 1995. John Harvey, *Men in black* (University of Chicago Press)

Hauser 2008. Mark. W. Hauser, *An archaeology of black markets: local ceramics and economies in eighteenth century Jamaica* (Gainesville: University Press of Florida)

Havard and Vidal 2003. Gilles Havard and Cécile Vidal, *Histoire de l'Amérique française* (Paris: Flammarion)

Heckewelder 1876. John Heckewelder, *History, manners, and customs of the Indian nations who once inhabited Pennsylvania and the neighbouring states*, new and rev. edn. (1818; Philadelphia: Historical Society of Pennsylvania)

Hennepin 1683. Louis Hennepin, *Description de la Louisiane* (Paris: Veuve Sebastian Huré)

Hennepin 1698. Louis Hennepin, *A continuation of the new discovery of a vast country in America* (London: M. Bentley et al.)

Hennepin 1880. Louis Hennepin, *A Description of Louisiana*, ed. and trans. John G. Shea (New York: John G. Shea)

Henry 1809/1969. Alexander Henry, *Travels and adventures in Canada and the Indian territories, between the years 1760 and 1776* (1809; Rutland, Vt.: Charles E. Tuttle)

Higman 1988. Barry W. Higman, *Jamaica surveyed: plantation maps and plans of the eighteenth and nineteenth centuries* (Kingston: Institute of Jamaica Publications)

Hilliard d'Aubertuil 1777. Michel Réné Hilliard d'Aubertuil, *Considérations sur l'état présent de la colonie française de Saint-Domingue*, 2 vols. (Paris: Grangé)

Hilton 1985. Anne Hilton, *The kingdom of Kongo* (Oxford: Clarendon Press)

Hirsch 2004. Alison Duncan Hirsch (ed.), *Early American Indian documents: treaties and laws, 1607–1789*, vol. III: *Pennsylvania and Delaware treaties, 1756–1775* (Bethesda, Md.: University Publications of America)

Historical statistics 1975. *Historical statistics of the United States: colonial times to 1970* (Washington, DC: Bureau of the Census)

Holmes 1896. William Henry Holmes, "Prehistoric textile art of the eastern United States," in *Thirteenth annual report of the Bureau of American Ethnology to the Secretary of the Smithsonian Institution, 1891–1892* (Washington, DC: Government Printing Office), 3–46

Honychurch 2004. Lennox Honychurch, "Chatoyer's artist: Agostino Brunias and the depiction of St Vincent," *Journal of the Barbados Museum and Historical Society* 50: 104–28

Hood 2003. Adrienne Hood, *The weaver's craft: cloth, commerce, and industry in early Pennsylvania* (Philadelphia: University of Pennsylvania Press)

Hopkins 1973. A. G. Hopkins, *An economic history of West Africa* (New York: Columbia University Press)

Hornsby 2005. Stephen J. Hornsby, *British Atlantic, American frontier: spaces of power in early modern British America* (Hanover, NH: University Press of New England)

Howell 2010. Martha Howell, *Commerce before capitalism in Europe, 1300–1600* (Cambridge University Press)

Hudson 1976. Charles Hudson, *The Southeastern Indians* (Knoxville: University of Tennessee Press)

Hudson 1985. Samuel Hudson, "Auctions – their good and evil tendency," ed. Robert Shell, *Quarterly Bulletin of the South African Library* 39: 147–51, 40: 12–18

Hunt 1996. Alan Hunt, *Governance of the consuming passions: a history of sumptuary law* (New York: St. Martin's)

Hvidt 1980. Kristian Hvidt (ed.), *Von Reck's voyage: drawings and journal of Philip Georg Friedrich von Reck* (Savannah, Ga.: Beehive Press)

Inikori 2002. Joseph Inikori, *Africans and the Industrial Revolution in England* (Cambridge University Press)

Iselin 1994. Regula Iselin, "Reading pictures: on the value of the copperplates in the 'Beschryvinghe' of Pieter de Marees (1602) as source material for ethnohistorical research," *History in Africa* 21: 147–70

Jackson 2010. Jason Baird Jackson, "The Southeast," in Tortora 2010a (unpaginated)

Jacobs 1966. Wilbur R. Jacobs, *Wilderness politics and Indian gifts: the northern colonial frontier 1748–1763* (1950; Lincoln: University of Nebraska Press)

Jaenen 1985. Cornelius J. Jaenen, "The role of presents in French–Amerindian trade," in Duncan Cameron (ed.), *Explorations in Canadian economic history: essays in honour of Irene M. Spry* (University of Ottawa Press), 231–50

Jensen 1963. Arthur L. Jensen, *The maritime commerce of colonial Philadelphia* (Madison: University of Wisconsin Press)

Jenss 2010. Heike Jenss, "Secondhand Clothing," in Skov 2010 (unpaginated)

Johnson 1921–65. *The Papers of Sir William Johnson*, 14 vols. (Albany: University of the State of New York)

Johnson 1979. Lyman L. Johnson, "Manumission in colonial Buenos Aires, 1776–1810," *HAHR* 59: 258–79

Johnson 2009. Laura E. Johnson, "'Goods to clothe themselves': Native consumers and Native images on the Pennsylvania trading frontier, 1712–60," *Winterthur Portfolio* 43: 115–40

Jolicoeur 1941. [Joseph-Charles Bonin, *dit* Jolicoeur] J. C. B., *Travels in New France*, ed. Sylvester K. Stevens, Donald H. Kent, and Emma Edith Woods (Harrisburg: Pennsylvania Historical Commission)

Jones 1774. David Jones, *A journal of two visits made to some nations of Indians on the west side of the River Ohio, in the years 1772 and 1773* (Burlington, N.J.: Isaac Collins)

Jones 1982. Adam Jones, "Double Dutch? A survey of seventeenth-century German sources for West African history," *History in Africa* 9: 141–53

Jones 1986. Adam Jones, "Semper aliquid veteris: printed sources for the history of the Ivory and Gold Coasts, 1500–1750," *Journal of African History* 27: 215–35

Jones 1990. Adam Jones, "Decompiling Dapper: a preliminary search for evidence," *History in Africa* 17: 171–209

Jordán Pérez 2010. Manuel Jordán Pérez, "Angola," in Eicher and Ross 2010 (unpaginated)

Joseph and Szuchman 1996. Gilbert M. Joseph and Mark D. Szuchman (eds.), *I saw a city invincible: urban portraits of Latin America* (Wilmington, Del.: SR Books)

Kalm 1772. Peter [*sic*] Kalm, *Travels into North America*, trans. John Reinhold Forster, 2 vols., 2nd edn. (1753–61; London: T. Lowndes)

Kalm 1977. Pehr Kalm, *Voyage de Pehr Kalm au Canada en 1749*, ed. and trans. Jacques Rousseau and Guy Béthune (Montreal: Pierre Tisseyre)

Kamermans 1999. Johan A. Kamermans, *Materiële cultuur in de Krimpenerwaard in de zeventiende en achttiend eeuw: ontwikkeling en diversiteit* (Wageningen: Landbouwuniversiteit)

Katzew 1996. Ilona Katzew et al., *New world orders: casta painting and colonial Latin America* (New York: Americas Society Art Gallery)

Katzew 2004. Ilona Katzew, *Casta painting: images of race in eighteenth century Mexico* (New Haven, Conn.: Yale University Press)

Kea 1982. Ray Kea, *Settlement, trade, and polities in the seventeenth century Gold Coast* (Baltimore, Md.: Johns Hopkins University Press)

Kellogg 1916. Louise Phelps Kellogg (ed.), *Frontier advance on the upper Ohio 1778–1779* (Madison: Wisconsin Historical Society)

Kelsay 1984. Isabel Thompson Kelsay, *Joseph Brant, 1743–1807, man of two worlds* (Syracuse University Press)

Kenny 1761–63/1913. "Journal of James Kenny, 1761–1763," *Pennsylvania Magazine of History and Biography* 37: 1–47, 152–201

Kent 1979. Donald H. Kent (ed.), *Early American Indian documents: treaties and laws, 1607–1789*, vol. I: *Pennsylvania and Delaware treaties, 1629–1737* (Washington, DC: University Publications of America)

Kidd 2006. Colin Kidd, *The forging of races: race and scripture in the Protestant Atlantic world 1600–2000* (Cambridge University Press)

Kindersley 1777. Mrs. Kindersley, *Letters from the island of Teneriffe, Brazil, the Cape of Good Hope, and the East Indies* (London: J. Nourse)

King 2001. Stewart R. King, *Blue coat or powdered wig: free people of color in pre-revolutionary Saint Domingue* (Athens: University of Georgia Press)

Kinietz 1940. W. Vernon Kinietz, *The Indians of the western Great Lakes 1615–1760* (Ann Arbor: University of Michigan Press)

Klooster 2009. Wim Klooster, "Inter-imperial smuggling in the Americas, 1600–1800," in Bernard Bailyn and Patricia Denault (eds.), *Soundings in Atlantic history: latent structures and intellectual currents, 1500–1830* (Cambridge, Mass.: Harvard University Press), 141–80

Kolb 1719/1738. Peter Kolb, *The present state of the Cape of Good Hope . . .*, 2 vols. (1719; London: W. Innys and R. Manby)

Konrad 2011. Joel Konrad, "'Barbarous gallants': fashion, morality, and the marked body in English culture, 1590–1660," *Fashion Theory* 15: 29–48

Kraak 2000. Deborah Kraak, "Variations on 'plainness': Quaker dress in eighteenth-century Philadelphia," *Costume* 34: 51–63

Kriger 2005. Colleen Kriger, "Mapping the history of cotton textile production in precolonial West Africa," *African Economic History* 33: 87–101

Kriger 2006. Colleen Kriger, *Cloth in West African history* (Lanham, Md.: Altamira)

Kriger 2009. Colleen E. Kriger, "'Guinea cloth': production and consumption of cotton textiles in West Africa before and during the Atlantic slave trade," in Riello and Parthasarathi 2009, 105–26

Kriz 2008. Kay Dian Kriz, *Slavery, sugar, and the culture of refinement: picturing the British West Indies, 1700–1840* (New Haven, Conn.: Yale University Press)

Krzesinski-De Widt 2002. Annemarie Krzesinski-De Widt, *Die boedelinventarisse van erflaters in die distrik Stellenbosch, 1679–1806*, 5 vols. (Stellenbosch Museum)

Kuchta 2002. David Kuchta, *The three-piece suit and modern masculinity: England, 1550–1850* (Berkeley: University of California Press)

Kupperman 1997. Karen Ordahl Kupperman, "Presentment of civility: English reading of American self-presentation in the early years of colonization," *WMQ* 3rd ser. 54: 193–228

Kwass 2014. Michael Kwass. *Contraband: Louis Mandrin and the making of a global underground* (Cambridge, Mass.: Harvard University Press)

Labat 1722. Jean Baptiste Labat, *Nouveau voyage aux isles de l'Amérique*, 6 vols. (Paris: Guillaume Cavelier)

Laborie 1798. P. J. Laborie, *The coffee planter of Saint Domingo; with an appendix, containing a view of the constitution, government, laws, and state of that colony, previous to the year 1789* (London: printed for T. Cadell and W. Davies)

Lafitau 1724. Joseph-François Lafitau, *Moeurs des sauvages américains comparées aux moeurs des premiers temps*, 4 vols. (Paris: Saugrain l'aîné et Ch. E. Hochereau)

Lambert 2004. Miles Lambert, "'Cast-off wearing apparell': the consumption and distribution of second-hand clothing in northern England during the long eighteenth century," *Textile History* 35: 1–26

Lamikiz 2010. Xabier Lamikiz, *Trade and trust in the eighteenth-century Atlantic world: Spanish merchants and their overseas networks* (Woodbridge, UK: Boydell & Brewer)

Lamp 2010. Frederick John Lamp, "Dress, undress, clothing, and nudity," in Eicher 2010 (unpaginated)

Lara 1997. Silvia Hunold Lara, "The signs of color: women's dress and racial relations in Salvador and Rio de Janeiro, ca. 1750–1815," *Colonial Latin American Review* 6: 205–24

Lara 2000. Silvia Hunold Lara, "Sedas, panos e balangandãs: o traje de senhoras e escravas nas cidades do Rio de Janeiro e de Salvador (século XVIII)," in Maria Beatriz Nizza da Silva (ed.), *Brasil: colonização e escravidão* (Rio de Janeiro: Nova Fronteira), 177–91

Lara 2001. Silvia Hunold Lara, "Legislação sobre escravos africanos na América portuguesa," in Andrés-Gallego 2001, separately paginated 1–680

Lara 2002. Silvia Hunold Lara, "Customs and costumes: Carlos Julião and the image of black slaves in late eighteenth-century Brazil," in Thomas Wiedemann and Jane Gardner (eds.), *Representing the body of the slave* (London: Frank Cass), 125–46

Lara 2007. Silvia Hunold Lara, *Fragmentos setecentistas: escravidão, cultura e poder na América portuguese* (São Paulo: Companhia das Letras)

Laverdière and Casgrain 18/1/1973. C. II. Laverdière and II. R. Casgrain, *Le journal des Jésuites publié d'après le manuscrit original conservé aux archives du Séminaire de Québec*, 3rd edn. (1871; Montreal and Laval: Éditions François-Xavier)

Lavradio 1972. Marquês do Lavradio, *Cartas da Bahia 1768-1769* (Rio de Janeiro: Arquivio nacional)

Laws of Jamaica 1683. *The laws of Jamaica* (London: Charles Harper)

Laws of Jamaica 1716. *The laws of Jamaica* (London: W. Wilkins)

Le Gouic 2012. Olivier Le Gouic, "La contrebande des indiennes à Lyon au temps de la prohibition (1686–1759)," in Marguerite Figeac-Monthus and

Christophe Lastécouères (eds.), *Territoires de l'illicite et identités portuaires et insulaires: du XVIe siècle au XXe siècle* (Paris: Armand Colin), 55–93

Lebrero 1992. Rodolfo E. González Lebrero, "Las pulperias de Buenos Aires 1580–1640" (unpublished conference paper)

Lebrero 2002. Rodolfo E. González Lebrero, *La pequeña aldea: sociedad y economía en Buenos Aires (1580–1640)* (Buenos Aires: Editorial Biblos)

Lemire 2003. Beverly Lemire, "Domesticating the exotic: floral culture and the East India calico trade with England, *c.* 1600–1800," *Textile* 1: 65–85

Lemire 2009. Beverly Lemire, "Revising the historical narrative: India, Europe, and the cotton trade, *c.* 1300–1800," in Riello and Parthasarathi 2009, 205–26

Lemire 2010. Beverly Lemire, "Introduction: fashion and the practice of history: a political legacy," in Beverly Lemire (ed.), *The force of fashion in politics and society: global perspectives from early modern to modern times* (Aldershot, UK: Ashgate), 1–19

Lemire 2011. Beverly Lemire, *Cotton* (Oxford and New York: Berg)

Lemon 1972. James T. Lemon, *The best poor man's country: a geographical study of early southeastern Pennsylvania* (Baltimore, Md.: Johns Hopkins University Press)

Lender and Martin 1982. Mark E. Lender and James Kirby Martin, *Citizen soldier: the revolutionary war journal of Joseph Bloomfield* (Newark: New Jersey Historical Society)

Léon 1970–80. Pierre Léon, "L'élan industriel et commercial," in Fernand Braudel and Ernest Labrousse (eds.), *Histoire économique et sociale de la France*, 4 vols. (Paris: Presses Universitaires de France), II: 499–528

Léry 1578/1990. Jean de Léry, *History of a voyage to the land of Brazil, otherwise called America*, ed. and trans. Janet Whatley (1578; Berkeley: University of California Press)

Leslie 1739. Charles Leslie, *A new and exact account of Jamaica* (Edinburgh: R. Fleming)

Lespagnol 1982. André Lespagnol, "Cargaisons et profits du commerce indien au début du XVIIIe siècle: les opérations commerciales des compagnies malouines 1701–1720," *Annales de Bretagne et des pays de l'Ouest* 89: 313–50

Lespagnol 1996. André Lespagnol, "Des toiles bretonnes aux toiles 'bretagnes': conditions et facteurs d'émergence d'un 'produit-phare' sur les marchés ibériques," in Bottin and Pellegrin 1996, 179–92

Lettre 1682/1922. "Lettre de l'Intendant de Meulles au Ministre (12 novembre 1682)," *Bulletin de recherches historiques* 28: 292–303

Levinton 2009. Norberto Levinton, *El espacio jesuítico-guaraní: la formación de una región cultural* (Asunción: Universidad Católica "Nuestra Señora de la Asunción")

Lockyer 1711. Charles Lockyer, *An account of the trade in India: containing rules for good government in trade, price courants, and tables* ... (London: the author)

Loewald, Starika, and Taylor 1958. Klaus Loewald, Beverly Starika, and Paul Taylor, "Johann Martin Bolzius answers a questionnaire on Carolina and Georgia, Part II," *WMQ* 3rd ser. 15: 218–61

Long 1774. Edward Long, *The history of Jamaica*, 3 vols. (London: T. Lowndes)

Lopez 1976. Roberto Lopez, *The commercial revolution of the Middle Ages, 950–1350* (Cambridge University Press)

Louisiana Code Noir 1724, www.centenary.edu/french/codenoir.htm

Lovén 1935/2010. Sven Lovén, *Origins of the Tainan culture, West Indies* (1935; Tuscaloosa: University of Alabama Press)

Loyer 1714. Godefroy Loyer, *Relation du voyage du royaume d'Issyny, Côte d'Or, Païs de Guinée, en Afrique* (Paris: Chez Arnoul Seneuze et Jean-Raoul Morel)

Lucca 1953. Lorenzo da Lucca, *Relations sur le Congo du Père Laurént de Lucques (1700–1717)*, ed. J. Cuvelier (Brussels: Institut Royal Colonial Belge, 1953)

Mackie 1999. Erin Skye Mackie, "Cultural cross-dressing: the colorful case of the Caribbean creole," in Jessica Munns and Penny Richards (eds.), *The clothes that wear us: essays on dressing and transgressing in eighteenth-century culture* (Newark: University of Delaware Press), 250–70

Macquarrie 2000. Charles W. Macquarrie, "Insular Celtic tattooing: history, myth and metaphor," in Caplan 2000a, 32–45

Main 1975. Gloria Main, "Probate records as a source for early American history," *WMQ* 3rd ser. 32: 89–99

Malan 1998/99. Antonia Malan, "Chattels or colonists? 'Freeblack' women and their households," *Kronos* 25: 50–71

Malheiro 1866/1976. Perdigão Malheiro, *A escravidão no Brasil: ensaio histórico, jurídico, social*, 3 vols., 3rd edn. (1866; Petrópolis: Editora Vozes)

Manganelli 2012. Kimberly Snyder Manganelli, *Transatlantic spectacles of race: the tragic mulatta and the tragic muse* (New Brunswick, NJ: Rutgers University Press)

Marees 1912. Pieter de Marees, *Beschryvinghe ende historische verhael van het Gout koninckrijck van Gunea anders de Gout-Custe de Mina genaemt liggende in het deel van Africa*, ed. S. P. L'Honoré Naber (1602; The Hague: Mouton)

Marees 1987. Pieter de Marees, *Description and historical account of the Gold Kingdom of Guinea (1602)*, ed. and trans. Albert van Dantzig and Adam Jones (Oxford University Press)

Martin 1972. Phyllis Martin, *The external trade of the Loango coast 1576–1870: the effects of changing commercial relations on the Vili kingdom of Loango* (Oxford: Clarendon Press)

Masquelier 2005. Adeline Masquelier (ed.), *Dirt, undress and difference: critical perspectives on the body's surface* (Bloomington: Indiana University Press)

Mathieu 1981. Jacques Mathieu, *Le commerce entre la Nouvelle-France et les Antilles au XVIIIe siècle* (Montreal: Fides)

Mauss 1923–24/2000. Marcel Mauss, *The gift: the form and reason for exchange in archaic societies* (1923–24; New York: W. W. Norton)

Maxwell 1993. Kenneth Maxwell, "The Atlantic in the eighteenth century: a southern perspective on the need to return to the 'big picture,'" *Transactions of the Royal Historical Society*, 6th ser. 3: 209–36

Mbow 2010. Mary-Amy Mbow, "Prehistory to colonialism," in Eicher and Ross 2010 (unpaginated)

McClellan 1992. James E. McClellan, *Colonialism and science: Saint-Domingue in the Old Regime* (Baltimore, Md.: Johns Hopkins University Press)

McCord 1840. David James McCord (ed.), *The statutes at large of South Carolina*, vol. VII (Columbia: A. S. Johnston)

McCracken 1988. Grant McCracken, *Culture and consumption: new approaches to the symbolic character of consumer goods and activities* (Bloomington: Indiana University Press)

McCullough 1992. A. B. McCullough, *The primary textile industry in Canada: history and heritage* (Ottawa: National Historic Sites Publications, Environment Canada)

McDonald 1993. Roderick McDonald, *The economy and material culture of slaves: goods and chattels on the sugar plantations of Jamaica and Louisiana* (Baton Rouge: Louisiana State University Press)

McDowell 1955. W. L. McDowell (ed.), *Journals of the Commissioners of the Indian Trade, September 20, 1710–August 29, 1718* (Columbia: South Carolina Archives Department)

McDowell 1958. W. L. McDowell (ed.), *Documents relating to Indian affairs May 21, 1750–August 7, 1754* (Columbia: South Carolina Department of Archives and History)

McDowell 1970. W. L. McDowell (ed.), *Documents relating to Indian affairs 1754–1765* (Columbia: University of South Carolina Press)

McKendrick, Brewer, and Plumb 1982. Neil McKendrick, John Brewer, and J. H. Plumb (eds.), *The birth of a consumer society: the commercialization of eighteenth-century England* (Bloomington: Indiana University Press)

Meinig 1986. D. W. Meinig, *The shaping of America: a geographical perspective on 500 years of history* (New Haven, Conn.: Yale University Press)

Meléndez 2005. Mariselle Meléndez, "Visualizing difference: the rhetoric of clothing in colonial Spanish America," in Regina A. Root (ed.), *The Latin American fashion reader* (Oxford and New York: Berg), 17–30

Menard 1991. Russell Menard, "Transport costs and long-range trade, 1300–1800: was there a European 'transport revolution' in the early modern era?" in James Tracy (ed.), *The political economy of merchant empires* (Cambridge University Press), 228–75

Mentzel 1785–87/1921–44. O. F. Mentzel, *A geographical and topographical description of the Cape of Good Hope*, 3 vols. (1785–87; Cape Town: Van Riebeeck Society)

Merolla 1726. Girolamo Merolla da Sorrento, *Breve, e succinta relazione del viaggio nel regno di Congo* (Naples: n.p.)

Meuwese 2011. Mark Meuwese, *Brothers in arms, partners in trade: Dutch–Indigenous alliances in the Atlantic world, 1595–1674* (Leiden: Brill)

Michelant and Ramé 1867. H. Michelant and A. Ramé (eds.), *Relation originale du voyage de Jacques Cartier au Canada en 1534* (Paris: Librairie Tross)

Miller 1988. Joseph C. Miller, *Way of death: merchant capitalism and the Angolan slave trade 1730–1830* (Madison: University of Wisconsin Press)

Mintz 1974. Sidney W. Mintz, *Caribbean transformations* (Chicago: Aldine)

Miquelon 1975. Dale Miquelon, "Havy and Lefebvre of Quebec: a case study of metropolitan participation in Canadian trade, 1730–1760," *Canadian Historical Review* 56: 1–24.

Miquelon 1978. Dale Miquelon, *Dugard of Rouen: French trade to Canada and the West Indies, 1729–1770* (Montreal and Kingston: McGill-Queen's University Press)

Mittelberger 1898. Gottlieb Mittelberger, *Journey to Pennsylvania in the year 1750 and return to Germany in the year 1754*, trans. Carl Eben (Philadelphia: Joseph Jeanes)

Montaigne 1580/2009. Michel de Montaigne, *Essais*, ed. Emmanuel Naya, Delphine Reguig, and Alexandre Tarrête, 3 vols. (1588; Paris: Gallimard)

Montigny 2008. Jean-François-Benjamin Dumont de Montigny, *Regards sur le monde atlantique 1715–1747*, ed. Carla Zecher, Gordon M. Sayre, and Shannon Lee Dawdy (Sillery, Québec: Septentrion)

Moore 1988. Alexander Moore (ed.), *Nairne's Muskhogean Journals: the 1708 expedition to the Mississippi River* (Jackson: University Press of Mississippi)

Moreau de Saint-Méry 1784–90. Médéric Louis Élie Moreau de Saint-Méry, *Loix et constitutions des colonies françoises de l'Amérique sous le vent*, 6 vols. (Paris: Chez l'Auteur et al.)

Moreau de Saint-Méry 1797. Médéric Louis Élie Moreau de Saint-Méry, *Description topographique, physique, civile, politique et historique de la partie française de l'isle de Saint-Domingue*, 2nd edn., 2 vols. (Philadelphia: Chez l'Auteur)

Moreno 2006. José Luis Moreno, "Españoles y criollos," in Romero and Romero 2006, 79–90

Morgan 1984. Philip D. Morgan, "Black life in eighteenth-century Charleston," *Perspectives in American History* New ser. 1: 187–232

Morgan 1998. Philip D. Morgan, *Slave counterpoint: black culture in the eighteenth-century Chesapeake and Lowcountry* (Chapel Hill: University of North Carolina Press)

Morgan 2000. Kenneth Morgan, "Business networks in the British export trade to North America, 1750–1800," in John J. McCusker and Kenneth Morgan (eds.), *The early modern Atlantic economy* (Cambridge University Press), 36–62

Morgan 2007. Kenneth Morgan (ed.), *The Bright–Meyler papers: a Bristol–West India connection, 1732–1837* (Oxford University Press)

Morrison 1751. John Morrison, *Account of the robberies committed by John Morrison, and his accomplices, in and near Philadelphia, 1750 ...* (Philadelphia, Pa.: n.p.)

Moutoukias 1988. Zacarias Moutoukias, *Contrabando y control colonial en el siglo XVII* (Buenos Aires: Centro Editor de América Latina)

Mui 1989. Hoh-Cheung Mui and Lorna H. Mui, *Shops and shopkeeping in eighteenth-century England* (Kingston and Montreal: McGill-Queen's University Press)

Muldrew 1998. Craig Muldrew, *The economy of obligation: the culture of credit and social relations in early modern England* (Basingstoke: Macmillan)

Müller 2010. Mechthild Müller, "Early history of dress and fashion in continental west Europe," in Skov 2010 (unpaginated)

Mullin 1992. Michael Mullin, *Africa in America: slave acculturation and resistance in the American South and the British Caribbean, 1736–1831* (Urbana: University of Illinois Press)

Nash 2009. R. C. Nash, "Domestic material culture and consumer demand in the British Atlantic world: colonial South Carolina, 1670–1770," in David S. Shields (ed.), *Material culture in Anglo-America: regional identity and urbanity in the Tidewater, Lowcountry, and Caribbean* (Columbia: University of South Carolina Press), 221–66

Nicolas 2011. *The Codex Canadensis and the writings of Louis Nicolas: the natural history of the New World*, ed. François-Marc Gagnon (Kingston and Montreal: McGill-Queen's University Press)

Nicolson 1776. [Le père] Nicolson, OP, *Essai sur l'histoire naturelle de l'isle de Saint-Domingue* (Paris: Chez Gobreau)

Nieuhof 1682. Johan Nieuhof, *Gedenkweerdige Brasiliaense zee- en lant-reize* (Amsterdam: Widow Jacob van Meurs)

Novais 1997. Fernando A. Novais (ed.), *História da vida privada no Brasil*, 2 vols. (São Paolo: Companhia Das Letras)

O'Brien, Griffiths, and Hunt 1991. Patrick O'Brien, Trevor Griffiths, and Philip Hunt, "Political components of the Industrial Revolution: Parliament and the English cotton textile industry, 1660–1774," *EcHR* New ser. 54: 395–423

Olwell 1996. Robert Olwell, "'Loose, idle and disorderly': slave women in the eighteenth-century Charles Town marketplace," in Gaspar and Hine 1996, 97–110

O'Reilly 2011. William O'Reilly, "Movements of people in the Atlantic world, 1450–1850," in Canny and Morgan 2011, 305–23

Orlin 2002. Lena Cowen Orlin, "Fictions of the early modern English probate inventory," in Henry S. Turner (ed.), *The culture of capital: property, cities and knowledge in early modern England* (New York: Routledge), 51–83

Oury 1971. Dom Guy Oury (ed.), *Marie de l'Incarnation, Ursuline (1599–1672): correspondance* (Solesmes: Abbaye Saint-Pierre)

Pagden 1982. Anthony Pagden, *The fall of natural man: the American Indian and the origins of comparative ethnology* (Cambridge University Press)

Pagden 2009. Anthony Pagden, "The peopling of the New World: ethnos, race and empire in the early-modern world," in Miriam Isaac, Benjamin H. Ziegler, and J. Eliav-Feldon (eds.), *The origins of racism in the West* (Cambridge University Press), 292–312

Pastoureau 2000/2001. Michel Pastoureau, *Blue: the history of a color* (2000; Princeton University Press)

Pastoureau 2009. Michael Pastoureau, *Black: the history of a color* (Princeton University Press)

Paterek 1994. Josephine Paterek, *Encyclopedia of American Indian costume* (Denver, San Diego and Oxford: ABC-CLIO)

Patterson 1982. Orlando Patterson, *Slavery and social death: a comparative study* (Cambridge, Mass.: Harvard University Press)

Pellegrin 1993. Nicole Pellegrin, "Le vêtement comme fait social total," in Christophe Charle (ed.), *Histoire sociale, histoire globale?* (Paris: Éditions de la Maison des Sciences de l'Homme), 81–94

Peltz 2007. Lucy Peltz, "Basire, Isaac (1704–1768)," *Oxford Dictionary of National Biography*, online edn. (Oxford University Press, 2004)

Pigafetta 1591. Filippo Pigafetta, *Relatione del reame di Congo et delle circonvicine contrade, tratta dalli scritti e ragionamenti di Odoardo Lopez portoghese* (Rome: Bartolomeo Grassi)

Piso and Markgraf 1648. Willem Piso and Georg Markgraf, *Historia naturalis Brasiliae* (Leiden and Amsterdam: Hackius and Elzevier)

Podruchny 2006. Carolyn Podruchny, *Making the voyageur world: travelers and traders in the North American fur trade* (Lincoln: University of Nebraska Press)

Pointon 1993. Marcia Pointon, *Hanging the head: portraiture and social formation in eighteenth-century England* (New Haven, Conn.: Yale University Press)

Pomeranz and Topik 2012. Kenneth Pomeranz and Steven Topik, *The world that trade created: society, culture, and the world economy, 1400–the present*, 3d edn. (Armonk, NY: M. E. Sharpe)

Post 1990. *Frans Post, 1612–1680* ([Basel]: Kunsthalle Basel)

Pouchot 1781/1994. Pierre Pouchot, *Memoirs on the late war in North America between France and England*, ed. Brian L. Dunnigan (1781; Youngstown, NY: Old Fort Niagara Association)

Powell 2008. Richard J. Powell, *Cutting a figure: fashioning black portraiture* (University of Chicago Press)

Pratt 2005. Stephanie Pratt, *American Indians in British art, 1700–1840* (Norman: University of Oklahoma Press)

Praz 1971. Mario Praz, *Conversation pieces: a survey of the informal group portrait in Europe and America* (University Park: Pennsylvania State University Press)

Pritchard 2004. James Pritchard, *In search of empire: the French in the Americas, 1670–1730* (Cambridge University Press)

Proyart 1776. Abbé Liévin-Bonaventure Proyart, *Histoire de Loango, Kakongo, et autres royaumes d'Afrique* (Paris: Berton and Crapart; Lyon: Bruyset-Ponthus)

Quaife 1947. Milo Milton Quaife (ed.), *The Western Country in the 17th century: the memoirs of Lamothe Cadillac and Pierre Liette* (Chicago, Ill.: Lakeside Press)

Quaife 1958. Milo Milton Quaife (ed.), *The siege of Detroit in 1763: the journal of Pontiac's conspiracy and John Rutherfurd's narrative of a captivity* (Chicago: R. R. Donnelley)

Ramos 1990. Hector R. Feliciano Ramos, *El contrabando inglés en el Caribe y el Golfo de Mexico (1748–1778)* (Seville: Diputación Provincial de Sevilla)

Randle 2007. Tracey Randle, "Patterns of consumption at auctions: a case study of three estates," in Worden (ed.), 53–74

Ratelband 1953. K. Ratelband (ed.), *Vijf dagregisters van het kasteel São Jorge da Mina (Elmina) aan de Goudkust (1645–1647)* (The Hague: Martinus Nijhoff)

Reports 1918. *The Reports of Chavonnes and his Council, and of Van Imhoff, on the Cape, with incidental correspondence* (Cape Town: Van Riebeeck Society)

Ribeiro 2005. Alexandre Vieira Ribeiro, "O tráfico atlântico de escravos e a praça mercantil de Salvador, *c.* 1680–*c.* 1830," MA dissertation (Universidade Federal do Rio de Janeiro)

Rich 1949. E. E. Rich (ed.), *James Isham's observations on Hudsons Bay, 1743* ([Toronto]: Champlain Society for The Hudson's Bay Society)

Richter 2001. Daniel Richter, *Facing east from Indian country* (Cambridge, Mass.: Harvard University Press)

Riello 2010a. Giorgio Riello, "Footwear," in Skov 2010 (unpaginated)

Riello 2010b. Giorgio Riello, "Materials," in Skov 2010 (unpaginated)

Riello 2013. Giorgio Riello, *Cotton: the fabric that made the modern world* (Cambridge University Press)

Riello and Parthasarathi 2009. Giorgio Riello and Prasannan Parthasarathi (eds.), *The spinning world: a global history of cotton textiles, 1200–1850* (Oxford University Press)

Rinchon 1964. Dieudonné Rinchon, *Pierre-Ignace-Liévin van Alstein, Capitaine négrier, Gand 1733–Nantes 1793* (Dakar: IFAN, 1964)

Robert 1960. Henri Robert, *Les trafics coloniaux du port de La Rochelle au XVIIIe siècle* (Poitiers: Oudin)

Robertson 1992. Roland Robertson, *Globalization: social theory and global culture* (London: Sage)

Robinson 2001. W. Stiff Robinson (ed.), *Early American Indian documents: treaties and laws, 1607–1789,* vol. XIII: *North and South Carolina treaties, 1654–1756* (Bethesda, Md.: University Publications of America)

Roche 1989/1994. Daniel Roche, *The culture of clothing: dress and fashion in the 'ancien regime'* (1989; Cambridge University Press; Paris: Éditions de la Maison des Sciences de l'Homme)

Roche 1997. Daniel Roche, *Histoire des choses banales: naissance de la consommation XVIIe–XIXe siècle* (Paris: Fayard, 1997)

Roche 1998. Daniel Roche, "Between a 'moral economy' and a 'consumer economy': clothes and their function in the 17th and 18th centuries," in Robert Fox and Anthony Turner (eds.), *Luxury trades and consumerism in ancien régime Paris: studies in the history of the skilled workforce* (Aldershot, UK: Ashgate), 219–29

Rochemonteix 1904. Camille de Rochemonteix (ed.), *Relation par lettres de l'Amérique septentrionale (années 1709 et 1710)* (Paris: n.p.)

Rogers 1765. Robert Rogers, *A concise account of North America* (London: the Author)

Rogers 2007. Dominique Rogers, "Entre lumières et préjugés: Moreau de Saint-Méry et les libres de couleur de Saint-Domingue," in Dominique Taffin (ed.), *Moreau de Saint-Méry ou les ambiguïtés d'un créole des Lumières* (Fort-de-France: Archives départementales de la Martinique), 77–93

Rogers and King 2012. Dominique Rogers and Stewart King, "Housekeepers, merchants, rentières: free women of color in the port cities of colonial Saint-Domingue, 1750–1790," in Douglas Catterall and Jody Campbell (eds.), *Women in port: gendering communities, economies, and social networks in Atlantic port cities, 1500–1800* (Leiden: Brill), 357–97

Romano 1649. Giovanni Francesco Romano, *Breve relatione del successo della missione de' Frati Minori Capuccini . . . al regno del Congo* (Milan: Francesco Mognaga)

Rømer 2000. Ludewig Ferdinand Rømer, *A reliable account of the coast of Guinea (1760)*, ed. and trans. Selena Axelrod Winsnes (Oxford University Press)

Romero 2006. Luis Alberto Romero, "La lucha por el puerto," in Romero and Romero 2006, I: 61–78

Romero and Romero 2006. José Luis Romero and Luis Alberto Romero (eds.), *Buenos Aires: historia de cuatro siglos*, 2 vols., 3rd edn. (Buenos Aires: Altamira)

Rosecrans 2000. Jennipher Allen Rosecrans, "Wearing the universe: symbolic markings in early modern England," in Caplan 2000a, 46–60

Rosenthal 2006. Angela Rosenthal, *Angelica Kauffman: art and sensibility* (New Haven, Conn.: Yale University Press)

Ross 2007. Robert Ross, "Sumptuary laws in Europe, the Netherlands and the Dutch colonies," in Worden 2007, 382–90

Ross 2008. Robert Ross, *Clothing: a global history* (Cambridge: Polity Press)

Rowland, Sanders, and Galloway 1927–84. Dunbar Rowland, Albert G. Sanders, and Patricia Galloway (eds.), *Mississippi Provincial Archives, French Dominion*, 5 vols. (Jackson: Press of the Mississippi Department of Archives and History; Baton Rouge: Louisiana State University Press)

Rushforth 2003. Brett Rushforth, "'A little flesh we offer you': the origins of Indian slavery in New France," *WMQ* 3rd ser. 60: 777–808

Rushforth 2012. Brett Rushforth, *Bonds of alliance: indigenous and Atlantic slaveries in New France* (Chapel Hill: University of North Carolina Press)

Ryder 1969. A. C. Ryder, *Benin and the Europeans 1485–1897* (New York: Humanities Press)

Saadani 2005. Khalil Saadani, "Gift exchange between the French and Native Americans in Louisiana," in Bradley Bond (ed.), *French colonial Louisiana and the Atlantic world* (Baton Rouge: Louisiana State University Press), 43–64

Sagard 1632/1990. Gabriel Sagard, *Le grand voyage du pays des Hurons*, ed. Réal Ouellet and Jack Warwick (1632; Québec: Bibliothèque Québecoise)

Saint-Vallier 1688. Jean Baptiste de la Croix Chevrierès de Saint-Vallier, *Estat présent de l'Église et de la colonie françoise dans la Nouvelle France* (Paris: Robert Pepie)

Sala-Molins 1993. Louis Sala-Molins, *Le Code Noir ou le calvaire de Canaan* (Paris: Presses universitaires de France)

Salmoral 2001. Manuel Lucena Salmoral, "Leyes para esclavos: el ordenamiento jurídico sobre la condición, tratamiento, defensa y represión de los esclavos en las colonias de la América española," in Andrés-Gallego 2001, separately paginated 1–1384

Santos 1956. Lycurgo de Castro Santos, *Uma comunidade rural do Brasil antigo (Aspectos da vida patriarchal no sertão da Bahia nos séculos xviii e xix)* (São Paulo: Companhia Editora Nacional)

Sarreal 2014. Julia J. S. Sarreal, *The Guaraní and their missions: a socioeconomic history* (Stanford University Press)

Sassatelli 2007. Roberta Sassatelli, *Consumer culture: history, theory and politics* (Los Angeles, Calif.: SAGE)

Savary 1742. Jacques Savary des Bruslons, *Dictionnaire universel de commerce: contenant tout ce qui concerne le commerce qui se fait dans les quatre parties du monde ...* , new edn. by Philémon-Louis Savary, 3 vols. in 5 parts (Geneva: les Héritiers & Freres Philibert)

Sayre 1997. Gordon Sayre, *Les sauvages américains: representations of Native Americans in French and English colonial literature* (Chapel Hill: University of North Carolina Press)

Scammell 2000. V. G. Scammell, "'A Very profitable and Advantageous Trade': British smuggling in the Iberian Americas circa 1500–1750," *Itinerario* 24: 135–72

Schapera and Farrington 1933/1970. Isaac Schapera and E. Farrington (eds.), *The early Cape Hottentots: described in the writings of Olfert Dapper (1668), Willem Ten Rhyne (1686) and Johannes Gulielmus de Grevenbroek (1695)* (1933; Westport, Conn.: Negro Universities Press)

Schaw 1939. [Janet Schaw], *Journal of a lady of quality; being the narrative of a journey from Scotland to the West Indies, North Carolina, and Portugal, in the years 1774 to 1776*, ed. Evangeline Walker Andrews, 3rd edn. (New Haven, Conn.: Yale University Press)

Schevill 2010. Margot Blum Schevill (ed.), *Berg encyclopedia of world dress and fashion*, vol. II: *Latin America and the Caribbean* (Oxford: Berg), online edition

Schoeman 2007. Karel Schoeman, *Early slavery at the Cape of Good Hope, 1652–1717* (Pretoria: Protea)

Schoeser 2003. Mary Schoeser, *World textiles: a concise history* (London and New York: Thames & Hudson)

Schuurman and Walsh 1994. Anton Schuurman and Lorna Walsh (eds.), *Material culture: consumption, life-style, standard of living, 1500–1900* (Milan: Università Bocconi)

Schwartz 1974. Stuart B. Schwartz, "The manumission of slaves in colonial Brazil: Bahia, 1684–1745," *HAHR* 54: 603–35

Schwartz 1985. Stuart B. Schwartz, *Sugar plantations in the formation of Brazilian society: Bahia, 1550–1835* (New York: Cambridge University Press)

Schwartz 1992. Stuart B. Schwartz, *Slaves, peasants, and rebels: reconsidering Brazilian slavery* (Urbana: University of Illinois Press)

Schwartz 2007. Stuart Schwartz, "The economy of the Portuguese empire," in Francisco Bethencourt and Diogo Ramada Curto (eds.), *Portuguese oceanic expansion, 1400–1800* (Cambridge University Press), 19–48

Séguin 1973. Robert-Lionel Séguin, *La civilisation traditionnelle de l' 'habitant' aux 17e et 18e siècles*, 2nd edn. (Montreal: Fides)

Sekora 1977. John Sekora, *Luxury: the concept in Western thought, Eden to Smollett* (Baltimore, Md.: Johns Hopkins University Press)

Shames 2010. Susan P. Shames, *The Old Plantation: the artist revealed* (Colonial Williamsburg Foundation)

Shammas 1990. Carole Shammas, *The pre-industrial consumer in England and America* (Oxford: Clarendon Press)

Shammas 1994. Carole Shammas, "The decline of textile prices in England and British America prior to industrialization," *EcHR* New ser. 57: 483–507

Shannon 1996. Timothy J. Shannon, "Dressing for success on the Mohawk frontier: Hendrick, William Johnson, and the Indian fashion," *WMQ* 3rd ser. 53: 13–42

Shannon 2009. Timothy J. Shannon, "King of the Indians: the hard fate and curious career of Peter Williamson," *WMQ* 3rd ser. 66: 3–44

Shawe-Taylor 2009. Desmond Shawe-Taylor, *The conversation piece: scenes of fashionable life* (London: Royal Collection Publications)

Shell 1991. Robert Shell, "The short life and personal belongings of one slave: Rangton of Bali, 1673–1720," *Kronos* 18: 1–6

Shell 1994. Robert C.-H. Shell, *Children of bondage: a social history of the slave society at the Cape of Good Hope, 1652–1838* (Hanover and London: University Press of New England)

Sheridan 1995. Richard B. Sheridan, "Strategies of slave subsistence: the Jamaican case reconsidered," in Mary Turner (ed.), *From chattel slaves to wage slaves: the dynamics of labour bargaining in the Americas* (Bloomington: Indiana University Press), 48–67

Shovlin 2006. John Shovlin, *The political economy of virtue: luxury, patriotism, and the origins of the French Revolution* (Ithaca, NY: Cornell University Press)

Silverstein 2000a. Cory C. Silverstein, "Clothed encounters: the power of dress in relations between Anishnaabe and British peoples in the Great Lakes region, 1760–2000," Ph.D. dissertation (McMaster University)

Silverstein 2000b. Cory C. Silverstein, "Bright baubles and blue broadcloth: color symbolism in the aesthetics of Anishnaabe fur trade dress," paper presented at meeting of the American Society for Ethnohistory, October 21

Simmel 1904. Georg Simmel, "Fashion," *International Quarterly* 10: 130–55

Skov 2010. Lise Skov (ed.), *Berg encyclopedia of world dress and fashion*, vol. VIII: *West Europe* (Oxford: Berg), online edition

Sloane 1707–25. Hans Sloane, *A voyage to the islands Madera, Barbados, Nieves, S Christophers and Jamaica*, 2 vols. (London: B.M.)

Smith 1799. James Smith, *An account of the remarkable occurrences in the life and travels of Col. James Smith* (Lexington, Ky.: John Bradford)

Smith 1947. Abbot Emerson Smith, *Colonists in bondage: white servitude and convict labor in America 1607–1776* (Chapel Hill: University of North Carolina Press)

Smith 2002. Woodruff D. Smith, *Consumption and the making of respectability, 1600–1800* (New York: Routledge)

Smith and Pheiffer 1993. Andrew B. Smith and Roy H. Pheiffer, *The Khoikhoi at the Cape of Good Hope: seventeenth-century drawings in the South African Library* (Cape Town: South African Library)

Socolow 1975. Susan M. Socolow, "Economic activities of the Porteño merchants: the viceregal period," *HAHR* 55: 1–24

Socolow 1991. Susan M. Socolow, "Buenos Aires: Atlantic port and hinterland in the eighteenth century," in Franklin W. Knight and Peggy K. Liss (eds.), *Atlantic port cities: economy, culture, and society in the Atlantic world, 1650–1800* (Knoxville: University of Tennessee Press), 240–61

Socolow 1996. Susan M. Socolow, "Economic roles of the free women of color of Cap Français," in Gaspar and Hine 1996, 279–97

Socolow and Johnson 1981. Susan M. Socolow and Lyman L. Johnson, "Urbanization in colonial Latin America," *Journal of Urban History* 8: 27–59

Sousa 1992. Avanete Pereira Sousa, *Salvador, capital da colônia*, 4th edn. (Bahia: Editora Atual)

Sparrman 1975. Anders Sparrman, *A voyage to the Cape of Good Hope … 1772–1776*, 2 vols. (Cape Town: Van Riebeeck Society)

Spufford 1984. Margaret Spufford, *The great reclothing of rural England: petty chapmen and their wares in the seventeenth century* (London: Hambledon Press)

Spufford 1990. Margaret Spufford, "The limitations of the probate inventory," in John Chartres and David Hey (eds.), *English rural society 1500–1800: essays in honour of Joan Thirsk* (Cambridge University Press), 139–74

Staden 1557/2008. Hans Staden, *Hans Staden's true history: an account of cannibal captivity in Brazil*, ed. Neil L. Whitehead and Michael Harbsmeier (1557; Durham, NC: Duke University Press)

Standen 1994. S. Dale Standen, "'Personnes sans caractère': private merchants, post commanders and the regulation of the western fur trade, 1720–1745," in Hubert Watelet (ed.), *De France en Nouvelle-France: société fondatrice et société nouvelle* (Presses de l'Université d'Ottawa), 265–95

Stedman 1796/1988. John Gabriel Stedman, *Narrative of a five years expedition against the revolted Negroes of Surinam*, ed. Richard Price and Sally Price (1796; Baltimore, Md.: Johns Hopkins University Press)

Steger 2013. Manfred Steger, *Globalization: a very short introduction*, 3rd edn. (2003; Oxford University Press)

Stern and Wennerlind 2013. Philip J. Stern and Carl Wennerlind (eds.), *Mercantilism reimagined: political economy in early modern Britain and its empire* (Oxford University Press)

Stewart 2007. Charles Stewart (ed.), *Creolization: history, ethnography, theory* (Walnut Creek, Calif.: Left Coast Press)

Stols 1996. Eddy Stols, "L'âge d'or du déshabillé: échanges et cultures vestimentaires au Brésil colonial du XVIIIe siècle," in Bottin and Pellegrin 1996, 277–94

Strutt 1975. Daphne Strutt, *Fashion in South Africa 1652–1900* (Cape Town and Rotterdam: A. A. Balkema)

Styles 2007. John Styles, *The dress of the people: everyday fashion in eighteenth-century Britain* (New Haven, Conn.: Yale University Press)

Surrey 1916. N. M. Miller Surrey, *The commerce of Louisiana during the French régime, 1699–1763* (New York: Columbia University Press)

Sutton 2012. Elizabeth A. Sutton, *Early modern Dutch prints of Africa* (Farnham, UK: Ashgate)

Svendsen 2004/2006. Lars Svendsen, *Fashion: a philosophy* (2004; London: Reaktion)

Swanton 1946. John Swanton, *The Indians of the Southeastern United States* (Washington, DC: Smithsonian Institution Press)

Tanguy 1994. Jean Tanguy, *Quand la toile va: l'industrie toilière bretonne du 16e au 18e siècle* (Rennes: Éditions Apogée)

Tanner 1994. Helen Hornbeck Tanner, "The career of Joseph La France, *coureur de bois* in the upper Great Lakes," in Jennifer S. H. Brown, W. J. Eccles, and Donald P. Heldman (eds.), *The fur trade revisited* (East Lansing: Michigan State University Press), 171–87

Tarrade 1972. Jean Tarrade, *Le commerce colonial de la France à la fin de l'Ancien Régime: l'évolution du régime de "l'Exclusif" de 1763 à 1789*, 2 vols. (Paris: Presses Universitaires de France)

Tarrant 2010. Naomi E.A. Tarrant, "Early history of dress and fashion in Great Britain and Ireland," in Skov 2010 (unpaginated)

Taylor 2008. John Taylor, *Jamaica in 1687: the Taylor manuscript at the National Library of Jamaica*, ed. David Buisseret (Kingston: University of the West Indies Press)

Teychenie 1960. Henry Teychenie, "Les esclaves de l'habitation Belin à Saint-Domingue, 1762–1793," *Revista de ciencias sociales* 4: 237–68

Thévet 1558. André Thévet, *Les singularitez de la France Antarctique, autrement nommee Amerique, & de plusieurs terres & isles decouvertes de nostre temps* (Antwerp: Christophle Plantin)

Thomas 1690. Sir Dalby Thomas, *An historical account of the rise and growth of the West-India collonies* [sic] (London: Jo. Hindmarsh)

Thomas 1989. Daniel Thomas, *Fort Toulouse, the French outpost at the Alabama on the Coosa* (Tuscaloosa: University of Alabama Press)

Thomas 1991. Nicholas Thomas, *Entangled objects: exchange, material culture, and colonialism in the Pacific* (Cambridge, Mass.: Harvard University Press)

Thomson 1992. James K. J. Thomson, *A distinctive industrialization: cotton in Barcelona 1728–1832* (Cambridge University Press)

Thomson 1996. James K. J. Thomson, "Marketing channels and structures in Spain in the first half of the eighteenth century: two contrasting cases," in Bottin and Pellegrin 1996, 335–57

Thornton 1983. John K. Thornton, *The kingdom of Kongo, civil war and transition, 1641–1718* (Madison: University of Wisconsin Press)

Thornton 1998. John Thornton, *Africa and Africans in the making of the Atlantic world, 1400–1800*, 2nd edn. (Cambridge University Press)

Thunberg 1986. Carl Peter Thunberg, *Travels at the Cape of Good Hope 1772–1775*, ed. V.S. Forbes (Cape Town: Van Riebeeck Society)

Timberlake 1765. Henry Timberlake, *The memoirs of Lieut. Henry Timberlake* (London: J. Ridley, W. Nicoll, C. Henderson)

Tobin 1999. Beth Tobin, *Picturing imperial power: colonial subjects in eighteenth-century British painting* (Durham, NC: Duke University Press)

Torra 1997. Lidia Torra Fernández, "Comercialización y consumo de tejidos en Cataluña (1650–1800)," *Revista de historia industrial* 11: 177–95

Torra 1999. Lidia Torra Fernández, "Pautas de consumo textil en la Cataluña del siglo XVIII: una visión a partir de los inventarios *post-mortem*," in Torras and Yun Casalilla 1999, 89–105

Torras and Yun Casalilla 1999. J. Torras and Bartolomé Yun Casalilla (eds.), *Consumo, condiciones de vida y comercialización: Cataluña y Castilla, siglos XVII–XIX* (Valladolid: Junta de Castilla y León, Consejería de Educación y Cultura)

Tortora 2010a. Phyllis Tortora (ed.), *Berg encyclopedia of world dress and fashion*, vol. III: *The United States and Canada* (Oxford: Berg), online edition

Tortora 2010b. Phyllis G. Tortora, "History and development of fashion," in Eicher 2010 (unpaginated)

Trentmann 2012. Frank Trentmann (ed.), *The Oxford handbook of the history of consumption* (Oxford University Press)

Trigger 1985. Bruce Trigger, *Natives and newcomers: Canada's "heroic age" reconsidered* (Montreal and Kingston: McGill-Queen's University Press)

Trudel 2004. Marcel Trudel, *Deux siècles d'esclavage au Québec* (Montreal: Hurtubise HMH)

Turner 1969. Victor Turner, *The ritual process: structure and anti-structure* (Chicago: Aldine)

Unger 2011. Richard W. Unger (ed.), *Shipping and economic growth, 1350–1800* (Leiden: Brill)

van Baerle 1647/2011. Caspar van Baerle, *The history of Brazil under the governorship of Count Johan Maurits of Nassau, 1636–1644*, trans. Blanche T. van Berckel-Ebeling Konin (1647; Gainesville: University Press of Florida)

Van Dantzig 1999. Albert Van Dantzig, *Forts and castles of Ghana* (Accra: Sedco)

van den Heuvel and Ogilvie 2013. Danielle van den Heuvel and Sheilagh Ogilvie, "Retail development in the consumer revolution: the Netherlands, *c.* 1670–*c.* 1815," *Explorations in Economic History* 50: 69–87

Van Duin and Ross 1987. Pieter Van Duin and Robert Ross, *The economy of the Cape Colony in the 18th century* (Leiden: Centre for the History of European Expansion)

van Gennep 1909/1960. Arnold van Gennep, *The rites of passage* (1909; University of Chicago Press)

van Lottum and van Zanden 2014. Jelle van Lottum and Jan Luiten van Zanden, "Labour productivity and human capital in the European maritime sector of the 18th century," *Explorations in Economic History* 53: 83–100

Van Young 1996. Eric Van Young, "Material life," in Louisa Schell Hoberman and Susan Migden Socolow (eds.), *The countryside in colonial Latin America* (Albuquerque: University of New Mexico Press), 49–74

Vaughan 2006. Alden T. Vaughan, *Transatlantic encounters: American Indians in Britain, 1500–1776* (Cambridge University Press)

Ventosa and Lawton 2010. Silvia Ventosa and Lucy Lawton, "Spain," in Skov 2010 (unpaginated)

Verger 1968. Pierre Verger, *Flux et reflux de la traite des nègres entre le Golfe de Bénin et Bahia de Todos os Santos, du XVIIe au XIXe siècle* (Paris and The Hague: Mouton).

Vicente 2009. Marta Vicente, "Fashion, race, and cotton textiles in colonial Spanish America," in Riello and Parthasarathi 2009, 247–60

Vigarello 1988. Georges Vigarello, *Concepts of cleanliness: changing attitudes in France since the Middle Ages* (1985; Cambridge University Press)

Vilhena 1969. Luís dos Santos Vilhena, *A Bahia no século xviii*, 3 vols. (Bahia: Editôra Itapuã)

Villeneuve 1814. René Claude Geoffroy de Villeneuve, *L'Afrique, ou histoire, moeurs, usages et coutumes des africains: le Sénégal*, 4 vols. (Paris: Nepveu)

Vincent 2003. Susan J. Vincent, *Dressing the elite: clothes in early modern England* (Oxford: Berg)

Vincent 2009. Susan J. Vincent, *The anatomy of fashion: dressing the body from the Renaissance to today* (Oxford: Berg)

Vogt 1975. John Vogt, "Notes on the Portuguese cloth trade in West Africa, 1480–1540," *International Journal of African Historical Studies* 8: 623–51

Vogt 1978. John Vogt, *Portuguese rule on the Gold Coast, 1469–1682* (Athens: University of Georgia Press)

Waldstreicher 1999. David Waldstreicher, "Reading the runaways: self-fashioning, print culture, and confidence in slavery in the eighteenth-century mid-Atlantic," *WMQ* 3rd ser. 56: 243–72

Walvin 1997. James Walvin, *Fruits of empire: exotic produce and British taste, 1660–1800* (New York University Press)

Ward 1988. J. R. Ward, *British West Indian slavery, 1750–1834* (Oxford: Clarendon Press)

Waselkov and Braund 1995. Gregory A. Waselkov and Kathryn E. Holland Braund, *William Bartram on the Southeastern Indians* (Lincoln: University of Nebraska Press)

Weatherill 1988. Lorna Weatherill, *Consumer behaviour and material culture in Britain 1660–1760* (London: Routledge)

Weaver 2011. Jace Weaver, "The red Atlantic: transoceanic cultural exchanges," *American Indian Quarterly* 35: 418–63

Weiner and Schneider 1989. Annette B. Weiner and Jane Schneider, "Introduction," in Jane Schneider and Annette B. Weiner (eds.), *Cloth and human experience* (Washington, DC, Smithsonian Institution Press), 1–11

Welters 2010. Linda Welters, "The Northeast," in Tortora 2010a (unpaginated)

White 1991. Richard White, *The middle ground: Indians, empires, and republics in the Great Lakes region, 1650–1815* (New York: Cambridge University Press)

White 2003. Sophie White, "'Wearing three or four handkerchiefs around his neck, and elsewhere about him': sartorial constructions of masculinity and ethnicity among slaves in French colonial New Orleans," *Gender & History* 15: 527–49

White 2004. Sophie White, "'This gown ... was much admired and made ladies jealous': fashion and the forging of elite identities in French colonial New Orleans," in Tamara Harvey and Greg O'Brien (eds.), *George Washington's South* (Gainesville: University Press of Florida), 86–118

White 2006. Sophie White, "'A baser commerce': retailing, class, and gender in French colonial New Orleans," *WMQ* 3rd ser. 63: 517–50

White 2012. Sophie White, *Wild Frenchmen and Frenchified Indians* (Philadelphia: University of Pennsylvania Press)

White and White 1995. Shane White and Graham White, "Slave clothing and African-American culture in the eighteenth and nineteenth centuries," *Past and Present* 148: 149–86

Wien and Pritchard 1987. Thomas Wien and James Pritchard, "Canadian North Atlantic trade," in Harris 1987

Williams 1969. Glyndwr Williams (ed.), *Andrew Graham's observations on Hudson's Bay, 1767–1791* (London: Hudson's Bay Record Society)

Williamson 1758. Peter Williamson, *French and Indian Cruelty*, 2nd edn. (York, UK: J. Jackson)

Willmott 2005. Cory C. Willmott, "From stroud to strouds: the hidden history of a British fur trade textile," *Textile History* 36: 196–234

Wilson 1963. Samuel Wilson, Jr., "Louisiana drawings by Alexandre de Batz," *Journal of the Society of Architectural Historians* 22: 75–89

Windley 1983. Lathan A. Windley, comp., *Runaway slave advertisements: a documentary history from the 1730s to 1790*, 4 vols. (Westport, Conn.: Greenwood Press)

Winsnes 1992. Selena Axelrod Winsnes (ed. and trans.), *Letters on West Africa and the slave trade: Paul Erdman Isert's journey to Guinea and the Caribbean Islands* (1788; Oxford University Press)

Wood 1974. Peter Wood, *Black majority: Negroes in colonial South Carolina from 1670 through the Stono rebellion* (New York: Knopf)

Worden 2007. Nigel Worden (ed.), *Contingent lives: social identity and material culture in the VOC world* (Cape Town: Historical Studies Department, University of Cape Town)

Worden, van Heyningen, and Bickford-Smith 1998. Nigel Worden, Elizabeth van Heyningen, and Vivian Bickford-Smith, *Cape Town: the making of a city: an illustrated social history* (Kenilworth: David Philip)

Worden and Worden 2005. Nigel Worden and Gerald Worden (eds.), *Trials of slavery: selected documents concerning slaves from the criminal records of the Council of Justice at the Cape of Good Hope, 1705–1794* (Cape Town: Van Riebeeck Society)

Young 1995. Kathryn A. Young, *Kin, commerce, community: merchants in the port of Quebec, 1717–1745* (New York: Peter Lang)

Yun 1994. Bartolomé Yun, "Peasant material culture in Castile (1750–1900): some proposals," in Schuurman and Walsh 1994, 125–36

Zahedieh 1986. Nuala Zahedieh, "The merchants of Port Royal, Jamaica, and the Spanish contraband trade, 1655–1692," *WMQ* 3rd ser. 43: 570–93

Zimmerman 1966. Albert G. Zimmerman, "The Indian trade of colonial Pennsylvania," Ph.D. dissertation (University of Delaware)

Zucchelli 1712. Antonio Zucchelli, *Relazioni del viaggio e missione di Congo* (Venice: Bartolomeo Giavarina)

Index

Textiles and garments frequently found in Atlantic dress regimes are noted only when first mentioned and/or defined.